T0330338

African Hosts & their Guests

African Hosts & their Guests
Cultural Dynamics of Tourism

Edited by
Walter van Beek & Annette Schmidt

JC JAMES CURREY

James Currey is an imprint of Boydell & Brewer Ltd
PO Box 9, Woodbridge, Suffolk IP12 3DF (GB)
and of Boydell & Brewer Inc.
668 Mt Hope Avenue, Rochester, NY 14620-2731 (US)
www.jamescurrey.com

First published 2012

ISBN 978-1-84701-049-0

A CIP catalogue record for this book is available
from the British Library

Papers used by Boydell & Brewer Ltd are natural, recyclable products
made from wood grown in sustainable forests

Designed and set in 11/13 pt Warnock Pro by
Kate Kirkwood, Long House Publishing Services
Printed and bound in Great Britain by
CPI Group (UK) Ltd, Croydon, CR0 4YY

Contents

PART III   INTENSIVE CONTACT

List of Illustrations

Tables

Foreword

Valene Smith

The scientification of tourism began in March 1974 when I inserted a one inch notice in the Fellow Newsletter of the American Anthropological Association (AAA) asking: 'Is anyone else interested in the study of tourism?' Twenty-eight replies came quickly, and with the aid of Western Union telegraph and Special Delivery mail (in the era before email and fax), an agenda was established for the forthcoming AAA meetings in Mexico City that November. Following the two sessions, all participants gathered in a hotel suite to review our thoughts. Nelson Graburn commented: 'We have REALLY done something *special*.' Discussion turned to the next move: a book. Theron Nunez named it: *'Hosts and Guests – The Anthropology of Tourism'.* I took on the task as editor. Authors diligently edited their articles. The manuscript went out for review, and an offer came immediately from University of Pennsylvania Press, founded by the eminent Benjamin Franklin and respected as the second oldest Press in the USA.

We became a close knit group, with some of us meeting at other AAA sessions and with other specialty groups that recognised the growing importance of tourism. At the 1975 AAA meeting, Jafar Jafari appeared, to inquire if his neophyte journal *Annals of Tourism Research* could succeed? I was elated as our new book would soon be in print and already there was a new journal to support ongoing research... The initial research was basic: what were the agents of culture change and how did these changes affect social interaction and group stability? Most of the original articles tended to be passive in their evaluation of tourism, to the degree that there were accusations of wanting to keep our indigenous study groups in an 'anthropological zoo'.

At that early stage, classification systems, terminology and disciplinary concerns dominated the research. Jafari provides an excellent concise summary of the scientification progress during the early decades (Smith 2001: 28-33). As I read and listened to colleagues, it soon became apparent that the widely read and cited original *Hosts and Guests* was out of date. All authors agreed, with one exception (Reiter, who chose to withdraw), to revise their original chapter, and the second edition appeared in 1989. In accord with Jafari, the new outlook on tourism was Adaptancy, and with a readiness to develop knowledge-based tourism. The interest in tourism had spread rapidly from anthropology to economics, geography and sociology.

I continued to teach the Anthropology of Tourism and observed the felt need for a student text book that consolidated the varying theoretical aspects of cultural tourism. The literature was in varied, scattered journal articles to which students had very little access; thus, *Hosts and Guests Revisited: Tourism Issues of the 21st Century* (2001) was my effort to consolidate the many new themes in tourism research. An error in judgment, the book was too long and too expensive for many students to purchase and might better have been divided in two volumes; one for theory and one for case studies. In addition, the book did not attract widespread attention because it was promoted as a third addition rather than as a new book. The scientification of tourism is not yet complete. Proposed for 2014, in celebration of the 40th anniversary of the initial symposia is at least one book, including retrospective thoughts from the original authors, and one or more conference Special Sessions.

The economic crisis of 2008 to the present is changing the established patterns of tourism dramatically which, coupled with the economic power of emerging nations in Asia and Africa, will create new 'golden hordes' who wish to see in reality what they view on TV. Their traditional cultures often have different cuisines and other preferences that successful hosts must recognise as they redesign facilities to receive new guests. The need to establish techniques to measure these values is increasingly important as demonstrated by the essays in this volume.

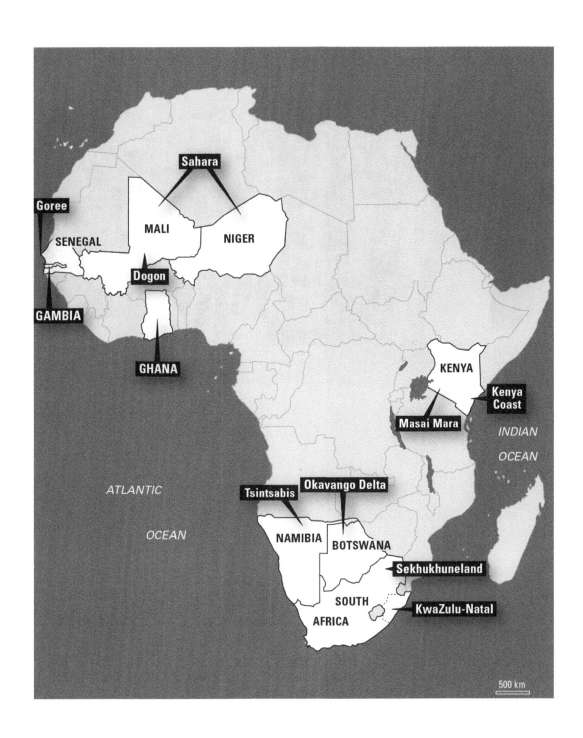

Map showing location of case studies

1.1 Tourists in Sanga, Dogon country Mali, during ethnographic filming of Desmond Morris's The Human Animal, 1994   (© Walter van Beek)

1 · African dynamics of cultural tourism

Walter van Beek & Annette Schmidt

'We are all Africans'
(Sign welcoming tourists in Ghana)

Africa as a parallel universe

Although Africa is not the centre of world tourism and will not be for the foreseeable future, tourism is important for Africa[1]. African tourism has grown in international tourist arrivals, but its present 3-5% share in world tourism[2] is, viewing its land surface and population, a clear underrepresentation. The great magnet for global tourism still is the Mediterranean area, where over 40% of all world tourism is destined for, but also tourism to Asia amounts to 15% of arrivals. The prognostics of the UNWTO before the credit crisis suggested a doubling of tourism arrivals and revenues in the next 15 years, a growth of over 3-5% per year and after the crisis does so again. During the crisis in 2009 global tourism slumped with – 4%, but African tourism continued to grow, 8% for Sub-Saharan Africa, 4% for North Africa, with a prognosis of 5.5 market share for 2010, boosted slightly by the WC 2010. The data on the first half of 2011 show a general increase of 5% in arrivals, and a steady growth of 9% for Africa[3]. Though Africa does show a gap between tourist arrivals and expenditures,[4] income from tourism is crucial and tourism investments are considered to be the most profitable.

Not only is tourism unevenly distributed among continents, also within Africa the distribution of tourists between sub regions and countries is extremely skewed; roughly speaking, Northern Africa takes one third of the market share, southern Africa one third, Eastern Africa a quarter, Western Africa 10%, and the whole of Central Africa has to do with the remaining 1%. These proportions have changed little. No African country shows up in the global top 25

1 A tourist is defined by the World Tourist Organisation as someone who travels to another place or country and stays at least a night over.
2 The African proportion of international tourist arrivals mounted from 2.6 in 1980, 3,3 in 1996, to 5.1 in 2008. The proportion of tourism receipts grew less: 2.6 in 1980, 1.8 in 1996 and 3.2 in 2008. All numbers derive from the UNWTO Barometer of the years 1998- 2010. With thanks to Ton van Egmond. See also Pieter U.C. Dieke, *The Political Economy of Tourism in Africa* (Washington: Cognizant Communication Corporation, 1999).
3 www.UNWTO.org, accessed 18-11-2011.
4 Several reasons may account for the lower income per tourist in Africa: family visits, small merchant travelling, or increase in leakage.

of destination countries, but three countries (South African, Morocco and Tunisia) take more than half of all African arrivals. Why this is so, and what the consequences from these large scale figures are for local populations, can only be seen when we look at the specific features of African tourism. So, in order to develop general insights about the interchanges between 'hosts' and 'guests', we have to view the specific character of specifically African tourism.

Romanticism has been a crucial feature in the development of long range tourism in Europe, and characteristically, the majority of international tourists still stem from North-western Europe where the influence of the Romantic ideals on the elite has been strongest (Ton van Egmond, 2005). Child of an affluent Europe – and relevant only for the affluent minority in society – the Romantic view turned our attention away from ourselves towards our environment. As the wilds around us had been transformed and tamed, the forests of Europe changed from wild and dangerous places full of wolves into well kept gardens. So the concept of 'nature' was domesticated and thus became open for aesthetical considerations: nature was no longer to be conquered, mastered and tamed but to be admired, protected and cherished (Drenthen, Keularz, Proctor eds., 2009). As a critique on the conditions of early industrialism and the futility of human endeavour, Romanticism deplored the fleetingness of human existence and our distance from the surroundings. It is this view of nature, as something beyond us, something fragile and wonderful, that is still dominant in tourism in general, and in African tourism in particular.[5]

History is full of irony. Romanticism coincided also with the start of the colonial expansion of Europe, thus with the subsequent 'pillage of Africa'. Our major focus in this book is on the receiving population. Of course, mass tourism took off well after decolonization, but the similarities between the colonial situation and tourism are evident. Taking the concept of 'dependencia' (in this volume represented by Joseph Mbaiwa as postcolonial theory), came the notion that post-colonial developments tended to recreate colonial dependencies into complex but unequal relations between metropolis and satellite. In this light, the tourist experience in Africa is recognizably 'postcolonial': the rich tourists from the North descend on the poor South to gallivant in their pristine territories.[6] Africa is the prima donna of 'nature'. Here the 'West' goes to find its adventures in the splendour of the African game parks: the vast herds of wildebeest thundering through the immense plains of untouched wilderness, the elusive 'big five'

5 The view of Africa as a romantic universe fits in with one of the main approaches in the anthropology of tourism, tourism as a kind of pilgrimage, see Graburn, 'Secular ritual: a general theory of tourism' in Valene Smith & M. Brent eds., *Hosts and Guests Revisited* (2001: 42-50).
6 For a more elaborated treatment of the neo-colonial aspect see: Graburn, 'Tourism and leisure: a theoretical overview', in Valene Smith (1989: 21-36); M.-F. Lanfant, 'International tourism, internationalization and the challenge to identity', in M.-F. Lanfant, J.B. Allcock & E.M. Bruner eds., *International Tourism: Identity and Change* (1995: 1-43). See also Valene Smith, 'The nature of tourism', in Smith & Brent, eds., *Hosts and Guests Revisited* (2001: 53-68).

every traveller must have spotted and photographed. But Africa is also the continent of colourful, strange cultures, picturesque people, thatched huts in savannah surroundings, where one can encounter a truly 'other' culture. That is the romantic-*cum*-(neo)colonial mix that dominates African tourism: elephants and Bushmen, lions and Maasai, camels and Tuareg.

In this way Africa is for the West a parallel universe, or as Amselle calls it a theme park.[7] One fascination is its sheer vastness. For people from the well-filled European countries, those plains of emptiness and the timelessness of travelling through vast stretches of unchanging landscapes are fascinating, with the Sahara (Klute, this volume) as the extreme example.[8] It is this vastness that allots space for the strangeness of the prima inhabitants, the animals, those that are not native in Europe and America, and thus emblematic for the African wilds. The big five form the main attraction because they are fundamentally alien: large, wild, and in a world totally of their own. They are, in a certain sense, on a par with human beings: they have their own world in which humans do not belong and would be in mortal danger. Of course, a meerkat burrow is just as wild and alien, but too reminiscent of a human family, and they are afraid of humans, not the reverse. The big beasts' in the tourist focus symbolise our fascination but also our awe and fear for the African wilderness as an alien society, a parallel universe.

The African cultures that do command the tourist attention have the same element of strangeness. Maasai, for instance, are described as people that belong in the parks, not outside them,[9] and Wijngaarden's contribution focuses on this. In general, the cultures of Africa are interesting as long as they are 'authentic', which means 'different', 'not European'. So in this book we gaze at Africa in a wide circle around the animals, because that is where the Africans live, sometimes forcefully separated from the animals, as the middle section in this volume shows. But the notion of the parallel universe is always there, the wildness, untamedness, or 'authenticity' as brochures call it. An estimated 80% of tourists come for wildlife, but they never come for one reason only: if they are presented with a choice they opt for 'wildness'-*cum*-culture. Few places are more wild and alien than the Sahara, inhospitable, endless, mysterious, a perennial challenge for any traveller. Tuareg, the blue men of the desert, share this wildness image, and, as Klute shows in his contribution to this volume, they exploit this to the full, thanks to the desert, an observation that holds also for the Dogon and the Bushman.

7 J.-L. Amselle, 'L'Afrique, un parc à thèmes', *Les Temps Modernes* 620-21 (2002: 46-60).
8 An interesting perspective here is Godfrey Baldacchino 'Re-placing matriality. A Western anthropology of sand, *Annals of Tourism Research* 37, 3 (2010), 763-78.
9 See Bruner & Kirschenblatt-Gimblett, 'Maasai on the lawn: Tourist realism in East Africa', *Cultural Anthropology* 9, 4 (1994): 435-70; Raymond Corbey *Wildheid en beschaving de Europese verbeelding van Afrika* (1989), and Isaac Sindiga, *Tourism and African Development. Change and Challenge of Tourism in Kenya* (Aldershot: Ashgate/ASC, 1999).

One corollary of wildness is apprehension, even fear. A tourist brochure describes an African holiday as 'comfortable adventure', highlighting the paradoxical nature of travelling in 'the wilds', while keeping the wilderness at arm's length. Africa is daunting, full of dangers, wild animals, strange people, deadly diseases, without security, a 'wilderness'. Although that is part of its attraction, apprehension is the constant companion of the traveller and may be one reason why 'Africa' is for the tourist branch one destination. 'Africa is a country', a tour operator remarked, 'people choose between going to France, Mexico or Africa' – not Kenya, South Africa or Mali, but *a priori* 'Africa'. Later, through the tour operator, a particular country is chosen. The only exception is 'the Sahara' which is marketed as a destination on its own, separate from 'Africa'.[10] For 'Africa' as such, after the end of apartheid, South Africa has quickly gained dominance on the tourist scene, elbowing Kenya and Tanzania out of their former lead positions, while Zimbabwe has put itself out of the race owing to its political instability. South Africa is seen as a white man's Africa, which generates confidence. African guides, also local ones, see this problem of 'fear' or apprehension quite clearly, often interpreting it as a question of trust, but then cross-cultural trust. In Rhumsiki, the centre of the tourism to the Mandara Mountains of North Cameroon,[11] the guides are acutely aware of the importance of 'trust' (*confiance*), as the basis of the tourist encounter. Characteristic is their low evaluation of fellow Cameroonians. Such stereotypes by Africans on Africans abound: 'The African will sell goat meat as steak'. They recognised that tourism was at its peak when the main hotel had a white *gérant*, and even they themselves felt more at ease with a European running the hotel, just because of trust.

African tourism studies

Anthropology was rather late in studying tourism, 'reluctant adventurers in a new field', as Nash calls them,[12] even if some adventure has always been associated with anthropological fieldwork. But, the anthropology of tourism has taken on well since, and the title of our volume emphasises the continuity of this new enterprise, ever since Valene Smith highlighted it in her Foreword to the seminal publication of *Hosts and Guests* in 1977. Elsewhere in the world, studies of the dynamics of the tourist presence in small scale societies have been proliferating, often framed as indigenous or ethnic tourism. The appellation of indigenous, and to some extent 'ethnic', has the definite slant of a minority situation, a small besieged and marginal group

---

10 See Sébastian Boulay, 'Le tourisme de désert en Adrar mauritanien: réseaux "translocaux", économie solidaire et changement sociaux, *Autrepart* 40 (2006): 75.
11 See Walter E.A. van Beek, 'African Tourist Encounters: Effects of Tourism on Two West African Societies', *Africa* 73, 2 (2003): 251-89.
12 Dennison Nash ed. *The Study of Tourism Anthropological and Sociological Beginnings* (Amsterdam: Elsevier, 2007).

of people holding onto their 'indigenous' culture. Should tourism to local cultures be called cultural tourism, as we refer to it, or indigenous or ethnic tourism?[13] In the literature, ethnic tourism overlaps with cultural tourism referring to activities that engage tourists in the experience of cultural events,[14] while cultural tourism is used for the vanishing life-styles of peasant or 'tribal' cultures.[15] In the latter case the term 'indigenous tourism' is used as well, sometimes defined as part of ethnic tourism or as 'alternative' tourism. These rubrics do not fit well in Africa, where most cultures are 'indigenous' in the sense of 'having lived there always'. In Mali, the Bambara or Malinke are no less 'indigenous' than the Dogon, a people all the tourists head for. 'Ethnicity' is everywhere in Africa and is not a way to distinguish those cultures that merely possess more 'appeal' for the sightseer.

The problem with these terminological distinctions is that cultural tourism has expanded into a wide array of touristic activities, and is branching out in many directions.[16] Isolated communities, local festivals, participatory treks, home-comings, or chieftaincy for show: the array of tourist destinations defies easy classification. This concurs with the varied experience of tourists themselves; those coming to Africa want a broad palette of activities and sights, so that each tourist may be categorised in several ways. In this book, therefore, we use 'cultural tourism' as an inclusive category, also visits to museums and monuments, which are rare in Africa. Viewing this broad array in African hosts-guests relations, we feel that the division into stages of 'indigenous' tourism, as in Weaver's work on Africa, would be premature and unproductive.[17]

Most introductions to Third World cultural tourism hardly mention Africa focusing instead on Latin America, Asia and Oceania.[18] If Africa is in the picture[19] it is mainly in the fringe of the parks, highlighting the plight of the Maasai, the dynamics of community-based wildlife exploitation, such as CAMPFIRE and its recent derivatives, or the problems of cultural villages as tourism projects.[20] South African

13 Valene Smith, 'Introduction', in V. Smith, ed. *Hosts and Guests. The Anthropology of Tourism* (Oxford: Basil Blackwell, 2nd ed. 1989): 4.

14 E. Chambers ed. *Tourism and Culture. An Applied Perspective* (NY: State University of New York Press, 1997): 100.

15 Smith, 'Introduction', 1989.

16 G. Richards 'Introduction: Global Trends in Cultural Tourism', in G. Richards, ed. *Cultural Tourism: Global and Local Perspectives* (New York and London: Routledge, 2007) 1-25.

17 David Weaver 'Indigenous tourism stages and their implications for sustainability', *Journal of Sustainable Tourism*, 18, 1 (2008): 44.

18 For instance, see R. Butler & T. Hinch *Tourism and Indigenous Peoples* (London: International Thomson Business Press, 1996) and more recently Chris Ryan & Michelle Aicken, eds., *Indigenous Tourism: The Commodification and Management of Culture* (Oxford: Elsevier, 2005). Also, of the 31 plates in David Telfer & Richard Sharpley, eds. *Tourism and Development in the Developing World* (London: Routledge, 2008), just two pertain to Africa and both are from South Africa.

19 The Association for Tourism and Leisure Education, ATLAS, has an African section which has hosted conferences on African tourism. It has produced an important series of thematic proceedings on conservation, wealth creation, sustainable development, community empowerment, all in relation to tourism.

20 Mowforth, Martin & Ian Munt, eds., *Tourism and Sustainability. Development, Globalisation*

studies of tourism are different; they address a wide range of types of tourism, including beach holidays, sports, small town, township and 'dark' tourism (to Robben Island),[21] as well as backpacking studies, quite like tourism studies elsewhere.[22] Therefore, this collection of the views from below aims to complement studies done elsewhere on local perceptions, appreciations and creations of tourism, seen from the receiving part of a world system of 'visiting the other'.

Most tourism studies in Africa focus, just as the tourists themselves do, on nature. The main approach is a combined conservation and development perspective, with a development orientation towards the local 'communities' in areas such as empowerment, gender and poverty reduction. Often written from a planning platform, these studies form the logical outcome of the development of this new field, tourism studies, institutionalised now in professional schools at centres of higher learning. This new field is dominated by management issues, the trend that Nash notices in tourism studies in general.[23] Nature conservation looks closely at the relationship between 'nature' and human society as the main occupation and problematic.[24] The principal quandary is between conservation and exploitation: how to manage parks, how to draw income out of tourist visits to parks or safari tourism and yet preserve the holy grail of conservation and ecological diversity. Providing the most telling images, the parks are the principal attraction and most of the cultural tourism discussed in the literature is performed in the slipstream of the powerful fascination of their animals. The combination of parks and surrounding cultural activities are increasingly studied as one system, sometimes called 'tourismscapes' especially in Southern and Eastern Africa,[25] evoking the image of theme parks.

Yet, as the literature points out, the definitions of nature by the conservationist and by the tourist are not the same. The tourist defines African nature by visual standards of wildness, while the conservationist sees systems of interspecies interaction.[26] Anyway, the distinction between nature and culture seems clear, but is not. Although the parks are defined in the tourist scene as well as in popular imagery as 'nature', even as the epitome of nature, many of them are in actual fact cultural constructs, the results of planning, (post)colonial

and New Tourism in the Third World (London: Routledge, 2nd edn, 2009).

21 See Smith, 'Hostility and Hospitality: War and Tourism' in Valene Smith & M. Brent, eds., Hosts and Guests Revisited (Washington: Cognizant Communication Corporation, 2001), 367-79.

22 E.g. Christian Rogerson, 'Backpacker Tourism: Policy Lessons for South Africa from International Experiences', Africa Insight, 37, 4 (2007/8): 27-46.

23 Nash, ed. (2007).

24 V. R. van der Duim & M.E. Kloek, eds., Tourism, Nature Conservation and Wealth Creation in Africa. Thematic proceedings of Atlas Africa Conference, Volume 4 (Arnhem, ATLAS, 2008).

25 V.R. van der Duim, 'Performing African Tourismscapes', in Bob Wishitemi, Anne Spencely & Harry Wels, eds., Culture and Community. Tourism Studies in Eastern and Southern Africa (Amsterdam: Rozenberg, 2007), 25–48.

26 Martin Drenthen, Joseph Keularz and James Proctor, eds, New Visions of Nature: Complexity and Authenticity (Dordrecht, Springer Netherlands, 2009).

intervention, top-down policy and tourist development. The great parks of Africa are in large part culturally created wildernesses, indeed, colonial products resulting from shutting off areas, ousting people, limiting hunting rights and struggling against 'poaching' (i.e., the standard local use of bush area). But human involvement can go much deeper. Parks relate to each other from niche-like positions, both from a management and conservationist perspective: for example small parks without major predators can serve as breeder parks for certain types of animal species. Waterberg Park in Namibia has eliminated all predators, resulting in a park where the tourists can trek on foot, for an additional bodily experience of the wilds of Africa. But it also leads to over-breeding of grazers, especially rhino. New conservancies, such as described in this volume by Brooks, Spierenburg and Wels, rely on these older niche parks to provide stock in order to become privately owned pieces of nature. Here, even the notion of 'reconversion' does not apply: the farms are changed into something they never were in human memory. Not only can nature be commoditised; it can be bought, shaped and managed. So 'Nature' is not only a romantic emotional construct, it is also an invention as well as a fabrication of human culture.

The other reason for the blurring of nature and culture is the selection of what constitutes the relevant cultural expression for tourists: the Maasai (see Wijngaarden), the Bushmen (Koot), and the Tuareg (Klute, all in this volume). They all are more or less equated with nature itself, or with a state of culture close to nature. In the only stretch of wilderness in Africa that is not man made, the Sahara, the Tuareg living there epitomise 'wildmen', as natural masters of an ungovernable universe. And even the Dogon, living with a complete absence of wildlife, are considered a 'natural culture', a notion that we shall explore further when discussing the driving myth of cultural tourism: authenticity. So with some exaggeration one could say that all African tourism is cultural tourism.

The 'gaze' on Africa

Tourism is not a new phenomenon, as many authors have pointed out, with roots in medieval pilgrimage and even older forms of leisure travel,[27] but its explosive growth in the 20th century is an unprecedented phenomenon. Tourism has moved more people over larger distances and to more destinations than all the wars in history together. This travel explosion, made possible by a revolution in technology, is impacting Africa in many ways, including tourism, one major product of globalisation, which came to the continent rather late. African tourism has been of any importance for just half a century, completely dependent as it is on cheap mass air transport.

---

27   Michael Stausberg, *Religion in Modernen Tourismus* (Berlin: Verlag der Weltreligionen 2010).

So visitors are cultural aliens, and the tourist gaze descends from the guest down to the host. In Foucauldian terms, the gaze is an aspect of domination: power is an inherent aspect of any social formation, and so are power imbalances. Tourism is such a 'complex strategic situation'[28] characterised by the omnipresence of power, relational networks and finally, the gaze. The latter is dominant in tourism, the 'inspecting gaze'. In Urry's influential work, *The Tourist Gaze*,[29] he points out the power imbalances in this gaze upon the 'other', one that simultaneously identifies, constructs and judges the tourist destination. The visited know themselves to be watched and judged by people who are not accountable to them.

Tourists are 'eye beasts', with the dominance of the visual under-scored by the omnipresent camera; photo 1.1 on page xii serves as an emblem here, for the large camera belongs in fact to a film crew that had nothing to do with the two tourists. So, even a double gaze is present. The tourist couple daringly stand near the 'masks of the wilds' in order to be photographed; however, their photo-op in itself is shot by a camera team investigating the dynamics of tourism in Dogon country. The first gaze is the tourist looking at the mask, the second one highlights this process of the production of 'alterity', offering a reflexive commentary on the power inequalities of the gaze itself. In this way, tourism forms a postmodern expression of globalisation, not just a diffusion of western products, but also an encounter between two unequal power positions, a bodily encounter that inevitably produces reflexivity. What is missing in the picture, at least not visible, is the 'reverse gaze'.[30] The Dogon dancers in the picture all see what is happening, but they do not look, as part of the performance. They are not people, but masks, and they play their role till the end of the session a few minutes later, undressing well out of sight of the tourists. But they do have their commentaries, afterwards, if they deign to view their visitors at all. This return or reverse gaze is not part of the performance, but each tourist destination has its discourse on visitors, often collectively, sometimes individually. African hosts routinely distinguish between kinds of tourists, sometimes on the basis of colour, often of nationality, definitely of generosity. Their reaction may even endanger a proper performance.

One incident in Dogon: a group of Japanese tourists had ordered a mask dance, which was duly performed. But the Japanese girls in the group, afraid that the scorching sun of Africa would render their skin yellowish,

28 Michel Foucault, cited in So-Min Cheong & Marc L. Miller. 'Power and Tourism: a Foucauldian Approach', *Annals of Tourism Research* 27, 2 (2000): 371-90.
29 J. Urry, *The Tourist Gaze: Leisure and Tracvel in Contemporary Societies* (London: Sage, 2nd ed. 2002). See also J. Urry, 'Globalizing the Tourist Gaze', in Babu, Sutheeshna, Sitikantha Mishra & Bivra B. Parida eds., *Tourism Development Revisited. Concepts, Issues and Paradigms* (New Delhi, Response/Sage, 2009), 152-63.
30 See for instance Deepak Chabra, 'How They See Us: Perceived Effects of Tourist Gaze on the Old Order Amish', *Journal of Travel Research*, 49, 1 (2010: 93-105), as well as Daniel Maoz, 'The Mutual Gaze', *Annals of Tourism Research*, 33. 1 (2006): 221-39.

not only had put up parasols, but wore face masks as well, fully covering them with just slits for the eyes. For the Dogon performers this was almost a bridge too far: masked visitors watching masked dancers! Some of the dancers had to hide behind a rock, laughing their hearts out, and it took some time before the dance had picked up its habitual vigorous rhythm. They talked about it for a week.

Each tourist destination has its 'hidden transcripts' to deal with the power imbalances of the tourist situation, ranging from a front stage performance and backstage gossip (Dogon), to outright rejection.[31] Thus, the local population also contributes to the formation of the gaze. The other party in the gaze are the brokers, the tour operators, the guides, the 'experts', in short the people of the 'tourist bubble' (see below). In many ways the tourist gaze is guided, formed and directed by these agents, defining beforehand how the destination should look, selecting what is of 'touristic importance', and what locals should be on the scene. The encounter between tourists and locals is more complex than a mere host-guest relationship, involving as it does intricate power imbalances in a tripartite system.

In Africa the ambivalence about the phenomenon of tourism takes the form of a discourse on neo-colonialism or post-colonialism. And not without reason. The image of rich Northerners regaling themselves on the wilds of Africa, gazing at the indigenous straw huts in order to go home with pictures of fierce lions, bare breasted 'ebony' women plus the views from their safari lodge, easily generate value judgments on the 'negative effects' of tourism. After all, the difference in wealth between 'hosts' and 'guests' is huge, so a discourse on the tourist threat is easy, defining the former as an environmental hazard and a pernicious moral influence (see Kibicho and McCombes, this volume). This power imbalance is all the more visible by the very absence of internal, domestic tourism in Africa. More than in any other continent, people from the North fly in to view the people of the South. Many authors have commented upon the neo-colonial aspects of this situation, and in our volume this is taken up in several articles, in the terminology of postcolonial theory (Mbaiwa), and as organised hypocrisy on the corporate level (Brooks, Wels & Spierenburg). Peter Burns highlights the continuities between colonial and postcolonial tourism, showing that the power relations between the international tourists-cum-operators and the local recipients, closely mirror the general political and economic imbalance between the First and the Third World.[32]

This post- or neo-colonial aspect shows in the power of definition of what is a suitable tourist destination, in the first place. Second, the

31 I.e. the Suri of Ethiopia: Jon Abbink, 'Tourism and its Discontents. Suri-Tourist Encounters in Southern Ethiopia'. *Social Anthropology*, 8, 1 (2000): 1-17.
32 Peter M. Burns, 'Some reflections on Tourism and post-colonialism', 64-75, Hazel Tucker & John Akama, 'Tourism as Postcolonialism', in Tazim Jamal & Mike Robinson, eds., *The Sage Handbook of Tourism Studies,*(London: Sage, 2009), 504-20.

Northern gaze on Africa comes into full force when international tourism imposes its standards for the hospitality on the selected destination. The shape and quality of the 'bubble' – the infrastructure designed to host the 'guests' – is determined from the outside. The same holds for the country as a whole; tourism is an industry which is vulnerable to problems of insecurity, and the operators deal with governments and national planning offices: 'The existence of tourism affirms the nation's legitimacy and a faith in its internal security.'[33] Those lines between the North and the South can be very short in Africa:

> Early 2011 the French government issued a code red warning for tourism to Mali: the country was unsafe for proper tourists, both the North (which has been unstable for over a decade) and the 4rth region, with the touristic highlights of Djenné and the Dogon area. Tourism plummeted, both destinations losing 60% of their clientele. Actual conditions in the 4th region did not at all warrant the severe warning, and those tourists that defied it toured the area safely. The reason for the code red, Malians were convinced, was political. France wanted a military presence in the Malian Sahel for counter-terrorism purposes, like the USA Sahelcom. When the Malian government bristled against such a neo-colonial military outpost, the French killed off tourism. In July 2011 President Touré of Mali visited France, together with a Dogon mask troupe which was to perform at the opening of the Dogon exhibition at the Musée Branly. Touré made an impassioned plea to the French to lift the code red. Early November the travel restriction was lifted. However, the recent abductions and killing put Mali back on the 'do not visit' list, and neither does the recent coup.

This case encapsulates the power imbalance, even sheer dependency, of an African country on its former coloniser, so a postcolonial perspective is an obvious response. However, a similar imbalance may reign inside the country. The local groups that are interesting for tourists are seldom in a position of power and within their own country are either marginalised or exploited: Bushmen in Namibia (Koot, this volume), Maasai in Kenya (Wijngaarden) and the Kapsiki in Cameroon[34] suffer this predicament. Postcolonial theory concentrates on the international relation more than on the national scene, but the dynamics are quite similar. In any case, the planning of tourism takes place at the political centre, not in the margins; African national tourist planning and development is 'a policy area only if the political elites decide it to be.'[35] This process of internal exclusion is replayed in the formation of the conservancies, as Brooks, Spierenburg and Wels (this volume) show for South Africa. To some extent, at least, one main

33 Richter in Peter M. Burns, 'Some Reflections on Tourism and Post-colonialism', 65.
34 Walter E.A. van Beek, 'Walking wallets? Dogon at the Dogon falaise, in Stephen Wooten ed., *Wari Matters: Ethnographic Explorations of Money in the Mande World* (Münster, LIT Verlag 2005), 191-216, as well as Walter E. A. van Beek, Pacal Lemineur & Olivier Walther, 'Tourisme et patrimoine au Mali. Destruction des valeurs anciennes ou valorisation concertée?' *Swiss Journal of Geography*, 4 (2007): 249-58.
35 Richter, in Peter M. Burns, 'Some Reflections', 68.

difference resides in accountability and political clout; the colonial powers were not accountable to their African local subjects, just to their colonial homeland governments, but present-day entrepreneurs in South Africa are accountable to a post-apartheid society and to general norms of corporate social responsibility, and have to bend over backwards in order to combine the economics of scale with social welfare. Governments are players in this arena, either through their presence, or through their absence, as in the case of the Sahara. All in all, in African tourism governments are not heavily involved, as Ypeij remarks in her 'Afterword', at least not compared to Inca trail tourism.

The focus of the present volume is to view African cultures as the result of a long interaction between societies, environment and history, shaped by intense interaction among themselves, as well as by major exchanges with the rest of the world. In the long list from slavery to colonialism and from liberation to globalisation, international tourism is one of the latest global dynamics engaging the people of the continent. The postcolonial situation has large repercussions for the economy of tourism as well as for its development potential. Although in general tourism is a job creator of repute – albeit mainly of lower income jobs – the actual revenues for both the national level and for the local participants depend heavily on the power structures and the level of control of the local participation over the tourism enterprise. Percentages over 70% leakage (return of earnings from the destination to the tourist sending countries) circulate in the literature,[36] but here too differences are large, with South Africa operating as both a first and third world country in this respect. A rule of thumb in Africa, as far as leakage is concerned, would be that tourism is all the more profitable when the country does not really need it. But, for many countries not having tourism is not an option.

One popular antidote to leakage is the appearance of the numerous community-based operations in many tourist receiving African countries; they either are government initiated, often with considerable aid money, such as in the contribution of Mbaiwa on Botswana, or NGO initiatives working with local people. Many tourists prefer to have a 'cultural village' in their safari programme, even at additional cost.[37] In our volume the articles by Koot, then Finlay & Barnabas are examples of the latter. Though our book is not about the economy as such, it is clear that these endeavours are important for local earnings, albeit never easy to manage. When we move outside the shadow of the parks, leakage seems to diminish and the control over the tourist encounter increases. The Dogon do earn a considerable income, at

36   Isac Sindiga. *Tourism and African Development* (1999). See also Kibicho, this volume.
37   P. Chamonika, R.A. Groeneveld, A.O. Selomane & E.C. van Ierland. 'Tourist Preferences for Ecotourism in Rural Communities Adjacent to Kruger National Park: a Choice Experiment Approach', *Tourism Management* 33 (2012) 1: 168-76. See also Joseph E. Mbaiwa & Amanda L. Stronza, 'The Challenges and Prospects for Sustainable Tourism and Ecotourism in Developing Countries', in Tazim Jamal & Mike Robinson eds., *The Sage Handbook of Tourism Studies* (London: Sage, 2009), 333-53.

least some of them, and for a large part have their own tour operators, usually small businesses with an increasing say in the operation. The same holds, in principle, for the Tuareg, who are hard to replace by foreigners anyway in their severe environment.

Foucault indicates that power imbalances are not just restrictive, but can also be productive. Several authors in this volume focus on creative solutions, in which the receivers of tourism have grabbed opportunities offered by the postcolonial situation itself. Thus, the new Ghanaian institution of development chiefs (Westra, this volume) can be viewed as a creative response to a postcolonial situation. Building on the stereotype of African chieftainship, the Ghanaians cash in on their position at the receiving end of the tourism chain, converting their symbolic capital – chieftaincy – into economic capital. The same holds for the Afro-American tourism, called 'roots tourism', described by Warren & MacGonagle (this volume). Here another African myth, and a quite recent one, gives the hosts a symbolic handle on the identity construction of the visitors, who in this case would like to be called real guests, not tourists. The discourse on 'homecoming' by Afro-Americans is used in inventive ways to generate income, even if the myth of the 'Africanness' of the American visitors is shown to be very fragile. Volunteerism, a part of the tourist industry only recently receiving adequate attention, also plays on the self definition of the volunteers/tourists, or 'voluntourists'.[38] Finally, in 'romance tourism' a similar conversion of mythic tales into cash is evident, although this is a part of the tourist industry which is not particular to Africa. All these examples not only play on some mythic tale on Africa, but also on the problematic self- definitions of tourists. These creative local adaptations to the postcolonial situation all respond to the fact that many visitors want to escape from the tourist label, and would rather be perceived as the 'traveller', 'development chief', 'returning brother', 'volunteer-helper', or 'personally involved in Africa'. Of course, even if their local guides will tell them that they are 'not tourists', they are just that, according to all definitions, and as such are included here.

The bubble

Although the postcolonial situation seems to be a faithful inheritor of the old colonial one, there are marked differences. A tourist is not a coloniser, and does not have a colonial power behind him. Also, although the tour operator is sometimes endowed with consider-able economic clout, s/he has to negotiate with national and local authorities, and has to perform according to mutually accepted standards. The hegemonic power of the coloniser has given way to a

---

38 K. Tomazos & R. Butler, Volunteer Tourists in the Field; a Question of Balance?, *Tourism Management*, 33, 1 (2012): 177-87. Stephen Wearing & Jess Penning, 'Breaking Down the System: how Volunteer Tourism Contributes to New Ways of Viewing Commodified Tourism', in *The Sage Handbook of Tourism Studies* (London: Sage, 2009), 254-68.

competitive system, albeit a skewed one. The sending countries have the power of definition of what constitutes the proper hospitality structure, as well as of the 'sights to be seen', but the agency of the receiving partners is much larger than it was in the actual colonies. The differences stand out in what constitutes the heart of this book, the actual encounter in the field between 'hosts' and 'guests'.

For that encounter, one major concept is the 'tourist bubble', which informs the contributions in this volume. The 'environmental bubble'[39] as it is also now called, consists of the means created to host visitors, the arrangements made for their travel , stay, well-being and above all for their safe return home. This volume looks at the modalities of interchange between the two populations, the local groups and the tourists, who go under the flags of 'hosts' and 'guests', but the 'bubble' concept directs our attention to the brokering third party. The simple model 'traveller meets foreign culture' is inadequate. A sensitive travel writer told at a symposium of her train trip to Riga, Latvia:

> The whole trip and my whole stay in Riga I walked between two rows of people who were facing me, eager to accommodate my every wish, trying to make me comfortable. At one moment I realized that I could not see Riga because of them: they stood between me and Riga, between me and the Latvians, even if they were Latvians themselves. They made my stay possible while preventing me from really being there.[40]

This tourist 'bubble' consists of those infrastructural arrangements that permit the professional reception of guests – such as hotels, lodges, personnel, and general logistics. Inside this 'bubble', the tourist travels, arrives and is housed, an intermediary organisational layer protecting the visitor from the unfortunate features of the destination while permitting some view to the outside. It is the 'bubble' that interacts with the guest society, and thus stands central in the dynamics of the tourist encounter.

There are several sides to it. On the one hand, the bubble enables the tourist to encounter 'Africa' without fully experiencing it. MacCannell calls this the 'empty meeting place':[41] one arrives at the destination, but all meaningful and aimed-for interactions are elsewhere. And when finally an encounter is staged, both parties perform according to the expectations of the other, thus emptying the meeting place of any content that is not contingent on the encounter itself. On the other hand it involves 'surrender' to the agents that control the bubble. The tourists surrender control over their daily decisions, and especially their mobility – the very thing that makes them tourists – to the tour operator, the travel agency, or the tour guide. During their journey they are continually told what to do, when to do it, and when to stop doing it: 'Surrender makes the details of travel so much easier, but in the

---

39 Malcolm Crick, 'Representations of International Tourism in the Social Sciences,' *Annual Review of Anthropology*, 18 (1989): 327.
40 Symposium on tourism, Breda Ethnological Museum, June 1994.
41 Dean MacCannell, *Empty Meeting Grounds. The Tourist Papers* (London: Routledge, 1992).

bargain, the tourists also surrender their control of their relationship with the ... people.'[42]

Usually the bubble is the creation of the middlemen who set up an itinerary and infrastructure guaranteeing comfort and some distance from reality. But also the host culture sets the stage for tourists, to show their life as they want to portray it, in particular as they think the tourists want to see it: a local culture tailor-made for visitors. Other authors speak about the 'tourist culture';[43] the tourist as a 'natural victim of his own definition of reality';[44] or the above-mentioned 'staged authenticity'. The bubble not only produces comfort in the wilderness, it also filters and produces information about the other party in the encounter: on what is 'interesting' and 'authentic', on best spots, sights and scenes. It provides a total and uncontested image of the other, both for the guests and for the hosts, images that respond to each other in what French anthropologists with a nice expression call 'regards croisés' in 'zones tampons de négociacions identitaires'.[45]

There are many kinds of tourist arrangements, and some bubbles have thin, permeable walls, where people may pass through (such as a backpackers' lodge or local family guest accommodation), while others firmly enclose their guests. The clearest examples of the latter are the cruise ship or the isolated resort such as Club Med. In this volume we will gather many bubble varieties in Africa, ranging from the more inclusive ones – usually in the perimeter of game parks – to those where individual tourists try to integrate as much as possible with Africans, in the 'love-bubble'. In African tourism the bubble consists of two parts, one organised by the sending country – the operators – and the other one consisting of local arrangements for travel and stay, local travel agencies, guides, game wardens etc. Here we focus on the second part, on the interaction through the bubble wall at the destination, in the tourist encounter. As it is the bubble that interacts with both tourists and local communities, these dynamics lie at the core of the cases described in this volume. Thus the effect of the bubble on the larger host society is part of the dynamic to be examined here.

Generally, in Africa tourists seem to cherish their bubble more than in other destinations. Tourist brochures on Africa have three kinds of pictures: the majority is of wildlife, then a few shots of a nice sleeping arrangement (if possible with a half-drawn mosquito net and a view on the outside), then a view of a terrace alongside a swimming pool, and finally, one or two photos of smiling, authentic Africans. The largest picture is always of a cheetah, lion or elephant. The tourist is directed to see strangeness, and is then comforted, put at ease:

42   Edward M. Bruner, 'The Maasai and the Lion King: Authenticity, Nationalism, and Globalization in African Tourism', *American Ethnologist* 28, 4 (2001): 906.
43   R. Butler & T. Hinch, *Tourism and Indigenous Peoples* (London: International Thomson Business Press, 1996); M. Picard *Bali, tourisme culturel et culture touristique* (Paris, Harmattan, 1992).
44   Malcolm Crick, 'Representations of International Tourism in the Social Sciences', 327.
45   Anne Doquet & Sara Le Menestrel, 'Introduction' *Autrepart* 40 (2006): 10, 12.

Africa is 'the other', but it can be trusted, or at least the bubble can be trusted.

What we like to call 'bubble authenticity' is important: in Africa the bubble should look 'African'. The hotel lodges are thatched, the woodwork has an African flavour, the mosquito nets have to be very evident, both as an emblem of *Africanité* and as a reassurance that the well-being of the tourist is the first priority. As the sleeping and eating arrangements have to be very near the main attractions, the animals, the view from the veranda is essential. The contributions of Koot and Finlay & Barnabas are good examples of this closeness, with the 'heart of Africa' open to the tourist gaze from the very bubble. For the more adventurous tourist, the bubble is represented by a picture of the four-by-four drive and a comforting photo of a well-rigged tent.

Although backpackers tend to keep their distance from the habitual definition of 'tourists', in Africa even these visitors are quite attached to the bubble of their lodges, and follow the same itinerary as mainstream tourists (van Egmond, this volume). In the words of Hannan and Knox: 'Many forms of backpacking are intimately entwined with forms of mass tourism',[46] and in African tourism that holds *a fortiori*. But for a backpacker, giving up the myth of being a traveller and not a tourist is never easy: 'The individual traveller has overcome a series of rites of passage in order to move from being a tourist to a fully accomplished traveller in an exotic world',[47] and that cultural capital, called 'road status', is too important and has been too expensively acquired to be given up.

Under what conditions and through what dynamics are tourist bubbles created, what are their characteristics, and how 'governable' are they? In the first section of this volume 'Culture, Identity and Tourism' our African hosts, in their joint quest for identity, seem to stimulate their own type of processes in bubble formation, governed by several factors, one of which we would characterise as 'bubble width'. If the host himself is interesting for the tourist, the bubble will be versatile and diversified, but also profitable for the host. For example, the Amish in the USA, a community of fifteen thousand, is shielded from millions of tourist visits per year by a well-developed bubble,[48] and of course Bali is the Asian epitome. In Africa, the Dogon case is relevant (van Beek, this volume).[49] These bubbles tend to be quite large, taking in a maximum array of activities, covering a wide range of cultural activities, productions and landscape features.

46 Kevin Hannan & Dan Knox. *Understanding Tourism. A Critical Introduction* (Los Angeles, Sage, 2010), 52.
47 Ibid., 117.
48 M. Fagence, 'Tourism as a Protective Barrier for Old Order Amish and Mennonite Communities,' in Smith & Brent, eds., *Hosts and Guests revisited* (Washington: Cognizant Communication Corporation, 2001), 201-234.
49 For an overview of local views on the bubble, see Eric Francis, 'Lay Concepts of Tourism in Bosomtwe Basin, Ghana', *Annals of Tourism Research* 37 1(2010): 34-51.

If the host just lives in or near an attractive landscape, the niche width will be narrower and the bubble will be restricted, separated from the community itself, with more leakage and less bolstering of cultural self-confidence. African communities living near game parks exemplify this: here the local culture is an added item on a different agenda. The Kapsiki of Cameroon are a case in point,[50] as is much of the Inca trail (Ypeij, this volume).

The dominant issue here is the image of the host community, as 'authentic', interesting, essentially an attraction *per se*, a factor leading to cultural self confidence in the host community: they know their culture is interesting and exude that belief. This can be 'culture' as in the case of the Dogon, but also 'pure wilderness', as in Sahara tourism (Klute, this volume). A particularly fascinating case is the creation of the bubble around Afro-Americans who come to Ghana and The Gambia to retrace their own pre-slavery roots (Warren and MacGonagle, this volume). Ghana is also the stage for another 'bubble formation process', which uses one specific African cultural feature as its main attraction: the 'African Chief'. In all four cases the bubble is formed by the creative response of the local population, who not only make the tourist stay possible but also meaningful, adapting themselves to tourist expectations. Bubble formation can even start without any attraction to speak of whatsoever, but merely inspired by the local idea that the creation of a bubble generates tourists, as is demonstrated in the contribution to this volume from Ineke van Kessel.

A second set of factors is environmental: geographic isolation, the place in the tourist circuit, the place within the national state, the volume of tourism and the provenance of the tourists (internal or international) and safety. An isolated marginal situation with a rapidly increasing tourist flow is not conducive to the formation of an adequate reception structure and lead to conflicts. The Ethiopian Suri, for example, dislike being visited and photographed and may react violently against tourists who do not pay up.[51] A tourist industry that is crucial for the nation and with a long history of gradual expansion will generate processes of creative and diversified bubble formation. The game parks of East and South Africa are in this position, but at quite some social cost. Brooks, Spierenburg & Wels describe a process of bubble formation in its incipient phase, analysing the plight of local people whose livelihood is threatened by the creation of new game parks.

The most 'classic' bubbles are in the fringe of such parks, as discussed in our second section. Chapters by Mbaiwa; Finlay & Barnabas; Koot, and Wijngaarden all highlight the effects of the bubble on neighbouring peoples. The deep, historical impact has been the loss of hunting land: the bubbles described have been created to cushion

50 Walter E.A. van Beek, 'Tourist Encounters', *Africa* (2003).
51 Jon Abbink, 'Tourism and its Discontents', 1-17.

that shock. At the same time, local arrangements around the parks have to live up to tourists' high expectations.

A third factor is the permeability of the bubble. Tourists are quite aware of it, and even if they cherish its existence, they do want sometimes to go through its wall or at least engage in more interaction with local hosts than the bubble produces. Our third section examines those who want to experience Africa not 'as tourists', but as backpackers (or 'travellers') (van Egmond), romance tourists (McCombes and Kibicho), as well as the typically intermediate category of 'volunteers' (Swan). Although these encounters may be varied and seemingly bubble-less, in the end they are still inside one, with the local amenities of backpackers' lodges, sex workers and guest families making up a versatile array of bubble amenities. Tourism is an industry of images and one sector of that industry capitalises on the idea of an absent bubble, on direct contact as well as on a concrete contribution to local societies. The articles in this volume show that this entails its own contradictions and problems.

Fragility

Tourists first construct an image of Africa and then go and discover the 'real Africa', constructed as wild, non-human and pristine. Africa is the continent before the coming of man, or before the coming of 'civilisation': the African myth, with its varied versions (see Koot, Mbaiwa, Finlay & Barnabas, Klute, this volume). For some, it is the continent of their roots (i.e. for the Afro-Americans, MacGonagle and Warren, this volume), but for most it is the 'ultimate elsewhere'. This image of Africa is easy to construct. The media show Africa in essentially two ways. The first, through the news channels and documentaries, is as a continent of suffering and crisis, with hunger and war reducing people to recipients of much needed charitable donations. Africa has to be helped, at least the people in Africa have to be kept alive by the rich north, and one contribution to this volume, from Eiliadh Swan, discusses those tourists who try to combine helping with enjoying Africa: volunteers. The alternative route is through television adventure channels such as National Geographic, Animal Planet and Discovery: there, Africa is large animals, plus people giving their best efforts to preserve the precious wildlife resources. These animal riches are considered as a part of the world heritage, not the property or responsibility of Africans themselves. Usually, it is white people who interact with the African game, not blacks (though they may help as game wardens) and most documentaries feature white people whispering tidbits of interesting information about the animals close-focus to the camera. Here, as well, the message is clear: Africa is wild and has to remain that way, through our concerted (Northern) intervention.

Thus, the Romantic illusion is still dominant in this image of

Africa.[52] Africa means time travel, back to the era of our not-yet-existence; African wildlife safaris are the present day alternative for the Grand Tour. The gentleman from Britain, gazing upon the ruins of the Parthenon to ponder upon the foundations of European civilisation, finds his present counterpart in the couple from Germany training their long telephoto lens on a shy rhino, savouring the pre-human universe. The Romantic lie, as René Girard calls the bucolic life in rural arcadia of early Europe, continues in the pictures of 'authentic African life' in the villages bordering the game parks. Franklin criticises Urry for his singular focus on the 'tourist *gaze*', arguing that today's tourist is much more 'embodied', seeking experiences with all senses, not just through the eyes.[53] It is, as Bruner calls it, 'the sheer materiality of being there'.[54] However, in Africa, with the exception of romance tourism, the gaze is still absolutely dominant, implying an enduring distance between the observer and the observed. And even the 'experience hunger' of the backpacker gives way to the exigencies of the African situation (van Egmond, this volume).

The Romantic view idealised a fleeting past, its very fragility a crucial appeal to the emotions. From the start tourism has been an emotional, judgment-loaded subject, and 'negative' or 'adverse' effects of tourism were routinely adduced, tourism often being evaluated as detrimental to local culture or regional ecologies. In the European context – the dominant one in international tourism – the beaches of the Mediterranean, the museums of the great cities and the few unspoilt places of the old continent would be trampled by mass tourism. It seems the world was still good at the time of the Grand Tour, when the English gentleman, who never had to earn a farthing, visited the cultural shrines of Southern Europe, experiencing his own renaissance as a cultural connoisseur. But mass tourism has been depicted as a moral catastrophe, a scourge on the land, disrupting local mores and commoditising local cultures.

In cultural and ethnic tourism the notion of fragility dominates. For instance, in tourism to the Dogon area in Mali, until a decade ago, tourists were convinced the Dogon culture would change rapidly because of the tourist (i.e. their own!) presence, still counting themselves 'among the first' to visit the pristine area. Lately, the tenor has subtly changed. Well aware of the intensity of Dogon tourism and its history, quite a few say that they are the last to see and witness 'authentic' Dogon culture. Of course, the main tourist spots in Africa are game parks, where the separation between sight and seer is artificially guaranteed, with full agreement of the tourist, not primarily to protect him, but to protect the animals. The idea that

---

52 See for an in-depth analysis of the concept of nature, Drenthen, Keularz and Proctor eds., *New Visions of Nature* (2009).
53 Adrian Franklin, *Tourism, an Introduction* (London: Sage, 2003).
54 Edward Bruner, *Culture on Tour. Ethnographies of Travel* (Chicago Ill.: University of Chicago Press, 2005), 26.

the tourist is a stranger who puts the very existence of the destination in jeopardy, is very strong. But it is unwarranted.

An increasingly important notion in cultural tourism is 'heritage'. The UNESCO world cultural heritage list is intended to be an inducement for conservation, but also serves as a boost for tourism, thus highlighting the fragility of the very values it tries to protect. In most European countries, UNESCO recognition is viewed as the official stamp of *national* heritage and culture, but in African countries with heritage sites, these are usually taken as more global than national. African tourism lacks internal national tourism and relies only on international visitors. Thus, the heritage becomes international property, which even holds for the tales about the sites. Tourists visiting Dakar routinely go to Gorée, as one of the UNESCO-recognised World Cultural Heritage Sites. The high point of the Gorée tour is a visit to the '*maison des esclaves*'. This serves as a splendid backdrop to the blood curdling tales about the export of slaves, the 'voyage sans retour' (see Warren & MacGonagle, this volume). The actual historical fact that the smallish house did not serve as housing for the merchants and the slaves, as the main trade was elsewhere, and that such an arrangement would have been quite impossible, is of little import and does not detract from the grand unifying story of the slave trade. Relevant is the invention of 'history on the spot'. And essential in the invention of the past is its very fragility: our roots are always in danger of being uprooted, and UNESCO recognition enhances that sense of scarcity and fragility. As *lieux de mémoire* are rare in Africa, so inventive storytelling is called for. It is the story which is dominant, not the architecture, a situation highlighted by the opportunism of this kind of tourism, which focuses mainly on English speaking countries, as if no slaves were ever exported from Africa's Francophone shores.

Romanticism has no part in the heritage of the African continent itself, and the distanced, sentimental evaluation of nature and history are alien to most African cultures. When Africans become tourists, they do not visit their own country: few Malians from Bamako make a holiday trip to view the famous Mosque of Djenné, and all visitors to the Dogon country, the tourist hotspot in Mali, are from overseas, either Europe, America, or Japan. Africans visit family abroad, or the great cities of Europe and generally are little interested in the historical and cultural repertoire of other nations. South Africa and maybe Kenya form exceptions, but only to some extent. Kenya is reported as having some internal and regional tourism, but that too seems to be dominated by family visits.[55] South Africa enjoys considerable internal tourism, but here the white and Indian sub-populations dominate the tourist scene. This absence of internal tourism in other African countries precludes both a suitable and flexible infrastructure

55 Isac Sindiga, *Tourism*, 1999.

and a sense of the 'normalcy of the tourist': the tourist remains the stranger, the alien, and crossing the bubble wall will remain difficult.

Host–guest interactions

African hosts vary from conventional suppliers of hospitality as part of the attractions, whether as cultural performers to long-lost brothers or from fellows-in-need to sexual partners. Hosts in Africa are part of the story, for tourism in Africa is based upon a myth, a discourse about the 'other' and ourselves, about wildness, danger and roots. The various contributors give their own name to this myth, but the main point is who holds the power of definition. The constant reconstitution of Africa in European eyes, called indeed postcolonial by Mbaiwa (this volume), shows that this power definitely resides in the North, fed by the media and followed by the hosts. Motivated both by the ever-present authority of 'whiteness' (see Swan, this volume) and by well understood economic need, the hosts redefine their own identity in terms of the visitors. This may lead to an ambivalence between host and guest, and the complicated triangulation (ego, other and the other's view of ego) results in various outcomes.

The tourist encounter is an exchange of images, for the tourist is armed with notions how 'the other' should look stemming from media, travel books and guides, with the photographic high ground of the National Geographic Magazine as the ultimate yardstick. However, the tourist is not expected to show that to his host, but to accept whatever is offered or told: 'The role of the tourist is to be... adventurous, wide-eyed and curious.'[56] With this creative performance of proper tourist behaviour, the host-guest interaction may stimulate collective self-esteem at the hosts' side, as for the Tuareg and Dogon (Klute, van Beek, this volume), select specific institutions, such as chieftaincy (Ghana, Steegstra this volume), or create ambivalence, as in the heritage tourism of Afro-Americans (Warren & MacGonagle, this volume). An interesting case is the volunteer who is in a classical ambivalent position, between tourist and development worker, helping on the one hand, but independently defining what help the other needs (Swan, this volume).[57] These mirror images from the guests shape the self-definition of the host community in quite diverse ways. On the one hand, the people at the rim of the parks tend to be defined as belonging to that centre of wildness, thus as 'primitive', 'pristine', 'children of nature´ (Koot, Warren & Barnabas, Mbaiwa, Wijngaarden). Of course, they tend to play out their own identity *vis à vis* the tourists, but that is neither fully comfortable nor completely isolated from their society beyond the bubble. In Africa,

56   Kevin Hannan & Dan Knox, *Understanding Tourism.* (2010): 76.
57   For an overview see Stephen Wearing & Jess Penning, 'Breaking Down the System: How Volunteer Tourism Contributes to New Ways of Viewing Commodified Tourism' in Jamal & Robinson, eds., *The Sage Handbook of Tourism Studies* (London: Sage 2009) 254-68.

the hosts who form the bubble are not isolates but belong to local communities. So, foreign definitions of identity tend to spill over into local definitions of self. This process even shows in the appreciation of the environment. For a long time anthropologists have reported how their informants defined and appreciated their territory in terms of use and usefulness, not aesthetics,[58] but how Northern definitions also tend to spill over into the local ones. Thus, the Tuareg tend to reevaluate their desert from a dangerous place into captivating scenery (Klute, this volume).

One factor in this complicated equation is the concept of 'cultural self-confidence', i.e. the way in which people define their own identity in terms of their own cultural content. The Tuareg form a good example of this, as they use the tourist evaluation of their culture to counteract negative national connotations. The Dogon, who cherish their *tèm* (custom) view the tourist as a welcome stranger, as he is interested in the same performance as the Dogon are themselves[59]. When local cultures are a principal attraction, tourism implies cultural selection; from among the many cultural expressions the most spectacular are chosen as the most 'characteristic' and become show performances, touristic products, that become the iconic core of the culture.[60] Thus, the camel ride in the Sahara, the mask dance in Dogon country, the healing ceremony of the Hai//om, the dance of the Maasai, and the baskets of the Botswana San have become the core of their culture. But the power of definition is elsewhere. Even when hunting is a central issue, the performance is either an imitation of the hunt, or a tale about former hunts: tourism has redefined hunters into people who are allowed only the story of the hunt. Or, as in the Maasai case, as people who have to deny hunting in order to protect their image as guardians of game. This selection and commoditisation has been decried in the past as inauthentic and as 'staged authenticity', but is a reality in itself. After all, staging oneself does change oneself, especially when the 'tourist border zone' is close to the living community and not a show location[61]. All in all, one should not underestimate local creativity, as Africans pick up new tourist ideas quickly; the Ghanaian chieftaincy and roots tourism, exemplify the creative ways in which the Africans have reshaped the bubble to tourist expectations and towards economic profit.

The notion of authenticity long has haunted the study of tourism.

58   Walter E.A. van Beek, 'Eyes on Top? Culture and the Weight of the Senses, in Anne Storch, ed., *Invisible Africa, Sprache und Geschichte in Afrika* 21, (Koppe: Köln, 2010) 245-70.

59   Internationally, the clearest case of a large cultural self confidence would be Bali, which as McKean argues did not become 'less Balian' through its massive tourism, but 'more Balian': Phil McKean, 'Towards a Theoretical Analysis of Tourism: Economic Dualism and Cultural Involution in Bali', in T.V. Singh, L. Theuns & M. Go, eds., *Towards Appropriate Tourism: The Case of Developing Countries* (Frankfurt: Peter Lang, 1989),120.

60   See also Chris Ryan and Michelle Aicken, eds., *Indigenous Tourism: The Commodification and Management of Culture* (Oxford: Elsevier, 2005).

61   Like for instance Shakaland in South Africa, a old film set turned into a tourist show ground. The performances are a mix of dances from several ethnic groups in South Africa.

McCannell conjured up this ghost with his theory that the modern tourist experiences alienation in his modern, industrial life and travels on a quest for authenticity, trying to bond with nature and a simpler life during his holidays.[62] The tourism industry then more or less tricks the traveller by a performance of otherness, a 'staged authenticity'. Tourists are aware of that staging, 'tourists believe that the "real" authentic parts of the world are to be found backstage, hidden from view'.[63] But when they try to look backstage, that again is staged, so tourists fail in their quest for authenticity. And throughout, the lack of authenticity is linked with the decried 'commoditisation' of culture.[64] Since that first start, the question of authenticity shifted more to the destination, for two reasons. The first is that tourism has become so engrained in our postmodern identity, that it no longer generates the question why we travel. In the 1970s scholars still could be astonished that people left comfortable homes for uncomfortable destinations, in the 21st century travel is considered a basic fact of life. Second, tourism has 'discovered' the truly different other, long the province of anthropology, but how different and how 'real' is he? The notion of authenticity has become a sales pitch for tour operators as well as a basis for cultural capital of the experienced tourists, the definition of out-there-ness.

What authenticity does mean is hard to establish. In itself authenticity implies a contradiction. No living community will define itself as authentic or inauthentic; the question only surfaces when a third party comes in with a preconceived idea and then extends judgment. That very fact of the encounter with the other with a dominant gaze, in principle means that no authenticity is ever possible; as Katherine Whitehorn long ago wrote in the UK Guardian: 'The only unspoilt village is the one no outsider has ever visited, including you.'[65] *Stricto senso*, any discourse on authenticity belies itself. Authenticity is the way we think that the past should inform the present.[66] Authenticity is a myth, in fact the foundational myth of tourism and a powerful driving myth in the case of Africa, and as such reflects something of the fundamental paradoxes of this global industry. Bruner sums it up: 'Authenticity is a red herring, to be examined only when the tourists, the locals, or the producers themselves use the term'[67].

However, anthropologists should realise that 'authenticity' resonates with the concept of 'tradition', which has long been a leading concept in the discipline. The image of oldness, of knowledge handed

62   Dean MacCannell, *The Tourist. A New Theory of the Leisure Class* (London: MacMillan, 1976).
63   Naomi Leite & Nelson Graburn, 'Anthropological Interventions in Tourism Studies' in Jamal & Robinson, eds., *The Sage Handbook of Tourism Studies*, 43.
64   Dean MacCannell, 'The Commodification of Culture,' in Smith & Brent, eds., *Hosts and Guests Revisited*, 380-90.
65   Cited in Martin Mowforth & Ian Munt, *Tourism and Sustainability,* 224.
66   Keir Martin, 'Living pasts. Contested Tourism Authenticities', *Annals of Tourism Research* 37,2 (2010): 549.
67   Edward M. Bruner, *Culture on Tour* (2005): 5.

over unchanged through the generations and of historic authority that the notion of 'tradition' invokes, has been proven just as erroneous and mythical as 'authenticity' is now. But myths are important, even when everyone knows it is a myth. Many studies have shown that tourists are not deceived, but relish the performance of 'authenticity' nevertheless[68]. So, even if anthropology has by now deconstructed the notion, the appeal of 'authenticity' will remain, so the concept will continue to haunt us. In this volume van Kessel shows us how the advent of authenticity driven tourism can become an economic chimera.

Being a host demands knowledge of the guests, information as well as creativity. African hosts do know their guests, making subtle distinctions between the different nationalities, in all host situations, not only in romance. Sometimes the hosts travel Europe in order to gain additional knowledge and see for themselves the life word of their clientele. The tourist who comes armed with stereotypes, is met by a similar array of stereotypical images about what to expect of that type of white person. Sometimes, this stereotype clashes with the self image of the tourist, as in the case of heritage tourism, where the Afro-American enters an arena of contradictory definitions, 'who is African?', a source of deep ambivalence on the tourist side (Warren and MacGonagle). The Northern definition of Africa is met by a definition of 'whiteness' (Swan), which in the volunteer situation is all the more relevant as there the tourists pretend to come for reasons beyond themselves, to 'help' people, thus mixing the romantic Africa with the image of the suffering one, a mixture making from some awkward and ambivalent relations between hosts and guests, and consequently, between guests and middlemen[69].

Gender is an underexplored issue in tourism. Crucial in the forms of 'romance tourism' in Africa, of which we have the Eastern and Western as representatives (Kibicho and McCombes) in this volume, for the remainder gender is quite absent. The African bubble population is predominantly male (even in romance tourism!) and tourists interact very little with African women, or the reverse. Language constraints are one issue, but so is the definition of wildness, easier embodied in an African male than in a woman with children. From the hosts' side as well, interaction with foreigners knows its circumscribed rules and restrictions, in which gender lays an important role. African woman form a backdrop of tourism, a photo op, a quick view but with very little interaction: the feminine whiteness of the visitors to the bubble is met by varicoloured male Africans. In our examples we see the blue Tuareg men with camels, Dogon men with red masks, Ghanaian guides with stories of the past, chiefs with stools and *kente* cloth, Maasai men with spears (Klute, van Beek, Warren & MacGonagle,

68   Naomi Leite & Nelson Graburn, 'Anthropological Interventions', 42. See also Eric Cohen 'Authenticity and Commoditization in Tourism', *Annals of Tourism Research*, 15 (1988): 467-86.
69   Wearing & Penning, 'Breaking Down the System'.

Steegstra, and Wijngaarden respectively) and even the virtual space is populated with men (van Kessel). Also the various Bushmen groups and farm hands are predominantly male, even if they sell women's products.

The essays

African tourism is draped around the parks, so we have positioned our papers around the parks as well. In the first section, culture and identity form the main focus, starting deep inside one village dispute in Mali, then moving out into the wide open Sahara, and across the Atlantic, ending in virtual space. The tourist bubbles differ, but are defined as inclusive as possible, and all impinge upon processes identity construction.

Walter van Beek's case study narrates the conflict about the access to a tourist performance. Here, the reader is drawn deep inside a local community that offers a close-up view of an intricate arena of small scale in-fighting, in which tourist issues mingle with personal ones. Because the revenues from tourism have become substantial, access to tourism is an important issue. This extended case shows the relationships between tourist performances of the Dogon mask dances in Tireli, and the traditional masked dances that form a crucial part of Dogon death rituals. The question on hand is whether young men who dance for the tourists have to be initiated. The two village halves were, and still are, divided on the issue, with a drawn social battle between the 'orthodox' and the 'heterodox'. The conflict – into which the author was drawn quite closely – as well as its eventual solution, not only highlights some important values of Dogon culture and religion, but also examines the relation between the bubble the Dogon have created for their tourists, with the 'real life' in the village. This case also highlights that the impact of tourism, through the medium of the tourist bubble, is part of a wider process of social change in host communities.

Georg Klute attempts to bring together a political economy and a semiological approach to tourism research. In Saharan tourism and for the Tuareg, the economic transactions between migrants from a nomadic background and their hosts are based on the principle of 'foreignness'. Klute highlights the rather surprising relationship between Saharan tourism and the Tuareg upheavals in Mali and Niger. Tourist guides became members of the rebel movements; as former rebels they found employment in the tourist industry. It is argued that the importation of the image of the extreme world of the Sahara and its untamed inhabitants is by no means limited to those inside the 'tourist bubble'. It penetrated Tuareg society, contributed to the political notion of a Tuareg territory, and reinforced nationalism.

The contribution from Elizabeth MacGonagle and Kim Warren argues that the quest for a homeland for African-American pilgrims is fraught with complicated relationships surrounding the trans-atlantic slave trade and multiple definitions of the meaning of race and identity. In their exploration of identity formation in West Africa and the Diaspora, the divergent states of mind of the pilgrims relate to contested interpretations of the past. Local tour guides at heritage sites design tours not only to provide a palatable historical narrative of slavery, but also to meet the expectations of tourists. The pilgrimages of the 'heirs of slavery' to West Africa arouse the hope of recovering a connection to an African homeland. We observe the creation of fictive pasts and identities by those who seek to redefine their African heritage and view West Africa as a place of 'return'. Ghanaian responses to the presence of tourists from the Diaspora show the different conceptions of race, belonging, and heritage that have developed since Ghana's independence.

Ineke van Kessel takes us on a virtual tour of Sekhukhuneland in South Africa. Tourism is South Africa's fastest growing industry and many nationals are eager to gain their share of tourist revenue. There are numerous initiatives to capture even a trickle from the ever increasing inflow of tourists. Prominent among the relatively new sectors is cultural or heritage tourism, with the potential to involve not only tour operators, but local residents as well. Ordinary South Africans see pots of gold at the end of the rainbow, but have little understanding of what will attract the influx. What to do if there is no game park anywhere nearby, or if local historical imagery is not as colourful as the archetypical Zulu warrior or the staunch Boer commando? Many South African municipalities develop elaborate websites, hoping to attract tourists. The proudly presented virtual heritage tour on the website of the Fetakgomo municipality in Sekhukhuneland is tempting, but how does the virtual tour compares to the real-life experience?

At the fringe of the parks we are confronted with beneficiaries as well as 'victims of tourist development'. Displacement and loss of control, but also the shaping of the self to the view of the other, are the main themes in bubble formation around the parks. Thus this section surveys first the results of the process of park construction, i.e. the 'production of wilderness', and then provides a critique of the processes themselves as they stand at present. In the park fringe the bubbles have to conform to rigorous standards set by the North, and the gaze of the visitor dominates.

International tourism in the Okavango Delta, Botswana, is defined by Joseph Mbaiwa in Chapter Six through the three myths of the unchanged, unrestrained, and uncivilised. These explain the behaviour of tourists as 'guests' and their expectations of those local people who are the 'hosts'. International tourism in the Okavango Delta is designed to meet the needs and interests of tourists from developed countries. Tourists' expectations are centred on an enjoyment of a complete wilderness, full of dangerous animals set aside for the indulgence of tourists, staying in luxurious accommodation resorts. In the myth of the uncivilised, tourists stereotype a primitive, untamed nature onto natives such as the San or 'Bushmen' peoples. But tourists' stereotypes and expectations do not represent reality. While tourism has a positive socio-economic impact in destination areas, sustainable tourism should reduce the unfair expectations and behaviours of visitors and promote a tourism industry that is sensitive to the socio-cultural, economic and political setting of the people they come to 'see'.

Kate Finlay and Shanade Barnabas pursue issues of representation and development involving cultural tourism at !Xaus Lodge, a venture partly owned by the ≠Khomani San and situated in the Kgalagadi Transfrontier Park. The historical representation of the San has proved influential in the way in which the current ≠Khomani community present themselves and articulate their culture when engaging with 'outsiders'. The romantic primitivist inclination of governments towards preservation instead of development has contributed to the misuse of the land they won through their 1999 land claim. Although the ≠Khomani were awarded land they were not given training in how to use the land profitably. A number of the ≠Khomani seem to construct their authenticity in relation to the romantic myth.

Taking the Treesleper camp at Tsintsabis, Namibia as his topic, in the following chapter Stasja Koot looks at a community-based tourism project. Treesleeper illustrates the changing culture of the Hei//om, since tradition and modernisation are strong forces within the project. Treesleeper Camp and the Hei//om Bushmen make use of the possibilities within the growing industry of tourism in Namibia, by using the proximity of Etosha and its tourists to generate income. They use their possibilities, traditional as well as modern, within the prevalent tourism's environmental bubble of the 'African Myth'. But the Hei//om Bushman's relationship with wildlife, and the current situation of the latter has changed dramatically. Tourists can hunt game on designated farms as part of their 'African Myth', while Bushmen are restricted to hunting for survival; traditional hunting techniques have thus become performances and as such the source of a completely different revenue. At the same time, the village tour of the specially developed Treesleeper Camp is an example of an attraction where tourists can get closer to 'real Africa'.

The changing relationship between people and wildlife in Kenya is described by Vanessa Wijngaarden in her chapter on the Maasai hunting paradox. In tourist settings, Maasai living near Masai Mara National Reserve speak out strongly against hunting and the consumption of wild animal products. Privately however, they do obtain and use these products on a regular basis. This paradox largely derives from the tourist bubble between local 'hosts' and their 'guests'. Strict conservation efforts fuelled by international conservationists as well as tourism have disturbed the hierarchy between animals and people. Locals are however unable to discuss their interdependent relations with wild animals in an open arena. The stereotype of the ignoble savage poacher is a constant threat, while the stereotype of the noble savage, though important in obtaining a tourist income, does not compensate for the loss of land, crops and livestock through conservation efforts and tourism. In order to remain an attractive object of tourism the Maasai have to continue to present themselves exclusively as herders who have safeguarded the savannah wildlife for tourists to come and view.

'Is this the organization of hypocrisy?' is the question that Marja Spierenburg, Harry Wels and Shirley Brooks ask themselves in their contribution on game farming in South Africa. It is important to take into account that the concept of 'hypocrisy' is used here in a more neutral sense, i.e. the 'difference between words and deeds, the eventuality that organisations may talk in one way, decide in another and act in a third'. Perceived antagonistic demands by (international) tourists for 'pristine African landscapes' on the one hand, and for farm dwellers on the other to have a 'place to live and belong' are met by private wildlife conservationists and more particularly game farmers in KwaZulu-Natal, South Africa, by consciously organising and managing the differences between the 'front stage' and the 'back stage' of private wildlife production. They do this by presenting a perhaps over-polished image of corporate social responsibility to outside audiences, while persisting in deliberate changes to the landscape to create a 'pristine' wilderness landscape, with all the messy issues of land and labour rights that this entails.

The bubble is meant to contain the tourists, but stepping out of it is always tempting. The third section of this volume offers the most 'embodied' discussion, moving gently from the backpacker's lodge, via the helping white hands establishing 'life-long' connections through 'development chiefs and queen mothers', as well as to the more profound involvement in the African romance. Although it is an open question whether the tourists in this category are really leaving the bubble – after all, intense contacts are also 'catered for' in the ´love-bubble´ – this tourism leads to quite different definitions of ownership and power relations inside it.

Unfortunately, studies on the interaction of backpackers with local residents or 'hosts' in Africa are almost entirely missing. Therefore Tom Egmond had to concentrate on the guests' side of the story. Backpacker tourism is a recent phenomenon in Africa, originating in the 1960s and 1970s, breaking through in the 1990s, yet still appearing in only a few countries. The drifters or nomads of the early 1970s were almost exclusively drawn from the countercultures in western society. By the turn of the 21st century, backpacking had undergone a transformation from an 'alternative' to an increasingly mainstream form of tourism. Destinations are objects of a generalised curiosity and backpackers seem to be driven into the far corners of the globe by the restless search for ever-new experiences. Romanticism appears to be an extremely important concept in explaining the long-haul travel of Westerners and 'authenticity' becomes a key word among travellers in developing countries. 'Tourist traps' refer to staged authenticity, i.e. adaptations of local culture to the tastes of visitors.

In Eiliadh Swan's study on volunteers in South Eastern Ghana, the engagement of the guest looks profound but is often misunderstood. The traditional separation of tourism and development as modes of travel via emergent forms of international volunteering are differently perceived by Western volunteering organisations, volunteers themselves and their Ghanaian 'hosts'. A growing number of mainly European and American volunteers pay thousands of dollars to American organisers for the chance to 'help' Africans and be 'immersed' in a different culture. The position of volunteerism, as situated somewhere in-between tourism and development, looks increasingly fraught and untenable. For Ewe hosts, the presence of volunteers in their town reminds them of other differences: those between being a Westerner and being a Ghanaian, or being rich and staying poor. Discussions with both sides of the situation reveal that the 'hosts' and their 'guests' are often still at odds over the nature and purpose of international volunteerism itself.[70]

Marijke Steegstra shows that sometime Ghanaian communities try to establish 'life-long' connections with foreigners by installing them as so-called 'development chiefs' and 'development queen mothers'. These are honorary positions bestowed on commoner-foreigners in order to commend and secure their contribution to local development efforts. Critics fear that the installation of foreigners as chiefs will have a negative impact on Ghanaian culture and will lead to an erosion of chieftaincy. Nevertheless the installation of foreign development 'chiefs' and 'queens' is flourishing in Ghana. But what happens in the interaction between foreign development chiefs or queen mothers and their hosts, and what is the impact of this practice on local culture? Although the proliferation of development chiefs might contribute to an erosion or folklorisation of the title itself, it does not weaken the position of the Ghanaian hereditary rulers and their office. Rather, the advisory foreign development chiefs seem to add to the grandeur of the court.

In romance tourism, guest and host are closely interwoven and at the same time 'miles apart'. Wanjohi Kobicho demonstrates that in Kenya, local people's views on sex (trade)-oriented tourism varies depending on their interests and experiences. In order to illustrate

---

70 Another region where tourism often is combined with development assistance is, curiously enough, the Sahara, see Boulay 'Tourisme en Adrar', 79 and Emmanuel Grégoire, 'Tourisme culturel, engagement politique et actions humanitaires dans la région d'Agadès (Niger)', *Autrepart*, 40 (2006): 95-113.

the nexus between the tourism industry and the sex profession, Kobicho uses data from a leading tourism destination in the country, Malindi. Local residents view tourism as the source of the sex trade, and the encounter between the tourists and their host community has challenged behavioural patterns in Kenya. These one-time or long-term relationships between visited/hosts and visitors/hosted enable the locals to be part of the tourist bubble, albeit momentarily. The bubble has offered new roles for local men and women, exposing weaknesses within the norms of the local social spheres. Sex (trade)-oriented tourism entails the willingness of the (foreign) tourists to engage with the 'other' entailing a profound involvement with contrasting cultures to some degree on the former's terms.

Lucy McCombes describes the Gambian 'love-bubble' and asks the controversial question, whether it is desirable or possible to burst this particular bubble, to stop this sex or romance tourism trade. By highlighting some of the complexities of 'romantic' host-guest encounters in Gambia, she adds depth to the existing popular debate on whether they are about sex or love. 'Bumsters' and their associations with sex or romance tourism in Gambia are popularly derided. This typically reflects the perspective of those who judge that such relations are not about romance but rather about sex tourism and prostitution. However, this popular view is only one of many perspectives and such host-guest encounters are not as black or white as they might seem. They represent a complex social phenomenon. The focus of this study is not just the debate on whether the sexual encounters between tourists and bumsters are about true love and romance or prostitution, but to add some depth by highlighting the voices or perspectives of the bumsters and tourists involved, and the impact of these sexual host-guest encounters on relations with the host community.

Annelou Ypeij's *Afterword* is a reminder that Africa is not an island and that despite the peculiar constellation of tourism features in Africa, similar aspects can be found on other continents. So, this volume is rounded off by a brief comparison with Latin American tourism. Ypeij compares her research on the Inca trail around Cusco, Peru, with the findings in this book. Many processes are similar, but one major difference lies in the intense involvement of the Peruvian state in tourist planning and implementation, with a stronger state and a more detailed involvement than is usually the case in Africa. That very involvement easily becomes an arena of conflict in Latin America, generating local resistance. Another telling difference is the larger role of women in the tourist bubble, both as producers and as sellers of cultural artefacts, whereas in African tourism women are usually invisible.

The anthropology of tourism started out as a sideline in classic field work, when anthropologists happened to work in areas where tourists came in, usually welcomed by the local population although definitely uninvited by the field worker. This had the advantage that the impact of tourism could be followed closely as a relatively new phenomenon also experienced by the researcher. At first it had the disadvantage that as many researchers resented the intrusion, their analysis was sometimes coloured by that feeling. Since that time, tourism studies have become a separate discipline, no longer evoking value judgments, for tourism can no longer be seen as a foreign intruder but as a self-evident globalising force. Thus, gradually the tourist encounter itself has moved to the centre stage of research, with the researcher in a new participant/observer role. Valene Smith, in her Foreword, gives a fascinating insight into the birth of this anthropological sub-discipline.[71]

This book exemplifies the dynamics within the anthropology of tourism in several ways. First, the project started with the panel 'Tourism in Africa' at the 2007 AEGIS/ECAS conference which the African Studies Centre hosted in conjunction with the National Museum of Ethnology, both in Leiden, the Netherlands. After the conference, a selection of the panel participants was supplemented by a series of invited contributors to provide more comprehensive coverage of various host-guest relations. Second, the authors of this volume themselves reflect this development. Some, such as van Beek, van Kessel and Klute, started out long ago on other projects and were gradually confronted with tourism. With their decades of involvement in their study populations, they can trace tourism dynamics through time. Other researchers set out from the start to study the tourist encounter as an important aspect of a globalising world: Wijngaarden, McCombes, Spierenburg, Wels and Brooks, Steegstra, van Egmond and Ypeij write from this position. Swan, Warren and MacGonagle demonstrate that this can go hand in hand with very personal motivations, either with chance encounters or with existential searches for deep identities. Some authors, for example Koot, Finley and Barnabas, are actively involved in tourism projects, reporting from a more participant than observer role. Alternatively, as is the case for Kibicho and Mbaiwa, they write from a deep commitment to their own African compatriots while they themselves are professional academics. Thus, the collection shows how both the development of the sub-discipline and the broad array of involvement anthropologists have evolved with their study populations.

71 For a very detailed and just as fascinating account of coming of age of the anthropology of tourism, see Dennison Nash, *The Study of Tourism* (2007).

REFERENCES   Abbink, Jon. 'Tourism and its Discontents. Suri-tourist Encounters in Southern Ethiopia', *Social Anthropology*, 8, 1 (2000): 1-17.

Amselle, J.-L. 'L'Afrique, un parc à thèmes', *Les Temps Modernes* 620-621 (2002): 46-60.

Babu, Sutheeshna, Sitikantha Mishra & Bivrai B. Parida, eds. *Tourism Development Revisited. Concepts, Issues and Paradigms* (New Delhi: Response/

Sage, 2009).

Baldacchino, Godfrey. 'Re-placing Materiality. A Western Anthropology of Sand', *Annals of Tourism Research* 37, 3 (2010): 763-78.

Beek, W.E.A. van. 'African Tourist Encounters: Effects of Tourism on Two West African Societies', *Africa*, 73, 2 (2003): 251-89.

—— 'Walking wallets? Tourists at the Dogon falaise', in Stephen Wooten, ed., *Wari Matters: Ethnographic Explorations of Money in the Mande Eorld* (Münster: LIT Verlag, 2005), 191-216.

—— 'Eyes on top? Culture and the Weight of the Senses', in Anne Storch, ed., *Invisible Africa, Sprache und Geschichte in Afrika* (Köln: Koppe, 2010) 21, 245-70.

Beek, W.E.A. van, P. Lemineur & O. Walther. 'Tourisme et patrimoine au Mali. Destruction des valeurs anciennes ou valorisation concertée?' *Swiss Journal of Geography*, 4 (2007): 249-58.

Boulay, Sébastien. 'Le tourisme de désert en Adrar mauritanien: réseaux «translocaux», économie solidaire et changements sociaux', *Autrepart* 40 (2006): 75.

Bruner, Edward M. 'The Maasai and the Lion King: Authenticity, Nationalism, and Globalization in African Tourism', *American Ethnologist* 28, 4 (2001): 881-908.

—— & B. Kirschenblatt-Gimblett. 'Maasai on the Lawn: Tourist Realism in East Africa', *Cultural Anthropology* 9, 4 (1994): 435-70.

—— *Culture on Tour. Ethnographies of Travel* (Chicago Ill: University of Chicago Press, 2005).

Burns, Peter M. 'Some Reflections on Tourism and Post-colonialism', in Babu, Sutheeshna, Sitikantha Mishra & Bivrai B. Parida, eds., *Tourism Development Revisited. Concepts, Issues and Paradigms* (New Delhi, Response/Sage, 2009), 64-75.

Butler, R. & T. Hinch. *Tourism and Indigenous Peoples* (London: International Thomson Business Press, 1996).

Chabra, Deepak. 'How They See Us: Perceived Effects of Tourist Gaze on the Old Order Amish', *Journal of Travel Research*, 49, 1 (2010): 93-105.

Chambers, E. (ed.). *Tourism and Culture. An Applied Perspective* (NY: State University of New York Press, 1997).

Chamonika, P., R.A. Groeneveld, A.O. Selomane & E.C. van Ierland. 'Tourist Preferences for Ecotourism in Rural Communities Adjacent to Kruger National Park: a Choice Experiment Approach', *Tourism Management* 33, 1 (2012): 168-76.

Cheong, So-Min & Marc L. Miller. 'Power and Tourism: a Foucauldian Approach', *Annals of Tourism Research* 27, 2 (2000): 371-90.

Cohen, Eric. 'Authenticity and Commoditization in Tourism', *Annals of Tourism Research*, 15 (1988): 467-86.

Corbey, Raymond. *Wildheid en beschaving: de Europese verbeelding van Afrika* (Baarn: Ambo, 1989).

Crick, M. 'Representations of International Tourism in the Social Sciences', *Annual Review of Anthropology*, 18 (1979): 307-44.

Dieke, Peter U.C. *The Political Economy of Tourism in Africa* (Washington: Cognizant Communication Corporation, 1999).

Doquet, Anne & Sara Le Menestrel. 'Introduction', *Autrepart* 40 (2006): 1-15.

Drenthen, Martin, Joseph Keularz, James Proctor, eds. *New Visions of Nature:*

Complexity and Authenticity (Dordrecht, Springer Netherlands, 2009).

Duim, V.R. van der & M.E. Kloek, eds. *Tourism, Nature Conservation and Wealth Creation in Africa*. Thematic proceedings of Atlas Africa Conference , Volume 4, (Arnhem, ATLAS, 2008).

Duim, V.R. van der. 'Performing African Tourismscapes', in Bob Wishitemi, Anne Spencely & Harry Wels, eds., *Culture and Community. Tourism Studies in Eastern and Southern Africa* (Amsterdam: Rozenberg, 2007), 25-48.

Egmond, Ton van. *Understanding the Tourist Phenomenon. An Analysis of 'West'–'South' Tourism* (Breda: NHTV, 2, 2005).

Fagence, M. 'Tourism as a Protective Barrier for Old Order Amish and Mennonite Communities' in Smith & Brent eds., *Hosts and Guests Revisited* (2001), 201-34.

Francis, Eric. 'Lay Concepts of Tourism in Bosomtwe Basin, Ghana', *Annals of Tourism Research* 37, 1 (2010): 34-51.

Franklin, Adrian. *Tourism, an Introduction* (London: Sage, 2003).

Graburn, Nelson H. 'Tourism and Leisure: a Theoretical Overview', in Smith and Brent eds., *Hosts and Guests. The Anthropology of Tourism* (Oxford: Basil Blackwell, 1989), 21-36.

—— 'Secular Ritual: a General Theory of Tourism', in Smith and Brent, eds., *Hosts and Guests Revisited* (2nd edn 2001) 42-50.

Grégoire, Emmanuel. 'Tourisme culturel, engagement politique et actions humanitaires dans la région d'Agadès (Niger)', *Autrepart*, 40 (2006): 95-113.

Hannan, Kevin & Dan Knox. *Understanding Tourism. A Critical Introduction* (Los Angeles, Sage, 2010).

Jamal, Tazim & Mike Robinson, eds. *The Sage Handbook of Tourism Studies* (London: Sage, 2009).

Lanfant, M.-F. 'International Tourism, Internationalization and the Challenge to Identity', in M.-F. Lanfant, J.B. Allcock & E.M. Bruner, eds., *International tourism. Identity and change* (London: Sage, 1995), 1-43.

Leite, Naomi & Nelson Graburn. 'Anthropological Interventions in Tourism Studies' in Tazim Tazim & Robinson, eds., *The Sage Handbook of Tourism Studies* (2009), 35-64.

MacCannell, Dean. *Empty Meeting Grounds. The Tourist Papers* (London: Routledge, 1992).

—— 'The Commodification of Culture', in Smith & Brent, *Hosts and Guests Revisited* (Washington: Cognizant Communication Corporation 2001) 380-90.

—— *The Tourist. A New Theory of the Leisure Class*, (London: MacMillan, 1976)

McKean, Ph.M. 'Towards a Theoretical Analysis of Tourism: Economic Dualism and Cultural Involution in Bali', in T.V. Singh, L. Theuns & M. Go, eds., *Towards Appropriate Tourism: The Case of Developing Countries* (Frankfurt: Peter Lang, 1989), 101-25.

Maoz, Daniel. 'The Mutual Gaze', *Annals of Tourism Research*, 33, 1 (2006): 221-39.

Martin, Keir. 'Living Pasts. Contested Tourism Authenticities', *Annals of Tourism Research* 37, 2 (2010): 549.

Mbaiwa, Joseph E. & Amanda L. Stronza. 'The Challenges and Prospects for

Sustainable Tourism and Ecotourism in Developing Countries, in Jamal & Robinson, eds., *The Sage Handbook of Tourism Studies* (London: Sage, 2009) 333-53.

Mowforth, Martin & Ian Munt, eds. *Tourism and Sustainability. Development, Globalisation and New Tourism in the Third World* (London, Routledge, 2nd edn 2009).

Nash, Dennison, ed. *The Study of Tourism. Anthropological and Sociological Beginnings* (Amsterdam: Elsevier, 2007).

Picard, M. *Bali, tourisme culturel et culture touristique* (Paris, Harmattan, 1992).

Richards, G. 'Introduction: Global Trends in Cultural Tourism', in G. Richards, ed., *Cultural Tourism: Global and Local Perspectives* (New York and London: Routledge, 2007) 1-25.

Rogerson, Christian. 'Backpacker Tourism: Policy Lessons for South Africa from International Experiences', *Africa Insight*, 37, 4 (2007/8): 27-46.

Ryan, Chris and Michelle Aicken, eds. *Indigenous Tourism: The Commodification and Management of Culture* (Oxford: Elsevier, 2005).

Sindiga, Isac. *Tourism and African Development. Change and Challenge of Tourism in Kenya* (Aldershot: Ashgate/ASC, 1999).

Smith, Valene. 'Hostility and Hospitality: War and Tourism', in Valene Smith & M. Brent eds., *Hosts and Guests Revisited* (Washington: Cognizant Communication Corporation, 2001).

—— 'The Nature of Tourism', in Smith & Brent eds., *Host and Guests Revisited* (Washington: Cognizant Communication Corporation, 2001), 53-68.

—— 'Introduction', in V. Smith, ed., *Hosts and Guests. The Anthropology of Tourism* (Oxford: Basil Blackwell, 2nd edn, 1989), 1-15.

Stausberg, Michael. *Religion in Modernen Tourismus* (Berlin: Verlag der Weltreligionen, 2010).

Telfer, David J. & Richard Sharpley, eds. *Tourism and Development in the Developing World* (London: Routledge, 2008).

Tomazos, K, & R. Butler, 'Volunteer Tourists in the Field; a Question of Balance?' *Tourism Management*, 33, 1 (2012): 177-87.

Tucker, Hazel, & John Akama, 'Tourism as Postcolonialism', in Jamal & Robinson eds., *The Sage Handbook of Tourism Studies* (London: Sage, 2009), 504-20.

Urry, J., *The Tourist Gaze: Leisure and Travel in Contemporary Societies*, (London: Sage, 2nd edn. 2002)

—— 'Globalizing the Tourist Gaze, in Babu, Sutheeshna, Sitikantha Mishra & Bivrai B. Parida eds., *Tourism Development Revisited. Concepts, Issues and Paradigms* (New Delhi, Response/Sage, 2009), 152-63.

Wearing, Stephen, & Jess Penning, 'Breaking Down the System: How Volunteer Tourism Contributes to New Ways of Viewing Commodified Tourism' in Jamal & Robinson, eds., *The Sage Handbook of Tourism Studies* (London: Sage, 2009), 254-68.

Weaver, David, 'Indigenous Tourism Stages and their Implications for Sustainability', *Journal of Sustainable Tourism*, 18, 1 (2008): 44

Wishitemi, Bob, Anne Spencely & Harry Wels eds. *Culture and Community. Tourism Studies in Eastern and Southern Africa* (Amsterdam: Rozenberg, 2007).

PART I
Culture, Identity & Tourism

2 · To dance or not to dance?
Dogon masks as a tourist arena

Walter van Beek

This is a story about masks. But the masks themselves do not form the centre of this tale, but the question of dancing 'rights': who may dance with them and who may not. And for the Dogon of Mali this fight is not about just any masks, but theirs! Dogon masks may be well known in the world of museum exhibitions and art dealers; for the Dogon themselves masks form the main fascination in their culture.

The general setting is the village of Tireli, nestled at the foot of the Bandiagara cliff, a village where tourists come regularly during the cool season in order to see mask dances. Tireli is on the tourist trail because of its renown as a mask dancing village ever since the 1980s when the tourist market was opened up (as part of the structural adjustment implementations in Mali[1]). Before that time only the central village of Sangha, a cluster of villages at the end of one of the few roads into Dogon country, hosted all visitors. Dogon country and culture had already been on the tourist agenda for decades, as the publications of the French anthropologists Marcel Griaule and Germaine Dieterlen had made Dogon culture famous in the period 1938-1956.[2] Their esoteric descriptions fired the imagination of many Northerners, and provided the background stories for the first waves of visitors. In effect, one reason why I chose the Dogon as my second field of study was precisely the fact that their reports on Dogon culture had become an anomaly in West African ethnography, out of sync with what anthropology had learned on African local cultures.[3]

1 In the '80s the so-called structural adjustment policy of the IMF and the World Bank, i.e. of development policies in general, demanded the opening up of internal markets. Hence, a series of monopolistic state organisations, such as for the production chain of cereals and cotton, were de-nationalised. One of these so-called 'parastatals' was the SMERT, (*Société Malienne d'Exploitation des Ressources Touristiques*) the state tourist organisation which had run all tourist enterprises until that time; it had to sell its hotels and no longer organised tourist performances or rented out guides.
2 Marcel Griaule, *Masques Dogons*, (Paris: Travaux et Mémoires de l'Institut d'Ethnologie, 33, 1938) ; Marcel Griaule, *Dieu d'eau: Entretiens avec Ogotemmêli* (Paris: Éditions du Chêne, 1948) ; Marcel Griaule & Germaine Dieterlen, *Le renard pâle. Tome I: Le mythe cosmogonique. La création du monde* (Paris: Travaux et Mémoires de l'Institut d'Ethnologie, 72, 1956.)
3 And most anthropologists. I came out in 1979 on a project of cultural ecology, but soon realised I had to do a total restudy of the Dogon, as in fact only the literature before 1948 was reliable, such as Marcel Griaule, *Masques Dogons* (Paris: Institut d'Ethnologie, 1938). For the 'debunking' of the exoticisms in Dogon ethnography see Walter E. A. van Beek, 'Dogon Restudied: A Field Evaluation of the Work of Marcel Griaule', *Current Anthropology* 32, 2 (1991): 139-67; 'Haunting Griaule: Experiences from the Restudy of the Dogon', *History in Africa* 31, 1 (2004): 43-68;

When I came to the area in 1978 I chose Tireli as my central research village for several reasons, one on them being the distance from the tourist centre, Sangha. However, tourism quickly expanded along the cliff and I soon found myself in the thick of it, leading, among other things, to a photo book I co-published in 1982.[4] Though I was neither the first nor the last anthropologist in the Dogon region, and the book surely not the final coffee table book on the Dogon, it had a wide distribution and got the attention of the new tour companies, who now wanted to avoid the well-trodden trail of Sangha. So there they came, the European operators, with their Landcruisers, to have mask performances arranged in Tireli.

However, it was not a wholly new idea. A few years earlier, in 1974, an early tour operator from Sweden had already sounded out the idea of holding mask dances out of Sangha, arranging with SMERT, the state tourist organisation controlling all tourist activities at the time, to stage a few dances in Tireli.[5] After huge deliberations, the village agreed and in 1975 the first mask dances for tourists were held in Tireli. Those dances were organised at the largest dancing space in the village, in the southern half of the village, the ward Teri Ku Dama, which could boast a great *toguna* or men's house, next to a spacious *tèi* or dancing place. Several operators found their way to Teri Ku ('the head of Tireli') and until 1982 the dances went smoothly, with the southern half of the village as performers and SMERT as the official organiser, raking in most of the revenues. In 1982, Teri Ku started realise that it received precious little for the performances and complained to SMERT. Almost immediately the northern half of the village stepped in, telling SMERT that they were willing to take up the task, and thus the performances moved to the main dancing place in Sodanga, the northern half of Tireli, which could boast an even more photogenic setting for the dances. When in 1982 the Time-Life book appeared and market liberalisation followed in 1984, the tourist traffic towards Tireli (read 'Sodanga'), increased substantially. In the following years Sodanga had a virtual monopoly on the tourist dances, which became even more important when droughts hit the area between 1982 and 1994. With crops failing with some regularity, aid organisations stepped in, a response that underscored the importance of external contacts.

Jan Jansen & Walter E.A. van Beek, 'La mission Griaule à Kangaba (Mali)', *Cahiers des études africaines* 7 (2000): 363-76.
4   Stephen Pern, Bryan Alexander & Walter E.A. van Beek, *Masked Dancers of West Africa: the Dogon* (London: Time Life, 1982).
5   For an assessment of tourism among the Dogon see Paul Lane. 'Tourism and Social Change among the Dogon', *African Arts*, 21, 4 (1988): 66-9; Walter E.A. van Beek, 'African Tourist Encounters; Effects of Tourism in Two West-African Societies', *Africa* 73, 3 (2003) 251-89; Walter E.A. van Beek. 'Walking Wallets? Tourists at the Dogon falaise', in Stephen Wooten, ed., *Wari Matters: Ethnographic Explorations of Money in the Mande World,* (Münster, LIT Verlag, 2005), 191-216; Philippe Lemineur, Olivier Walther & Walter E.A. van Beek. 'Tourisme et patrimoine au Mali. Destruction des valeurs anciennes ou valorisation concertée?' *Geographica Helvetica* 4, (2008): 249-58

Sodanga had such contacts and kept the lead, so in short, Teri Ku was left out and Sodanga flourished.

Tourist performances, however, are connected with the regular mask performances, an essential part of the *dama*, the 'second funeral'. Dogon death rituals are complicated. A death is announced by gunshots, the sound ricocheting against the cliff. Actual burial is done quickly. The corpse is sewn into a white shroud around which a blue-white death blanket is wrapped. The young men of the village improvise a stretcher and together they carry the deceased in honour, 'like riding a horse' to his grave, a cavern high up in the cliff side. A few days of condolences follow, and then people wait for the first funeral rites. Once a year, or straight away in the case of the death of a clan elder, all the deceased of that year are honoured in the funeral rites, the *nyû yana*, usually in January or February after the harvest is in. This is the most complicated of all Dogon rituals, lasting three days and nights for the men and another two days and nights for the women, thus involving the whole village. Though some masks do feature in the dances, the rituals are dominated by mock battles, the men decked out in their finest dance with flintlock guns and spears, mimicking the wonderful game of war.[6] At night some of the great songs of the Dogon cultural repertoire are sung, the *baja ni* [7] and the *gumo*: (the latter is important in our tale). These songs take all night to sing, their long and complicated texts underscored by a simple, captivating melody, and are sung by the older men, those who know and are essential for a funeral. And they have to be sung by the whole village, both halves, in this case Teri Ku as well as Sodanga.

Each twelve years, give or take a few, the final rites of death are held, the *dama* with the 'real' mask dances. At the foot of the cliff, *dama* rituals are only held about every twelve years, whereas on top of the cliff, the villages have small as well as large *dama* rituals. But Tireli as a cliff village is on a twelve-year schedule. When I arrived in 1979, the last *dama* was already ten years in the past, so I had every reason to expect a *dama* pretty soon in my 'own' village. It would turn out quite differently. During my first field stay, 1979-80, I witnessed the *dama* in neighbouring Komakan, and realized that participation in a neighbouring village meant participation as a stranger, a welcome guest surely, but not on the inside. At the time I was not aware of some of the earlier happenings in Tireli, and while the tensions between

6 For descriptions see Eric Jolly. *Boire avec esprit. Bière de mil et société Dogon* (Nanterre: Société d'Ethnologie, 2004) ; Anne Doquet. *Les masques Dogon. Ethnologie savante et ethnologie autochtone* (Paris: Karthala, 1999). Stephanie Hollyman, & Walter E.A. van Beek. *Dogon. Africa's People of the Cliffs* (New York: Abrams, 2001). Marcel Kervran. *La vie et la mort en pays Dogon. Rites et célébrations chez les Donnon* (Paris: Jourdier, 1999). Walter E.A. van Beek. 'Enter the Bush: a Dogon Mask Festival', in Susan Vogel, ed., *Africa Explores; 20th Century African Art* (New York & Prestal Munich: Centre for African Art 1991), 56-73.

7 Walter E.A. van Beek. 'In Memory of a Great Singer: the Dogon *baja ni* as a Cultural-historical Performance', in Stephen Belcher, Jan Jansen & Mohamed N'Daou, eds., *Mande Mansa, Mande Worlds* 2 (2008), 193-215.

2.1 *Part of the audience of the 2008 Teri Ku mask dance, including a tourist*
(© Walter van Beek)

Teri Ku and Sodanga quickly became apparent, some of the deeper causes of the conflict only surfaced very gradually.

The first time something of the real problem came to the fore was in 1987, when Dègubèrè, the chief of the masks, died. Tireli has one clan in charge of the masks, indeed of the mask altar, and that clan happens to be in Sodanga, *ginaboro*, the 'behind clan', with good old 'Dèbè' as its elder. His funeral, which I could not attend at the time, was a huge affair, with many masks performing during the *nyû yana*. But then the conflict struck home when Teri Ku refused to attend his funeral. This, for Dogon, is an affront, and a terrible one at that. After the usual time, two years, the next oldest man of the clan, Pôla, entered the clan house as the new one responsible for the mask altar. I knew Pôla very well, as he was my host's closest mother's brother, and thus by adoption mine as well. I had been adopted as the younger brother of Dogolu Tigemu Say, the *de facto* leader of Sodanga, who had organised the show dances in Sodanga. His mother, a famous potter, was Pôla's sister, so on each market since I had first arrived, as a dutiful sister's son, I had presented him with some small gifts, usually money for beer. His personality is important in the story: whereas Dogolu is the quintessential organiser, a natural leader and go-between, the new clan elder was a proud, self-contained and sometimes stubborn man, a purist in religious matters. He kept the taboos of his office meticulously, was never very talkative – which was a pity – and it took me a long time to gain his confidence.

Two years later, two other important clan elders died, Yèngulu and Amingènè, both close friends of mine. Their funeral also included Dogolu's mother, who had died the same year, and as 1989 produced one of the first really good harvests in many years, this became a very large funeral. I expected the *dama* to take place later this same year (the funeral was in January, the *dama* could have been in April). But in the event it was neighbouring Amani that organised a *dama*, not Tireli.[8] Why? Because Teri Ku refused to sing the *gumo* at the funeral. This was one funeral in which I participated intensely, so the issue became very clear, a real conflict between the two village halves. People talked about it at some length, but mainly in terms of the insults offered by the other party. The Teri Ku insult seemed clear, but there was another one behind it. At some stage, the men from Teri Ku seemed to have said that the men from Sodanga were 'like women' (because they danced uninitiated), a huge and unforgivable insult for almost any African man, and surely for the Dogon. In order to understand this insult, we have to go into the masks themselves, i.e. into what happens during the *dama* dances.

'Legal' and 'illegal' masks

The dances are complex, but so are the masks themselves. In principle a Dogon man does not wear a mask; he *is* an *imina*, which is in fact common in Africa. The mask is not just the head piece, but the whole person with the complete costume which consists of a cover of coloured fibres on arms, legs and torso, something in the hand to dance with, plus, indeed, a headpiece.[9] The most important element, ritually, are the fibres which define the costume as a mask. Just before a funeral, some women spotted a small roll of fibres at the entrance of a waterhole and asked me to remove it, as they could not enter because a 'mask' was there. Masks, especially these fibres, are indeed taboo for women, the core taboo of the mask festival, and the very word '*dama*' just means 'taboo'. The head pieces are needed to cover the head, also essential, and the oldest masks seem to have been just head coverings with a spike or tuft on top. But the differences in head pieces are what defines the mask as representing something specific; most masks represent animals (or people) from the bush. As argued

8   For a description of that funeral see Walter E.A. van Beek. 'Enter the Bush: a Dogon Mask Festival. 1991); Stephanie Hollyman & Walter E.A. van Beek. *Dogon*. 2001).
9   See also Barbara De Mott. *Dogon Masks, a Structural Study of Form and Meaning* (Ann Arbour, Michigan: UMI Research Press, Studies in the Fine Arts, Iconography, no 4, 1980), Doquet, *Les masques Dogon. Ethnologie savante et ethnologie autochtone* (Paris: Karthala,1999), 2, and Polly Richards, Polly. 'Imina Sangan' or 'Masque à la Mode'. Contemporary Masquerade in the Dogon Region', in Karel Arnaut, ed., *Re-Visions: New Perspectives on the African Collections of the Horniman Museum* (The Horniman Museum and Gardens, London and the Museum of Anthropology, Coimbra, 2000), 107-23.

elsewhere, there is a strong association between masks and bush, which is considered the source of plenty, the origin of fertility, power and knowledge.[10] Those identifications are not crucial: in principle a mask is a mask, and only secondary it is a specific mask. The shortest definition for a Dogon mask would be: 'Something weird out there.' A mask has a degree of strangeness, unfamiliarity and threat, especially for women, but never absent for men either. The *imina* represent power, force and as such are not to be slighted. Masks are serious business as they are also closely connected with death; even if the *dama* as a whole can be read as a ritual of regeneration, death is first. Although men sometimes use masks as a means to discipline women in the so-called *puro*,[11] masks remain liminal matter, never to be engaged in facetiously.

How does this relate to tourist mask dances? Dancing with power objects for tourists to gaze at and take photographs is no light matter. In Sangha, masks had danced for tourists for decades already, and the twin villages of Ogo Lè and Ogol Donyu (high and low Ogol) which are situated at the centre of the Sangha cluster, near the hotel and the administration buildings, had already solved the problem a long time ago. The masks for the tourists were made especially for the show dances, both the costumes and the head pieces. Anybody who danced for the tourists should have participated in one proper *dama*, but as Ogol holds both large and small mask rituals, this did not pose a problem. Also, through the years this rule had been watered down, with uninitiated youngsters dancing as well. So in Sangha, for the young Dogon men who danced, for the elders who drummed and sang, as well as for the spectators the situation was clear: this was just a performance, a show dance. Furthermore, they had chosen the part of the final day in which the foreigners, i.e. people from other villages, are invited to watch, as the performance piece for the dance. So the tourist dance was modelled on the most public part of the *dama*, avoiding the more private, even hidden rituals that also are part of the total ritual.

When the mask performances were first taken to Tireli, this was the model. For the first year, Sangha furnished the head pieces but these were soon replaced by their own production. More important was the question of initiation. A *dama* is a second funeral but also an initiation: young men have to dance first in a *dama* in order to be fully initiated, and from that participation they derive the familiarity with the masks needed for other performances. Having youngsters dance for tourists before participating in a proper *dama* would invert the normal course of events. That was exactly the position taken by Teri Ku: first the *dama*, then the show. At the time, their last *dama* was

10 Walter E.A. van Beek. 'Boys and Masks among the Dogon', in Simon Ottenberg & D.A. Binckley, eds., *Playful Performers. African Children's Masquerades* (New Brunswick & London, Transaction Publishers, 2006), 67-88.

11 Walter E.A. van Beek & Pieteke Banga. 'The Dogon and their Trees', in Elisabeth Croll & David Parkin, eds., *Bush Base, Forest Farm. Culture, Environment and Development* (London, Routledge, 1992), 57-75.

10 years behind them, and they had enough initiated men still young enough to perform the vigorous and athletic dances of the major masks. So the 'orthodox' position was the natural option for them.

When the performances were transferred to the other village half, Sodanga, they too had still enough initiated men, but many youngsters had left to settle in the plains or to find work in the big cities. The 1980s were the time that migrant labour really took off, young men doing a work stint of two or three years in the thriving economy of Ivory Coast, mainly in Abidjan. The supply of potential dancers had dwindled, and a council was called in the *toguna*, the palaver house of Sodanga. After long discussions, Dègubèrè, as chief of the masks, easy-going as he was, assured the others that whatever the infraction was by uninitiated dancing for tourists, he would afterwards purify the dancers through his altar, and purify them again when the proper *dama* would be held.[12] Thus the decision was made for the 'heterodox masks', with youngsters dancing first for the tourists, and later in the *dama*. Among the first dancers were the son of Dèbè and the sons and nephews of Dogolu, the Sodanga leader. As they told me, they were scared at the time, and had to be assured that they would be properly purified afterwards; still, when performing for the first time, they were not at ease. It was only with later performances that they grew accustomed to the act and the 'heterodox masks' became a common issue. Teri Ku reacted with indignation, of course. Not only was their business taken from them, Sodanga was doing it 'wrong', watering down the *tèm*, the customs of the Dogon with 'illegal' masks. One of their reactions, evidently, was to withdraw support for the funerals of the mask chief and the two other ritual elders. Other reactions were more direct and verbal, aimed at the 'illegal' masks themselves. Dancing uninitiated is like dancing as a women, so the accusation that the men of Tireli were 'like women' surfaced readily. By now the die was cast, the two village halves set on a collision course.

In 1990, the year after the large *nyû yana*, Yagalu, a prominent man from Teri Ku who had political ambitions, tried to mend the matter by soothing wounded feelings. He came with a small retinue of kinsmen and drank the dregs of the beer from the brewing vats at the three clan houses involved, those of Yèngulu, Amingènè and Dègubèrè. This sign of contrition, drinking from the brewing vat in which the old beer has long ceased to be drinkable, was appreciated by all, and some calm descended on the village. In the meantime the tourist trade flourished, and Teri Ku also developed its links with the main operators, mainly through Eli, who built his hotel at the south entrance of Teri Ku and managed to attract customers and groups

12 That particular meeting has generated some diverging stories. According to my informants from Sodanga, the people from Teri Ku were also present, and the decision to have 'liberal' mask dances was unanimous. However, the elders from Teri Ku vehemently deny this: this was only a Sodanga meeting. Weighing the evidence and the interests, I am inclined to give Teri Ku most credence as they would have little to gain by breaking such an arrangement; on the contrary they would put themselves in a lose-lose situation.

2.2 Tigemu, a month before his death before the gina of the mask altar, 2008.
(© Walter van Beek)

who ordered mask dances in the village. In the period up to 1995, however, little changed as Pôla was adamant that he did not want to have a joint *dama* with the 'others'; he had not really forgiven the insults. After his death in 1995 things started to look better with the crops, so the possibility of effectively organising a *dama* grew.

Tourism continued to intensify, stimulated also by another photo book I co-produced[13] and by the appearance of a series of small Dogon-led tourist operations. Further, a major archeological project in Teli, as well as the activities of the Mission Culturelle of the Malian government, based in Bandiagara, started to bear fruit. A small museum in Nombori resulted, and though not overly successful, the whole enterprise fell well into pace with the continuing rise of the Dogon on the tourist agendas. The death of the Aru Hogon in 1989,[14] the long strife for a successor, and the many film teams visiting the area for this and other reasons, all contributed to the sense of the Dogon as a focus of world attention.

In the meantime, however, the dancers in Teri Ku were growing old; the young dancers of the early eighties had given way to adult dancers, ageing visibly at the end of the century. Teri Ku asked Tigemu, Pôla's successor, once more but although the latter was an easy personality

13   Hollyman & van Beek. *Dogon. Africa's People of the Cliffs* (New York: Abrams, 2001).
14   For a great memorial to this elder and to his successor see Germaine Dieterlen. *Le titre d'honneur des Arou (Dogon-Mali)* (Paris: Harmattan, 1982) and Eric Jolly & Nouhoum Guindo, eds., *Le pouvoir en miettes. Récits d'intronisation d'un Hogon (Pays Dogon, Mali)* (Paris: Servédit, 2003).

to deal with and very harmony-oriented, he was still loyal to his predecessor and refused. So in 2002 a delegation of Teri Ku went over to Yugo, the village from where the masks originated and which still commands the major mask altar, origin of all local ones.[15] The Teri Ku request to have their own altar, delegated straight from Yugo, was in fact a demand for the division of Tireli into two villages. That very same demand had already come to Yugo from other villages, such as Ireli, also a village with internal problems, and the elders of Yugo were not at all inclined to divide any villages. One additional reason was that political developments in Mali stimulated local governance and decentralisation, a complicated process in which the government tried the curb tendencies towards fragmentation. After huge deliberations, the canton Sangha, i.e. the string of villages from Sangha to Tireli, had decided to remain one 'commune' with one mayor. Though masks do not depend on political units but on traditional definitions of villages, the fragmentation that Teri Ku wanted did not sit well with the official administration either, which made the decision easy for Yugo: no separate mask altar for Teri Ku. Realising that the *dama* had become a political issue, Eli, the hotel owner at Teri Ku proposed to Dogolu that they split the village between them, separating from Sangha. Dogolu and his many sons reacted furiously, as if this were treason. Thus, Teri Ku and Sodanga remained each other's hostages in politics as well as in the mask dances.

Due to the ageing of its dancers, Teri Ku started to suffer from its less attractive show dances, and mounted the pressure on Sodanga, but from 2002 till 2007 Tigemu, well briefed by the elders from Sodanga, kept refusing. As the crops had been good enough for the *dama* several times over the past few years, Teri Ku grew desperate. If they had ever considered changing their standpoint on who could dance with the masks, the current battle with their neighbours had eliminated all such possibilities. At the start of 2007 the dancers of Teri Ku decided to take matters into their own hands. In the cave where the men put on their masks and garb, under their *toguna*, they performed divination, with the cowry shells, the oldest form of divination in Dogon society. The shells gave them the option to perform their own *dama*, just as Teri Ku, with or without Sodanga participating. Dutifully they presented the oldest man of Tireli (at the time), Orisî, with a gift of food and cola nuts. Being of Sodanga and also well instructed, he refused the gift. Undaunted, the elders from Teri Ku proceeded with their preparations, advising the youngsters all over the country that the *dama* would be held. After the 2007-8 harvest they followed custom again, in handing over the traditional gift for the elder of the mask altar and thus handed Tigemu a rooster and bag of millet, using all the proper respect such an occasion called for. Then the impossible happened: Tigemu refused the gift. He left the

15   For the first rendition of this mask myth see Griaule *Masques Dogons*, 1938.

2.3   *Preparing for the* dama: *a kanaga mask being painted in Teri Ku 2008*
(© Walter van Beek)

rooster at the side of the *toguna*, its feet tied, and the millet in corner nearby. Nobody touched either of the offerings. The rooster gradually died, and the birds and mice ate the millet from the bag, which by all accounts still lies there, a poignant reminder of a hardheaded refusal. This was, of course, the final straw. Anyone remotely knowledgeable on African cultures immediately realises that this is the greatest affront possible between two ritual partners, and indeed it was the point of no return. Teri Ku was set on doing their dance, Sodanga unified in not participating, even trying to ignore the fact that something was going on in Teri Ku.

At last, the real dama

This was the situation I found when coming in March 2008 to Tireli, and immediately I was drawn into the battle. And did I find myself in the thick of it! Of course, Dogolu assumed I was pro-Sodanga, but the elders from Teri Ku thought I was pro-Tireli, which in fact was closer to the truth. At first I had a naïve notion of trying to bring the two parties together, but that bridge had already been burnt long ago. But I had been waiting for 27 years for the *dama* in 'my own' village, and I was not going to let the quarrel rob me of my participation in the festival, however defined. Another complication arose in my immediate surroundings. Dogolu has been the natural leader of Tireli for decades and had been village chief twice. In Tireli, the son or close relative of the oldest living man in the village becomes village chief,[16] and Dogolu had been that on the basis of his grandfather some decades ago, and lately on behalf of an uncle (actually the older brother of his father), who himself resided in the plains. But his uncle had died. After him the oldest man was Orisî, the uncle (in the same way) of another important man in the village (and for me), Apomi Say. The latter is the nephew of Dogolu, but also had been my assistant in all those years and had profited hugely from his many contacts with Europeans in becoming the director of a major development NGO in the region. When Orisî became the oldest[17] in the village, Apomi became chief. He was doing well in life; although deferential to his uncle, he had grown too important, too rich and too independent to play second fiddle to Dogolu. Throughout the conflict he considered himself chief of all Tireli, not just of Sodanga, and rightly so, of course.

So Apomi did nothing to thwart the Teri Ku mask endeavour, an issue beyond his mandate anyway. So, there I was, living with my host and older brother Dogolu, also my next door neighbour, and working with my assistant-turned NGO director Apomi, who were thoroughly at odds with each other. Dogolu's sons, representing a good share of

---

16 The classical Dogon way, nowadays becoming less common,
17 In most Dogon villages the oldest is called '*Hogon*'. In Tireli the eldest is also village priest, but is not called *Hogon*, as Tireli resides directly under the 'great *Hogon*' of the Dogon area, the one in Aru.

the ward, sided with their father against their cousin, even if he was formerly their good friend. All of the parties, Dogolu, his sons as well as Apomi, had stakes in tourism, having built their own 'hotel' for the tourists, and all of them knew that the Teri Ku *dama* would 'cost them clients'. But while Dogolu was set on thwarting the Teri Ku *dama* project, declaring it illegal at many occasions, Apomi realised that he had a duty to assist both village halves.

The situation was complicated again by a similar conflict in Teri Ku itself. Eli, the upstart hotel owner, was in fact the natural leader of the youngsters, i.e. of the dancers, with his hotel serving as the centre of their leisure time. For the masks, however, the old men were in charge, as they always are, but in this case the number of elders who had actually witnessed the last *dama* was scarce after the long interval of 39 years. The long delay of the *dama* in Tireli became the nagging problem of Teri Ku: how exactly did we do in it in 1969? Normally, the representatives of the mask clan would be the ones to know and to decide, but they had refused all cooperation. No Sodanga elder would help them out, Dogolu kept explaining to me: 'They know nothing about it. They are making many mistakes, this is not a real *dama* at all.' Yet he was curious about what happened in the other half, and for once I as 'younger brother' could inform him, the elder one, conferring, just the two of us, hidden from sight and out of earshot. Of course, the major liturgy was still well known, as the *dama* of most villages follow the same general programme, but the devil is in the details, especially in the exact order of the rituals: which came first, which later? So they continuously deliberated and in doing so delayed the ritual, till they had the programme pretty secure.

I do think Teri Ku made one mistake: in the sequence two rites appear to have been reversed, at least that is what Dogolu and his elders gleefully told me: 'Wrong! They know nothing.' It might have been the case, but mattered little, as the main proceedings were well done, and – just as important – with great enthusiasm and by a huge number of initiates. Sodanga made a last attempt to block the ritual at the first stage of the mask rituals, during the night when the initiates have to visit the sacred spots of the other village half, beating their little slit drums. The people from Sodanga tried to stop them from entering their 'space' and here Apomi intervened, allowing them to finish the ritual as it should be done, a proper gesture for a chief of the whole village. Dogolu was not amused: 'Apomi has spoilt our village', meaning by 'village' clearly only Sodanga, so the battle between the two halves continued.

Then disaster struck for Sodanga: Tigemu, the chief of the masks died, right in the heart of the very *dama* he had refused to sacrifice for. The people from Sodanga tried to play down the issue: 'Tigemu had been ill for a long time, and this was just natural.' Of course, the other half saw it quite differently: 'That is what happens, when one muddles with masks. He should have done his duty, not blocked a proper

2.4 *Dogolu with a new rifle for the funeral, Tireli 2008* (© Walter van Beek)

2.5 *Teri Ku* dama: *Two rabbit masks, with an antelope behind them, Tireli 2008*
(© Walter van Beek)

dama, not refuse our gift.' His funeral rites, plus those for an old man in Teri Ku about the same time – someone not related to the mask altar at all – had to be performed first, and the mask proceedings were postponed. Apomi and his brothers took advantage of the delay, and organised the *nyû yana* they still had to do for their father, Balugo, the younger brother of Orisî, the oldest villager. Apomi being the rich and important man he is in Tireli, this was not just a funeral, it was a giant one. These funeral proceedings, mentioned above, are much too complicated to be described here, but did amount to an enormous show of wealth for the village. For one thing, having a herd of cattle, Apomi included in the proceedings a spectacular and rare ritual called *na uro*, mounting the cattle. This is an option only for a rich man, and involves the sacrifice of a bull. Not only is the bull sacrificed, it is first mounted on an improvised stretcher, alive, and then carried by a host of young men from the plains to the dancing place up in the village. Women shout, ululate and sing, men fire their guns, while the throng with the kicking bull slowly winds its way uphill trough the narrow paths of the village, a spectacle to be seen to be believed. It was the third time I had seen it, but it was now organised by my sister's son! During the first day of the dance, the bull is sacrificed, and left at the dancing place throughout the next day, as a proper decoration and piece of the ritual during the great war dances that make up the bulk of the ritual. Eventually, the beast is cut up and the meat divided.

Back to the *dama* as such: after the *nyû yana* the masks proceeded in their proper fashion, so the reality of the Teri Ku *dama* became inevitable for the people in Sodanga. Each night they heard the initiates with their slit drums, the staccato rhythms ricocheting off the cliff in a weird, strange sound, signalling the coming of the masks, those 'weird things from out there'. The start of the final procedures was set when the *dani*, the temporary mask altar marked by a straight pole decorated like a mask, was set up during one particular night, conforming to *tèm*, custom. From that moment onwards the *dama* marched in its time-honoured course. No Sodanga man – except Apomi – visited Teri Ku, though Dogolu and the others became ever more curious, and I had to 'report' each night. One item still had to settled: I had been accepted as an initiate, but true initiates do not film or take pictures, they just dance. So, if I wanted to 'film' – for the Dogon there is no difference between film and photo – then I still had to pay. And I did want to film, and take my own pictures. I was not the only one, however, as an anthropologist from LSE had come, revisiting the Dogon on whom she had just defended her thesis.[18] Further, there were also some visitors from Mopti, and a few hoteliers among the Dogon who wanted their own recording of the *dama* had also sent their own person with a camera. The elders came up with a reasonable price, a fixed amount for anyone for each

18 Laurence Douny

day's 'filming', enquired how many days each of us would be filming, and took cash in advance. That settled, one question remained after the first day. The Dogon who were filming: would they have to pay as well? Of course, they argued that it was their own *dama*, and they had every right to film. However, characteristic of the high self-esteem with which the Dogon cherish their own culture, the elders surmised that their brothers would sell their pictures and become rich, like the white people, so they too had to pay. In the end, the Dogon did not film. I did.

The *dama* then proceeded through the many dances at the various dancing grounds in the village, up upon the cliff side, and was finally drawn towards it apotheosis, the various arrivals of the masks at the foot of the cliff.[19] And an imposing spectacle is was: over sixty masks arriving from the bush, lined up in a huge file, entering the large dancing ground dancing, charging and shrieking, the drums leading them, the elders shouting and chanting. Everywhere people watched, at the side, on the scree, on top of the houses, in the trees; spectators were everywhere. I had waited 27 years for this spectacle, and felt all of these waiting years fall away as I was totally immersed in this explosion of colour, movement and sound.

None of the Sodanga people (except Apomi) ever saw one mask. I kept Dogolu abreast, and of course did show him the pictures, one of the advantages of a digital camera, photo as well as film. When viewing, he grew silent, sighed and had to admit that this was a real *dama*, a *dama* proper, in fact a challenge for Sodanga to do at least as well. I do not think he regretted his stance, at least he did not state as much, but masks are immensely wonderful, and are always fascinating for the Dogon themselves. And were there a lot of masks, and did they dance well! No words about illegal masks any more, just some comments on what Sodanga should do. So the resolve set in: next year in Sodanga, and even better. Mask dances are competitive anyway, but Dogolu and the others fully realised that Teri Ku had stolen a march on them. From now on, the show dances would be over there, using the plethora of masks available, even some masks that had not been seen for a long time. And they had the Dogon *tèm* on their side now, so the ball was in Sodanga's court. Next year, surely!

It was not to be next year, however. After all, Tigemu had died, so the *gina* of the masks had no elder. Succession to elderhood of a *gina* is complicated and takes at least two years. First, the son of Tigemu took over the clan house, but as caretaker, not successor. This is standard procedure, and he would remain there till the next in age settles into the *gina* and takes over, usually about two years later. Of course there was pressure on the son of Tigemu to allow the masks and perform the sacrifices as Tigemu should have done. But the son remembered the death of his father during the Teri Ku *dama*, and made no move:

19   See Hollyman & van Beek, *Dogon*, 2001.

too risky for a youngster who is not properly the elder. The decision would have to be taken by his successor, the now oldest member of that clan. His ward mates had to respect this, and realised that the new elder would also need some time to be installed, as he even had to reconvert. As a Christian he had to become 'traditional' again, which he was fully prepared to do, but it would also take him time to settle in the *gina* and to learn about the proceedings of which he knew next to nothing. At the end of the 2009-2010 seasons, in mid-2010 he came into the *gina*, and then the decision to proceed was made. The matter is almost decided in principle (August 2010) but waits final approval, depending also on the harvest in the next years. In the end, Sodanga might have been wiser to accede to the *dama* together with Teri Ku, but as an anthropologist I have nothing to complain about: the fighting of the masks became a wonderful tale of two dances.

In the meantime fate struck again: Dogolu died from pancreatic cancer in February 2010, three days after my wife and I had had the chance to bid him farewell before we left Mali. So the ironies of life and the vagaries of death have dictated that he will not witness the *dama* in Sodanga, the very *dama* he had been instrumental in postponing. Before Dogolu's death, Apomi's position had also changed, as Orisî, his father's older brother, died and a new eldest of Tireli, someone in Teri Ku, succeeded him as the ritual elder of the village. This resulted in a change of village chief, too, with Apomi stepping down, no longer standing in the way of his uncle or his cousins. Thus, the conflict between the kinsmen has been laid to rest, and the close harmony of the kinship reigns again. Dogolu's oldest son, Atime, assured me in February 2010 that there had really never been a problem, and that the relationships between the two halves of the village were never under serious pressure. I know the orientation of Dogon culture to attain harmony well enough to appreciate such a gentle rewriting of history, and surely this will become reality. The burial of Dogolu was also a major opportunity for reconciliation. So, if rains are good the next years, the story will continue in May 2013 with the *dama* in Sodanga. Then, finally, the question remains, what the village will do in the future: have one joint *dama* again, or continue with two separate rituals?

Discussion: the bubble and the village

The fighting on masks in Tireli raises a number of questions. Is the Tireli case unique or exceptional? What is the impact of such a conflict on the Dogon view of their masks, on the *dama* in the long run, as well as on the village in general? Is this kind of conflict inevitable with increasing tourism? The first question is the easiest. A few other villages have conflicts over the tourist dances as well, though not as severe as in Tireli. Elsewhere the main issue is also who may dance, but usually it is about which ward or village-half is in charge of the dances, as any ward is home to enough qualified dancers. So the conflict usually is, indeed, about access to the tourist organisations.[20] In the Tireli case this is one of the issues at hand, but the conflict has been complicated by several factors: the specific history of tourist dances, the clash between orthodoxy and heterodoxy, the personalities involved and certain inopportune deaths.

The other questions are more complex. First, any conflict, also one over masks, tends to heighten the value of the focus of the conflict. So, a struggle over masks will reinforce the importance of masks, both the tourists' masks and the 'genuine' ones, and that is in fact what happened. Masks and the *dama* dominated the village discourse. As for the impact on the *dama* itself, what has been affected in Tireli is not the programme of the ritual, nor its emotional importance, and definitely not the place of the ritual in the general religious setting of the Dogon culture. What has been changed is the date and frequency of the ritual. The conflict has in fact eliminated the holding of one proper *dama* cycle: the past decades should have seen two *dama* taking place in Tireli, not just one. It may be that the order of the rituals was slightly altered, but that is a type of change that is common in oral religions.

Did this threaten the *dama* as such? *Dama* rituals are never run-of-the-mill events, but through the conflict, the Tireli one had accrued almost mythical proportions; compared to their neighbours in Amani and Komakan, the people from Tireli have become almost besotted by the idea of their *dama*. Its increasing economic weight, the polarisation of village politics around the *dama*, and the emotions generated by the conflict almost made the actual performance of the *dama* seem a chimera. Teri Ku breaking the stalemate was not only an economic as well as a religious necessity, it also brought a return to normal *dama* proportions. Also, when a conflict has to be fought, it better be over an issue of importance. The issue at hand was the right to the ritual itself, first of all, but secondly the access to dances for tourists, and thus for themselves as well, and at stake was the very basis of mask performances: the authority of the elders, the ascendancy of Yugo and the unity of the village (halves) in the performance. Of course, the outcome could have been different, but for Teri Ku the only other way out would have been to deny that masks have any religious value at all, which would have meant to break with their religion. The choice they made to get out of their impasse heightened the importance of the masks, of Dogon religion, boosted the position of the elders (of their own half) and united Teri Ku more effectively than anything else.

20 Despite the harmony orientation in Dogon culture, conflicts are not rare. See for a well described case, Jacky Bouju, *Graine de l'homme, enfant du mil* (Paris: Société d'Ethnographie, 1984); Eric Jolly, 'Diffusion de trois cultes dans le sud du pays Dogon: 'juru', 'ina' et 'ara-monu-na',' *Journal des Africanistes* 64 (1994): 3-38, and Gilles Holder, 'De la 'cité-état' en Afrique noire: L'espace et le politique chez les Saman du pays Dogon (Mali)', *Cahiers d'études africaines* 42 (2002): 257-83, Eric Jolly, *Boire avec esprit. Bière de mil et société Dogon* (Nanterre: Société d'Ethnologie, 2004).

Also, the overall effect on the village as such might not be as bad as the conflict suggests. After all these years, it might be just as well that this long-delayed *dama* is split over the two village halves. The normal programme, in which both Sodanga and Teri Ku have their *dama* together, would generate an almost unmanageable number of masks, weighing heavily on the ecological resources of the village. After all, masks demand wood, fibres, sesame, millet, beer, and decorations such as cowry shells in huge quantities, which from now on can be divided over a few years. This notion of the *dama* having become too large had already been voiced by some informants, but in itself is a reflection of a more general issue inside large villages. Tireli is one of the largest alongside the cliff; the usual Dogon village is considerably smaller. The other villages with mask conflicts characteristically are the large ones. Dogon villages vary from a few hundred to the 7000 of Tireli. Such a large community generates its own dynamics, and eventually, in the classic African sense, is expected to split. Right now Tireli consists in fact of two villages meeting each other at the weekly market, and incidentally performing rituals together. I expect that after the *dama* of Sodanga – which will be held eventually[21] – the *dama* in both halves will continue to be held apart, as processes of traditional religion favour imitation of the last example, not a return to an older situation.[22] So it might well be that this complicated conflict is a convoluted way of one village becoming two.

There remains the question of tourism. Is it a threat to Dogon culture? The tourists coming into the Dogon area show two general attitudes: one is that they are visiting an authentic African tribe, a culture with a deep history and intricate cosmology,[23] seeing themselves as trailblazers of the deep African wilds. The other attitude is the reverse. Viewing the many arrangements made for tourists and the general renown of the Dogon, they reckon that they are not the first, but might be the last ones to see the Dogon in their 'natural state', because all those tourists, like themselves, are ruining this African culture. Both versions are mistaken. The first has already been refuted, but the second, the spoiling tourist, has long been the topic of heated debate in tourism theory. The present consensus is that host communities are less vulnerable and much more resilient than imagined and usually adapt creatively to the new presence. The reason for this resilience is the 'tourist bubble',[24] which consists of

21 Probably in May 2013.
22 Pascal Boyer, *Tradition as Truth and Communication* (Cambridge University Press, 1990).
23 Inevitably, tour operators are not overly interested in academic refutations and the Griaule myths linger on in their travel booklets: *si non è vero, non è mal trovato*; after all, tour guides need stories, and none are more suited than the mythical fantasies of this old Dogon ethnography.
24 M. Crick. 'Representations of international tourism in the social sciences', *Annual Review of Anthropology* 18 (1989): 327; see for this debate Ton van Egmond, *Understanding the Tourist Phenomenon. An Analysis of 'West'-'South' Tourism* (Wageningen University Press, 2005). A. Franklin, *Tourism, an Introduction* (London: Sage, 2003). D. McCannell. 'The Commodification of Culture', in V. Smith & M. Brent, eds., *Hosts and Guests Revisited* (Washington: Cognizant Communication Corporation, 2001), 380-90 and Valene Smith, 'The Nature of Tourism.' in ibid. 53-68.

2.6 A real dama, *and no doubt about it!*
(© Walter van Beek)

those infrastructural arrangements that permit the reception of guests
– such as hotels, personnel, logistics – plus the travel arrangements for
the tourists from the sending country.[25] This 'bubble' hosts the tourists
and protects them from the unfortunate aspects of the destination
while permitting some view to the culture in question, here the Dogon.
In Tireli, all major protagonists were part of that bubble: Dogolu,
Apomi and Eli. In fact I was part of it as well, in several functions. First,
I stimulated tourism to Tireli through the 1982 and 2001 illustrated
books on the Dogon and through some documentary film productions;
second, I was part of the Dogon crew of the bubble as younger brother
to Dogolu, uncle to Apomi – and after all my research house now is the
old wing of a hotel. In fact I was, and still am, part of both halves of the
bubble, the receiving and the sending half.

So in the conflict between the village halves most of the in-fighting
was done inside the bubble, between just a few people, who admittedly
are important in the village, but whose dealings fall beyond the scope
of interest of most of their co-villagers. Of course, it did spill over from
the bubble into the village community through the issue of heterodox
versus orthodox dancing, but even that was also part of the bubble,
not of normal village life. The habituation of the frightened Sodanga
youngsters to their uninitiated dancing is a good example of the
emerging definition of the tourist phenomenon as a separate reality,

25 Meaning travel agencies in the sending as well as in the host countries, transport facilities and
a massive internet information business.

set apart from daily life in the village. This intra-bubble conflict did put the *dama* at risk for some time, but in the end the proper *dama* defeated the show dances, as well it should.

The final question is how these bubble politics inform the relationship between show and ritual and how this might develop in the near future. As the participation in the ritual was the key for the show performances, the link between show and ritual was extremely close, albeit in only that one aspect. But, as the Sodanga case highlights, that is a link that could quite easily be severed: Teri Ku's position was more anomalous than the Sodanga – or for that matter Sangha – one. In principle, both performances could be separated completely, as is the case in many folklore performances, where religious issues are absent. At present, in the case of the Dogon masks, the mask performance is at the very heart of their ritual competence, so emotions attached to masks are transferred to the shows. Probably that connection will become weaker. In the short-term future, reflecting on the fight that the men from Tireli put up with their masks, the *dama* will remain, maybe even longer than the religious context surrounding it. The show dances are there to stay as well, and I expect they both go their own ways, creating, as so often in tourist performances in other cultures, a separate reality for tourists to revel in, totally apart from the Dogon ritual life, thus not an arena in which to fight other Dogon, but a stage for the Dogon to 'play themselves' for an appreciative audience.

REFERENCES

Bouju, Jacky. *Graine de l'homme, enfant du mil* (Paris: Société d'Ethnographie, 1984).

Boyer, Pascal. *Tradition as Truth and Communication* (Cambridge: Cambridge University Press, 1990).

Crick, M. 'Representations of International Tourism in the Social Sciences', *Annual Review of Anthropology* 18 (1989): 307-44.

De Mott, Barbara. *Dogon Masks, a Structural Study of Form and Meaning* (Ann Arbour, Michigan: UMI Research Press, Studies in the Fine Arts, 1980), Iconography, No 4.

Dieterlen, Germaine. *Le titre d'honneur des Arou (Dogon-Mali)* (Paris: Harmattan, 1982).

Doquet, Anne. *Les masques Dogon. Ethnologie Savante et ethnologie autochtone* (Paris: Karthala, 1999).

Egmond, Ton van. *Understanding the Tourist Phenomenon. An Analysis of 'West'-'South' Tourism* (Breda, NHTV Academic Studies, 2005, no. 2).

Franklin, Adrian. *Tourism, an Introduction* (London: Sage, 2003).

Griaule, Marcel. *Masques Dogons* (Paris: Travaux et Mémoires de l'Institut d'Ethnologie, no. 33, Institut d'Ethnologie, 1938).

—— 1948. *Dieu d'eau: Entretiens avec Ogotemmêli* (Paris: Éditions du Chêne, 1948).

Griaule, Marcel and Germaine Dieterlen. *Le renard pâle. Tome I: Le mythe cosmogonique. La création du monde* (Paris: Travaux et mémoires de l'Institut d'Ethnologie, 1965).

Holder, Gilles. 'De la «cité-état» en Afrique noire: L'espace et le politique chez les Saman du pays Dogon (Mali)', *Cahiers d'études africaines* 42

(2002): 257-83.

Hollyman, Stephanie & Walter E.A. van Beek. *Dogon. Africa's People of the Cliffs* (New York: Abrams, 2001).

Jansen, Jan & Walter E.A. van Beek. 'La mission Griaule à Kangaba (Mali)', *Cahiers des études africaines* 7 (2000): 363-76.

Jolly, Eric. 'Diffusion de trois cultes dans le sud du pays Dogon: «juru», «ina» et «ara-monu-na»', *Journal des Africanistes* 64 (1994): 3-38.

—— *Boire avec esprit. Bière de mil et société Dogon* (Nanterre: Société d'Ethnologie, 2004).

Jolly, Eric & Nouhoum Guindo, eds. *Le pouvoir en miettes. Récits d'intronisation d'un Hogon (Pays Dogon, Mali)* (Paris: Servédit, 2003).

Kervran, Marcel. *La vie et la mort en pays Dogon. Rites et célébrations chez les Donnon* (Paris: Jourdier, 1999).

Lane, Paul. 'Tourism and Social Change Among the Dogon', *African Arts*, XXI 4 (1988): 66-9.

Lemineur, Philippe, Olivier Walther & Walter E.A. van Beek. 'Tourisme et patrimoine au Mali. Destruction des valeurs anciennes ou valorisation concertée?' *Geographica Helvetica* 4, (2008): 249-58.

MacCannell, D. 'The Commodification of Culture', in Smith V. & M. Brent, eds., *Hosts and Guests Revisited* (Washington DC: Cognizant Communication Corporation, 2001), 380-90.

Pern, Stephen, Bryan Alexander & Walter E.A. van Beek. *Masked Dancers of West Africa: the Dogon* (London: Time Life, 1982).

Richards, Polly. 'Imina Sana' or 'Masque à la Mode.' Contemporary Masquerade in the Dogon Region.' in Karel Arnaut, ed., *Re-Visions: New Perspectives on the African Collections of the Horniman Museum* (The Horniman Museum and Gardens, London and the Museum of Anthropology, Coimbra, 2000), 107-23.

—— 2006 'Dogon Masks at the Turn of the Millennium', *Arts Afrique*, 37.

Smith, Valene L. 'The Nature of Tourism', in Smith V. & M. Brent, eds., *Hosts and Guests Revisited* (Washington DC: Cognizant Communication Corporation, 2001), 53-68.

Van Beek, Walter E.A. 'In Memory of a Great Singer: the Dogon *Baja Ni* as a Cultural-historical Performance', in Stephen Belcher, Jan Jansen & Mohamed N'Daou, eds., *Mande Mansa, Mande Worlds* 2 (2008) 193-215.

—— 'Boys and Masks among the Dogon' in Simon Ottenberg & D.A. Binckley, eds., *Playful Performers. African Children's Masquerades* (New Brunswick & London: Transaction Publishers, 2006), 67-88.

—— 'Walking Wallets? Tourists at the Dogon falaise', in Stephen Wooten, ed., *Wari Matters: Ethnographic Explorations of Money in the Mande World* (Münster: LIT Verlag, 2005), 191-216.

—— 'Haunting Griaule: Experiences from the Restudy of the Dogon', *History in Africa* 31, (2004): 43-68.

—— 'African Tourist Encounters; Effects of Tourism in Two West-African Societies', *Africa* 73, 3 (2003) 251-89.

—— 'Dogon Restudied: A Field Evaluation of the Work of Marcel Griaule', *Current Anthropology* 32, 2 (1991): 139-67.

—— 'Enter the Bush: a Dogon Mask Festival' in Susan Vogel, ed., *Africa Explores; 20th Century African Art* (New York & Prestal Munich: Centre for African Art, 1991) 56-73.

Van Beek, Walter E.A. & Pieteke Banga. 'The Dogon and their Trees', in Elisabeth Croll & David Parkin, eds., *Bush Base, Forest Farm. Culture, Environment and Development* (London: Routledge, 1992), 57-75.

3 · Semiotics
& the political economy of tourism
in the Sahara

Georg Klute

In a conversation I had with Jeremy Boissevain and Tom Selwyn about the anthropology of tourism at the Mediterranean Summer School in Piran, Slovenia, 2002, Tom Selwyn suggested that anthropological research on the topic should bring together political economy and (imaginative) semiological approaches.[1] As I was fascinated by Tom's suggestion, I sat down and tried to write an essay on the issue for a lecture at the Free University of Berlin.[2] Despite the fact that I had never conducted fieldwork specifically on tourism in the Sahara, I became, interested in the topic, however, during my research on the Tuareg upheavals against the governments of Niger in Mali in the 1990s.[3] While doing fieldwork in Southern Algeria on Tuareg migrants from Mali and Niger in 1992, I realised that most Tuareg migrants found employment in fields they are particularly accustomed with, or at least are believed to be, by members of the host society. Nomadic migrants actually look for and are searched for those occupations which are in accordance with a particular nomadic identity or associated with particular nomadic properties and values, such as night-watchmen, herders, soldiers (mercenaries), trans-border traders or tourist-guides. Economic transactions between migrants from a nomadic background and their hosts obviously seemed to be based on the principle of 'foreignness,'[4] a principle that also applies to transactions between 'host and guest' in the field of tourism.

---

1   See also the discussion on this issue between Tom Selwyn and Donald MacLeod (Donald MacLeod & Tom Selwyn, 'The Scope of the Anthropology of Tourism: A response to Tom Selwyn', *Anthropology Today* 18, 2 (2002): 27).
2   The lecture later on was published in a German social science journal. See Georg Klute, 'Die Faszination des Fremden und der einheimische Blick. Semiotik und politische Ökonomie des Saharatourismus,' in Gerhard Hufnagel, ed., *Sonderheft Sowi. Das Journal für Geschichte, Politik, Wirtschaft und Kultur: Reisen – die Welt erfahren* (Seelze: Erhard Friedrich Verlag, 2003), 13-23. The present text is a revised version of the German publication. I am grateful to Walter van Beek for his criticism and suggestions.
3   For an overview of the so-called Tuareg rebellions, see Pierre Boilley, *Les Touaregs Kel Adagh. Dépendances et révoltes: du Soudan français au Mali contemporain* (Paris: Karthala, 1999); Georg Klute & Trutz v. Trotha, 'Roads to Peace. From Small War to Parastatal Peace in the North of Mali,' in Marie-Claire Foblets & Trutz v. Trotha, eds., *Healing the Wounds. Essays on the Reconstruction of Societies after War* (Oxford: Hart Publishing, Oñati International Series in Law and Society, 2004), 109-43
4   Elisabeth Boesen and Georg Klute, 'Direkt von der Wüste in die Stadt. Moderne Migration von Nomaden aus dem Sahara-Sahelraum,' *Das Parlament* Beilage 'Aus Politik und Zeitgeschichte' 10 (2004).

A second phenomenon with regard to tourism in the Sahara that I came across during fieldwork was a particular relation between tourism and rebellion. Quite a number of former tourist guides actually became members of the various rebel movements in the two countries, just as quite a number of former rebels found or tried to find employment in the tourist industry. I wondered what kind of relationships might exist between the decision to take up arms against the government in order to fight for (political) autonomy, social and economic rights, or even a Tuareg state on the one hand, and the decision to work in the field of tourism, on the other. What kind of impact do the encounters with tourists have on processes of Tuareg identity building, given the fact that the various upheavals of the Tuareg in the two countries, including the most recent one in northern Mali at the beginning of 2012, are, for a large part, a struggle to preserve their own identity as Tuareg? How is the political economy of both fields of activity linked, given the fact that the upheavals in the two countries are also economic enterprises?

My reflections on these questions are divided in three parts. Firstly, I will briefly outline some of the features characterising tourism in the Sahara. I will then explore the causes that motivate Western tourists to travel into the Sahara and to visit the Tuareg culture. Thirdly, I will attempt to elucidate the impact the encounters with tourists may have on Tuareg society in general and on Tuareg identity building in particular.

Features of Sahara tourism

Tourism in the Sahara has some special features: (1) It is clearly conditioned by political circumstances. (2) It is a voyage into an 'extreme world' and an encounter with its exotic inhabitants. (3) It is an exclusive form of tourism, involving but a comparatively small number of people, and it is thus relatively expensive. Rucksack tourism that was at its height in the 1970s and 1980s, and 'second-hand car tourism' scarcely plays any role today, since Africans buy directly on the European used-car market and send the vehicles to West Africa by sea. The Sahara is indeed not 'trampled' by 'golden hordes'[5] of tourists.

Since tourism in the Sahara is conditioned by political circum-stances, it is a recent phenomenon. It only began in the 1930s, after the European colonial powers had finally 'pacified' the Sahara. From 1931 onwards, the 'Touring Club de France' organised trans-Saharan tourist circuits.[6] The circuits were preceded by tests with a newly constructed and luxuriously equipped bus owned by the 'Compagnie Générale

---

5 Louis Turner & John Ash, *The Golden Hordes: International Tourism and the Pleasure Periphery* (London: Routledge, 1975).

6 Claude Blanguernon, *Le Hoggar* (Paris: Arthaud, 1983).

Transsaharienne' from Colomb-Béchar in Algeria to Bourem on the river Niger (in today's Mali) and back in the winter-season of 1926.[7] Tourist circuits with cars were, however, limited to prepared tracks; visits to Tuareg encampments were done, if at all, on camel-back. It was not until the middle of the 20th century, that 'automobiles had developed technically in such a way as to exceed camels in speed and range nearly everywhere' (in the Sahara).[8] Western tourists then had technical tools at their disposal that allowed confronting the 'extreme world' of the Sahara without much danger. From 1951 onwards the 'Touring Club de France' proposed circuits in the Hoggar mountains (Algeria) by car, during which the tourist was given the opportunity to visit Tuareg nomads. The new Algerian state continued the tourist enterprises of the French colonial power. The 'Touring Club Algérien' organised the same circuits in the south of the country as its French counterpart had done before. It was a decade later in Niger,[9] and only in the 1990s in Mali, that a specific Sahara tourism began to evolve in Algeria's neighbouring countries.

The vulnerability of tourism in the Sahara due to political circumstances – perhaps more than anywhere else – becomes clear if we consider the past two decades: there is indeed an obvious connection between the number of tourists and the current political situation in the Sahara. As relevant events let us mention: the Gulf War in 1991; the election victory of the 'Islamic Salvation Front' (FIS) in Algeria in 1992, with the stopping of the elections by the government and subsequent threats against foreigners; numerous acts of kidnapping of tourists in the Algerian, Tunisian, Malian and Nigerien Sahara by Islamist groups, namely by the Groupe Salafiste pour la Prédication et le Combat (GSPC) which started this activity in 2003 with the kidnapping and ransoming of a group of European tourists in Southern Algeria and continues this profitable 'business' to the present day,[10] and above all the armed struggle of the Tuareg against the states of Mali and Niger which was repeatedly interrupted by various peace treaties, only to flare up again after a while. The fighting lasted from mid-1990 to the end of 2009, when the last of the Tuareg rebel movements in Niger, the 'Front des Forces de Redressement' (FFR) laid down its arms in town of Arlit.[11] The above-mentioned events caused a sharp drop in the number of tourist expeditions to the southern Sahara, especially to the desert regions of Algeria, Mali and Niger. This was compensated only to a small degree by the fact that tourists turned to Libya when it

7 Werner Nöther, *Die Erschließung der Sahara durch Motorfahrzeuge 1901-1936. Chronik einer Pionierepoche* (München: belleville Verlag Michael Farin, 2003).

8 Georg Klute, 'The Technique of Modern Chariots: About Speed and Mobility in Contemporary Small Wars in the Sahara,' in Jan Bart Gewald, Sabine Luning and Klaas van Walraven, eds., *The Speed of Change. Motor Vehicles and People in Africa, 1890-2000* (Leiden: Brill, 2009), 199.

9 Marko Scholze, *Moderne Nomaden und fliegende Händler. Tuareg und Tourismus in Niger* (Berlin: LIT, 2009).

10 In 2007, the GSPC declared its affiliation to Al-Qaeda and is since then known as 'Al-Qaeda of the Maghrib'.

11 (http://issikta.blogspot.com/2009/12/desarmement-du-ffr-arlit.html). * See p. 72 update.

was opened up to international tourism (partly as a result of the UN embargo following the Lockerbie bombing), and then increasingly to Mauritania.

However, the main destination of tourists in the Sahara was and still is the southern Sahara: southern Algeria, south-east Libya, northern Niger and northern Mali. This is the region within which the Tuareg move about and have their settlements; tourism in the Sahara is essentially tourism in the land of the Tuareg and to the Tuareg themselves.

Fascination of the desert: an extreme world

Tourists who travel to the southern Sahara are essentially seeking two things: an encounter with wild, untamed nature, the extreme world of the desert, and an encounter with the 'blue knights' (meaning men) of the desert. As we shall see, both kinds of encounter are bound up with ambivalent, even contradictory, expectations, whose ambivalence is attractive and at the same time threatening: on the one hand the expectation of the 'wild' and 'uncivilized', and on the other that of the 'natural', 'unspoilt' and 'pure'.

Obviously the extreme desert environment holds a special fascination for European tourists. This fascination is based in the first place on the fact that members of industrialized cultures do see 'nature'[12] whereas pastoral nomads or gardeners in an oasis do not. Where the latter see fodder plants for camels or good conditions for cultivating, western tourists are fascinated by the untamed environment. Because they do not see with the eyes of a peasant, 'nature' is for them a special sphere that is separate from the rest of the world, and which seems to have no importance for their own existence. As the environment in Europe has been tamed since long ago and has lost all dangerous and threatening appearances, it can be admired as something wonderful,[13] a fragile thing to be protected from human greed. Certain aesthetic notions relating to shape, colour, light and sound can be projected onto this sphere of 'nature'. The extreme desert is particularly suitable for such a projection, because no vegetation covers its surface, which often forms bizarre shapes,

12 The notion of a sphere 'nature' of non-human things and beings, as opposed to 'culture' or 'civilization' as in the realm of man, is a quite recent phenomenon in western thinking. Even in Montaigne's time in the 17th century, no distinction whatsoever was made between 'nature' and 'culture' See Thomas Bargatzky, 'Introduction,' in Thomas Bargatzky and Rolf Kuschel, eds., *The Invention of Nature* (Frankfurt, Berlin, Bern, New York, Paris, Wien: Peter Lang, 1994), 9-25. It was Descartes' distinction between *res cogitans* and *res extensa* that laid the basis of the binary principle of western epistemology. While most binary oppositions stemming from Descartes' distinction, such as mind-body, subject-object, or individual-society have been criticised in anthropological discourse, the nature-culture dichotomy seems to be particularly resistant. See Philipe Descola and Gísli Pálson, 'Introduction,' in Descola and Pálson, eds., *Nature and Society. Anthropological Perspectives* (London and New York: Routledge, 1996), 1-21.

13 Walter van Beek, 'Approaching African Tourism; paradigms and paradoxes', in P. Chabal, U. Engel and L. de Haan, eds., *African Alternatives* (Leiden, Brill, 2007), 145-72.

eroded by the wind. Tourists find the desert fantastically beautiful.

A second reason for the fascination of the desert for members of industrialised cultures is the fact that it belongs to the extreme worlds. Comparable to high mountains, the ocean, or the cold deserts of the polar circles, the forces of nature here are not fully under control. While all other worlds have come to terms with nature to such an extent that it is only very rarely a threat, and exposing oneself to its forces is hardly possible, even if one should wish to, in extreme worlds there is still the thrill of danger. European travellers react to the perils of wayfaring in the desert in two contradictory ways. On the one hand, they try to reduce the risks by planning their journey carefully, and through the use of technical equipment; and on the other hand, they loudly invoke the risks that remain, despite their preparations. The thrill of trekking in the desert results from this ambivalence. The attraction of the challenge to cope with the extreme world of the desert is directly proportionate to the associated risks. Tourists from the industrialised north are therefore faced with a dilemma: the dangers and the fascination of the desert are reduced in proportion to the sophistication of their preparation and their technical equipment. Members of industrialised cultures find two ways out of this dilemma of controlling an extreme world by technical means and thus destroying its fascination: on the one hand, they may deliberately refuse to use existing technology in order to keep the level of danger high, and on the other, they may talk about the mortal dangers to which others expose themselves through less careful planning and inferior technical equipment. Stories about people who have died of thirst are therefore a ubiquitous topic of conversation among desert travellers, because they show the dangerousness of the desert and at the same time reveal the speakers' own careful management and good technical equipment.

Desert tourists, in the sense of people driving off-road vehicles whose destination is the extreme desert, must be distinguished from people, mainly used-car dealers, who are only passing through, and for whom the desert is no more than an obstacle to be overcome on the way to reaching their real destination. The great majority, over 90 per cent of those who die of thirst, are passing travellers. On the section of the central trans-Sahara highway between Tamanrasset and Arlit, the police of Tamanrasset district used to have an annual record of over fifty (Europeans) dead or missing, most of them used-car dealers. However, since the beginning of the second Gulf War, the central trans-Sahara highway is no longer frequented by Europeans.

The western imaginary of the desert as an extreme world of an untamed nature is reflected in the descriptions of travel guides, producing a particular 'tourist gaze'[14] specific to the Sahara and its inhabitants. In an (unpublished) study of French travel guides to the Sahara, the historian Pierre Boilley shows that this literature has been

14 John Urry, *The Tourist Gaze* (London: Sage, 1990).

shaped by similar, in some cases even identical, discourses from its first appearance around 1938 up to today. At first, the Sahara and its inhabitants were considered from a romantic point of view. The Sahara was painted as a place of adventure and at the same time as a place of mystical purity. In these texts, its inhabitants disappeared behind the descriptions of the desert itself. It was the landscape which permitted a ,double journey': on the one hand a journey to unlimited space, and on the other hand a journey into an extreme world, which, because of the hardships involved, was comparable to the heroic journeys of other, long past ages, and placed Sahara tourists on a level with the heroes of that past. If the inhabitants were mentioned at all, then only as living witnesses of those other heroic times, as the 'knights of the desert', recalling those figures of medieval Europe.

This discourse was interrupted by the independence of the African states in the 1960s and in particular by the Algerian war of independence (1954-1962). It was only resumed, in a different form, several years later. However, at that time it was not the journey into a heroic past that was emphasised, but the mystic journey into oneself, a search for an authenticity that has been lost in western industrialised societies.[15] It is not a coincidence that this aspect of the desert journey – at least as represented in the travel guides – appeared at the time when beatniks and hippies were travelling to India to seek themselves. The pure, empty desert – for the most part also empty of people – is presented as a place where one can find oneself.[16]

The local view: danger & death

The local inhabitants of the desert have a view of the extreme desert that is very different from that of tourists. They are not attracted by it; on the contrary, they fear it more than anything else. The extreme desert is without vegetation, it offers no food to the animals of the desert nomads and even camel riders can only cross it after careful preparation and at great speed. In the desert death is waiting. And there is something else that makes the extreme desert so terrifying for the local people: in it live and reign the 'spirits of solitude' (*Kal-assuf*), who tease travellers, lead them astray, and can drive them insane.

At first sight, the peasant understanding of 'nature' of Tuareg nomads and caravan traders seems to be primarily based on utilitarian considerations: green valleys full of fodder plants are opposed to sterile dunes with no vegetation. This division of the surroundings into 'useful' and 'useless' domains, however, is embedded in more far-reaching ideas of a religious (or cosmic) kind, centring around the

---

15 See also: Dean MacCannell, *The Tourist. A New Theory of the Leisure Class* (London: Mac-Millan, 1976).

16 In an overview of contemporary (French and German) tourist catalogues and travel guides, Marco Scholze comes to similar conclusions. He argues in a rather functionalistic manner, however, stating that differences in the descriptions correspond mainly to the type of trips offered: see his *Moderne Nomaden und fliegende Händler. Tuareg und Tourismus in Niger* (Berlin: LIT Verlag, 2009), 63ff.

notion of 'God's blessing' (*albaraka*), which in turn is reflected in the well-being of people, animals and other living beings.[17]

The presence or absence of 'God's blessing' is also expressed through the terms beautiful and ugly. These are categories of a religious nature, and only Westerners interpret 'beautiful' and 'ugly' as aesthetic categories projected on 'nature'. Indeed, the clear-cut divide between the human ('culture') and non-human ('nature') realm as in Western thinking does not exist. The conception of 'God's blessing', however, is not limited to human beings; on the contrary, these terms divide the whole world of the nomads into life-giving areas and areas that are hostile to life, on a kind of continuous scale. At the 'beautiful' end of the scale are green valleys, full of fodder plants, plump animals ('even donkeys'), well-nourished women, where even 'the mountains' (which are otherwise regarded only as landmarks) 'become beautiful when the rain beats on them and washes them; when there are clouds over the mountains, that is very beautiful!'[18] At the 'ugly' end of the scale are dried up vegetation during the hot season, emaciated animals, people who are excessively thin or those showing bad behaviour. The epitome of ugliness is the extreme desert, not only because it is lifeless itself, but because it is a threat to all living things. While tourists see the desert as extremely beautiful, for nomads it is extremely ugly.

Tourist-Tuareg encounters[19]

Tuareg who have regular contact with Europeans, however, react to the desert in a different way from the nomadic cattle keepers. In the southern Sahara, our area of study, this applies above all to those who work in the tourist industry. The paying European tourists want to be led into the extreme desert, in other words precisely into that area which nomadic cattle keepers avoid and caravans cross as quickly as they can. While the desert is a hostile environment for the nomadic Tuareg, it is a place of work for tourist guides, and provides them with an income. Therefore, they praise the beauty of the desert in the same way as that of a woman or a camel.

It would be too short-sighted, however, to reduce these various relations between the Tuareg and the desert to purely functional explanations. European tourists from the industrialised north have introduced an understanding of nature that is in contrast to the pre-industrial, peasant relationship to the world around them of the nomads and caravan traders; at least some of them have acquired a conception of 'nature', based indeed on the occidental nature-culture

---

17 Georg Klute, 'Wo liegt Gottes Segen? Natur und Arbeit bei Nomaden der Sahara', in Ute Luig & Achim von Oppen eds., *Naturaneignung in Afrika als sozialer und symbolischer Prozeß* (Berlin: Klaus Schwarz Verlag, 1995), 51-64.

18 Interview held in the Adagh in northern Mali in May 1988, cit. in Georg Klute, *Die schwerste Arbeit der Welt. Alltag von Tuareg-Nomaden* (München: Trickster Verlag, 1992), 119.

19 I borrowed the concept of the tourist encounter from Walter van Beek, 'African tourist encounters: Effects of tourism on two West African societies,' *Africa* 73, 2 (2003): 251-89.

3.1 (Above) Tourist
in Southern Algeria
(Tikokobawen), 2008
(© Dida Badi)

3.2 (Left) Tuareg
tourist guide and
former rebel with
tourist, Northern
Mali (near Gao),
2003
(© Georg Klute)

dichotomy, which conceives a ‚natural environment‘ as a separated sphere that exists independent of the normal daily environment and which has replaced the division between a life-giving and a life-threatening domain.

To give an example: Mano Dayak, the well-known (now deceased) Nigerien rebel leader and former head of a tourist agency (one of the organizers of the Paris-Dakar Rally), completely adopted the European, 'industrialised' view of the extreme desert. In a short text entitled 'The Desert',[20] he describes the desert in the same terms that a European tourist would use:

> For me the desert is extraordinarily beautiful and pure, confusing and magical at the same time. Each time I find myself face to face with the desert; it takes me on a moving journey into myself, where nostalgic memories, fears and hopes collide. [...] The desert is the mystery of the wind, driving the dunes before it and giving them strange shapes with pure lines. It is the mystery of the acacia tree, lost in the middle of the sandy wastes, like something forgotten from another era.[21]

While Mano Dayak has been an outstanding figure among the Tuareg,[22] a career progressing from tourist guide to armed rebel (or vice versa) is by no means a singular phenomenon. It is striking that quite a number of the later rebels worked in the tourist industry before the outbreak of fighting in 1990, or at least had sporadic contact with tourists. The leader of the first Nigerien rebel movement, Rhissa ag Boula, had worked for many years in a tourist agency before taking up the struggle for the 'land of the Tuareg'. His career after the conclusion of peace is also typical: Rhissa became the minister of tourism in the government of Niger. Other later rebel leaders, either in Niger and Mali, or as migrant labourers in exile in Algeria or Libya, had similar contacts with western tourists.[23]

The switching between the two careers is surely facilitated by the fact that desert trips with tourists bear some resemblances with many occupations of the Tuareg outside the tourist realm. Desert guerrilla, caravan trading, or smuggling indeed reveal a high degree of 'compatibility'[24] with tourist desert trips. Many Tuareg migrants in the border zones between Mali, Niger, Algeria and Libya were and are involved in smuggling, following the old tradition of nomadic raids, in the sense of swift looting attacks on caravans or oasis settlements. Long and risky journeys covering more than a thousand kilometres, some⁻

20 Mano Dayak, *Je suis né avec du sable dans les yeux* (Paris: Fixot, 1996), 233-35.
21 Ibid., 234.
22 See: http://en.wikipedia.org/wiki/Mano_Dayak
23 See: Georg Klute, 'Der Tuaregkonflikt in Mali und Niger', in Joachim Betz and Stefan Brüne, eds., *Jahrbuch Dritte Welt 1996. Daten, Übersichten, Analysen* (Hamburg: Deutsches Übersee-Institut, 1996), 146-61.
24 The term of compatibility has been proposed by Everett Rogers, in order to better grasp the 'degree to which an innovation is perceived as being consistent with the existing values, past experiences, and needs of the receivers.' See Everett Rogers and Floyd Shoemaker, *Communication of Innovations. A Cross-Cultural Approach* (London: Collier Macmillan Publishers / New York: The Free Press, 1971), 21.

times only with a single vehicle, are planned almost in the manner of military raids, for the purpose of smuggling light and expensive goods.

Indeed, guiding tourists in the Sahara requires similar skills and knowledge as caravan trading, or, more generally, travelling in the desert: a good sense of orientation, geographical knowledge, strength and endurance under difficult conditions. Also, these skills and (in part) hard physical labour are required only at certain times and not continuously. Just like the traditional camel caravan, the one-to-three week expedition with tourists is followed by a more or less long period of rest. In the tourist industry, just as in the caravan trade, the work is restricted to one part of the year only. In general, the tourist season is in the winter, because the temperatures are more comfortable (or more tolerable). In the other months of the year the guides can take a rest and recover from the hardships of these expeditions – just like the 'traditional' caravan traders – or engage in other work. As in the case of camel caravans, certain skills are needed on tourist expeditions that may seem incidental, such as setting up and striking camp quickly, preparing food with very simple aids, or building protection from wind, sand or cold: in short, the ability to cope in a natural environment, something that Europeans seem to have lost long ago.

The British traveller Angus Buchanan, who visited the Tuareg in the Air massif (Northern Niger) in the early 20th century, remarked on the great vigour and energy they show when travelling, but otherwise described them as a 'lazy race' and even referred to the Tuareg as the 'laziest people I have ever met', with the reservation: 'except when travelling.'[25]

Impacts of Saharan tourism

The western conception of nature as a separated sphere is not limited to some individuals or to tourist middlemen alone; it has moved beyond the 'tourist bubble'[26] and penetrated into parts of Tuareg society. My thesis in this regard is that tourist middlemen are not locked up in the tourist bubble their whole lifetime; they are leaving the bubble from time to time doing other things, and, as 'cultural brokers',[27] induce innovations.

Many (former) rebels speak of the desert in a manner similar to that of Mano Dayak, even if their descriptions are at times more ambivalent than his, and may still reflect the original 'peasant view' of the nomads and caravan traders. But both in the case of Mano Dayak and in the case of the rebels, a remarkable change has taken place in comparison

25 Angus Buchanan, *Out of the World of Northern Nigeria. Exploration of Air* (London: John Murray, 1921), 239.

26 Valene Smith, 'Introduction,' in V. Smith, ed., *Hosts and Guests. The Anthropology of Tourism* (Oxford: Basil Blackwell, 1989), 1-17.

27 Irwin Press, 'Ambiguity and Innovation: Implications for the Genesis of the Cultural Broker', *American Anthropologist* 71 (1969): 206-17.

with the 'peasant' view of the nomads, which is evident in the use of language: the word for 'extreme desert' (*tenere*) has become a metaphor for the 'land' or 'home' of the Tuareg or even the 'Tuareg state'. The political aspirations expressed in the term 'tenere' are heavily loaded with emotions, 'cette passion qu'éprouve le Touareg pour le désert [this passion that the Tuareg feels for the desert]'.[28] Such a strong bond with the desert, whole-hearted and positive in the case of Mano Dayak or slightly ambivalent in the case of others, is only very rarely found among 'traditional' nomads and caravan people. For them, the extreme desert is associated with ugliness and death and only a few, such as the caravan leader, Archi, mentioned by Spittler, feel at home in it.[29]

The encounters between western tourists and Tuareg have had another effect: they have reinforced ethnic and nationalist currents among the Tuareg, even though this was never the intention of the tourists and they are no doubt unaware of it. Western tourists undertake the long (and expensive) journey with the sole aim of seeing the beauties of the Sahara and the land of the Tuareg, and of learning something about their culture at first hand. For the Tuareg, the knowledge that their land and their culture are considered by others to be worth visiting is a source of increased pride in their desert home and ethnic origin. In general, western tourists do not distinguish between Algerian, Nigerian or Malian Tuareg, or between different regional groups. They know little about lineages, family groups and social strata, and the moral relations between them. They want to see the 'Tuareg', their culture and above all their land. This tends to encourage unifying political tendencies, something that the tourists are probably completely unaware of. They are interested only in the culture of the Tuareg, the 'being of the Tuareg'. They want to see what the Tuareg themselves call *temust en-majeghan* (the being, the nature of the Tuareg), an expression that, as a synonym of *tenere*, also means nation or land of the Tuareg.

To what extent can tourism be said to have influenced the Tuareg idea of power? While it was hitherto mainly conceived of as being related to persons, as power over people, the idea of power related to a particular space, the utopia of a future Tuareg state, gained ever clearer contours from the 1980s onwards. It was this concept that inspired the armed struggle, aimed at setting up a state with borders corresponding essentially to the area that was of interest to tourists in the southern Sahara. It was the western concept of desert dwellers in

---

28 Mano Dayak, *Je suis né avec du sable dans les yeux* (Paris: Fixot, 1996), 235. The fact that the term *tenere* has become a political notion is clearly shown in the first poem of the rebels: 'I am living in the deserts where there are neither trees nor shadow. Veiled friends, give up the indigo veil, the desert is waiting for you, where the blood of your relatives is shed. The *tenere* is our land and our future. [...]'. (Poet: Ibrahim ag Alkhabib 1979; transcription: Ehya ag Sidiyene 1995; translation: Ehya ag Sidiyene / Georg Klute 1995; in Georg Klute, *Die Rebellionen der Tuareg in Mali und Niger* (Siegen: University of Siegen, Habilitationsschrift, 2001).

29 Gerd Spittler, 'Wüste, Wildnis und Zivilisation - Die Sicht der Kel Ewey,' *Paideuma* 33 (1989): 285.

their own land – the desert – which was translated into the political demand for a Tuareg state.

The third impact of the encounter between the Tuareg and western tourists is that it counteracts the lack of respect felt by the Tuareg in two ways: from outside, for instance in the way they are treated by other Malians or Nigerians, and internally, in their own lack of self-esteem when they compare themselves with the rest of the world. Insults from outside may take the form of disparaging remarks or derogatory names used by members of neighbouring ethnic groups. The (nomadic) Tuareg are accused of having a mobile, unfixed way of life which is anachronistic and unproductive, so that they need to be 'developed' and persuaded to settle, which has led to attempts by the government to force them to do so. They are reminded of their past as cruel robbers, a legacy which some think has not been overcome and can never be overcome. This is why, during the armed Tuareg rebellions there were calls for the banishment or even the extermination of the Tuareg as a whole.

This image of the marauding and at the same time parasitical Tuareg is still widespread today in Niger and Mali. They are said to live not from their own labour, but from that of others, and the many raids carried out during the Tuareg rebellions helped to confirm the idea that 'greed' and 'rapacity' are essential, inherent features of the Tuareg. At best the Tuareg are seen as nomads who do not work hard but just watch their herds grow; forced or voluntary settlement is therefore seen as the right step away from a vagrant, unproductive and obsolete form of existence towards a more modern, 'civilised' way of life.

Since their defeats at the hands of the French colonial forces in the early 20th century, the Tuareg have felt inferior to the rest of the 'world'. From being political actors who played an important role in determining the fortunes of the central Sahara and the neighbouring areas of the Sahel, they were reduced to the status of subjects in states where they had to live as minorities under the rule of other ethnic groups. Ever since their experience of the great drought disasters in the Sahel zone in the 1970s and 1980s, they have come to the painful realisation that they are dependent on assistance when it comes to coping with famines. Food and aid projects came from outside, thus impressing the Tuareg with the overwhelming financial capacities and organisational abilities of western countries.

Thus, recognition from tourists, who show an interest in the desert and its inhabitants, and who admire their special skills in respect of surviving in a hostile environment, serves to counteract the disparaging way in which the Tuareg are treated in Mali and Niger. Tourist guides who can demonstrate that their knowledge and competence is superior to that of the western visitors, at least in certain areas, have greater pride and higher self-esteem. Tuareg nomads who act as tourist guides in the desert are, so to speak, enculturated: accompanying tourists on expeditions in the Sahara requires exactly those qualities which the Tuareg always needed to cultivate, whether on long journeys with trading caravans, during looting raids, or in war.

It is important not to underestimate the socio-psychological effects of tourism in the Sahara on the self-esteem of the Tuareg. The fact that tourists from the West, which they have learned to see as overwhelmingly superior, are willing to place themselves on the level of learners and thus, for the short period of the expedition, acknowledge the superior knowledge and skills of their Tuareg guides, inevitably counteracts their feeling of inferiority and increases their self-esteem. On the other hand, the Tuareg's own image of themselves, their culture and their environment, is certainly affected by the conceptions and expectations of the tourists, which encourage a kind of folkloric conservatism. The tourists know what image of the Tuareg and their culture they want to see, and so this is what they are shown (and what they pay for). It cannot be overlooked that recognition by western tourists, who place themselves on the level of learners in relation to their Tuareg guides and companions, at least during the expedition, not only raises the self-esteem of the Tuareg in general, but also changes their marginal and peripheral position in relation to neighbouring ethnic groups. There is a need for more detailed research into the question whether the interest of the western visitors, exclusively directed as it is towards the desert and its inhabitants, will cause the disparaging attitude of neighbouring ethnic groups towards the Tuareg to change into one of respect or envy.

The encounters between local guides and tourists during expeditions in the Sahara also have sensual connotations. About two thirds of those who take part in such expeditions are women.[30] This is not unconnected with the powers of attraction of the primitive, extreme world, the desert, and its wild, exotic inhabitants. Many Tuareg involved in the tourist business dress themselves in the traditional attributes of the Tuareg man, even though they no longer wear this traditional clothing in their daily life or have long ago stopped behaving like nomads 'from the desert'. In fact, rather than being encounters between western tourists and Tuareg in general, these are predominantly encounters between western women and Tuareg men. In the encounter with (foreign) European women, the Tuareg men stage themselves as 'primitive, wild men', underlining their exoticism by dressing in traditional clothing and veils, or presenting themselves as connoisseurs of the desert, mounted on camels, hoping at the same time to meet the expectations of the Europeans who are prepared to pay for their display.

The staging of primitive male exoticism and wildness in the transnational spaces (or in-between spaces) of the encounter clearly

30 According to telephone enquiries with three German tour operators, specialised in Saharan tourism, and the author's own observations.

contains some sensuality. This applies in the first place to the apparently banal commercial transaction of selling silver jewellery. Apart from (male) European traders, the buyers are almost exclusively European women, to whom the Tuareg sellers present themselves as mysterious men from the desert. Traditionally, Tuareg silversmiths, as an endogamous craft group, are strictly separated from other Tuareg and are regarded with a mixture of contempt and fear. But in the eyes of western women, even silversmiths represent the typical Tuareg man, not only in their clothing but also in their posture and attitude. By taking on the external appearance of pre-colonial noble warriors, the silversmiths are breaking with tradition.

It remains an open question, however, whether – and if yes to what extent – this outside (western) view is also projected inwards. Is there a real change in the position of these craftsmen who are commercially successful and appreciated by the superior Westerners, and who are even found desirable by some European women? This is especially relevant in the light of the fact that members of other Tuareg strata, who in the past clearly distanced themselves from the silversmiths, now also offer their products for sale. It is not improbable that such trans-cultural encounters will change the status and perception of jewellery makers as a group within Tuareg society. Some, at least, will probably begin to adopt the code of behaviour attributed to the Tuareg nobility, which includes despising the stratum of the vassals.

Outlook

It is not easy to assess the perspectives of tourism in the Sahara at the moment. Future developments will mainly depend on whether people in northern Mali reconcile, bringing peace back to the region. However, I argue that Tuareg-tourist encounters have already evoked social dynamics in the Tuareg society; tourists will remain to be fascinated by the Sahara, continuing to visit it via Algeria, Libya or Mauretania as soon as the situation improves. Although tourism will not break down in the long run, it will probably become more expensive and riskier.

It is not at all certain that Tourist expectations will lead to a re-traditionalisation of Tuareg society in a modern context. Quite to the contrary; in particular the mutual relationships of the sexes could be fundamentally changed. In the case of Tuareg nomads, the voice of the (married) woman carries great weight, which is not only a cultural phenomenon but also an economic reality: she is the owner of the tent and the household equipment, so that in the case of divorce the husband is left without a roof over his head, and a part of the family's herd belongs to her. In other words, men need to think twice before divorcing their wives. But as soon as the husband starts earning a good income as a tourist guide or travel agent, he gains economic independence and marriage is set on a different basis.

Traditional nomadic patterns of production may also be permanently changed. Camels, for instance, are no longer bred exclusively as milk or caravan animals, but also as docile mounts for tourists. In his study of tourism in northern Niger, Marko Scholze reports that these days not only the breeding but also the training of camels is designed in view of the needs of tourists: a smooth gait is more important than speed. The same applies to craft production, especially the well known silver jewellery of the Tuareg. Such jewellery is made to please not only Tuareg women, but also and above all western women. Designs and materials change, new things are created.[31]

The expectations of western tourists in respect of the wild, natural desert, and their image of the desert's inhabitants which is based mainly on primitive, male Tuareg warriors, are projected onto Tuareg society. These projections have an important politico-economic result, which is at the same time a precondition for the development of tourism in the Sahara. Tourism in the Sahara has already brought about a clear economic differentiation in Tuareg society and will continue to do so. The investments needed to set up a local tourist agency are substantial, and it is therefore no coincidence that local travel agents are often former rebels (or rebel leaders), who acquired their first capital during the rebellion. Travel agents can earn good money in the growing tourist sector, which clearly differentiates them economically from most other Tuareg.

The local tourist industry, however, requires not only capital but also organisational skills, especially of the political and military kind. This applies particularly when national borders are crossed or in areas where bandits or rebel groups are a threat to security. For this reason the local tourist industry is dominated by groups that have precisely these specialised skills. Thus all western tour operators offering expeditions to the southern Sahara must work together with Tuareg partners. If they do not, their expeditions run the risk of being attacked and their clients being robbed. Ironically, local travel agents and their employees can also use their skills, their capital and their vehicles in the profitable cross-border smuggling trade during the tourist off-season, which is in the hot months of the year from April to September. The same vehicles that serve to transport tourists in the desert winter are used in the other seasons to smuggle cigarettes or black African migrants.

It is possible that tourism in the Sahara is encouraging, among other things, the development of a new elite, oriented towards the image of the pre-colonial nobility. This is supported by tourist expectations in respect of posture, attitude and dress. Like the former nobility, the new elite profits from transit services, as well as from transnational, intra-Saharan and trans-Saharan trade, and continues to differentiate Tuareg society.

31 Marko Scholze, *Moderne Nomaden und fliegende Händler. Tuareg und Tourismus in Niger* (Berlin: LIT, 2009).

Shortly before finishing this article, the area has been shattered by political turmoil again. In January 2012, the Tuareg led 'Mouvement national pour la libération de l'Azawad' (MNLA) attacked army positions and towns in northern Mali. Unsatisfied with what they called too liberal attitudes towards the Tuareg rebels, soldiers in the south of the country, in March 2012, drove Malian President Amadou Toumani Touré to resign. The resulting breakdown of the military hierarchy demoralised troops in the north and helped the rebels to occupy the entire northern Mali and declare independence in beginning of April. These events will have important impacts on tourism development in the region as the main destination of tourists in the Sahara was and is the southern Sahara: southern Algeria, south-east Libya, northern Niger and northern Mali. This is the region within which the Tuareg move about and have their settlements; tourism in the Sahara is essentially tourism in the land of the Tuareg and to the Tuareg themselves. Thus, taking recent political developments into account, this article confines itself to the situation before January 2012. Its line of argumentation, however, foreshadows some of the developments that we can observe today. It brings together contemporary politics and tourism in a rather unexpected way.

REFERENCES

Bargatzky, Thomas. 'Introduction', in Thomas Bargatzky and Rolf Kuschel, eds., *The Invention of Nature* (Frankfurt, Berlin, Bern, New York, Paris, Wien: Peter Lang, 1994), 9-25.

Blanguernon, Claude. *Le Hoggar* (Paris: Arthaud, 1983).

Boesen, Elisabeth and Georg Klute. 'Direkt von der Wüste in die Stadt. Moderne Migration von Nomaden aus dem Sahara-Sahelraum' *Das Parlament*, Beilage 'Aus Politik und Zeitgeschichte' 10 (2004).

Boilley, Pierre. *Les Touaregs Kel Adagh. Dépendances et révoltes: du Soudan français au Mali contemporain* (Paris: Karthala, 1999).

Buchanan, Angus. *Out of the World of Northern Nigeria. Exploration of Air* (London: John Murray, 1921).

Dayak, Mano. *Je suis né avec du sable dans les yeux* (Paris: Fixot, 1996).

Descola, Philipe, and Gísli Pálson. 'Introduction', in Philipe Descola and Gísli Pálson, eds., *Nature and Society. Anthropological Perspectives* (London and New York: Routledge, 1996), 1-21.

Klute, Georg, and Trutz v. Trotha. 'Roads to Peace. From Small War to Parastatal Peace in the North of Mali', in Marie-Claire Foblets and Trutz von Trotha, eds., *Healing the Wounds. Essays on the Reconstruction of Societies after War* (Oxford: Hart Publishing, Oñati International Series in Law and Society, 2004), 109-43.

Klute, Georg. *Die schwerste Arbeit der Welt. Alltag von Tuareg-Nomaden* (München: Trickster Verlag, 1992).

—— 'Wo liegt Gottes Segen? Natur und Arbeit bei Nomaden der Sahara', in Ute Luig and Achim von Oppen, eds., *Naturaneignung in Afrika als sozialer und symbolischer Prozeß* (Berlin: Klaus Schwarz Verlag, 1995), 51-64.

—— 'Der Tuaregkonflikt in Mali und Niger', in Joachim Betz and Stefan Brüne, eds., *Jahrbuch Dritte Welt 1996. Daten, Übersichten, Analysen* (Hamburg:

Deutsches Übersee-Institut Hamburg, 1996), 146-61.

—— *Die Rebellionen der Tuareg in Mali und Niger* (Siegen: University of Siegen, Habilitationsschrift, 2001).

—— 'Die Faszination des Fremden und der einheimische Blick. Semiotik und politische Ökonomie des Saharatourismus', in Gerhard Hufnagel, ed., *Reisen – die Welt erfahren. Sonderheft Sowi. Das Journal für Geschichte, Politik, Wirtschaft und Kultur,* 1/03 (Seelze: Erhard Friedrich Verlag, 2003) 13-23.

Klute, Georg. 'Technique of Modern Chariots: about Speed and Mobility in Contemporary Small Wars in the Sahara,' in Jan Bart Gewald, Sabine Luning, and Klaas van Walraven, eds., *The Speed of Change. Motor Vehicles and People in Africa, 1890-2000* (Leiden: Brill, 2009), 191-211.

Lecocq, Sebastian. *'That Desert Is Our Country': Tuareg Rebellions and Competing Nationalisms in Contemporary Mali 1946–1996* (Amsterdam: Universiteit van Amsterdam, Proefschrift Maatschappij en Gedragsweten-schappen, 2002).

Luig, Ute, and Achim von Oppen. *Naturaneignung in Afrika als sozialer und symbolischer Prozess* (Berlin: Das Arabische Buch, 1995).

MacCannell, Dean. *The Tourist. A New Theory of the Leisure Class* (London: MacMillan, 1976).

MacLeod, Donald & Tom Selwyn. 'The Scope of the Anthropology of Tourism: A Response to Tom Selwyn', *Anthropology Today* 18, 2 (2002): 27.

Nöther, Werner. *Die Erschließung der Sahara durch Motorfahrzeuge 1901-1936. Chronik einer Pionierepoche* (München: belleville Verlag Michael Farin, 2003).

Press, Irwin. 'Ambiguity and Innovation: Implications for the Genesis of the Cultural Broker', *American Anthropologist* 71 (1969): 206-17.

Rogers, Everett M. & Floyd Shoemaker. *Communication of Innovations. A Cross-Cultural Approach* (London: Collier Macmillan Publishers / New York: The Free Press, 2nd edn 1971).

Scholze, Marko. *Moderne Nomaden und fliegende Händler. Tuareg und Touris-mus in Niger* (Berlin: LIT Verlag, 2009).

Smith, Valene. 'Introduction', in V. Smith, ed., *Hosts and Guests. The Anthro-pology of Tourism* (Oxford: Basil Blackwell: 2nd edn 1989), 1-17.

Spittler, Gerd. 'Wüste, Wildnis und Zivilisation – Die Sicht der Kel Ewey', *Paideuma* 33 (1989): 273-87.

Spittler, Gerd. 'Die Bewältigung von Todesangst. Krieg und Hungerkrisen bei den Tuareg', in Franz Bosbach, ed., *Angst und Politik in der europäischen Geschichte* (Dettelbach: Röll, 2000), 29-51.

Turner, Louis, and John Ash. *The Golden Hordes: International Tourism and the Pleasure Periphery* (London: Routledge, 1975).

Urry, John. *The Tourist Gaze* (London: Sage, 1990).

Van Beek, Walter E.A., van. 'Approaching African Tourism; Paradigms and Paradoxes', in P. Chabal, U. Engel & L. de Haan, eds., *African alternatives* (Leiden, Brill: 2007), 145-72.

—— 'African Tourist Encounters: Effects of Tourism on Two West African Societies', *Africa* 73, 2 (2003): 251-89.

4 • 'How much for Kunta Kinte?!'
Sites of memory & diasporan encounters in West Africa

Kim Warren & Elizabeth MacGonagle

In Juffureh, Gambia, in the summer of 2006, a Gambian man followed a group of European and American tourists back to the boat that had brought them to his village after a three-hour trip from the capital of Banjul. He held up two small, wooden, hand-carved statues, and when he caught up to the tourists, he called out a price of 300 *dalasi* (about twelve American dollars) for the pair. As he and the tourists drew closer to the dock where the boat waited, he lowered his asking price. By the time they reached the dock he reduced it again, and when he saw that the tourists where still not interested, he lowered the amount once more to a third of his original price. Seeing that the visitors were more concerned about eating their noontime meal on the boat than buying the statues that he had to sell, the man appealed to the disinterested group one last time. 'It's Kunta Kinte!' he yelled, hoping that the tourists would understand the value of his handiwork by naming the famous enslaved ancestor of Alex Haley, American author of a book that traced his roots back to Africa. Holding a statue high in each of his hands, the Gambian seller shouted to the unfazed crowd, 'How much for Kunta Kinte?!'

There is no intrinsic reason for a foreign tourist to visit the village of Juffureh on the River Gambia other than its link to Haley's best-selling book, *Roots: The Saga of an American Family*.[1] When Haley published *Roots* in 1976, he detailed how his family tree traced back over two centuries to a 17-year-old African ancestor named Kunta Kinte that slave traders had captured near that same village. The following year, the television mini-series captivated American audiences for eight nights in an unprecedented way. Haley's story also prompted millions of Americans to rethink their understanding of their own genealogies, encouraged the colloquial adoption of the term 'African American', and urged a generation of black Americans to think more specifically about their familial connection with a continent that otherwise received minimal attention in history books and leading newspapers.[2]

1 Alex Haley, *Roots: The Saga of an American Family* (Garden City NY: Doubleday, 1st edn 1976). The authors would like to acknowledge assistance for this project from Tami Albin and Rachel Jean-Baptiste, as well as financial support from the International Travel Fund for the Humanities, Office of International Programs and the Center for Teaching Excellence at the University of Kansas to conduct field research in Ghana, Gambia, and Senegal in 2006.
2 Although anthropologist Kamari Clarke argues that black nationalist narratives dating back to the 1960s had widely circulated a notion that black Americans were 'fundamentally embedded in genealogies of heritage' that encouraged them to think about ancestral membership in an African

Roots won Haley critical acclaim, was translated into several dozen languages, sold millions of copies, and earned the author a special Pulitzer Prize in 1976 as well as the National Association for the Advancement of Colored People's prestigious Spingarn Medal in 1977. But Haley also faced a barrage of criticism that challenged the authenticity, accuracy, and even the originality of his story.[3] Despite lingering controversy, Haley's act of tracing his own roots to uncover the name of a specific ancestor enslaved in Africa offered hope to many African Americans who wished to know their own African ancestors who were otherwise lost to history. If Haley could find the name of an ancestor who linked his American family tree to the continent of Africa, then others reasoned that details about their own lineages might be recovered from the confusing and often undocumented era of American slavery. In addition, African Americans, having experienced decades of discrimination and a sense of displacement in their own country, were now poised to claim the continent of their forbears as their own home.

In this essay we examine the enduring desire of many African Americans to envision the continent of Africa as a homeland and a geographical place that connects them to enslaved ancestors and families of origin. We first explore the notion of return: increased attention to Africa in literature such as *Roots* and popular magazines over the past several decades, as well as more recent access to DNA testing and heritage tours, have motivated blacks in the Diaspora to visit West African countries in hopes of feeling a connection to their own mythic Kunta Kinte. From both American and African perspectives, we show how the role of history as a framing mechanism has crafted different relationships onto stories about the transatlantic slave trade and has prompted varied responses to sites of memory, such as the *Maison des Esclaves* on Senegal's Gorée Island, the village of Juffureh in the Gambia, and the castles of Elmina and Cape Coast in Ghana – all of which have become pilgrimage destinations for African Americans. The second half of this chapter focuses specifically on Ghana, the country with the greatest number of slave forts and the largest number of tourists seeking a reunion with Africa through the long history of slavery. The large forts of Elmina and Cape Coast, as well as smaller structures such as those at Senya Beraku and Fort Amsterdam, not only provide opportunities to examine the motivations of tourists and Ghanaians, but also serve as the primary

community, she also acknowledges the importance of *Roots* in helping African Americans to embrace a common heritage linked to Africa through the history of slavery. See Kamari Maxine Clarke, 'Mapping Transnationality: Roots Tourism and the Institutionalization of Ethnic Heritage' in Kamari Maxine Clarke and Deborah A. Thomas, eds., *Globalization and Race: Transformations in the Cultural Production of Blackness* (Durham NC: Duke University Press, 2006), 133-40.

3   Donald Wright, *The World and a Very Small Place in Africa; A History of Globalization in Niumi, The Gambia* (London: M.E. Sharpe, 3rd edn 2010), 205; Jack Cashill, 'Alex Haley's Immaculate Roots', *WorldNetDaily Exclusive Commentary*, 1 July 2005, http://www.worldnetdaily.com/news/article.asp?ARTICLE_ID=45084. Alex Haley died in 1992 at the age of seventy; see his obituary in the *New York Times*, 11 February 1992.

places of encounter at which both groups contest the meaning of the slave forts and the history of slavery. Through these interrogations, we show how race and identity have multiple, conflicting, and at times confusing constructions throughout the Atlantic world.

Returning home

Increased attention to Africa in the media, in addition to amplified interest among African Americans about the possibility of discovering specific links to the African continent, have prompted the emergence of a new travel industry focused on 'roots', otherwise termed heritage tourism. The growing popularity of DNA testing, which often promises to identify the ethnic heritage of individuals, has provided a catalyst for African Americans to undertake a journey to Africa. American travel agencies, churches, and community groups have encouraged blacks in the Diaspora to travel to West Africa not simply as a vacation destination but specifically as an ancestral homeland where African Americans can make pilgrimages to fill in the gaps of their identities and family histories. Even as recently as 2009, developers hoped to profit from such tourism by announcing plans to build a multi-million-dollar slave history theme park and museum in Nigeria to entice tourists.[4]

African companies and governments have responded to this yearning for home by developing roots tourism and holding annual heritage festivals to celebrate the transoceanic link between West Africans and those of African heritage in the Diaspora.[5] Organisers and guides of heritage tours and celebrations are charged not only to sell a historical narrative of slavery, but also to attempt to meet the expectations of such pilgrimage tourists. In her travels from the United States to Senegal and the Gambia in the 1980s, anthropologist Paulla Ebron writes about one such journey sponsored by the fast-food corporation McDonald's. The company promoted an all-expenses-paid, ten-day trip designed mostly for African American contest winners as a 'pilgrimage' in which tourists would join members of the Haley family in 'going home'.[6] The tour organisers reminded tourists before they left the United States of their common purpose to recover a sense of 'historical ties to Africa'.[7] Guides in Senegal welcomed the travellers by stating, 'You are on a pilgrimage, not a safari', and they repeated

---

4 Andrew Walker, '[Marlon] Jackson Star in Nigeria Resort Row', 16 February 2009, *BBC News, Nigeria,* http://news.bbc.co.uk/2/hi/africa/7858010.stm.
5 See Paulla A. Ebron, *Performing Africa* (Princeton NJ: Princeton University Press, 2002); Palace Travel, http://www.panafest.us/ (accessed 21 June 2010).
6 Ebron, *Performing Africa*, 189-212. It is interesting to note that Ebron describes the motivation of Alex Haley's son, William Haley, who undertook the project as 'an entrepreneurial venture.' See Paulla Ebron, 'Tourists as Pilgrims: Commercial Fashioning of Transatlantic Politics', *American Ethnologist* 26 (November 1999): 915.
7 Ebron, 'Tourists as Pilgrims', 917.

that phrase almost daily during the trip.[8] In academic terms, Ebron describes the experience as 'a journey [that] takes place in mythical time; in this case, it involved a temporal displacement of the current moment.'[9] McDonald's was less sophisticated in its description of the trip however; Ebron notes that the word 'McMemories™' came into use.[10] Whether or not African Americans are able to trace their family to a specific ethnic group or region of Africa, tourists continually take trips to Senegal, Gambia, Ghana, and other African countries as pilgrims in an effort to feel at home.

The notion of returning home for black Americans continues to resonate in the popular imagination, but it also has historical ante-cedents that predate heritage tourism or even Haley's *Roots*. W. E. B. Du Bois, the pan-Africanist American intellectual who moved to Ghana in 1961 and lived there until his death in 1963, vocally endorsed migration to Africa, hoping that if African Americans returned to the continent some common unity or identity could be achieved.[11] The writer Maya Angelou held a similar belief when she lived in Ghana in the 1960s with other expatriate black intellectuals, whom she called 'Revolutionist Returnees'. In her initial estimation, she declared that she was 'home' again.[12] More recently, when the tennis player Serena Williams travelled to West Africa to finance the building of a school in Senegal, she declared, 'I felt I was finally able to go home.'[13]

Like Du Bois and Angelou, Williams expressed a desire for belonging that is similar to the yearning that prompts other African Americans – or 'Diasporans' as they are commonly called – to employ travel agencies that sell such tours from the United States to West Africa.[14] Travel agencies market to black clients who possess the economic means necessary for a transatlantic voyage by offering them a chance to remember and honour their ancestors. One agency promises visitors a 'return trip' by boat to Cape Coast Castle where they can enter 'through the door that was the last door African ancestors passed through on their way to board the ships to the new world.'[15] They are also encouraged to think of such passageways (nearly always

8 Ibid., 916; Ebron, *Performing Africa*, 195.
9 Ebron, 'Tourists as Pilgrims', 920.
10 Ebron, *Performing Africa*, 197.
11 W. E. Burghardt Du Bois, *Dusk of Dawn: An Essay toward an Autobiography of a Race Concept* (New York: Schocken Books, 1968), 122.
12 Maya Angelou, *All God's Children Need Traveling Shoes* (New York: Vintage Books, 1986), 4. Other African Americans who were living in Ghana around the time of Independence included Sylvia Boone and Julian Mayfield. For a discussion of blacks in Ghana in the late 1950s and 1960s, see Kevin K. Gaines, *American Africans in Ghana: Black Expatriates and the Civil Rights Era* (Chapel Hill: University of North Carolina Press, 2006).
13 Williams quoted in Christopher Clarey, 'Serena Williams Acknowledges a Decline', *New York Times*, 14 January 2007.
14 In 2003, the Ministry of Tourism expanded and changed its name to the Ministry of Tourism and Diasporan Relations. In 2009, the government reverted to using the original name of the office. See Ministry of Tourism-Ghana Tourism Homepage, http://www.touringghana.com/mot.asp (accessed 21 June 2010).
15 Land Tours 10-Day Emancipation Pilgrimage Featuring Panafest and the Joseph Project, http://www.landtours.com/emancipation_iti.asp (accessed 21 June 2010).

labelled with a sign stating, 'Door of No Return') not simply as symbols of hopelessness. Instead, modern pilgrims can reconsider such portals in more healing terms, as a 'Door of *Return*', for example.[16] Local guides at Cape Coast Castle are even more specific when they point to a 'Door of Return' sign on the exterior and encourage tourists to walk ceremonially back into the fort from the sea just outside the door.

The growth of heritage tourism to Africa during the past several decades reflects a rising interest in the continent from within the African American community. When African American leaders were polled in 1990, for example, 47 per cent felt a close connection to Africa.[17] Almost 75 per cent of African Americans surveyed by Gallop in 2000 noted an interest in knowing more about the continent.[18] According to historian James Campbell, this is a very different and new perception of Africa, a continent that rarely ever made it into the leading African American magazines, including *Ebony*, before the 1960s.[19] When *Ebony* decided to send journalist Era Bell Thompson to West Africa in 1953, she hesitated, confessing, 'Had anyone called me an African, I would have been indignant. Only race fanatics flaunted their jungle ancestry or formed back-to-Africa movements.'[20] Today, however, the notion of returning to an ancestral homeland has found an accepted appeal among many African Americans, and *Ebony* devoted much of its December 2007 issue to Africa, claiming to offer 'the Africa you don't know' on its cover.[21] Over the past decade, Africa has reentered the Western mindset as both hip and cool. This confronts earlier perceptions – shared by both whites and people of colour – of the continent as a basket case or a hopeless continent.[22]

Popular magazines such as *Vanity Fair* and *National Geographic* have devoted cover stories to emerging issues and new challenges facing the continent. 'Africa, Whatever you thought, think again', reads a 2005 special issue of *National Geographic*. The rock star Bono met President George W. Bush at the White House in 2005 to discuss poverty and AIDS in Africa, and other activists have demanded an end to Africa's debt payments to the West. Bono guest edited the July 2007 issue of *Vanity Fair*, and in 2006 he launched the (Product) Red campaign that gives a portion of the profits from the sale of various goods (ranging from credit cards to clothes and computers) to the

16 Emphasis added. On Gorée Island, the sign above the gate reads, 'The door of the voyage from which no one returned' (*La porte du voyage sans retour*). See Virtual Visit of Gorée Island, http://webworld.unesco.org/goree/en/index.shtml (accessed 21 July 2009).

17 Ibrahim Sundiata's statistics are cited in David Northrup, *Crosscurrents in the Black Atlantic, 1770-1965* (New York: Bedford/St. Martin's, 2008), 26.

18 In the poll commissioned by the National Summit on Africa, 73 percent reported a desire to learn more. Ishmael Mensah, 'Marketing Ghana as a Mecca for the African-American Tourist', *Ghana Web*, 10 June 2004, http://www.ghanaweb.com/GhanaHomePage/features/artikel.php?ID=59447.

19 James Campbell, *Middle Passages: African American Journeys to Africa, 1787-2005* (New York: Penguin Press, 2006), 286.

20 Thompson quoted in Campbell, *Middle Passages*, 287.

21 Ironically, *Ebony*'s cover featured a photo of Michael Jackson.

22 See, for example, the cover story of *The Economist*, 13-19 May 2000.

Global Fund to Fight AIDS, tuberculosis, and malaria. Gap stores are just one global partner of the Product Red campaign, selling merchandise such as beaded safety pins whose labels claim to be 'inspired by historic African trade beads'. This initiative seeks to combine consumerism in the West with assistance for Africa's poor, but the idea has been severely criticised since Product Red serves as an intermediary in what could be a direct charitable contribution from the consumer instead.[23] Product Red allows the West to feel good about its purchases even though the advertising costs of the campaign are much higher than actual contributions made to Africa. Nonetheless, Product Red has increased awareness about Africa in the West, however slim, through its marketing techniques.

It is also in the popular media that scholars and celebrities explore how DNA testing might provide genetic connections to the continent. For example, in the 2007 issue of *Ebony* about Africa, scholar Henry Louis Gates, Jr. comments, 'We are all Africans', in his explanation about the ways that science can provide heritage information absent from other historical records.[24] That same year, Gates published *Finding Oprah's Roots: Finding Your Own* to encourage African Americans to reclaim their ancestries through cultural and biological investigations. In particular, his book notes the rise of 'genetic testing resources that can make it possible to know one's distant tribal roots in Africa'.[25] Magazines, television shows, and even the organisers of an academic meeting of the Association for the Study of African American Life and History have promoted teaming up with DNA testing companies to help members of the public trace their roots.[26]

Such testing, however, is problematic and does not always provide the information that Diasporans are seeking. For instance, the *Washington Post* noted that a study by geneticist Bert Ely published in *BMC Biology* concluded that fewer than 10 per cent of black Americans could learn of a match with a single African ethnic group, and 40 per cent could not make a match at all.[27] When *New York Times* reporter Ron Nixon set out to uncover his heritage for a story in 2007, he received five different answers about his African roots from five selected companies that trace ancestry.[28] And even

23 The Buy (Less) campaign encourages people to donate directly to charity and seeks to inspire less consumption overall: http://www.buylesscrap.org/ (accessed 21 June 2010). See also Curtis Keim, *Mistaking Africa: Curiosities and Inventions of the American Mind* (Boulder CO.: Westview, 2009), 148-50.
24 Henry Louis Gates, Jr., '"We Are All Africans": Genealogical Research and DNA Testing Can Reveal Your Ethnic Connection to Africa,' *Ebony* (December 2007): 132-6.
25 Quotation from cover flap of *Finding Oprah's Roots: Finding Your Own* (New York: Crown Publishing Group, 2007).
26 Association for the Study of African American Life and History, email to members, 30 December 2008.
27 Darryl Fears, 'Out of Africa – but from Which Tribe?: DNA Tests of Blacks Promise Ancestry Answers, but Report Adds to Critics' Doubts,' *Washington Post*, 19 October 2006; Bert Ely et al., 'African-American Mitochondrial DNAs Often Match mtDNAs Found in Multiple African Ethnic Groups,' *BMC Biology* 2006, 4:34, http://www.biomedcentral.com/1741-7007/4/34.
28 Ron Nixon, 'DNA Tests Find Branches but Few Roots', *New York Times*, 25 November 2007.

though Gates has embraced genetic testing and used it to explore the ancestry of famous African Americans including Oprah Winfrey, Tina Turner, and Chris Rock, he admitted to Nixon, 'The limitations of current genetic DNA tests mean you can't rely on this alone to tell you anything.'[29] Acknowledging the limitations of DNA testing, some geneticists argue that such tests are simply part of a toolkit in the search for one's identity. Megan Smolenyak studies DNA testing and promotes its use to trace family trees, but even she admits that 64 per cent of participants find 'surprises' in their genealogy.[30] The biologist Fatimah Jackson adds that at best most African Americans are only going to be able to make 'some general statements' about their lineage after DNA testing. However, she also argues that enhancing historical information with genetic data will help create a more convincing family story.[31]

Given the growing popularity of genetic testing and the swift rise of a new industry around it, there is concern 'that the marketing is coming before the science.'[32] The research of Ely concludes that Africans and African Americans share genetic similarities across ethnic groups and regions in Africa. These findings led the reporter Nixon to argue that it is 'impossible to match African Americans with a single ethnic group, as some companies assert they can do.'[33] In his own case, Nixon's various test results indicated that he might be related to over 25 different African ethnic groups across the continent. Other news stories stress concerns about prejudice emerging in our new 'DNA era' and the hesitation that may accompany the quest to learn about one's self.[34] Despite these misgivings, the popularity of genetic testing has grown in the United States, as evidenced by the attention given to the two PBS *African American Lives* documentaries hosted by Gates, and the 2010 debut of an NBC television show exploring the ancestry of famous American celebrities called 'Who Do You Think You Are?'

In his examination of racial negotiations and a call for racial sincerity (v. authenticity), the anthropologist John Jackson, Jr. argues that the results of DNA testing provide 'information that is impossible to contextualise significantly (historically, genetically, or culturally) in anything other than the most abstract and symbolic ways.'[35] Thus, test takers are often left with symbols and

29 Ibid.

30 Smolenyak interviewed in *African American Lives 2*, Episode 1, DVD, directed by Jack Youngelson (Pleasantville, NY: Kunhardt Productions, Inc., 2008). Also see Megan Smolenyak and Ann Turner, *Trace Your Roots with DNA: Using Genetic Tests to Explore Your Family Tree* (Emmaus PA: Rodale, Inc., 2004).

31 Jackson interviewed in *African American Lives 2*.

32 Troy Duster quoted in Nixon, 'DNA Tests Find Branches but Few Roots.'

33 Nixon, 'DNA Tests Find Branches but Few Roots'.

34 See, for instance, the two front-page reports by Amy Harmon, 'In DNA Era, New Worries About Prejudice', *New York Times,* 11 November 2007 and 'Learning My Genome, Learning About Myself,' *New York Times,* 17 November 2007.

35 John L. Jackson, Jr., *Real Black: Adventures in Racial Sincerity* (Chicago: University of Chicago Press, 2005), 140.

abstractions rather than realities. However, the co-founder of the American company African Ancestry told Jackson in the course of his research that they might offer tours to African countries as part of their attempt to educate African Americans about Africa and their ancestry.[36] Jackson notes that African Americans now imagine themselves as having 'a newly real stake in African issues, while Africans might be said to manipulate these rehabilitated African sentiments in the name of greater financial gain within otherwise truncated economic contexts'.[37] Despite these complicated – and sometimes contradictory – realities, many of those who can trace or even suspect a genetic link to West Africa persist with their vision of the region as their long-desired homeland.

Crafting stories about slavery

The craftsman who attempted to sell his Kunta Kinte figures in the Gambia had probably not seen the mini-series *Roots* or read Haley's book. An audio recording of *Roots* is on display at the Slave History Museum in the village of Juffureh, but in a village without electricity, it is unlikely that the local people have listened to that record album. And yet the craftsman, along with every tour guide in the village, knows the profound meaning of the name Kunta Kinte, and they know that his story might provide more economic prosperity to their village than the peanut crops that they cultivate in the region. In the Gambia, the average life expectancy falls below fifty years, and the country is the third poorest on the continent, but with tourism, foreign exchange can help an otherwise struggling economy. It is not surprising, therefore, that tour guides introduce themselves as descendants of the Kinte family, regardless of the various other family names prominently displayed on their nametags.[38]

The Roots Tour in Juffureh is tightly scripted. After visiting the Slave History Museum, tourists meet the chief of the village and make an offering if they want their picture taken with her. The highlight of the tour takes place in a cement-floored shelter, where the guides state their names and their relationship to the Kinte family, assure visitors that the structure was built on the site where Kunta Kinte was born, pass around framed photos of Alex Haley and LeVar Burton (the actor who played Kunta Kinte in the televised version of *Roots*), and then tell a tale that is familiar to anyone who has seen or read *Roots*. The story swiftly recounts the generations from Kunta Kinte to Alex Haley. Kunta Kinte was in the forest looking for wood for a drum

---

36 Ibid, 142.
37 Ibid., 143.
38 Guide books and flyers in 2006 still listed Binde Kinte, 'a descendant of Alex Haley's own forebear', as the speaker on the Roots Tour in Juffureh, even though she died in the late 1990s. See, for example, Andrew Burke and David Else, *The Gambia and Senegal* (Oakland CA: The Lonely Planet Publications, 2002), 166.

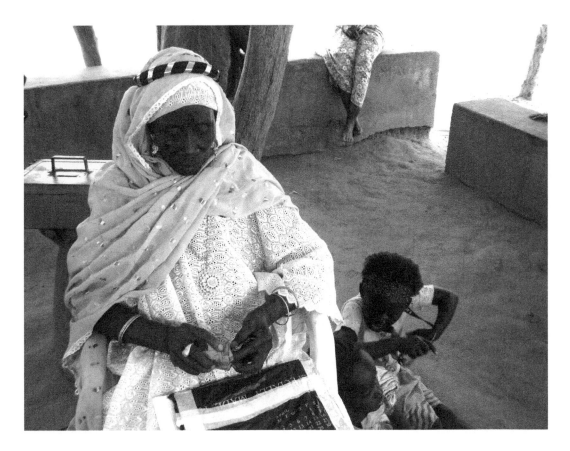

for his brother, he was captured, he survived the Middle Passage, and he was sold in America and renamed Toby. Because he tried to run away several times, part of his foot was cut off to prevent him from trying again. While enslaved, he had a daughter Kizzy, who then had Chicken George, who then fathered Tom, who fathered Cynthia, who mothered Bertha, who then had Alex Haley.

4.1 The chief of the village of Juffureh prepares to greet new visitors as part of the 'Roots Tour' in the Gambia.

(© K. Warren)

The story is a simplified recounting of Haley's narrative, but villagers in Juffureh have claimed it as theirs. They do not appear to be concerned about charges that *Roots* has fictional elements, because they understand the symbolic power of Kunta Kinte who has come to stand for *any* ancestor forcibly removed from Africa and taken to the Americas. Indeed, Haley provided the world with an 18th-century ancestor after visiting Juffureh and speaking with a Gambian man named Keba Fofana.[39] For guides on this Roots Tour, Kunta Kinte is

39   Haley met with Fofana in May of 1967 and claimed that he was a griot, but according to Donald Wright this was not the case. See *The World and a Very Small Place in Africa,* 202. Journalist Philip Nobile challenged Haley's authenticity in his article, 'Uncovering Roots', *Village Voice* (February 1993): 31-38. For a counter argument to Nobile, see Thomas A. Hale, *Griots and Griottes: Masters of Words and Music* (Bloomington: Indiana University Press, 1998), 244-64. Haley defended his work initially in 1976 by stating, 'Although it's advertised as nonfiction, perhaps we should call it "faction".' Every statement in *Roots* is accurate in terms of authenticity—the descriptions of the culture and terrain are based on valid material. The beginning is a re-creation, using novelistic techniques, but as it moves forward more is known and it is more factually based.' Mel Watkins, 'A Talk with Alex Haley', *New York Times Book Review* (September 1976): 2.

4.2 A sign immediately welcomes guests when they disembark from the boat that takes them to Juffureh on the Gambia River, 2006.
(© K. Warren)

as much theirs as he was Haley's, and they craft their tours around that claim.

Although tour guides at Gorée Island, Elmina, and Cape Coast cannot hang their stories on a single person's capture as the guides in Juffureh can, they are just as invested in crafting their narratives for use by tourists. Indeed, the ways in which tour guides have configured histories of slavery for tourist consumption is at the heart of how African Americans view their relationship with West Africa as a homeland. When travelling under the auspices of a heritage tour, many African Americans arrive in West Africa steeped in a desire to feel a deep connection to their African ancestors. However, several tour guides report their surprise over how little tourists know about the history of the transatlantic slave trade. The guides, then, are charged with recounting a history of slavery that includes an overwhelming amount of violence, cruelty and suffering. Although not identical to the tour in Juffureh, a standard narrative often emerges at the forts: the men's dungeons were separate from the women's; the condemned cell held slaves who were left to die in isolation rather than be shipped from the continent; Europeans slept and prayed in close proximity to their captives; and slaves left the continent through a portal widely referred to as the 'Door of No Return.'

In an attempt to reconcile the brutal stories of the enslaved at the forts, guides at Elmina allow tour groups to segregate according to race and hold special reenactments and healing ceremonies for descendants of slaves. 'We allow them to, as our brothers and sisters', reported Tetteh Amark, a guide at Elmina.[40] Visitors place wreaths in the dungeons of Elmina and Cape Coast from 'our dear brothers and sisters in the Diaspora' to honour those who died in the castle.[41] As a commemoration in the guest book at Cape Coast, an American from New York wrote, 'May "their" departed souls rest in perfect peace.'[42] Another American visitor, a white man, was surprised when an African American tourist rejected his greeting at a slave fort, but also admitted that he 'felt a little bit of guilt for having invaded some space that she considered very, very precious and valuable to her.'[43]

In addition to memorialising enslaved ancestors, some African Americans hope to leave the forts with a larger sense of who they are. However, that expectation – conceived in the United States and encouraged through the rhetoric of return and the perception of Africa as a homeland – is often impossible to meet. 'They want to know their roots but they *cannot*', said the Ghanaian tour guide Amark. With a hint of pity, he added, 'They can only know they came from here... when they come back to Ghana, we do not know their names, so we cannot show them where they came from.'[44] On Gorée Island, in 2006, the manager of the slave fort, Boubacar Joseph Ndiaye, stated that the main difference between African Americans and other tourists is that African Americans are the ones who cry. 'Most others don't cry', he commented.[45] Ndiaye suggested that the tears come from hearing stories of slavery that are deeply disturbing to learn for the first time. Hand-written posters cover the walls of holding cells and compare the experiences of those who suffered the brutality of the slave trade to the attempted annihilation of Jews in Europe during World War II. Ndiaye encourages visitors to use the powerful word 'holocaust' when referring to the transatlantic slave trade, but the comparison is shocking to some visitors, Ndiaye acknowledges.[46] Gorée Island is not the only site of memory where tears are often shed. A guide at Elmina, Augusta Ampem Darko, observed, 'Most African Americans, they cry.'[47] At Cape Coast and Elmina, where large numbers of African

---

40 Augusta Ampem Darko and Tetteh Amark, interview by authors, Elmina, Ghana, 9 June 2006; see also 'Ghana's Joseph Project Says "Come Home"' *The World*, National Public Radio, 7 June 2007, http://www.npr.org/templates/story/story.php?storyId=10802304.
41 Anonymous from Mt. Vernon, New York, Cape Coast guest book, Ghana, 22 May 2006.
42 American from New York, Cape Coast guest book, Ghana, 22 May 2006.
43 *Traces of the Trade: A Story from the Deep North*, DVD, directed by Katrina Browne, (Cambridge, MA: Ebb Pid Productions, LLC, 2008).
44 Darko and Amark, interview by authors.
45 Boubacar Joseph Ndaiye, interview by author, Gorée Island, Senegal, 27 May 2006.
46 Ibid. For other references that draw parallels between the slave trade and holocaust events, see Ebron, 'Tourists as Pilgrims,' 923; Paul Gilroy, *The Black Atlantic: Modernity and Double Consciousness* (Cambridge MA: Harvard University Press, 1993); Zygmunt Bauman, *Modernity and the Holocaust* (Ithaca NY: Cornell University Press, 1989).
47 Darko and Amark, interview by authors.

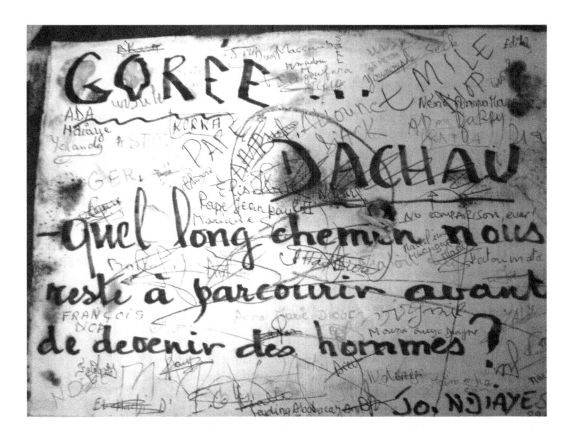

4.3 The manager of the Maison des Esclaves on Senegal's Gorée Island has hung signs throughout the fort urging visitors to think about the history of the slave trade as a global tragedy comparable to the Holocaust, 2006.

(© K. Warren)

American tourists visit, the experience of standing in a dungeon or being temporarily locked in a cell for the condemned can bring a visitor to tears. Indeed, Valerie Papaya Mann, an American who now lives in Ghana and escorts African American clients to slave forts, said that at times tourists refuse to go to a second fort after seeing their first one. 'It's enough', she sighed in reference to the emotional anguish that some experience.[48]

While the standard narrative explained at slave forts can move tourists to tears, those who work at Elmina observe that the responsibility of recounting a horrific past can lead guides to truncate their descriptions to make them more palatable to tourists who may be hearing about the atrocities of the transatlantic slavery in detail for the first time. A Gambian guide admitted that he does not provide as much information as he could for tourists because he does not want to 'hurt anyone.'[49] He explained that he tried to avoid offending both whites and blacks during his tour, but asserted that it is usually black tourists who feel hurt. Despite the risk of hearing heart-wrenching stories, tourists persist in attempting to locate what one visiting family at Cape Coast Castle has called 'a missing piece of the puzzle' of their identities.[50]

48 Valerie Papaya Mann, interview by authors, Accra, Ghana, 6 June 2006.
49 Lamin Ceesay, interview by author, Juffurreh, Gambia, 21 May 2006.
50 Family Kelley (Surinam, Holland, Dubai), Cape Coast guest book, Ghana, 18 May 2006.

If a desire to connect with an African homeland prompts Diasporan tourists to travel to West Africa, then it is important to examine the destinations to which travellers make their pilgrimages and where they meet Africans. In particular, it makes sense to investigate encounters between African Americans and Africans in Ghana, a country that has overtly welcomed such tourists and maintains the largest number of visited slave forts in West Africa. Along Ghana's coast, about one-third of more than sixty original structures built by Europeans over a span of 300 years from 1482 to 1787 still remain. The two large castles of Cape Coast and Elmina are preserved as memorials that attract a large number of visitors from around the world, and a significant number of smaller forts are also open to the public (albeit less frequently visited) with many used on a regular basis by local communities.[51] These historic buildings serve as crucial sites of memory that move beyond national confines to anchor the past for both Africans and those of African heritage in the Diaspora. Various parties are involved in the making of a national past in Ghana, as well as a global history of black people, and the ways in which they meet – and sometimes clash – reveal multiple meanings about identities and the interpretation of history at these physical vestiges of the transatlantic slave trade.[52]

Places, along with ideas, stories, and memories, shape our under-standing of both past and present. But there are assumptions and problems associated with the cultivation of heritage in the physical remains of slave forts recognised by the United Nations Educational, Scientific, and Cultural Organization (UNESCO) as World Heritage Sites for their outstanding cultural importance to humanity. As sites of memory steeped in history, physical structures such as slave forts and other spaces related to the slave trade serve as tangible reminders of a tortured past. The histories and memories emanating from such African sites reflect legacies of racism and oppression that both groups continue to face on either side of the ocean. And yet with monuments from the era of the slave trade serving as primary sites of encounter between African American tourists and African tour guides and visitors, there are struggles over interpretations of a past interwoven with the history of slavery. From these encounters, it is possible to understand nuances of a shared past and analyse the myriad constructions of race, belonging, heritage, and identities –

51   See Elizabeth MacGonagle, 'From Dungeons to Dance Parties: Contested Histories of Ghana's Slave Forts', *Journal of Contemporary African Studies* 24 (May 2006): 249-60; Edward M. Bruner, 'Tourism in Ghana: The Representation of Slavery and the Return of the Black Diaspora', *American Anthropologist*, New Series 98 (June 1996): 290-304; Cheryl Finley, 'Of Golden Anniversaries and Bicentennials: Convergence of Memory, Tourism and National History in Ghana', *Journeys: The International Journal of Travel and Travel Writing* 7 (November 2006): 15-32.
52   See Katherine McKittrick and Clyde Woods, eds, *Black Geographies and the Politics of Place* (Toronto: Between the Lines, 2007) for arguments about the existing globalisation of black peoples.

American and African – as history and memory are contested on the ground and in the imagination.

Finding a missing piece of their heritage might provide enough incentive for some travellers to Africa, but there are others who argue that blacks in the Diaspora should find motivation beyond their own desire for a homeland and focus on paying homage to enslaved ancestors while they fully reclaim their African heritage and identities. As one returnee, Seestah Imahküs, states, 'We are proud African people who are here where we're supposed to be. We make no apologies to anyone for what we are doing or how we are doing it.'[53] For Imahküs, identifying as a proud African means settling in Ghana for the long term and appealing to the Ghanaian government to make it easier for African Americans to establish permanent homes in the country. Whether African Americans travel to Africa in response to racial strife in the United States (as Du Bois and Angelou did in the 1960s) or to 'retreat from city life' and escape 'Diasporan Stress' (as Imahküs encouraged in 2007 on the website for her guest house on the coast), tourism among African Americans in Ghana is on the rise.[54]

For the most part, Ghanaians encourage African Americans to visit (on short-term or long-term bases) because, at the very least, they bring US dollars with them. As United States citizens, African Americans are beneficiaries of the very divide between the West and the global South that perpetuates an ongoing Ghanaian need for foreign currency.[55] The glaring difference in the level of wealth between African Americans and Ghanaians suggests that American citizenship, however problematic for African Americans, does afford a lifestyle that many Africans desire. This awkward reality may add to levels of tension or misunderstanding between African Americans and Ghanaians. Still, the Ghanaian government has taken steps to make it easier for many Diasporans to tour in Ghana, including plans to offer a lifetime visa for the descendants of slaves, new measures for dual citizenship, and even greater possibilities for land ownership. Thousands of African Americans do live in Ghana for at least part of the year, according to Valerie Papaya Mann, President of the African American Association of Ghana.[56] And perhaps more will return if Ghana's Ministry of Tourism has its way. 'We want Africans everywhere, no matter where they live or how they got there, to see Ghana as their gateway home', declared Tourism Minister Jake Otanka Obetsebi-Lamptey in 2005. Citing cultural projects, including

---

53 Seestah Imahküs quoted in Eric Campbell, 'Ghana Slavery', *Foreign Correspondent*, original airdate 20 March 2007, http://www.abc.net.au/foreign/content/2007/s1903382.htm. See also Seestah Imahküs, *Returning Home Ain't Easy but It Sure Is a Blessing!* (Cape Coast, Ghana: One Africa Tours and Specialty Services, Ltd, 1999).

54 One Africa Guest House and Restaurant, http://www.oneafricaghana.com/lodging.htm (accessed 20 August 2007).

55 See Jackson, *Real Black*, for more on this troubled situation.

56 Mann, interview by authors; see also Lydia Polgreen, 'Ghana's Uneasy Embrace of Slavery's Diaspora', *New York Times*, 27 December 2005.

pan-African celebrations designed to encourage African American tourism, he added, 'We hope we can help bring the African family back together again.'[57]

Perhaps because of the explicit welcome from Ghana's government, or possibly because the English-speaking country is one of the easier ones for middle-class Americans to navigate in West Africa, some African Americans clearly want to identify specifically with Ghana as their homeland. There is, in turn, a general consensus among Ghanaians to encourage those feelings. But when African American tourists and Ghanaians meet, cultural fissures can occur around issues of race, home, and identity. Conflicts occur in part because African Americans are so invested in their link with the history of slavery as their defining connection to Africa. Ghanaians, on the other hand, do not feel that investment from the past equally. In fact, anthropologist Jennifer Hasty notes, 'Some Ghanaian intellectuals refer to foreign scholarly and diasporan preoccupation with slavery as the "Americanization of African history".'[58] She suggests that events such as Emancipation Day are activities centred on the Diaspora that suppress local histories, even though they are often sponsored by the state. A range of reactions to black tourists includes a 'strange mix of envy and contempt', from embracing them as brothers and sisters, seeing them simply as rich foreigners, or even having disdain for their connections to slave ancestors.[59] Weighted with the assumption that their primary connection to Africa traces back to an ancestor taken from the continent, the association that black tourists have with Africa tends to be fixed in the past. Therefore, African Americans travelling to Africa often expect to be treated as long-lost relatives. Upon arrival, however, they are shocked to realise that they are as likely to be labelled a 'foreigner', and even a 'white' person (*obruni* in Ghana or *muzungu* elsewhere), as they are to be called a 'sister' or a 'brother'. A trip to Ghana allows African American visitors to remain within the tourist bubble on the one hand, while also denying the existence of the bubble since they are returning 'home'. By calling upon an ancestral link, albeit possibly not to Ghana specifically, African American guests and their local hosts sidestep the traditional notion of the tourist bubble.

There is ample travel literature written by African American return-ees that offers warnings about possible disappointment in store for Diasporans. Maya Angelou, for example, expressed her sadness over how she was 'overlooked by the Ghanaians' and did not feel embraced there.[60] Angelou recalled, 'We had come home, and if home was not what we had expected, never mind, our need for belonging allowed us

---

57 Obetsebi-Lamptey quoted in Polgreen, 'Ghana's Uneasy Embrace of Slavery's Diaspora'.
58 Jennifer Hasty, 'Rites of Passage, Routes of Redemption: Emancipation Tourism and the Wealth of Culture', *Africa Today* 49 (Fall 2002): 62.
59 Ibid., 63-4.
60 Angelou, *All God's Children Need Traveling Shoes*, 18-19.

to ignore the obvious and to create real places or even illusory places, befitting our imagination.'[61] Paul Robeson also expressed a similar frustration when he wrote of his surprise in discovering that the connections between African American and African identities seemed obvious on the one hand but proved to be 'an extremely complicated matter' on the other.[62] Paulla Ebron heard a chorus of '*Toubob, Toubob*', meaning 'white person', when her tour group arrived for the Roots Tour in Juffureh in 1989.[63] More recently, English scholar Saidiya Hartman has written a memoir of her travels in Ghana and noted her surprise when locals labelled her a foreigner: 'As I disembarked from the bus in Elmina, I heard it. It was sharp and clear, as it rang in the air, and clattered in my ear making me recoil. *Obruni*. A stranger. A foreigner from across the sea.'[64] Historian Lorelle Semley had more complicated experiences while travelling and working in Benin, Senegal, and Ghana when she noticed that at first encounter, Africans frequently tried to identify her in relation to specific countries. 'When they realized I was American, I looked different to them', she added.[65] Although she never expected to be considered a 'local', she came to accept that there would be times that she would be perceived as a 'stranger' or a 'Westerner'. Despite their conclusions, Semley still took comfort in the efforts that various Africans took to 'place' her identity in a particular region of the continent.[66] Another recent traveller to Ghana wrote about an exchange with a taxi driver that illustrates common misunderstandings between black tourists and Ghanaians about the nature of African American identity:

> In one taxi ride, my [driver] asked my nationality. I said 'African American.' He asked, 'Who is African? Your mother?' I said, 'No, my family came from here long ago.' I said this with the assumption that everyone here knows about the slave trade from West Africa to the Americas. He nodded, but then looked confused. 'You are African American?' he repeated it twice. Since he had nodded, I didn't understand his question. Then I realized to him, unless my mother or father was born in Africa, I was just American.[67]

Despite these different perceptions about the African *and* American identities of tourists, the desire to return persists for many in the Diaspora. Although African American tourists often seek to share a collective memory or a common experience with their African counterparts, economic realities prevent most Ghanaians from making a comparable journey to the Americas as leisure travellers.

61 Ibid.,19.
62 Paul Robeson quoted in Northrup, *Crosscurrents in the Black Atlantic*, 118.
63 Ebron, *Tourists as Pilgrims*, 925. *Toubob* is also spelt *toubab*.
64 Saidiya Hartman, *Lose Your Mother: A Journey along the Atlantic Slave Route* (New York: Farrar, Straus and Giroux, 2007), 3.
65 Lorelle Semley, email message to author, 24 June 2010.
66 Lorelle Semley, telephone interview by author, 9 February 2009. Also see the preface to her book, *Mother Is Gold, Father Is Glass: Gender and Colonialism in a Yoruba Town* (Bloomington: Indiana University Press, 2010).
67 Anonymous, 'Identity Dilemma', 30 August 2004, http://mezolife.blogspot.com/2004/08/identity-dilemma-american-obruni.html (accessed 20 August 2007).

Thus, West Africans do not flock to the eastern shores of the Americas to tour auction houses or rivers where newly imported slaves were moved to the interior.[68] There is no symbolic or real 'Door of Entry' on the eastern side of the Atlantic, even though slave forts on the African coast direct tourists to a 'Door of No Return' as a crucial and dramatic feature of their tours. Instead, African Americans are the ones who make the reverse voyage to West Africa. They usually visit one or more of the former castles and dungeons, and they often do so in the context of a pilgrimage. The coastal slave forts located next to Atlantic beaches are a prime spot for tourists, and although the forts are tangible objects with a fixed physical position, their attraction comes from their symbolic meaning. As art historian Cheryl Finley has argued:

> Beyond the mere sight of Africa as a symbolic motherland, the physical and imposing sites of the castles of Cape Coast and Elmina and the forts along the coast are claimed by roots tourists as tangible and necessary memorials, some of the very few places where material evidence of the legacy of slavery still stands before their eyes and is available to be touched, walked through, and experienced with all of their senses and with the movement of their bodies through the space.[69]

Tour guides know that tourists interpret such places as more than mere structures, thus they permit African Americans to segregate their tours from white tourists or have healing ceremonies to inform the ancestors that descendants are coming together after generations of separation.[70] At Elmina, Seestah Imahküs has permission to conduct 'commemorative ceremonies' for Diasporans that she refers to as 'returning African Ascendants'.[71] In her brochure, she notes, 'It has been said that this ceremony assists our people in making the connection with their ancestors as returned ascendants and not merely as Tourists'.[72] Memorial and atonement ceremonies often incorporate the laying of wreaths and the lighting of candles at Elmina or Cape Coast, and even call upon visitors to stroll down Elmina's beach 'where each pilgrim will throw bread into the waters in remembrance of ancestors'.[73]

Debates ensue, however, between Diasporans and Homelanders about how the forts should be used and maintained. One ongoing issue is the concern expressed by some visitors that cleaning, repairing, and painting of Cape Coast and Elmina misrepresents the horrific nature of slaves' experiences. Imahküs argues that painting the walls of the

---

68 A 2004 UNESCO initiative encouraged the development of 'Sites of Memory' websites for teachers around the world that included locations along the Eastern Seaboard and in the Caribbean. 'Breaking the Silence: Transatlantic Slave Trade Education Project', http://www.unesco.org/education/educprog/asp/tst/ (accessed 21 July 2010).

69 Finley, 'Of Golden Anniversaries and Bicentennials', 21.

70 Darko and Amark, interview with authors; 'Ghana's Joseph Project Says "Come Home"'.

71 Seestah Imahküs Njinga, 'Thru the Door of No Return—The Return', *Points to Ponder*, n.d., 5.

72 Ibid.

73 Land Tours 10-Day Emancipation Pilgrimage Featuring Panafest and the Joseph Project.

dungeon is as offensive as the act of planting flowers in the ovens at Auschwitz. To clean the forts is to 'white wash' the history of slaves, she claims.[74] The maintaining of forts, the packaging of stories, and even the selling of admission tickets might turn a sacred place of memory into what Paulla Ebron calls a 'commodified object'.[75] But potted plants are indeed placed in the courtyards of these spaces, both in the large castles of Cape Coast and Elmina, and at smaller forts out of the main tourist gaze. From a Ghanaian perspective, maintaining the structures so that tourists continue to visit is important. For example, one tourist identifying as a Ghanaian wrote in the guest book at Cape Coast, 'This place should be painted'.[76] For the most part, restoration projects are a priority. This is evident at Elmina Castle, where the Elmina Strategy 2015, launched in 2003, seeks to 'restore and manage the mutual heritage existing in Elmina'.[77] Funded with 1.5 million Euros by European and African sources, the restoration project aims to make Elmina Ghana's premier tourist destination. Thus, the focus of the investment is on Elmina's future through the marketing of its past.

Although Ghanaians would like to maintain Cape Coast and Elmina as prominent monuments that draw tourists, they have different ideas about the uses of the many other smaller and less prominent forts that dot the coast of Ghana. Past practices of using some structures as prisons and government offices during the colonial era continue today. Osu Castle, formerly Fort Christiansborg, has served as the main government building for much of its recent history. James Fort in downtown Accra is still a prison for men and women. The women's section is on the street side in full view of those – be they tourists or locals – passing by. Tourists visiting the Kwame Nkrumah Memorial in Accra can see a photograph of Nkrumah's release from James Fort Prison on 24 March 1951. The nearby Usher Fort in Accra functioned as a prison until recently, and then squatters occupied the fort. Ghanaians use other former forts along the coast as rest houses, community centres, and libraries. At these smaller sites there is a conscious desire to set aside the ghosts of the past to promote both tourism and community enrichment. As Ghanaians reclaim their own history by storing beer in the dungeons and holding dance parties in the courtyards of these historic spaces, various states of mind converge around discussions between hosts and guests over the appropriate use of these forts. One might ask if beer should be stored in the male slave dungeon at Senya Beraku, or, if locals should watch television or lift weights in the female slave dungeon there. Are these not sacred sites stained by the blood of those enslaved? In many

74 Seestah Imahküs, *Returning Home Ain't Easy*, 211.
75 Ebron, 'Tourists as Pilgrims', 910. See also Cheryl Finley, 'The Door of (No) Return', *Common-Place* (July 2001) http://www.common-place.org/vol-01/no-04/finley/finley-2.shtml.
76 Anonymous, Cape Coast guest book, 2 June 2006.
77 'The Elmina 2015 Strategy', http://awad.kitlv.nl/pdf//The%20Elmina%202015%20Strategy. pdf (accessed 16 July 2010).

4.4 Ghanaians use former slave forts in multiple ways, including storing beer in the male slave dungeon at Senya Beraku, 2006.
(© E. MacGonagle)

cases, the practical concerns of locals outweigh Diasporan issues of memory and cultural heritage at the smaller forts, demonstrating that there are different attachments to the past and distinct categories of meaning surrounding these sites.[78]

African American tourism does not inherently lead to discord among hosts and guests, particularly as the smaller sites are visited by the more adventurous tourists who travel beyond the typical stops on the tour bus route. For instance, the family of the famed musician Louis Armstrong visited a smaller fort in 1992 at the site of his ancestral home at Kormantse on the Etsi Lagoon, where Fort Amsterdam still stands.[79] The fort is open to the public and under the careful watch of Philip Atta-Yawson who serves as both guide and caretaker. He recalls that several other Diasporans have traced their roots to the village of Kormantse. Reflecting on the mid-1990s 'return' of Gary Bird, accompanied by a group of forty other Americans, Atta-Yawson said: 'To us it was touching to see people from that far away country to have the same cultural heritage as us.'[80] Atta-Yawson sleeps at the fort with two of his children even though his grandmother had warned him of spirits at the site. Unconcerned, he claims, 'That kind of fear

78 For more on the multiple uses of slave forts, see MacGonagle, 'From Dungeons to Dance Parties'.
79 The fort near Abandze is also known as Fort Cormantin. Philip Briggs, *Ghana: The Brandt Travel Guide*, (Guilford, CT.: The Globe Pequot Press, Inc., 3rd edn 2004), 146.
80 Philip Atta-Yawson, interview by authors, Fort Amsterdam, Abandze, 6 June 2006.

4.5. Whether open or barred shut, most former slave forts have a 'Door of No Return' that tourists view on their tour, 2006.

(© E. MacGonagle)

is gradually fading away', and also notes that one American dentist stayed in the fort for five years to prove that the site was habitable and safe to visit.[81] At some of the smaller forts, including Fort Amsterdam, the 'Door of No Return' is clearly marked, but it is either barricaded for security or walled up as the needs of the structure have changed over time.

Such multiple uses of the forts and varied meanings assigned to them by Ghanaians and Americans have often left black tourists feeling upset or dissatisfied. African Americans may have immense expectations that missing pieces of their heritage will be recovered

81 Doctors Robert and Sarah Lee moved from the United States to Ghana before Independence and they became naturalised citizens by 1963 after they renounced their United States citizenship. Robert Lee was involved in projects to refurbish slave forts and often travelled back to the United States to seek funding from African Americans. See Gaines, *American Africans in Ghana*, 170 and 245; Campbell, *Middle Passages*, 324-64.

during their travels, but this desire is often impossible to meet. For African Americans, a history of struggle over citizenship rights in the United States complicates a sense of constant negotiation faced in the Diaspora. For all involved, sharing stories of what Paulla Ebron calls 'collective trauma and African cultural healing' is deeply moving on an emotional level.[82] But as James Campbell notes, it can lead African Americans who are seeking an answer to the question, 'What is Africa to me?' to confront feelings of disappointment with their own country and also ask, 'What is *America* to me?'[83]

With such an emphasis by African Americans on slavery as the common denominator between Diasporans and Ghanaians, additional frustration (on the part of Ghanaians) and confusion (on the part of African Americans) develops when tourists do not take time to learn about Ghana's long past and rich culture. Independence from Britain in 1957 led to new ways of thinking about national identity in Ghana, but as the tour guide Augusta Darko points out, a citizenship group called 'Ghanaian' has only existed for a half century. She added, 'We're hoping to be here longer.'[84] Perhaps Darko's comment reflects a desire to continue developing a national identity for a relatively new and now democratic nation, but it probably also reveals her frustration that most Americans are not knowledgeable about Ghana's past and rich culture before 1957, or long ago before the era of the transatlantic slave trade. Do visitors know, for instance, that the modern country of Ghana takes its name from a pre-colonial African empire in another part of West Africa? Commenting on African Americans' understanding of Ghanaian history, tour guide Tetteh Amark said, 'They say they're African, but they don't know these things.'[85] He offered the example that tourists do not know the meaning and feeling of being welcomed by a word like *akwaaba*. Jennifer Hasty argues that learning Ghanaian terms creates opportunities for African Americans to 'send distinct messages of local historical identification and collaboration to Ghanaians.'[86] It appears that African hosts desire more of these messages from their guests.

In an interview with anthropologist Jemima Pierre, Tourism Minister Obetsebi-Lamptey argued that black Americans and Ghanaians need to work together for mutual understanding. 'Africans and African Americans don't know enough about each other', he said, adding, 'This is why there needs to be a process of education on both sides.'[87] Acknowledging that there is misunderstanding between the two groups, Obetsebi-Lamptey noted that the state has helped to educate the Ghanaian public about African American experiences by recently

82 Ebron, 'Tourists as Pilgrims', 911-12.
83 Emphasis added. Campbell, *Middle Passages*, xxiv.
84 Darko and Amark, interview by authors.
85 Ibid..
86 Hasty, 'Rites of Passage', 53.
87 Jemima Pierre, 'Beyond Heritage Tourism: Race and the Politics of African-Diasporic Inter-actions,' *Social Text* 98 (Spring 2009): 70-1.

broadcasting *Roots* on television and making plans to broadcast the PBS four-part series *Africans in America: America's Journey through Slavery*.[88] The tourist experiences of African Americans in Ghana are usually brief and temporary, however, making it difficult for them to leave their American sense of time and priorities behind. This was evident at one small, family-owned coastal resort when a tourist demanded of his waiter: 'I want an American breakfast, and I want it in 15 minutes.'[89]

Even though a return home for African Americans brings with it some cultural knowledge about their ancestral homeland, Ghanaians have expressed frustration when tourists lay claim to the history of slavery as a privilege reserved solely for themselves as descendants of the enslaved. The writer Richard Wright made this consideration before he embarked on his trip to Africa in the 1950s. He wondered, 'What would my feelings be when I looked into the black face of an African, feeling that maybe his great-great-great-grandfather had sold my great-great-great-grandfather into slavery?'[90] A divide in understanding is the result of two groups of people sharing a legacy that is experienced 'entirely differently', as Lydia Polgreen suggests in her reporting on Ghana's 'uneasy embrace' of the Diaspora.[91] Negotiations over the history of slavery and the legacies that linger today continue to take place at the forts as guides, locals, and foreigners interact day in and day out.

With a history of slavery at the centre of African American and Ghanaian encounters, negotiations over what it means to return and who is to interpret the histories of an ancestral past will continue at slave forts on Ghanaian shores and in other sites of memory. These tensions are manifested on a larger scale by recent public apologies for slavery and two-hundred-year commemorations of the ending of the slave trade. Several state governments in the United States have formally apologised for slavery, and in 2007, the United Kingdom commemorated the official end of their slave trade. In a controversial act, the founder of a pan-African human rights organization, Toyin Agbetu, disrupted the service at Westminster Abbey marking the 200th anniversary of the British abolition of the slave trade in 1807. He said to the crowd, which included Queen Elizabeth II and Prime Minister Tony Blair, 'This is an insult to us. You should be ashamed.'[92] After being escorted outside, Agbetu demanded an apology from the Queen, remarking 'The three major institutions involved in slavery – the monarchy, the government and the church – are all inside there, patting each other on the back. No one has had the decency to say the

88 Ibid.
89 Overheard at Birwa Beach Hotel during fieldwork in December 2002–January 2003.
90 Richard Wright quoted in Campbell, *Middle Passages*, 296.
91 Polgreen, 'Ghana's Uneasy Embrace of Slavery's Diaspora'.
92 Agbetu quoted in Paul Harris, 'Security Scare as Slavery Protester Is Just 10ft from the Queen', *Mail Online*, 28 March 2007, http://www.dailymail.co.uk/news/article-444941/Security-scare-slavery-protester-just-10ft-Queen.html#ixzz0qNsz15ZT.

word Sorry.'[93] These actions also lay bare the central role that slavery played in the rise of Britain and the United States as world powers. As debates over apologies and reparations continue, the President of Ghana focused on 'reconnections' with those in the Diaspora in 2007 rather than supporting reparation demands.[94] Such negations over memory, history, and identity 'enable the continuation of the transnational dialogue between Ghanaians and other members of the Black Atlantic', as Pierre argues.[95]

For Diasporans, a return to Ghana and encounters with Home-landers at slave forts can provide unexpected outcomes. The antici-pation of being greeted as a long-lost relative can be spoiled by a taxi driver or tour guide who does not recognise a common identity based on skin colour or distant ancestral ties. Diasporans may also be confused about why Ghanaians, who have maintained and reallocated the uses of some slave forts, are reluctant to think of the history of slavery as a history belonging solely to the heirs of slavery in the Diaspora. Many may be challenged to think beyond the history of slavery to a more distant past or the recent present after the end of slavery. African Americans are looking to the past when they visit Ghana, but West Africans are looking towards the future. President Barack Obama attempted to bridge this divide in perception during a trip to Ghana in 2009, his first official visit to a sub-Saharan African country. He stated that his family's tour of Cape Coast Castle offered a sense of hope in overcoming historical wrongs while noting that for African Americans the site has special meaning as a 'place of pro-found sadness ... where the journey of much of the African American experience began.'[96]

The conflicts and misunderstandings between Diasporans and Homelanders can ultimately lead African Americans to feel that they do not belong anywhere. As Saidiya Hartman has written,

> *Obruni* forced me to acknowledge that I didn't belong anyplace. The domain of the stranger is always an elusive *elsewhere*. I was born in another country, where I also felt like an alien and which in part determined why I had come to Ghana. I had grown weary of being stateless. Secretly I wanted to belong somewhere or, at least, I wanted a convenient explanation of why I felt like a stranger.[97]

Hartman's search for a homeland echoes those of others who most likely return to the United States with the realisation that a universal African identity is elusive. In addition, a common African American interest in Africa also remains ambiguous, despite growing access

93 Ibid.
94 'Reparation for Slave Trade Not Best Approach', *Ghana Web*, 26 March 2007, http://www.ghanaweb.com/GhanaHomePage/NewsArchive/artikel.php?ID=121462.
95 Pierre, 'Beyond Heritage Tourism', 74.
96 Barack Obama, 'Remarks by the President at Cape Coast Castle', Office of the Press Secretary, The White House, 11 July 2009, http://www.whitehouse.gov/the-press-office/remarks-president-cape-coast-castle.
97 Hartman, *Lose Your Mother*, 4.

to DNA testing and increased opportunities for tourism. Therefore, confusion can remain over the notion of what it means to be American or African, or a mixture of both African *and* American.

If sites of memory that commemorate the history of slavery 'can function in various combinations as museums, monuments, memorials and/or information centers', as anthropologist Paula Girshick notes, then such sites are conceptually framed 'as distinct types of cultural activity with distinct modes of representation'.[98] Thus, it makes sense that African Americans and Ghanaians might have different perceptions of the functions of slave forts and their own identities in relationship to them. History and remembering become muddled when framing strategies and devices are not socially shared by all constituents.[99] Idealised representations call into question issues of identity and nationalism, and competing perspectives emerge, for instance, between descendants of those who endured the Middle Passage (African Americans) and those who did not (Ghanaians). Given the very public and official presentation of history at the forts, tour guides are challenged to negotiate a terrain often contested by both the heirs of those who were enslaved and those who were not.

Histories and inventions

It is in the murky history of slavery that African Americans want to find their ancestors, and if they cannot do it through genealogical data, they can create some connection to an ancestral homeland with the help of Ghanaian, Senegalese, or Gambian guides. If the story of slavery, scripted and then sold to them, seems unsatisfying, tourists can also take a symbolic connection to the past in the form of a souvenir back to the United States. Slave forts and castles are the largest physical reminders of the history of slavery, and constructing a narrative of the past is nothing short of complicated, but other reminders of the slave trade are available for tourists to purchase. In addition to wooden figures such as the ones for sale in Juffureh, tourists can authenticate their pilgrimage with a certificate verifying that they toured either Kunta Kinte's village or the Ghanaian fort at Abandze. They can purchase photographs and books about Elmina and Cape Coast, and even wear a t-shirt with an image of Cape Coast castle on the front. Back in the United States, their children can attend Kunta Kinte Camp for fifty American dollars. In this four-day programme, participants 'learn about Kunta Kinte's West Africa by playing games, making crafts, dancing, eating African foods and dressing in

---

98   Paula Girshick, 'Ncome Museum/Monument: From Reconciliation to Resistance', *Museum Anthropology* 27 (March 2004): 28.
99   Ibid. Girschick makes this point for the Ncome site in South Africa drawing on the work of Iwona Irwin-Zarecka in *Frames of Remembrance: The Dynamics of Collective Memory* (New Brunswick, NJ: Transaction, 1994).

authentic garb' at the Chesapeake Children's Museum in Annapolis, Maryland.[100] African Americans' continued desire for a connection to real or imagined ancestors, and the willingness of Africans to claim and craft stories of slavery, demonstrate that the history of slavery holds symbolic power that continues to be produced and consumed throughout the transatlantic world. While the Kunta Kintes of past centuries were bought and sold as property, the memories of such slaves are sold over and over again today.

100   James Clemenko, 'Summer Camps: Just around the Corner', Bay Weekly.com 10 (22-28 May, 2003), http://www.bayweekly.com/year03/issuexi21/kidsxi21.html (accessed 15 August 2009). In August 2010, Camp Kunta Kinte was still operating at the Chesapeake Children's Museum.

REFERENCES

African American Lives 2, Episode 1, DVD, directed by Jack Youngelson. Pleasantville, NY: Kunhardt Productions, Inc., 2008.

Angelou, Maya. *All God's Children Need Traveling Shoes* (New York: Vintage Books, 1986).

Anonymous. 'Identity Dilemma', 30 August 2004, http://mezolife.blogspot. com/2004/08/identity-dilemma-american-oboruni.html.

Atta-Yawson, Philip. Interview by authors. Fort Amsterdam, Abandze, Ghana, 6 June 2006.

Bauman, Zygmunt. *Modernity and the Holocaust* (Ithaca, NY: Cornell University Press, 1989).

'Breaking the Silence: Transatlantic Slave Trade Education Project', http:// www.unesco.org/education/educprog/asp/tst/ (accessed 21 June 2010).

Briggs, Philip. *Ghana: The Brandt Travel Guide* (Guilford, CT.: The Globe Pequot Press, Inc., 3rd edn 2004).

Bruner, Edward M. 'Tourism in Ghana: The Representation of Slavery and the Return of the Black Diaspora', *American Anthropologist*, New Series 98 (June 1996): 290-304.

Burke, Andrew and David Else. *The Gambia and Senegal* (Oakland, CA: The Lonely Planet Publications, 2002).

Buy (Less) http://www.buylesscrap.org/ (accessed 19 June 2010).

Campbell, Eric. 'Ghana Slavery', *Foreign Correspondent*, original airdate 20 March 2007, http://www.abc.net.au/foreign/content/2007/s1903382.htm (accessed 29 August 2007).

Campbell, James. *Middle Passages: African American Journeys to Africa, 1787–2005* (New York: Penguin Press, 2006).

Cape Coast Castle guest book, Cape Coast, Ghana.

Cashill, Jack. 'Alex Haley's Immaculate Roots', *WorldNetDaily Exclusive Commentary*, 1 July 2005, http://www.worldnetdaily.com/news/article. asp?ARTICLE_ID=45084 (accessed 27 January 2009).

Ceesay, Lamin. Interview by author. Juffureh, Gambia, 21 May 2006.

Clarey, Christopher. 'Serena Williams Acknowledges a Decline', *New York Times*, 14 January 2007.

Clarke, Kamari Maxine. 'Mapping Transnationality: Roots Tourism and the Institutionalization of Ethnic Heritage', in Kamari Maxine Clarke and Deborah A. Thomas, eds., *Globalization and Race: Transformations in the Cultural Production of Blackness* (Durham NC: Duke University Press, 2006), 133-53.

Clemenko, James. 'Summer Camps: Just Around the Corner', *Bay Weekly. com* 10 (22-28 May, 2003), http://www.bayweekly.com/year03/issuexi21/kidsxi21.html (accessed 1 August 2009).

Darko, Augusta Ampem and Tetteh Amark. Interview by authors. Elmina, Ghana, 9 June 2006.

Door of Return, http://doorofreturn.com/home/?page_id=5 (accessed 22 June 2010).

Du Bois, W. E. Burghardt. *Dusk of Dawn: An Essay toward an Autobiography of a Race Concept* (New York: Schocken Books, 1968).

Ebron, Paulla A. *Performing Africa* (Princeton NJ: Princeton University Press, 2002).

—— 'Tourists as Pilgrims: Commercial Fashioning of Transatlantic Politics', *American Ethnologist* 26 (November 1999): 910-32.

The Economist, 13-19 May 2000.

'The Elmina 2015 Strategy', http://awad.kitlv.nl/pdf//The%20Elmina%20 2015%20Strategy.pdf (accessed 16 July 2010).

Ely, Bert, J.L.Wilson, F. Jackson and B.A. Jackson, 'African-American Mitochondrial DNAs Often Match mtDNAs Found in Multiple African Ethnic Groups', *BMC Biology* (2006): 4:34, http://www.biomedcentral.com/1741-7007/4/34.

Fears, Darryl. 'Out of Africa – but from Which Tribe?: DNA Tests of Blacks Promise Ancestry Answers, but Report Adds to Critics' Doubts', *Washington Post*, 19 October 2006.

Finley, Cheryl. 'The Door of (No) Return', *Common-Place* (July 2001), http://www.common-place.org/vol-01/no-04/finley/finley-2.shtml (accessed 21 June 2010).

—— 'Of Golden Anniversaries and Bicentennials: Convergence of Memory, Tourism and National History in Ghana', *Journeys: The International Journal of Travel and Travel Writing* 7 (November 2006): 15-32.

Gaines, Kevin K. *American Africans in Ghana: Black Expatriates and the Civil Rights Era* (Chapel Hill NC: University of North Carolina Press, 2006).

Gates, Henry Louis, Jr. *Finding Oprah's Roots: Finding Your Own* (New York: Crown Publishing Group, 2007).

—— '"We Are All Africans": Genealogical Research and DNA Testing Can Reveal Your Ethnic Connection to Africa', *Ebony*, December 2007.

'Ghana's Joseph Project Says "Come Home"', *The World*, National Public Radio, 7 June 2007, http://www.npr.org/templates/story/story.php?storyId= 10802304 (accessed 2 September 2007).

Gilroy, Paul. *The Black Atlantic: Modernity and Double Consciousness* (Cambridge MA: Harvard University Press, 1993).

Girshick, Paula. *Frames of Remembrance: The Dynamics of Collective Memory* (New Brunswick NJ: Transaction, 1994).

—— 'Ncome Museum/Monument: From Reconciliation to Resistance', *Museum Anthropology* 27 (March 2004): 25-36.

Hale, Thomas A. *Griots and Griottes: Masters of Words and Music* (Bloomington: Indiana University Press, 1998).

Haley, Alex. *Roots: The Saga of an American Family* (Garden City, NY: Doubleday, 1st edn 1976).

Harmon, Amy. 'In DNA Era, New Worries About Prejudice', *New York Times*, 11 November 2007.

—— 'Learning My Genome, Learning About Myself', *New York Times*, 17 November 2007.

Harris, Paul. 'Security Scare as Slavery Protester Is Just 10ft from the Queen', *Mail Online*, 28 March 2007, http://www.dailymail.co.uk/ news/article-444941/Security-scare-slavery-protester-just-10ft-Queen. html#ixzz0qNsz15ZT (accessed 2 September 2007).

Hartman, Saidiya. *Lose Your Mother: A Journey along the Atlantic Slave Route* (New York: Farrar, Straus and Giroux, 2007).

Hasty, Jennifer. 'Rites of Passage, Routes of Redemption: Emancipation Tourism and the Wealth of Culture', *Africa Today* 49 (Fall 2002): 47-76.

Jackson, John L., Jr. *Real Black: Adventures in Racial Sincerity* (Chicago IL: University of Chicago Press, 2005).

The Joseph Project-Ghana. http://www.thejosephproject.com (accessed 2 September 2007).

'The Joseph Project: Ghana reaches out to the Diaspora', http://www.info-ghana.com/joseph_project.htm (accessed 21 June 2010).

Keim, Curtis. *Mistaking Africa: Curiosities and Inventions of the American Mind* (Boulder CO: Westview, 2nd edn, 2009).

Land Tours 10-Day Emancipation Pilgrimage Featuring Panafest and the Joseph Project, http://www.landtours.com/emancipation_iti.asp (accessed 5 September 2009).

MacGonagle, Elizabeth. 'From Dungeons to Dance Parties: Contested Histories of Ghana's Slave Forts', *Journal of Contemporary African Studies* 24 (May 2006): 249-60.

Mann, Valerie Papaya. Interview by authors. Accra, Ghana, 6 June 2006.

McKittrick, Katherine, and Clyde Woods, eds. *Black Geographies and the Politics of Place* (Toronto: Between the Lines, 2007).

Mensah, Ishmael. 'Marketing Ghana as a Mecca for the African-American Tourist', *Ghana Web*, 10 June 2004, http://www.ghanaweb.com/Ghana HomePage/features/artikel.php?ID=59447 (accessed 18 June 2010).

Ministry of Tourism – Ghana Tourism Homepage. http://www.touringghana. com/mot.asp (accessed 15 June 2010).

Ndaiye, Boubacar Joseph. Interview by author. Gorée Island, Senegal, 27 May 2006.

Njinga, Seestah Imahküs. 'Thru the Door of No Return-The Return', *Points to Ponder: A Travel Guide* (n.d.).

Nixon, Ron. 'DNA Tests Find Branches but Few Roots', *New York Times*, 25 November 2007.

Nobile, Philip. 'Uncovering Roots', *Village Voice*, February 1993.

Northrup, David. *Crosscurrents in the Black Atlantic, 1770-1965* (New York: Bedford/St. Martin's, 2008).

Obama, Barack. 'Remarks by the President at Cape Coast Castle', Office of the Press Secretary, The White House, 11 July 2009, http://www.whitehouse. gov/the-press-office/remarks-president-cape-coast-castle (accessed 21 May 2010).

One Africa. http://www.oneafricaghana.com/lodging.htm (accessed 12 May 2006).

Pace, Eric, 'Alex Haley, 70, Author of "Roots", Dies', *New York Times*, 11

February 1992.

Palace Travel. http://www.panafest.us/ (accessed 27 January 2009).

Pierre, Jemima. 'Beyond Heritage Tourism: Race and the Politics of African-Diasporic Interactions', *Social Text* 98 (Spring 2009): 59-81.

Polgreen, Lydia. 'Ghana's Uneasy Embrace of Slavery's Diaspora', *New York Times*, 27 December 2005.

'Reparation for Slave Trade Not Best Approach', Ghana Web, 26 March 2007, http://www.ghanaweb.com/GhanaHomePage/NewsArchive/artikel.php?ID=121462 (accessed 29 March 2007).

Seestah Imahküs. *Returning Home Ain't Easy but It Sure Is a Blessing!* (Cape Coast, Ghana: One Africa Tours and Specialty Services Ltd. 1999).

Smolenyak, Megan, and Ann Turner. *Trace Your Roots with DNA: Using Genetic Tests to Explore Your Family Tree* (Emmaus PA.: Rodale, Inc., 2004).

Semley, Lorelle. *Mother Is Gold, Father Is Glass: Gender and Colonialism in a Yoruba Town* (Bloomington IN: Indiana University Press, 2010).

—— Telephone interview by author. 9 February 2009.

'This is Ghana – Welcome Home!' http://www.ghanaweb.com/Ghana Home Page/features/artikel.php?ID=16104 (accessed 23 June 2010).

Traces of the Trade: A Story from the Deep North, DVD, directed by Katrina Browne. Cambridge MA: Ebb Pid Productions, LLC, 2008.

Virtual Visit of Gorée Island. http://webworld.unesco.org/goree/en/index.shtml (accessed 23 June 2010).

Walker, Andrew. '[Marlon] Jackson Star in Nigeria Resort Row', *BBC News, Nigeria*, http://news.bbc.co.uk/2/hi/africa/7858010.stm (accessed 25 February 2009).

Watkins, Mel. 'A Talk with Alex Haley', *New York Times Book Review*, September 1976.

Wright, Donald. *The World and a Very Small Place in Africa; A History of Globalization in Niumi, The Gambia* (London: M.E. Sharpe, 3rd edn 2010).

5 • Imitating heritage tourism:
A virtual tour of Sekhukhuneland, South Africa

Ineke van Kessel

Tourism in South Africa has enjoyed rapid growth since the end of Apartheid. The number of foreign visitors increased more than tenfold over a period of ten years, from 640,000 in 1994 to more than 6.5 million in 2003, and reaching 9.2 million in 2007. It is now the country's fastest growing industry and accounts for just over 7% of its GDP.[1] With all eyes set on an expected influx of visitors for the World Cup in 2010, many South Africans were keen to tap their share of tourist revenue. It was projected that tourism would employ more than 1.2 million people, directly and indirectly by 2010.[2]

Game parks and Cape Town remain the most spectacular attractions but numerous other initiatives are attempting to capture their corner of the ever-increasing tourist market. Business and conference tourism is seen as the money-spinner of the future, while ecological tourism – ranging from bird watching to snorkelling and hiking – is currently the fastest growing segment of the industry. Prominent among relatively new ventures in the tourism sector is community tourism, sometimes labelled 'cultural tourism' or 'heritage tourism', with its potential to involve not only tour operators but local residents as well.

Township tours and cultural villages have been designed to allow tourists a glimpse of modern and traditional lives of ordinary black South Africans. More than a thousand people visit Soweto every day to see the two-bedroom house in Orlando where Nelson and Winnie Mandela lived, and the Hector Pietersen Museum, which commemorates the 1976 Soweto Uprising. The Department of Arts and Culture is promoting cultural tourism as part of its poverty-alleviation programme.[3] New heritage sites are being developed in addition to the traditional landmarks that celebrate South Africa's colonial history. Freedom Park in Pretoria, Lesedi cultural village, Makhosini cultural village in the Valley of the Kings in Zululand and the Mapoch Ndebele village have all emerged to take their place on the tourist route alongside the battlefields of Natal and the Voortrekker Monument.

---

1 Government Communications, *South Africa Yearbook 2004/05*, (Pretoria: Government Communications, 2004): 535; Statistics South Africa, *Stats in Brief 2008*, (Pretoria: Statistics South Africa, 2008). www.statssa.gov.za
2 *South Africa Yearbook 2004/05*: 535.
3 *South Africa Yearbook 2004/05*: 109.

However, the tourist business is also a mirage: ordinary South Africans see pots of gold at the end of the rainbow but have little understanding of what will attract tourists. What to do if there is no game park anywhere near and local historical imagery is not as colourful as the archetypical Zulu warrior or the staunch Boer commando? Many South African municipalities now sport elaborate websites in the hope of attracting tourists. What exactly is identified as 'heritage' and how are these sites and stories portrayed in the context of the tourist industry? This chapter explores the virtual heritage tour on the website of Fetakgomo Municipality in Sekhukhuneland and compares the virtual tour with the (attempted) real-life experience.

Sekhukhuneland: From obscurity to Google

I first went to Sekhukhuneland in 1990 when doing research on youth movements involved in organising resistance against Apartheid.[4] Sekhukhuneland is a poor, rural area in Limpopo Province, some 200 km northeast of Pretoria. Formerly part of the Lebowa Bantustan, it now is part of the administrative district Greater Sekhukhune, which has its district offices in the town of Groblersdal. In 1990, it was quite difficult to find any current information on Sekhukhuneland at all. The BaPedi of Sekhukhuneland have a long and interesting history of resistance against Afrikaner and British encroachments in the 19th century and against the imposition of Bantustan rule in the 1950s. Historians have recorded these struggles as well as the fractious politics of the BaPedi rulers, while Afrikaner ethnographers have described their customs and material culture.[5] But when I first set off for Sekhukhuneland in August 1990, I had almost no information on the current state of the region.

These days, a Google search for Sekhukhune comes up with some 56,900 hits, including the website of Greater Sekhukhune District.[6] To my surprise, this website invites the visitor to enjoy a tourist experience in Sekhukhune, notably in the region where I previously conducted my research. Sekhukhune District is subdivided into five new municipalities and my research area would have come within Fetakgomo Local Municipality, which has its newly established offices in the village of Apel. Previously, in the days of Bantustan rule, the chiefs were responsible for local government in rural parts of the

4 Ineke van Kessel, 'Beyond our Wildest Dreams': The United Democratic Front and the Transformation of South Africa (Charlottesville/London: University Press of Virginia, 2000).
5 D.R. Hunt, 'An Account of the Bapedi', Bantu Studies, December 1931; C.V. Bothma, 'The Political Structure of the Pedi of Sekhukhuneland', African Studies 35 (1976), 3-4: 177-205; Peter Delius, The Land Belongs to Us, (Johannesburg: Ravan Press, 1983) ; Peter Delius, A Lion amongst the Cattle: Reconstruction and Resistance in the Northern Transvaal, (Johannesburg: Ravan Press, 1996); H.O. Mönnig, The Pedi (Pretoria: Van Schaik, 1988).
6 www.sekhukhune.gov.za. In 2007, when I wrote a first draft of this paper, the headword Sekhukhune or Sekhukhuneland produced 53,500 hits. The websites of Sekhukhune District and Fetakgomo Municipality have since changed but this chapter is based on the 2007 websites.

Bantustans. Fetakgomo's municipal website proclaims the area as a 'land of legends and myths and of ancient civilizations that visitors find fascinating'. The website promises visits to a traditional village, a game reserve, a spring inhabited by water spirits, an echo stone that turns summer into winter, traditional dancing, God's footprint, the heritage site at Tjate (where the BaPedi fought battles with Boers and Brits) and 'mountains full of wild animals, reptiles of all sorts and songs of birds filled with the happiness of the day'.

I recollect having heard and seen a much wider variety of birds in Johannesburg than in Sekhukhune and, apart from a few scorpions, I never spotted a wild animal. Sekhukhune, an impoverished, arid and dusty landscape sheltered by the barren Leolo Mountains, is now described as a land of milk and honey.

> It is rich with cultural heritage and an abundance of wildlife and nature-based tourism opportunities, indeed a treasure chest waiting to be discovered.

This text is obviously inspired by a romanticised image of game parks and heritage. As if this was not persuasive enough, the website also borrows from the adventure industry with the promise of a 4x4 demonstration in the dry riverbed of the Olifants River:

> Great for your relaxation and entertainment. Boredom becomes a thing of the past. One may even forget to go back home.

It is not that I have ever been bored in Sekhukhuneland: there are always lots of interesting stories about the past and the present, and rumours and gossip abound. But after a dozen visits or so over an eighteen-year period, I do not ever recall any traditional villages, as for example in Venda or KwaZulu, picturesque dancing and drumming or even any attempts to provide tourist facilities.

Booking without the tourist bubble

I hasten to take up the invitation at the bottom of the website:

> We invite you to explore some of these places and suggest that you do so with Kodikodi, a trained guide who will explain the significance and history of them to you.
>
> Our people, the custodian of this wonderful legacy, are warm and hospitable and look forward to sharing the abundance of their municipality with you.
>
> Whether you are an international or a local tourist, we in Fetakgomo extend an invitation to you to pay a visit. The beauty and the diversity of culture that our municipality has to offer will overwhelm you.

The email I send off to book my heritage tour immediately bounces back with a message that the address is non-existent. After arriving in

Johannesburg, I phone Fetakgomo Municipality and ask for Kodikodi. I am told that he left a long time ago and that the only person who can possibly handle my request is on leave. I am becoming ever more determined to see the wonders of Sekhukhune and am not about to give up. There is no 'tourist bubble' in Sekhukhune, no intermediary service that can help fulfil my wishes.[7] But fortunately the region is, to some extent, familiar ground.

On my arrival in Apel, I tell my host family about these new adventures that I want to explore. Although my hosts are well connected locally, they have never heard anything about tourist trips in their area nor have they ever seen any tourists. They kindly take me to Fetakgomo Municipality's brand new offices and introduce me to some officials who could perhaps be of help.

A real live tourist who wants to book the advertised heritage tour causes considerable consternation. Like a hot potato, I get tossed around between various officials who have no idea as to how to handle this unexpected situation. While waiting in the hall for my next appointment, I hear solemn hymns in Afrikaans. Following the sound, I see a television in the entrance hall showing the SABC's live coverage of the late President P.W. Botha's funeral in George. It is utterly unreal: President Thabo Mbeki is seated in the front row of the church but hardly anybody in Fetakgomo Municipality is paying any attention to the funeral of the former president under whose rule Sekhukhuneland became a hotbed of resistance in the 1980s.

At one point, I am introduced to Mayor Coleman Marota. Without any introductory niceties, Mayor Marota launches into a diatribe against imperialism and the plundering of Africa's mineral resources by whites. 'Never trust a white person. They only come here to steal from us.' I am somewhat taken aback. This is not the red-carpet welcome tourists are promised on Fetakgomo's website. When the mayor has run out of steam, I cautiously make inquiries about the municipality's development plans and the tourist potential of Fetakgomo. Still agitated, Mayor Marota states that Fetakgomo offers a unique tourist package: 'The history of the BaPedi is as rich as the history of the Zulus.' I assure him of my interest in BaPedi heritage and explain my wish to book this unique package. I attempt to express my interest in learning more about local history and heritage but the mayor is not about to give me a chance to speak. The arrival of the manager of the newly opened shopping centre saves me from further harassment.

Now I am handed over to an engaging young man called Robert. I am told that he is the webmaster and therefore in a position to help

---

7   W.E.A. van Beek, 'Approaching African Tourism; Paradigms and Paradoxes', in P. Chabal, U. Engel & L. de Haan (eds.) *African Alternatives* (Leiden, Brill, 2007), 145-72. Van Beek defines the 'tourist bubble' as 'those infrastructural arrangements that permit the professional reception of guests – such as hotels, lodges, personnel, logistics – plus those arrangements making the travel of tourists possible: travel agencies in the sending as well as in the host countries, transport facilities and a massive internet information business'.

me. Robert takes me to his office and promises that he will show me the website. But I have already seen the website and now I want to see the real thing. I want to visit the sights described on the website. Robert is flabbergasted. He repeats incredulously: 'You want to see the real thing???' Without further ado, he takes me back to Garrison, the municipality's PR official, who produces a leaflet offering more or less the same information as the website. In addition to the wonders of the website, the leaflet promises overnight accommodation too.

> Those who may need overnight accommodation after feasting their eyes and minds on the beautiful tapestry of breathtaking sites of this cultural seat of Sekhukhuneland, can enjoy a well deserved rest in Potlake and the Municipal Guest House, which meets world standards. (...) Be with us when you wake up to shower beautiful municipality. The red carpet is there for you.

I nod enthusiastically: yes, that is precisely what I want, and of course I am willing to pay. All of a sudden, after a new round of consultations, Garrison promises that I can make the tour if I come back on Friday with my own car. On Friday morning I am welcomed by Jackson Lesufi, the official responsible for economic development (which includes tourism). His newly appointed right-hand man, Silence, will accompany me to God's footprint, the Potlake Game Reserve, and – as I insist on it – King Sekhukhune's statue at the Tjate battlefield. Nothing else is possible on a one-day trip, and this turns out to be quite true. However before we leave, we have to stop at the nearby Spar supermarket to consult a woman who can provide directions for getting to God's footstep.

After getting directions, we drive over a mountain pass to the other side of the Leolo mountain range and when we reach the end of the road we are in Ga-Maisela India. My companion – named Silence because he did not scream when he was born – asks around for directions but the villagers shake their heads. At long last, a woman accompanies us to see the chief, an elderly man in worn overalls. Chief Maime Maesela is quite enamoured by the visit of a municipal official and a real live white tourist. For him, this is obviously evidence confirming the tourist potential of his heritage site.

The chief immediately agrees to accompany us to God's footstep. We drive towards the edge of the village from where we walk along a goats' trail, crossing an arid and very hot plain towards a formation of rocks. On the way, Chief Maesela points to black spots on the rocks, explaining that these are the footprints of panthers and leopards. After some clambering over rocks in the blazing sun, we see a hollow space in a flat rock, the size of a human foot. This is the print of God's left foot; his right foot landed some considerable distance further away. Chief Maesela emphasises that he has not invented anything and is not showing off local folklore. The footprints were discovered around 2000 when a Mr Tladi from the Sekhukhune College of Education

5.1 God's footprint, 2007
(© Ineke van Kessel)

identified the step as God's footstep because he could see it was not a human footprint.

The chief uses this opportunity to complain to Silence that the municipality has neglected to build a fence around the site to prevent vandalism. And once there is a fence, the tourist potential of Modimo's footprint can be developed. Tickets and refreshments will be sold at the entrance with the revenue being administered by a community trust and used for community development. The chief is obviously well versed in development-speak. Silence remarks approvingly that this is a modern chief but is not quite sure whether God's footprint is mentioned in Fetakgomo's Integrated Development Plan. If so, it is indeed feasible that the municipality could provide fencing. The scheme would require dozens of kilometres of fence but it is not very clear why the footprints might be susceptible to vandalism. However, these questions do not concern the chief. Chief Maesela is adamant that there can be no development without fencing.

After taking our leave of the chief, we head for the Potlake Nature Reserve on the main road from Polokwane to Burgersfort. It dates back to 1975 when the Ucar Mining Group and the local traditional authority agreed to set 2,800 ha of bushveld and mountains aside for a nature reserve. Potlake does not have the 'Big Five' but boasts some ten species of game including giraffe, gems buck, kudu, impala, ostrich, water buck, red hartebeest and sable antelope. According to Fetakgomo's website, this is the place where tourists can enjoy a well-deserved rest and world-class comfort. It is a very hot November afternoon by the time we arrive at the entrance gate. We are referred to the manager in the information centre who is most willing to help (after he has woken up). In the information centre, we are shown stuffed animals in a landscaped setting behind glass. This is apparently a popular outing for school children. The manager then takes us on a brief trip by car to see some of the animals but when we ask to see the accommodation, he explains that apart from a camp site the nature park has no other accommodation for visitors. Some refreshments perhaps? A family-size bottle of Coca Cola is the only item available.

The visitors' registration book reveals that Potlake Nature Reserve receives an average of three visitors a week, plus an occasional visit from local schools. Staff members vividly remember the exotic appearance of the only foreign tourist who ever came to Potlake: a Spaniard on a bicycle! Clearly, the tourist potential of Potlake is very limited with the Kruger Park and many other well-stocked game parks only 100 km further east.

Next, we head for Sekhukhune's most important heritage site, Tjate, the place where the BaPedi warriors valiantly fought British regiments and their Swazi allies in 1878. The local chief is not at home and his wife admits to not knowing anything about history and statues. However, it is quite easy to find the statue of King Sekhukhune, not because the statue towers above the battlefield but because of the huge fence that is easily spotted from a distance, long before we can actually see the modest bronze statue.

A plaque on the pedestal reveals that the statue of King Sekhukhune I (1814–1882) was unveiled on 16 September 2004. In spite of the massive fence, a local group of 'concerned citizens' attempted to blow it up with spent explosives from the stocks at the nearby platinum mines in protest against the delay in the delivery of water and electricity to Tjate. Damage was limited to the cement base but since the incident two guards have been stationed at the statue. They emphasise that more and stronger fencing is needed. There is no guide available and the Sepedi-speaking guards tell us a long and complicated story about the dynasty of Pedi rulers and their heroic wars against the enemy. Who was 'the enemy'? The guards shrug and point to the plaque where the enemy is identified as 'colonialists and imperialists'. Silence finds all of this too complicated to translate. He says that the guards need to be 'workshopped' so that they can act as guides as well.

Somewhere near the fenced statue is a modest headstone in honour of the Scottish regiment that fought here with their Swazi allies in 1878 against King Sekhukhune's troops. The stone was erected many decades ago and even though there is no fence, nobody has ever vandalised it. ANC symbols have been painted on the rocks some way off but the memorial itself has never been damaged in spite of the nearby football field that attracts dozens of youngsters every day.

5.2 *The king's statue behind a fence, 2007*
(© Ineke van Kessel)

At Tjate, there are also dreams of fences and gates, refreshments and entrance tickets, in other words *community development*. Or, in the words of the 2025 Development Strategy of Greater Sekhukhune District:

> The vision of the proposed project is to create a major tourism anchor project and cultural icon in the district based on the formidable contribution of King Sekhukhune to the formation of an African empire. ... The tourism potential of Tjate could be compared with the Natal Battlefields, Thulamela and perhaps Mapungubwe to the North. Shakaland, which is also in a remote area, enjoys international support based on the fact that people can interact and participate in cultural events, and experience the lifestyle of local people.[8]

8 Greater Sekhukhune District Municipality, 2025 Development Strategy, synthesis report of the research: 36-40.

In previous centuries, the BaPedi did indeed once rule over a substantial empire stretching from the Limpopo to the Vaal River. The current acting paramount chief, KK Sekhukhune, likes to remind his visitors that his ancestors were as powerful as the Zulu kings and that they too fought valiant battles against Boers and Brits. For the paramount chief, this history serves as justification for his claim that he, as a descendent of the formidable BaPedi kings, is entitled to the same royal salary and substantial benefits as the post-apartheid state has accorded to the Zulu King Goodwill Zwelethini. However, the largesse bestowed on Zwelethini has a different rationale. In the early 1990s when Mangosothu Buthelezi, the then prime minister of the KwaZulu bantustan, attempted to derail the negotiations for a democratic South African constitution by threatening secession, the negotiators bought the compliance of traditionalist Zulus by offering tempting privileges for Zulu royalty.

The Zulu appeal to the tourist – domestic and foreign – is due largely to their former British arch foes. The British (including Anglophone white South Africans) produced an avalanche of books, movies, newspaper stories and memorabilia to popularise the stories of the Battle of Isandhlwana (which the Zulus won) and the subsequent military campaigns resulting in ultimate victory for the British. The production of such works still continues today, with movies regularly attracting large television audiences. One film even has Buthelezi starring as Shaka Zulu. The battlefields of Natal saw the first defeat of the imperial British army on African soil because they came ill-prepared having seriously underestimated the military strength and determination of their local opponents. To make defeat less humiliating, Zulu warriors were from then onwards always portrayed as formidable fighters. With typical British nostalgia, the Zulu impies and the British redcoats assemble every now and then on the green hills of Natal for a rerun of the famous battles.

The Natal battlefields are a popular destination on heritage tours in Natal. But unlike Sekhhukhune, Natal has visible tourist sites: the old hospital at Rorke's Drift has been converted into a museum, and burial monuments mark the battlefields. At Bloedrivier (Ncome), Afrikaner nationalists have constructed a weird lager of bronze Boer wagons to commemorate the 1838 Battle of Bloedrivier, the fountain of Afrikaner nationalist mythology. Apart from the battles between Zulus and Voortrekkers and between Zulus and the British, there are also the battlefields from the Anglo-Boer War. Like the Afrikaners and the British, Zulu traditionalists equally enjoy basking in their erstwhile glory and are willing partners in heritage tourism schemes.

The battlefields of Natal evoke a colourful imagery: there is an abundance of visual representation to prepare the tourist for a visit to the actual sites, even if there is not that much to see. More recent battles are less suitable for heritage tourism: the hills around Pietermaritzburg, where Inkatha youth and UDF-aligned youth enacted their bloody confrontations in the 1980s, do not feature on tourist programmes.

The BaPedi, however, are not benefiting from the massive PR machinery that has rendered international fame to the Natal battlefields. And although the BaPedi are proud of their long history of struggle against foreign invaders and impostors, few are able to recount even the basic outline of this history. Silence, in spite of his university degree, told me that King Sekhukhune I (1814-1882) was arrested by the Lebowa government (the Bantustan imposed under National Party rule in the 1950s). Most importantly perhaps, the 'battlefields' niche of heritage tourism has already been taken up by the Natal battlefields. In spite of BaPedi ambitions and dreams, there seems to be no space for yet another 'battlefields heritage' enterprise. The story of Tjate is not well known by overseas tourists and does not appeal to nostalgic sentiments among domestic tourists. Its other limitation is that it is far from other major tourist routes and so at best can only hope to become a destination for school excursions.

Tjate marked the end of my heritage tour. Silence asked to be dropped near his home village and I drove back to Apel. Thanks to my host family, my accommodation in Sekhukhune has never been a problem. I enjoyed my heritage tour in Sekhukhuneland immensely but for most aspiring heritage tourists this 'feast for the eyes and the minds' will probably remain a virtual adventure on the website. Although tourism was seen by all those I met on that day as an economic activity with income-generating potential for local communities, nobody at any of the sites asked me for any money.

By way of conclusion: What does it all mean?

There is more to this virtual adventure than the fantasies of webmaster Robert alone. The economic potential of tourism figures in all the Integrated Development Plans, Scenarios for 2025 and other policy plans produced by or for Sekhukhune District and its municipalities. Most of these have been drawn up by consultancy bureaus that so far seem to be the main beneficiaries of the mirage of tourism. The attractions are generally promoted as natural beauty, cultural secrets and 'age-old traditions and lifestyles'. However, in a country like South Africa with its plethora of well-developed, easily accessible and well-advertised tourist destinations, Sekhukhune faces significant competition. I must add however that other proposed developments seem more realistic, such as the development of the Loskop Dam and the new De Hoop Dam as family resorts catering for the domestic tourist market.

The 2025 Development Strategy of Greater Sekhukhune District has, as one of its five proposed anchor projects, a grandiose vision of entrance gates to the district. From these three entrance gates, tourists will be guided along routes with local attractions, 'and by so doing increase the length of stay and total expenditure in the area'. Here, inspiration is drawn from famous international icons.

> The entrance gates proposal is a new and unique tourism concept in South Africa although there are similarities with the Brandenburg Gate in Berlin (Germany) and the Arc de Triomph in Paris (France).

It is not clear which historical feats will be commemorated by the gates to Sekhukhune District but the planners acknowledge that 'the business model for the gates could be reconsidered' as 'the anticipated revenue stream from the gate proposal is insufficient to cover the capital requirement'.[9]

Tourism is viewed as an economic activity with job-creation potential although planners acknowledge that its employment potential is less than that in the mining and agricultural sectors in the province and in Sekhukhune District. The predicted job creation is described in minute detail, with the entrance gates being expected to generate 135 jobs in the construction phase and 60 jobs in the operational phase. The employment potential of the Tjate heritage site is more modest with 26 jobs foreseen in the construction phase and 11 jobs in its operational phase.

The prospect of lucrative employment has lured dozens of young people in Sekhukhune to attend 'tourism courses' provided by the infamous fly-by-night colleges: private institutions that dupe young people and their parents into paying large amounts of money for a worthless diploma. In the visitors' register at the Umsobumvo Youth Advisory Centre in Apel, a number of young jobseekers stated that they had a diploma in tourism studies. It seems unlikely that they will find employment in Sekhukhune District in this sector in the near future.

Heritage tourism in Sekhukhune is just one component of a more complex virtual reality. Most municipal websites in South Africa sport elaborate Integrated Development Plans (IDPs) with impressive graphs. Sekhukhune District and Fetakgoma Municipality are no exception. Excited about this wealth of data and policy plans – a stark contrast with the previous paucity of information – I read the IDP and attempted to engage municipal officials in a discussion. However, the IDP obviously was not the product of local policy processes, but of consultants parachuted in from elsewhere. In discussing the IDP, the municipal officer could not be drawn on the employment statistics, social services or agricultural extension services. He kept repeating the same mantra: 'there can be no development without funds'. When pressed for particulars, he responded likewise: 'What does your university do to promote development in Fetakgomo? Why don't you bring us funds?'

9 Ibid.: 35-40.

Obviously, both the heritage tour and the IDP are part of a virtual reality that has only tenuous links with the real-life policies and practices in these newly constituted municipalities. Websites and interactive links are part and parcel of the image of modernity and progress. Supposedly, the interactive links allow for citizen's input and community participation, very much in keeping with official ideology that stresses the importance of consultative policy processes and accountable government. However, numerous attempts to communicate via these website links confirm the impression that the link is a dead alley: either the link cannot be activated, or else no answer is forthcoming. It is not only the struggling rural municipalities that have spun a web of virtual realities. I have similar experiences with the website of Mogale City (ex-Krugersdorp), an urban municipality not far from Johannesburg.[10] In Mogale City, authorities as well as numerous local residents jealously watch the impressive flow of tourists to nearby Soweto and feel entitled to their slice of tourist revenue. The impressive achievements of South Africa's tourist industry have inspired a virtual world created by local authorities who claim their share of the ever-growing tourism cake.

10 Incidentally, bouncing or non-responding website links and addresses are of course a universal feature, all too common not only in South Africa but also in my own part of the world.

REFERENCES

Bothma, C.V. 'The Political Structure of the Pedi of Sekhukhuneland', *African Studies* 35 (1976), 3-4: 177-205.

Delius, Peter. *The Land Belongs to Us* (Johannesburg: Ravan Press, 1983).

—— *A Lion amongst the Cattle: Reconstruction and Resistance in the Northern Transvaal* (Johannesburg: Ravan Press, 1996).

Government Communications, *South Africa Yearbook 2004/05* (Pretoria: Government Communications, 2004).

Greater Sekhukhune District Municipality, 2025 Development Strategy.

Hunt, D.R. 'An Account of the Bapedi', *Bantu Studies*, December 1931.

Mönnig, H.O. *The Pedi* (Pretoria: Van Schaik, 1988).

Statistics South Africa, *Stats in brief 2008* (Pretoria: Statistics South Africa, 2008).

Van Beek, W.E.A. 'Approaching African Tourism; Paradigms and Paradoxes', in P. Chabal, U. Engel & L. de Haan, eds., *African Alternatives* (Leiden, Brill, 2007), 145-172.

Van Kessel, Ineke. *'Beyond our Wildest Dreams': The United Democratic Front and the Transformation of South Africa* (Charlottesville/London: University Press of Virginia, 2000).

PART II
At the Fringe
of the Parks

6 • Hosts & guests:
Stereotypes & myths of international tourism in the Okavango Delta, Botswana

Joseph Mbaiwa

Introduction

Developing countries of Latin America, Asia and Africa are the fastest growing destinations of international tourist. About 30 per cent of all international tourist arrivals are in developing countries; this proportion has nearly tripled over the past 20 years.[1] Marketing of tourism destinations in developing countries is largely done by multinational tour operators, travel agencies, and other intermediaries with origins in developed countries. Promotional materials used by these agencies create particular images about destinations in developing countries. As Morgan & Pritchard[2] state, the '...images of tourism destinations in developing countries ... tend to reflect a western, white, male, colonial perspective', whereby '... a dynamic First World contrasts itself with a static, timeless and unchanging Third World.' The representation of developing countries in tourism promotional materials has resulted in myths and stereotypes being formed by international tourists about destinations in developing countries. The images and representation of tourism destinations of developing countries are part of the tourist bubble, which, as Cohen[3] argues allows tourists 'to experience the novelty of the macroenvironment of a strange place from the security of a familiar environment.'

In the last 10-15 years, the Okavango Delta has become one of the major tourism destinations for international tourists in Botswana. Tourism attractions in the Okavango Delta include the rich wildlife diversity and scenic beauty of the area. Cultural tourism, though at infant stage, is beginning to take shape and is based on local culture especially that of the San (Basarwa) communities. The Okavango Delta as an international tourism destination has developed a recognisable tourist bubble in order for the tourist to experience their stay in the wetland comfortably. The tourist bubble in essence is a physical space[4]: 'a tourist bubble is a place designed exclusively for tourists and

---

1 Figures from WTO 1999-2009.
2 Nigel Morgan and Annette Pritchard, *Tourism Promotion and Power: Creating Images, Creating Identities* (Chichester: Wiley, 1998), 168, 242.
3 Cohen, Eric. "Towards a Sociology of International Tourism", *Social Research* 39, 1 (1972): 166.
4 See Cohen, 'Towards a Sociology'; Joseph E. Mbaiwa, 'Enclave Tourism and its Socio-economic Impacts in the Okavango Delta, Botswana', *Tourism Management*, 26(2005): 157-72;

those who serve them ... which presupposes some kind of territorial separation and home-like travel institutions premeditated to evade or soften the culture shocks or experience of otherness to which international travel and holiday displacement may lead' (Jaakson 2003: 46). Here I analyse the relationship between international tourists (guests) and locals (hosts) in the Okavango Delta, Botswana, focusing on the myths and stereotypes international tourists (guests) cherish about their hosts (locals) during safari visits there. In order to capture the specific and often contradictory nature of this tourist encounter, I use post-colonial theory, an approach in which the notion of the tourist bubble fits well.

Post-colonial theory

Post-colonial theory is built on the insight that colonialism has been and remains one of the most compelling influences on the industrialised countries' interpretations of and interactions with people from non-western cultures, and serves in several academic disciplines to explain the relationship and attitudes between former colonies in Africa, Latin America and Asia and their ex-colonisers. Thus it explores the polarities between industrialised and non-industrialised countries, 'civilised' and 'uncivilised' societies, 'developed' and 'undeveloped' countries. Post-colonial theory uses these polarities to analyse the historical stages exploration, exploitation, colonisation and civilisation of people in developing countries.[5]

Originating in cultural studies, the theory has expanded into other academic areas such as literature, cultural studies, political science, ethnology, education, history and tourism studies. Said's *Orientalism* (1978) is regarded as the paradigm study for post-colonial theory. Said's work uncovered the pejorative and romantic elements that emerged in the complicated encounter between the colonial European powers and colonies such as those in the Middle East. Hall & Tucker[6] indicate that post-colonial theory represents three main areas, language, place and identity.

In tourism studies, post-colonial theory is new and not yet widely used, but catching on. Echtner & Prasad[7] use it to describe myths created for marketing of tourism destinations in developing countries, Milne & Ateljevik[8] note the problems of colonial thinking

Dennis Judd, 'Constructing the Tourist Bubble', in D. Judd and S. Fainstein, eds., *The Tourist City* (New Haven: Yale University Press, 1999), 35-53.

5   Charlotte Echtner and Pushkala Prasad, 'The Context of Third World Tourism Marketing', *Annals of Tourism Research*, 30(2003): 660-82.

6   Michael Hall and H. Tucker, eds., *Tourism and Postcolonialism* (London: Routledge, 2004).

7   Echtner and Prasad, 'The Context'.

8   Simon Milne and Irena Ateljevik, 'Tourism, Economic Development and the Global-Local Nexus: Theory Embracing Complexity', *Tourism Geographies*, 3 (2001): 369-93.

in describing tourism and economic development. For McRae[9] post-colonialism provides a rethinking of tourism development in developing countries, particularly in issues of identity, authenticity, exile and displacement. The glaring distinction between international tourists from industrialised countries and the places, cultures and people they visit in developing countries, according to Hall & Tucker[10] easily lead into a post-colonial discourse through the very nature and implications of the cultural, political and economic encounters that are intrinsic to the tourist experience. After all, issues of identity, contestation and representation are increasingly recognised as central to the nature of tourism[11]. Lanfant[12] recognises that tourism occupies an increasingly central place within the North-South dialogue, as part of the new world economic order and as such a matter of debate in current global issues.

Post-colonial theory retrieves the colonial past through myths and attitudes which western societies construct about people in former colonies and developing nations. Echtner & Prasad[13] identify three myths, which will inform this chapter: the myth of the unchanged timeless local culture, traditional as it was supposed to be during the pre-colonial eras; the myth of the uncivilised backward cultures, different from the modernised western lifestyle; and, finally, the myth of the unrestrained, where western societies expect their actions (e.g. exploration or hunting) not to be controlled or prohibited. Through these myths, visitors expect local cultures and natural environments to be unaffected by western modernisation. Traditional cultures are expected to remain backward, uncivilised and static in an almost 'timeless' scenario. The physical environment is viewed as a complete wilderness, full of untamed and dangerous animals which form part of the tourist adventure and safari in developing countries, especially Africa. The myths described by Echtner & Prasad find their expression in the tourist bubble, as the materialisation of the expectations and experiences of tourists about their safari visits. Jaakson[14] argues that the term tourist bubble is also used with a psychological focus on the tourists' attitudes. So, the stereotypes and myths which international tourists harbour about, for example, the Okavango Delta, their motivations, attitudes and belief system, are part of the bubble. This chapter, therefore, interrogates the motivations, attitudes and belief system of international tourists about the people and the Okavango Delta.

9   Leanne McRae, 'Rethinking Tourism', *Tourist Studies*, 3 (2003): 235-51.
10 Michael Hall and H. Tucker, eds., *Tourism and Postcolonialism* (London: Routledge, 2004).
11 David Drakakis-Smith and Wyn Williams eds., *Internal Colonialism: Essays around a Theme* (Edinburgh, Institute of British Geographers, 1983); Chris Dixon and Michael Heffernam, *Colonialism and Development in the Contemporary World* (London: Mansell, 1991).
12 Marie-Francoise Lanfant et al., *International Tourism: Identity and Change*, (London: Sage Publications, 1995).
13 Echtner & Prasad 'The Context'.
14 Reiner Jaakson, 'Beyond the Tourist Bubble? Cruiseship Passengers in Port', *Annals of Tourism Research*, 31(2003): 45.

The Okavango Delta

I carried out this study in the Okavango Delta, in north-western Botswana (Figure 6.1). If a tourist bubble is 'a place designed exclusively for tourists and those who serve them',[15] then the Delta fits very well into this description. The Okavango Delta is the physical space or environment which international tourists visit to satisfy their psychological needs and in recent years it has become a key destination in Botswana. The Delta is formed by the inflow of the Okavango River which originates from the Angolan Highlands, and drains into north-western Botswana in the huge wetland known as the Okavango Delta, covering an area of about 16,000 square kilometres. The landscape is characterised by large stretches of open water and grasslands which sustain human life, plant life, wildlife, birds, insects, a huge biodiversity: 1300 identified plant species, 71 fish, 33 amphibian, 64 reptile, 444 bird and 122 mammal species.[16] The Delta is also home to 124,712 people who live within and around it),[17] over 95 per cent of whom directly or indirectly depend on the natural resources of the wetland for their livelihoods (through the collection of plants, fishing and flood recession farming).[18]

Due to its rich wildlife diversity, permanent water resources, rich grasslands and forests and scenic landscapes,[19] the Okavango Delta has become one of the key international tourism destinations in Botswana, and it is here that I will apply the three myths identified above.

The myth of the unchanged

In the myth of the unchanged, destinations in Third World countries are firmly fixed in the past and are represented by timeless places, allowing tourists to seek 'exotic and authentic' cultural experiences. Through both the verbal and visual representations, the tourist expects to find the mystical secrets of legendary lands and to marvel at exotic people. In the Okavango Delta, this desire is met by the presence of traditional villages, dug-out canoes, handicraft, performances and heritage sites. Traditional villages are in fact tourist lodges that provide services such as accommodation in traditional huts,

15 Reiner Jaakson, 'Beyond the Tourist Bubble', 46.
16 Department of Environmental Affairs (2008).
17 Central Statistic Office, *National Population and Housing Census*, (Gaborone: Ministry of Finance and Development Planning, 2002). North West District Council, NWDC. *District Development Plan Six 2003/4-2008/9* (Maun: North West District Council, 2003).
18 Donald Letsholo Kgathi et al., *Rural Livelihoods, Indigenous Knowledge Systems, and Political Economy of Access to Natural Resources in the Okavango Delta, Botswana* (Maun: University of Botswana, 2004), 169.
19 Joseph E. Mbaiwa and Lollies Sakuze, 'Cultural Tourism and Livelihood Diversification: The Case of Gcwihaba Caves and XaiXai Village in the Okavango Delta, Botswana', *Journal of Tourism and Cultural Change*, 7 (2009): 61-75.

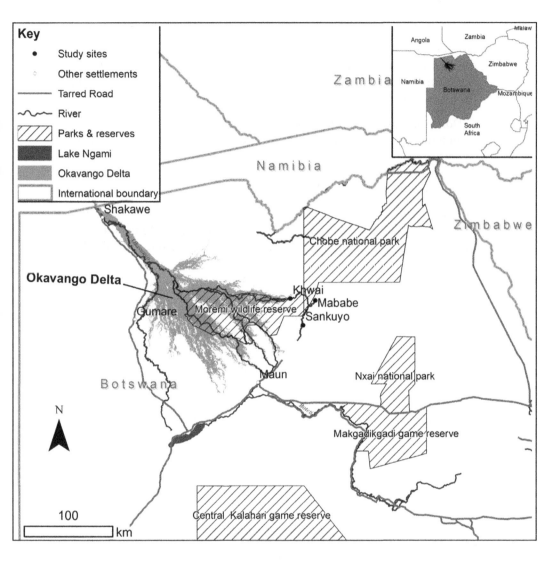

6.1 *Map of the Okavango Delta*

traditional dishes, music and dance, walking trails, animal tracking and traditional transportation in *mekoro* (wooden dug-out canoes) in river channels of the Delta. Curio shops sell traditionally made souvenirs such as baskets, wood engraved products, beads, bows and arrows. For instance, Mbiromo Lodge, owned by the Okavango Poler's Trust, is located in the northern parts of the Delta, and sports thatched chalets, where tourists can imagine themselves in an African traditional hut. The main tourist attractions include the *mekoro* safaris and accommodation in traditional huts. The dug-out canoe has been the traditional means of transport for communities living in the Okavango Delta for hundreds of years; for example, the Bayei used it for hunting hippos[20] and for transportation in the Okavango River channels.

20 Thomas Tlou, *History of Ngamiland: 1750 – 1906. The Formation of an African State* (Gaborone: Macmillan Publishing Company, 1985).

The *mokoro* has in recent years become very popular with international tourists who want to experience traditional travel within the channels of the Okavango River. In its September 2009 issue, Air Botswana's in-flight magazine known as *Peolwane* had an article of '10 must-do's of the Okavango Delta', stating:

> Don't pass up the *mokoro*. In this traditional dugout canoe, you will feel an intimacy with Nature such as you have never felt before. Your time in the water will be blissfully tranquil, and supremely relaxing, and you will glean some insights into incredible diversity of land and water vegetation in the Delta[21] (Peolwane 2009; 16).

The use of *mekoro* as a key tourist activity is one way in which the myth of the unchanged is expressed in the Okavango Delta, showing the history of the people while providing an appealing insight for visitors about local how people used to move in the Delta.

Traditional huts have also become a key item, especially regarding the San (Basarwa) or the so-called 'Bushmen'. Gudigwa Camp is one example where traditional Basarwa culture is sold to tourists, consisting of eight chalets in the form of traditional Basarwa huts. The Camp serves local dishes, walking trails that teach visitors about San animal tracking and hunting and sells bows and arrows as souvenirs. Although traditional villages play a significant role in reviving and preserving the local culture, they also serve as means to perpetuate the myth of the unchanged, providing tourists with a historic image of Botswana that has long passed.

Baskets are one traditional product that is popular among tourists. Basket making is a traditional activity for different ethnic groups, and baskets were traditionally produced for local use in most of Botswana before colonialisation of the country by the British.[22] Through tourist demand for 'authentic' cultural artefacts, baskets have become commercialised in the last 20-30 years (Mbaiwa 2004b), and are an icon of local cultural artefacts in Botswana tourism.

Of course, the local culture has changed, so has to be staged for tourists, even baskets. Terry argues that tourism development changes basket-making designs in the Delta, in order to suit the desires of tourists. Few traditional designs of the 1970s still exist, as traditional designs known as 'urine trail of the bull', 'night and day', 'tears of the giraffe', and 'back of the python' have disappeared. Terry shows that designs such as round and oval trays, French bread baskets, hot pad mats, table mats, waste paper baskets, gas cylinder covers, necklaces made with palm woven beads and wooden beads, which were developed and promoted in the 1980s and early 1990s are no longer

21 *Peolwane*, Air Botswana's In-flight Magazine, September Issue, (Gaborone: Air Botswana, 2009).
22 Elisabeth Terry, 'The Botswana Handicraft Industry: Moving from the 20th to the 21st Century', in John Hermans and Doreen Nteta, eds., *Botswana in the 21st Century*, (Gaborone: Botswana Society, 1994). Elisabeth Terry, 'The Economic and Social Significance of the Handicraft Industry in Botswana', (PhD diss., University of London, 1999).

available in the Okavango. The commodification of basket making led to some upgrading of basket weaving skills in the production of a small array of designs that sell well in the market.[23] This commoditisation of culture resulted in 'staged authenticity' where traditional products were modified products to suit tourist taste.

6.2 A Mosarwa man harvesting a wild fruit.
(© Steven W. Stockhall)

The myth of the unrestrained

The myth of the unrestrained, as part of the tourist bubble, hints at total indulgence in the wishes of tourists, an indulgence expressed in the marketing brochures and websites of tour operators. For example, a luxurious lodge in the Okavango Delta advertises its services in a brochure with the message: '*Let us spoil you.*' The same safari company advertises its five star accommodation facility of Xaranna Okavango Delta Camp as follows:

> The Okavango Delta is simply an unbeatable travel destination. Its stunning natural beauty, wealth of animal and bird life, coupled with its utter seclusion and wilderness surroundings, makes it an out-of-this-world experience. Add to it the exotic beauty of Xaranna, with luxurious tents, plush accessories and enchanting atmosphere, and you have the memory of a lifetime.

23   Joseph E. Mbaiwa, 'Prospects of Basket Production in Promoting Sustainable Rural livelihoods in the Okavango Delta, Botswana' *International Journal of Tourism Research*, 6 (2004a): 221-35.

Thus, in the myth of the unrestrained, the destination is portrayed as comprehensible, comfortable and completely enjoyable, with a pristine nature. The luxurious resorts entice tourist to be self-indulgent and sensuous. People in these areas are friendly, always smiling and are always willing to cater to every tourist need, and the resorts offer amenities to satisfy every sensual desire, whether active or passive, in short a 'paradise', 'unspoiled', and 'sensuous'.[24] In the Okavango Delta, tourist brochures and magazines (e.g. *The Tourist*) published by the Hospitality and Tourism Association of Botswana (HATAB) indicate that resorts in wildlife areas provide services such as game drives, walking trails, traditional dug-out canoe transportation, safari hunting, fishing, bird watching, motor boating cruises and many other nature tourism services, set in luxurious accommodation made of superior tents, reeds and thatched with local grass. Because of the services offered, marketing brochures of various companies and magazines such as *The Tourist* advertise wildlife areas such as the Okavango Delta as 'The Jewel of Africa, The Last Paradise, The Last Eden, The Exotic and Unspoiled Wilderness'. As an example, the text in the Air Botswana in-flight magazine on '10 must do of the Okavango Delta':

> Your game drives are the mainstay of the safari. Your encounters with the animals seem so immediate and intense. Here you clearly recognize that you are in their territory, on their terms, and you want to tread softly and leave as little impact as possible. The scenes can go from idyllic, as you watch a herd of zebra peacefully grazing the tall grasslands, to soft and tender, as you watch a mother lioness and her cubs ritually greeting each other, to amusing, as you watch a dominant male impala impatiently rounding up his harem.[25]

The location should resemble an 'unchanged' natural environment, so these facilities are constructed in the thickest of the forests along river channels and lagoons of the Okavango River. However, the tourist does not want to lose his habitual comfort, modern bedding, bath tubs, showers and toilets, hence all these facilities and services are provided in wilderness areas like the Okavango Delta.

Marketing brochures and tourism magazines provide pictures and images of a wild nature with meandering channels , forests and of course the large mammals: lion, elephant, buffalo, zebra, giraffe and flocks of antelopes and countless birds. They also show the accommodation located within forests, with restaurants overlooking channels or lagoons with wildlife converging at the water points. In the myth of the unrestrained the destination is not only romanticised and comfortable, but, as Echtner & Prasad note,[26] tourists are promised unfettered access to abundant nature, well-equipped amenities

---

24 Stephen Britton, 'The Political Economy of Tourism in the Third World', *Annals of Tourism Research*, 9 (1982): 318.
25 *Peolwane* Air Botswana inflight, 16
26 Echtner & Prasad 'The Context', 672

and submissive hosts. This holds well in Botswana's wildlife areas. Accommodation facilities and services in wildlife areas are designed to meet the expectations of visitors. These are of an exotic and unspoiled wilderness nature and nice food served to them in the hot African sun and wilderness. Some of the tourists also enjoy the experience of wild and dark African night where the sounds of different animals are heard throughout the night. For example, a mother with her family in *Peolwane* writes:

> Night game drives are allowed in many private concessions, but not in national parks. Here your world opens up to the myriad nocturnal species that begin their quest for food when the sun goes down – from kangaroo-like springhare, to the rabbit-like scrub hare, to the tree-hopping bush babies, to the whooping and howling hyenas, to the roaring lions...while you are at it, look up into the extraordinary night skies of Botswana. Try to remember to take along a book to identify the planets, constellations and galaxies of the southern skies, and have a go at identifying them – as you are bowled over by their brilliance.[27]

So, tourism operators do not want to restrain tourists in their experiences, day and night. Although night activities are not allowed by the Department of Wildlife and National Parks (Mbaiwa, 2002), the desire not to restrain tourist experience has resulted in some tour operators conducting illegal activities to serve the interest of their clients. The myth of the unrestrained is part of the tourist bubble, and life should be different in the bubble.

The myth of the uncivilised

In the myth of the uncivilised, the tourist undertakes an expedition into an almost primordial place, where civilisation is largely absent and the natives are savage. The landscapes are supposedly severe, covered with inhospitable and bizarre vegetation that harbours rare and often dangerous animals, Echtner & Prasad argue that the primordial, pristine nature of these Third World destinations must be presented. Bruner stresses that in this myth, the local inhabitants must appear in a primitive state 'despite the industrial revolution, colonization, wars of independence, nationalism, the rise of new countries, economic development, tourism and the entire production of modern technology'.[28] In the Okavango Delta, some Basarwa communities such as those of Khwai and Gudigwa have been relocated from the inner parts of the Okavango Delta to its peripheral areas in the establishment of Moremi Game Reserve.[29] However, the San culture

---

[27] *Peolwane*, Inflight 2009:16.
[28] Edward Bruner, 'Transformation of Self in Tourism', *Annals of Tourism Research*, 18(1991): 239.
[29] Mbaiwa et al., 2008; Joseph E. Mbaiwa, 'Tourism Development, Rural Livelihoods and Conservation in the Okavango Delta, Botswana', (PhD Diss., Texas A&M University, 2008). Joseph

6.3 *Basarwa women dressed in animal skins and walking in a line.*

(© Steven W. Stockhall)

of hunting and gathering remains very marketable for international tourists from developed countries visiting Botswana and Okavango Delta. In 2003, a marketing manager at Okavango Wilderness Safaris (one of the largest tour companies in Botswana, owning 22 lodges in the Delta) remarked about the San culture at Gudigwa Lodge as a tourist product: 'There is no doubt that the product is a hit. It is selling well to our clients.' Air Botswana's in-flight magazine in 2008 published articles about the hunting and gathering community of XaiXai in the Okavango Delta. The photographs in this chapter show this community. International tourists who visit the Okavango Delta expect to see this 'backward and uncivilised' culture that has managed to withstand all the influence of modern technology. The Basarwa are shown gathering wild foods while wearing animal skins, tracking wild animals during hunting expeditions and enjoying their night song and dances in the thickest of the forests . Thus tourists get a glimpse of the Basarwa as part of nature, undisturbed by any western influence, a 'staged authenticity'[30] that is an integral part of the tourist bubble.

Of course, the photographs do not show an actual situation, as Basarwa culture has changed over time. For example, they now wear western clothes, and no longer use bows and arrows for hunting, but rely on western-made guns.

E. Mbaiwa and Molefe Ranstundu, *A Socio-economic Baseline Study of the Bukakhwe Cultural Conservation Trust in the Okavango Delta* (Maun: University of Botswana, 2003).
30 Bruner & Kirschenblatt-Gimblett (1994) elaborated on this notion, writing about the commoditisation of culture among the Maasai in Kenya.

Figure 6.4 Basarwa hunting gear.
(© Steven W. Stockhall)

The need to enjoy an uncivilised and possible dangerous nature creates a sense of ambivalence in tourists. On the one hand they want to enjoy the wilderness while on the other hand they fear its hostile life. They are well aware that the wilderness where they take game drives and walking trails is also home to dangerous animals. The walking trails in the forests are a particular case in point. In these walks, tourists know that the forest is dangerous, for instance through snakes and dangerous animals, and have mixed feelings about the adventure. Nevertheless, tourists love to walk in these forests to experience the savageness of the African wilderness; it is an experience they cherish so that they can tell a story back home. This very ambivalence is crucial in any bubble, in Cohen's words:[31] 'Tourists would like to experience the novelty of the macroenvironment of a strange place from the security of a familiar environment.'

The three myths generate a notion of otherness that was and still is inextricably linked to the accounts of travels and explorations in imperial lands. So the mythical creation of a destination is the process by which places have become incorporated within the global tourist system.[32] In the myth of the uncivilised, destination areas in developing areas are presented as static and backward, associated with the age of colonial exploration and expeditions; so modern day tourists are like explorers, hunters, traders, scientists, anthropologists

31 Cohen, 'Towards a Sociology', 166.
32 Hall & Tucker, *Tourism and Colonialism*.

and missionaries of old, and in modern times can participate in expeditions to discover and explore these frontiers.

For the myth of the uncivilised, the variety of wildlife species in the Okavango Delta is crucial, as the abundance of wildlife provide tourists with a good frontier for sport or trophy hunting and photographic safaris. Thus, tourists who desire to hunt in wilderness areas like the colonial hunters and traders of old, pay handsome figures to get the experience of hunting for leisure in an African jungle. These tourists visit the Okavango Delta not only to see the Big Five (elephant, buffalo, leopard, rhino, lion) but also to shoot them as trophies. A website of a safari hunting company[33] notes:

> The term 'Big Five' refers to five of Africa's greatest wild animals - lion, leopard, elephant, buffalo and rhino. As during the bygone hunting era the term 'Big Five' still conjure[s] up the romance and excitement of Africa's exotic destinations and experiences.

The hunting industry in the Okavango Delta is largely shaped by western investors. Scout Wilson Consultants[34] note that safari hunting in the Okavango Delta started in the United States, and hunters and operators from all over the world attend the Safari Club International (SCI) convention in January every year to decide how many animals should be sold for hunting in Botswana. At this convention, safari hunting companies operating in the Okavango Delta sell their hunts for up to two or three years in advance. The majority of the safari hunters are Americans, followed by Spanish and Italians. The trade in hunting trophies and animals to be hunted is decided between safari hunting companies and safari hunters without the participation of local people in the Okavango Delta; in effect safari companies shape wildlife hunting policy in Botswana, thus perpetuating the colonial legacy where decisions about developing countries were taken in the colonial centres (in most cases without the involvement of local people).

Displacement of traditional societies was one of the characteristics of colonialism, as Hall & Tucker[35] note, because of the process of colonial settlement and migration, by slavery, or by cultural denigration and oppression by the colonial society. As stated, in Botswana, Basarwa (San) communities were displaced in the Okavango Delta, being relocated from inner parts of the Delta to their present site on the outskirts.[36] The aim of all these changes was to give way for wildlife and tourism development. As such, tourism development deeply affects the identity and history of local people, for in displacement, identities of places and individuals come to be

33 http://www.places.co.za/html/famousbig5.html
34 Scout Wilson Resource Consultants, *Environmental Impact Assessment of Veterinary fences in Ngamiland Report*, (Gaborone: Scott Wilson Resource Consultants and Environment and Development Group, (2000), 189.
35 Hall & Tucker, *Tourism and Colonialism*.
36 Mbaiwa 2002; Joseph Mbaiwa and Molefe Ranstundu, *A Socio-economic Baseline*; Mbaiwa, *The Socio-Economic and Environmental Impacts of Tourism Development in the Okavango Delta, Botswana: A Baseline Study* (Maun: University of Botswana), 144.

contested and negotiated. The cultural identity (e.g. in the burial grounds, hunting areas) of the people of Gudigwa and Khwai has been affected by their forced removal from the Moremi Game Reserve.[37]

The displacement of traditional societies in order to create wildlife sanctuaries and tourism zones has also been carried out by Botswana's post-colonial governments. The forced relocation of the Basarwa (San) from their ancestral land in the Central Kalahari Game Reserve (CKGR) by the Botswana Government to the new settlements of Kaudwane and New Xade, outside the reserve, in 1997 and 2002 demonstrates this phenomenon: the government's purpose was partly to promote wildlife conservation and international tourism in the CKGR.[38] As *The Sunday Standard* (one of Botswana's leading newspapers) in its issue of Sunday 2 May 2010, noted: 'The Government of Botswana has leased land to Wilderness Safaris (a multinational tourism company operating in Southern, Central and Eastern Africa), allowing them to build a lodge on Basarwa land, based on an agreement signed in 2008' (construction of the lodge has since been completed and it is currently in operation). While the Basarwa have been displaced from the CKGR, this reserve is being developed as an international tourism destination.

The response of hosts

The local communities and the general population of Botswana respond differently to international tourism in the Okavango Delta. For example, the Botswana Government perceives tourism as 'an engine of economic growth' and as a means to diversify Botswana's economy from reliance on mining – particularly diamond mining.[39] Thus the Botswana Government supports international tourism in places such as the Okavango Delta for its ability to generate foreign exchange, employment opportunities, encourage infrastructure development and promote rural development.[40] Some rural communities involved in community-based tourism projects such as those of Khwai, Sankoyo and Mababe, also perceive international tourism as a means to improve their livelihoods.

The government's view has led to an increase in accommodation and tourism activities to meet the growing demand of international tourists in the Okavango Delta. Data from the Department of Tourism[41]

---

37 Joseph Mbaiwa, *Tourism Development*.
38 Clifford Maribe, 'The Relocation of the Basarwa from the Central Kalahari Game Reserve'. Paper Presented at the South African Broadcasting Association's Eleventh General Assembly, Johannesburg, South Africa, 13 October 2003.
39 Government of Botswana, *The Tourism Policy. Government Paper No. 2 of 1990* (Gaborone: Government Printer, 1990).
40 Joseph Mbaiwa, *Tourism Development*.
41 Department of Tourism, DOT, *Botswana Tourism Master Plan: Final Report* (Gaborone: Department of Tourism, 2000).

indicate that the number of international tourists to Botswana's wilderness areas increased by 90 per cent over a five-year period: from 106,800 in 1993 to 203, 172 in 1998. In 2009, a total of 272, 799 tourists visited Botswana and of this total, 27 per cent, or 73, 656 tourists, visited the Okavango Delta in 2009,[42] making the Delta the second largest leisure destination in Botswana after the Kasane/ Chobe region. In 2009, Botswana had a total of 380 licensed and fixed tourist accommodation facilities providing 6,511 rooms and 11,275 beds. From this total, 116 accommodation facilities with 1,125 rooms and 2,129 beds were located in the Okavango Delta.[43] Apparently, in 1989 there were just 32 accommodation facilities in that region.[44] This increased to 63 accommodation facilities in 2001, 73 in 2004 and to 116 in 2009. The Okavango Delta is the second largest region in terms of the highest number of accommodation facilities, rooms and beds after the Gaborone City area (Botswana's capital city and environs). The growth of international tourism and international tourist numbers in Botswana's wildlife areas has in the process led to a booming tourist economy built around what is perceived internationally as a 'new' and 'exotic' wilderness destination. Up-market tourists visit the Okavango Delta and in the process have created an exclusive, enclave tourism in the wetlands, confirming observations by Judd[45] that 'The tourist bubble creates islands of affluence that are sharply differentiated and segregated from the surrounding urban landscapes'. High poverty levels in the outskirts of the Okavango Delta point to the separation between the affluence and exclusivity of tourism industry and sur- rounding poor communities. The CSO[46] notes that over 60 per cent of the households in the Okavango Delta live in poverty, earning less than one US dollar a day.

The image of Botswana's wildlife areas as 'exotic and unspoiled' can be attributed to the marketing strategy adopted by both the Botswana Government and tourism companies. The government has engaged 'professional marketing companies in North America, Germany and the United Kingdom to promote the country's tourism industry',[47] which explains why the majority of the tourists and operators come from Europe, North America, New Zealand and Australia. As Mowforth & Munt (1998) argue, tourism development in developing countries is about power and domination between developed and developing countries.[48] This suggests that tourist experiences in the Okavango Delta are somehow determined by international tourism

42 Department of Tourism, DOT, A Statistical Review of Tourism 2009 (Gaborone: Department of Tourism, 2010).
43 Department of Tourism, DOT, A Statistical Review of 2009 (Gaborone: Department of Tourism, 2010).
44 Joseph Mbaiwa, 'Enclave Tourism'.
45 Judd, 'Constructing the Tourist Bubble', 45.
46 Central Statistics Office, National Population.
47 NWDC. District Development, 243.
48 Martin Mowforth, and Ian Munt, Tourism and Sustainability: New Tourism in the Third World (London: Routledge, 1998).

companies with the support of the Botswana Government.

Some people in Botswana have responded negatively to international tourism mainly because of its enclave aims. That is, tourism that develops in remote areas and is largely owned and controlled by outsiders (e.g. expatriates) has in recent literature been referred to as 'enclave tourism',[49] set up in remote areas in which the types of facilities and their physical location fail to take into consideration the needs and wishes of surrounding communities. The goods and services available are beyond the financial means of local people and any foreign currency created may have only a minimal effect upon the economy of the host location. Enclave tourism has also been referred to as internal colonialism,[50] a phenomenon whereby natural resources in a host region mostly benefit expatriates or outsiders while the majority of the locals are marginalised, financially or otherwise. These facilities are characterised by foreign ownership and are geared to meet the needs and interests of foreign tourists, exactly as has happened in the Okavango Delta. Lanfant[51] notes that international tourism is largely a result of the demand from highly developed, tourist-sending countries, a power position that can be attributed to the globalisation process and higher rates of production and technology – especially the transport system – in the industrialised world.[52] So, in effect, the growth of international tourism in Botswana in the last two decades is a result of the high consumption rate in such countries. The wildlife-rich areas of Botswana, particularly in the Okavango Delta and Chobe regions, have thus become goods to be consumed by tourists from the 'first' world.

The expensive nature of the tourism industry in the Okavango Delta makes it difficult for citizens to invest in tourism because of lack of capital investment and entrepreneurship skills such as marketing and management. As such, non-citizen companies which have the necessary skills and capital to invest in tourism are the main owners of tourism facilities in the Okavango Delta, resulting in foreign domination of the industry and a loss of local control over resources.[53] The absence of autonomy is arguably the most negative long-term effect of tourism. A permanent dweller may suffer alienation, as his/her surroundings are transformed by a foreign-dominated tourism industry. The local people in the Okavango region feel that the delta has been taken from them by the government and given to foreign tour operators, so they view the domination by non-citizens as a

49 Hector Cebalos-Lascurain, *Tourism, Ecotourism and Protected Areas* (Gland: IUCN Publication, 1996).
50 Drakakis-Smith & Williams, *Internal Colonialism*; C. Dixon & M. Hefferman, *Colonialism and Development in the Contemporary World* (London: Mansell, 1991).
51 Lanfant et al., *International Tourism*.
52 Ning Wang, *Tourism and Modernity: A Sociological Analysis* (New York: Pergamon, 2000).
53 Jeffry Glasson et al., *Towards Visitor Impact Management: Visitor Impacts, Carrying Capacity and Management Responses in Europe's Historic Towns and Cities* (England: Avebury, 1995).

'sell-out' of their resources. Butler, Prosser and Ceballos-Lascurain[54] all note that resentment, antagonisms and alienation often emerge between the host communities and international tourism as a result of this exclusion. The resentment of local communities towards tourism development in the Okavango Delta became clearer in 2011 when the a Taskforce Committee of the Department of Museum and Monuments (of which I was a member) addressed a total of 36 public consultative meetings in various villages around the Okavango Delta as part of a process of listing the Okavango Delta as a World Heritage Site. In these meetings, locals asked rhetoric questions such as: 'who owns the delta and who derives most benefits from it? ... government took our delta and gave it to foreign tourism companies ... revenues from tourism in the delta are not used for rural development in the area', and so on.

The tendency of international tourists to indulge into whatever they want conflicts at times with local cultural taboos, showing disrespect for the people of Botswana. For example, in Botswana's wilderness areas, some foreign tourists and tour operators dress in a way that conforms to local norms, while others dress in offending and culturally unacceptable ways for local people. Thus, girls have been influenced to wear miniskirts and clothes that expose parts of their bodies such as the belly and the tops of their breasts. A manager in one of the main supermarkets in Maun in my survey indicated that some tourists pass through Maun to the Okavango Delta 'half-naked'. The man was worried that this way of dressing would be culturally unacceptable especially to the elderly in the area.[55] So by the myth of the unrestrained, tourists influence the dress code in developing countries.

Local writers such as Weinburg[56] comment on the 'false' authenticity of the Basarwa (San) culture, that is being staged rather than being made robust by international visitors: 'It is widely believed that the San or Bushmen still roam the Southern African interior in search of game, unaffected by the outside world.' Weinburg studied the Basarwa communities throughout Southern Africa for more than a decade in an attempt to demonstrate the reality behind the myth of the unchanged, unrestrained and uncivilised perpetuated in popular films, glossy picture books, and in tourism marketing. The result was a remarkable and moving portrayal of a people in transition, clinging to the last vestiges of their culture while trying to adapt to the pressures of the modern world. Weinburg concludes:

---

54   Richard Butler, 'The Concept of a Tourist Area Cycle of Evolution', *Canadian Geographer*, 24(1980): 5-12; Robert Prosser, 'Societal Change and the Growth in Alternative Tourism' in Erlet Cater and Gwen Lowman (eds.), *Ecotourism: A Sustainable Option*, (New York: John Wiley and Sons Ltd, 1994), 19-37; Cebalos-Lascurain, *Tourism, Ecotourism*.

55   Joseph E. Mbaiwa, 'The Socio-cultural Effects of Tourism Development in the Okavango Delta' *Journal of Tourism and Cultural Change*, 2(2004b): 163-184.

56   Paul Weinberg, *In Search of the San* (Johannesburg: The Porcupine Press, 1997).

The lives of the Bushmen have been thoroughly mythologized, obscuring their real circumstances and the fragility of their culture. It is assumed that to continue to function, hunter-gatherer economies require free access to land. The harsh truth is that the majority of the Bushmen have been dispossessed of their traditional land, and almost everywhere, they are struggling to survive, which is the legacy of colonialism.[57]

As noted earlier, the problems of the Basarwa and the loss of their land during British colonial rule of Botswana are being perpetuated by the post-colonial government of Botswana. The repossession of the ancestral land of the Basarwa in the CKGR by the Botswana Government indicates how post-colonialism, international tourism development and wildlife conservation coincide in Botswana, centred around wildlife as Botswana's main international tourist product.

Conclusion

Developing countries endowed with natural resources such as Botswana have increasingly become destination areas for international tourism. In this chapter, I have discussed the relationship between international tourism, destination communities, post-colonial theory and the notion of the tourist bubble. The latter two concepts have led to some effects of the commoditisation of local culture, such as staged authenticity and the dispossession of the inhabitants in destinations such as the Okavango Delta. The international tourists' need to experience novelty and otherness creates stereotypes about destinations in developing countries, and the three myths of the unchanged, unrestrained, and uncivilised determine tourist activities, as well the behaviours and relationships between the 'hosts', the local people in the Okavango, and the 'guests'. Tourists visit this region to experience an 'exotic and pristine' environment where there is unlimited self-indulgence, relaxation, solitude, and otherness to experience.

Finally, I have shown that tourist activities in the Okavango Delta are often staged,[58] as in those relating to the Basarwa culture. Products have been modified to meet to meet the demands and expectations of international tourists. This suggests that the commodification of culture and such activities as basket production for the tourism market have created a 'staged authenticity', undermining genuine cultural products. So the psychological aspects of tourist motivations, attitudes and belief systems, as suggested in the tourist bubble creates the commodification of culture which leads to this phenomemon. This analysis, however, does not undermine the positive socio-economic impacts of international tourism in the Okavango Delta, particularly

---

57 Ibid., ii
58 See Ning Wang, 'Rethinking Authenticity in Tourism Experience', *Annals of Tourism Research* 26 (1999): 349-70.

income generation, employment creation and the inflow of foreign exchange.[59] It is an open question whether the adoption by the Botswana Government of a sustainable tourism approach as a model to guide all forms of tourism development in the Okavango Delta, will really assuage these problems. Though the government aims to develop a tourism industry that promotes environmental conservation and is able to meet socio-cultural and economic needs of all the stakeholders[60] (e.g. tourists, safari companies, local people) in the Okavango Delta, the basic contradictions as shown here, will probably remain.

59 Mbaiwa, Joseph E. and Lollies Sakuze, 'Cultural Tourism and Livelihood Diversification: The Case of Gcwihaba Caves and XaiXai Village in the Okavango Delta, Botswana', *Journal of Tourism and Cultural Change*, 7(2009): 61-75.
60 Joseph E. Mbaiwa, Barbara Ntombi Ngwenya, & Donald Letsholo Kgathi, 'Contending with Unequal and Privileged Access to Natural Resources and Land in the Okavango Delta, Botswana', *Singapore Tropical Geographical Journal*, 29(2008): 155-72.

REFERENCES   Britton, Stephen. 'The Political Economy of Tourism in the Third World', *Annals of Tourism Research*, 9 (1982), 331-58.

Bruner, Edward and Barbara Kirshenblatt-Gimblett. 'Maasai on the Lawn: Tourist Realism in East Africa', *Cultural Anthropology*, 9 (1994): 435-70.

Bruner, Edward. 'Transformation of Self in Tourism', *Annals of Tourism Research*, 18 (1991): 238-50.

Butler, Richard. 'The Concept of a Tourist Area Cycle of Evolution', *Canadian Geographer*, 24 (1980): 5-12.

Cebalos-Lascurain, Hector. *Tourism, Ecotourism and Protected Areas* (Gland: IUCN Publication, 1996).

Central Statistics Office. *Botswana Poverty Map* (Gaborone: Ministry of Finance and Development Planning, 2008).

Central Statistics Office. *National Population and Housing Census* (Gaborone: Ministry of Finance and Development Planning, 2002).

Cohen, Eric. 'Towards a Sociology of International Tourism', *Social Research* 39, 1 (1972): 164-82.

Department of Tourism, DOT. *Botswana Tourism Master Plan: Final Report* (Gaborone: Department of Tourism, 2000).

Department of Tourism, DOT. *A Statistical Review of Tourism 2009* (Gaborone: Department of Tourism, 2010)

Department of Environmental Affairs. *Okavango Delta Management Plan of 2008* (Gaborone: Department of Environmental Affairs).

Dixon, Chris and Michael Heffernan. *Colonialism and Development in the Contemporary World* (London: Mansell, 1991).

Drakakis-Smith, David and Wyn Williams, eds. *Internal Colonialism: Essays around a Theme* (Edinburgh, Institute of British Geographers, 1983).

Echtner, Charlotte and Pushkala Prasad. 'The Context of Third World Tourism Marketing', *Annals of Tourism Research*, 30 (2003): 660-82.

Glasson, J., K. Godfrey, B. Goodey, eds. *Towards Visitor Impact Management: Visitor Impacts, Carrying Capacity and Management Responses in Europe's Historic Towns and Cities* (England: Avebury, 1995).

Government of Botswana. *The Tourism Policy. Government Paper No. 2 of*

1990 (Gaborone: Government Printer, 1990).

Hall, Michael and H. Tucker, eds. *Tourism and Postcolonialism* (London: Routledge, 2004).

Jaakson, Reiner. 'Beyond the Tourist Bubble? Cruiseship Passengers in Port', *Annals of Tourism Research,* 31 (2003): 44-60.

Judd, Dennis. 'Constructing the Tourist Bubble', in D. Judd and S. Fainstein, eds., *The Tourist City* (New Haven CT: Yale University Press, 1999), 35-53.

Lanfant, Marie-Francoise, J.B. Allock, E.M. Bruner. *International Tourism: Identity and Change* (London: Sage Publications, 1995).

Letsholo Kgathi, Donald, H. Bendsen, P. Balikie, J. Mbaiwa, B.N.Ngwenya & J. Wilk. *Rural Livelihoods, Indigenous Knowledge Systems, and Political Economy of Access to Natural Resources in the Okavango Delta, Botswana,* (Maun: Harry Oppenheimer Okavango Research Centre, University of Botswana, 2004), 169.

Maribe, Clifford. 'The Relocation of the Basarwa from the Central Kalahari Game Reserve.' Paper Presented at the South African Broadcasting Association's Eleventh General Assembly, Johannesburg, South Africa, 13 October 2003.

Mbaiwa, Joseph E. 'Tourism Development, Rural Livelihoods and Conservation in the Okavango Delta, Botswana', (PhD diss., Texas A&M University, 2008).

—— 'Enclave Tourism and its Socio-economic Impacts in the Okavango Delta, Botswana', *Tourism Management,* 26 (2005): 157-72.

—— 'Prospects of Basket Production in Promoting Sustainable Rural livelihoods in the Okavango Delta, Botswana', *International Journal of Tourism Research,* 6 (2004): 221-35.

—— 'The Socio-cultural Effects of Tourism Development in the Okavango Delta', *Journal of Tourism and Cultural Change,* 2 (2004): 163-84.

—— *The Socio-Economic and Environmental Impacts of Tourism Development in the Okavango Delta, Botswana: A Baseline Study* (Maun: University of Botswana, 2002), 144.

—— and Molefe Ranstundu. *A Socio-economic Baseline Study of the Bukakhwe Cultural Conservation Trust in the Okavango Delta* (Maun: University of Botswana, 2003).

—— Barbara Ntombi Ngwenya, & Donald Letsholo Kgathi. 'Contending with Unequal and Privileged Access to Natural Resources and Land in the Okavango Delta, Botswana', *Singapore Tropical Geographical Journal,* 29 (2008): 155-72.

—— and Lollies Sakuze. 'Cultural Tourism and Livelihood Diversification: The Case of Gcwihaba Caves and XaiXai Village in the Okavango Delta, Botswana', *Journal of Tourism and Cultural Change,* 7 (2009): 61-75

McRae, Leanne. 'Rethinking Tourism', *Tourist Studies,* 3 (2003): 235-51.

Milne, Simon and Irena. 'Tourism, Economic Development and the Global-Local Nexus: Theory Embracing Complexity', *Tourism Geographies,* 3 (2001): 369-93.

Mowforth, Martin and Ian Munt. *Tourism and Sustainability: New Tourism in the Third World* (London: Routledge, 1998).

Morgan, Nigel and Annette Pritchard. *Tourism Promotion and Power: Creating Images, Creating Identities* (Chichester: Wiley, 1998).

North West District Council, NWDC. *District Development Plan Six 2003/4-*

2008/9 (Maun: North West District Council, 2003).

Peolwane, Air Botswana's In-flight Magazine, September Issue. (Gaborone: Air Botswana, 2009).

Prosser, Robert. 'Societal Change and the Growth in Alternative Tourism', in Erlet Cater and Gwen Lowman, eds., *Ecotourism: A Sustainable Option* (New York: John Wiley and Sons Ltd, 1994), 19-37.

Said, Edward. *Orientalism* (New York: Pantheon, 1978).

Scout Wilson Resource Consultants. *Environmental Impact Assessment of Veterinary fences in Ngamiland Report* (Gaborone: Scott Wilson Resource Consultants and Environment and Development Group, 2000), 189.

Terry, Elisabeth. 'The Botswana Handicraft Industry: Moving from the 20th to the 21st Century', in John Hermans and Doreen Nteta, eds., *Botswana in the 21st Century* (Gaborone: Botswana Society, 1994).

—— 'The Economic and Social Significance of the Handicraft Industry in Botswana', (PhD diss., University of London, 1999).

Tlou, Thomas. *History of Ngamiland: 1750 – 1906. The Formation of an African State* (Gaborone: Macmillan Publishing Company, 1985).

Wang, Ning. 'Rethinking Authenticity in Tourism Experience' *Annals of Tourism Research*, 26 (1999): 349-70.

—— *Tourism and Modernity: A Sociological Analysis* (New York: Pergamon, 2000).

Weinberg, Paul. *In Search of the San* (Johannesburg: The Porcupine Press, 1997).

World Tourism Organization. *Year Book of Tourism Statistics* (Madrid: World Tourism Organization, 2000).

7 · *Kom 'n bietjie kuier*[1]
Kalahari dreaming
with the ≠Khomani San

Kate Finlay and Shanade Barnabas

We had been dreaming about seeing the Kgalagadi Transfrontier Park for many years. Names like the Nossob and Auob rivers have for a long time been only points on a map, and documentaries about wildlife along the two rivers and on the dunes have always attracted our attention... [but !Xaus Lodge] offered a lot more: contact with the ultimate Bushmen.[2]

Introduction

This chapter[3] seeks to discuss issues of representation, relationships between the hosts and tourists, and development involving cultural tourism at !Xaus Lodge; a venture partly owned by the ≠Khomani San.[4] The historical representation of the San has proved influential in the way in which the current ≠Khomani community represent and articulate themselves when engaging with 'outsiders'. We explore the reasoning behind the romantic representation of the ≠Khomani and describe the 'realities' at !Xaus Lodge through our own (as researcher-tourists) and through tourists' experiences.[5] As with tourists to any destination, expectations and resulting experiences vary widely,[6] so too do people's expectations and experiences of meeting with the ≠Khomani. Therefore we do not claim to have a complete understanding of the tourist experience at !Xaus.

1 The English translation of this Afrikaans phrase would be: *Come and visit awhile.*
2 Anna Crova, e-mail message to authors, February 5, 2009: Message to authors from a past guest to !Xaus Lodge. Throughout the rest of the chapter, respondents' names will not be used for reasons of anonymity.
3 The financial assistance of the KwaZulu-Natal University and the National Research Foundation: Social Sciences and Humanities is hereby acknowledged. Opinions and conclusions expressed are those of the authors and not the Foundation. Thanks also to Professor Keyan Tomaselli for his insightful comments.
4 We concentrate on the ≠Khomani community as opposed to the co-owners (the Mier) as a result of the historical representation of the San and the fact that the cultural tourism at the Lodge is largely based on San culture. Since we have received a mixed response from our indigenous respondents regarding the nomenclatures, 'San' and 'Bushman', we have used these terms co-terminously in this chapter.
5 The visitors that frequent !Xaus Lodge are not necessarily cultural tourists as most come to the KTP for the wildlife and the scenic isolation. The fact that !Xaus Lodge is owned by the Mier and ≠Khomani, and offers a ≠Khomani cultural experience through its reconstructed cultural homestead is an added bonus to visitors already interested in visiting the Park, who may desire more comfortable accommodation over a camping experience.
6 There are many international as well as national visitors of various ages (although visitors to the Lodge in their 20s and 30s are not as frequent as those of older age groups).

Our research falls under the *Rethinking Indigeneity* project founded and headed by Professor Keyan Tomaselli at the University of KwaZulu-Natal, South Africa. Research areas in this project include 'development communication, media production and reception, livelihoods and micro-enterprises, community radio as a development medium (particularly among the !Xun and Khwe)[7], and a specific development project: the genesis, establishment and performance of !Xaus Lodge'.[8] Our research is based on this latter development project. The longterm relationship between the research team and the ≠Khomani has produced a wealth of accessible ethnographic knowledge.[9] This, along with our own ethnographic tropes based on visits to the lodge in July 2007 and July 2008, will be included in the following analysis to enable a more nuanced understanding of the running of the lodge and the relationships involved.

The lodge

The lodge, !Xaus, is owned by the ≠Khomani and Mier[10] and was built as a direct outcome of their 1999 land claims. Land in the Kgalagadi Transfrontier Park (KTP) as well as in surrounding areas was awarded to both communities as a result of the South African land reform programme where restored land is granted to 'indigenous' communities that are able to prove that they were forcibly removed from land under the apartheid system . This programme endeavours to return land to people eligible under such acts as the Natives Land Act of 1913.[11] It only considers those who can prove that they were displaced after 1913.[12]

The Bushmen's displacement, however, had begun well before 1913 and had continued well after. Such events as the Cape's thirty-year war between 1770 and 1800 (in which many San became involved), and the private Bushman hunting parties that began in the 17th century, contributed to the near decimation of the southern Kalahari

7 These are Bushman groups formally from Angola and Namibia respectively, and are descendants of those who were co-opted into the South African Defence Force in the Namibian War. Currently, they live in a small settlement in the Northern Cape.

8 Culture, Communication and Media Studies, 'Rethinking Indigeneity', University of KwaZulu-Natal, http://ccms.ukzn.ac.za/index.php?option=com_content&task=view&id=735&Itemid=90.

9 Tomaselli began working with the ≠Khomani in 2000 but has been involved in research with people popularly known as Khoisan since the mid-1990s.

10 The local 'coloured' community who were also land-claim recipients. The term 'coloured' refers to an ethnic group who have a diverse heritage, including lineage from the sub-Sahara peoples, although not enough to be considered 'black' under apartheid (or post-apartheid) law. The four official racial groups in South Africa during and after apartheid remain classified as: African (previously Bantu), White, Indian and Coloured.

11 The Natives' Land Act of 1913 supported the structure of apartheid. It was passed by the South African legislature in order to regulate how 'natives' acquired land.

12 L. Dyll-Myklebust, Lodge-ical Thinking and Development Communication: !Xaus Lodge as a Public-Private Partnership for Community Development in Tourism, (PhD diss., University of KwaZulu-Natal, South Africa, in process).

San.[13] During the 19th and early 20th centuries, the Bushmen's autochthonous relationship with the land changed as a result of the penetration of both European and Baster[14] farmers into the northern periphery of South Africa. Privatisation of land included all natural resources upon it and so helped to enable a new form of wage and forced labour.[15] The creation of the Kalahari Gemsbok National Park (KGP)[16] in 1931, as well as the segregated land policies of apartheid, further stripped the San of their 'traditional' use of land as well as much of their knowledge of the natural environment.[17] These acts of genocide, appropriation of land and various other abuses were supported by the dominant Western representation of Bushmen as degenerates and vermin. In the 20th century, liberal Western opinions began to take hold and Bushmen were represented in a romantic light as a pre-modern hunter-gathering community. This view was popularised through various media and has been used by the Bushmen themselves in cultural tourism ventures over the last few decades. It is still used by cultural tourism ventures such as !Xaus Lodge and by non-governmental organisations (NGOs)[18] in order to obtain funding.

The ≠Khomani land claim settlement agreement was signed on 21 March 1999 and attracted the attention of the world media. Derek Hanekom, Minister for Agriculture and Land Affairs, referred to the first people status of the ≠Khomani in his speech:

> We are here today celebrating more than just the settlement of a land claim. We are celebrating the rebirth of the ≠Khomani San nation...The revival of the language and culture gives proof that ≠Khomani San are who they claim to be: the first people of this country who know the truth about the natural world and the truth about our painful history. Today's settlement emerges from our commitment as a democratic government to face our past and have justice done.

!Xaus Lodge was constructed roughly on the dividing line between the restituted lands of the two communities in the KTP. What

13 Nigel Crawhall, *Written in the Sand: Auditing and Managing Cultural Resources with Displaced Indigenous Peoples: A South African Case Study*, (South African San Institute (SASI), in cooperation with UNESCO's office in Windhoek, 2001), 7.
Andy Smith et al., *The Bushmen of Southern Africa: A Foraging Society in Transition* (Cape Town: David Philip Publishers, 2000), 47-9.
Nigel Penn. '"Fated to Perish": The Destruction of the Cape San', in Pippa Skotnes, ed., *Miscast: Negotiating the Presence of the Bushmen* . (Cape Town: University of Cape Town Press, 1996), 81-91, 83.
14 'Baster' is a term for someone of 'mixed' race (Crawhall 2001, 7).
15 M. C. Schenck, 'Land, Water, Truth, and Love, Visions of Identity and Land Access: From Bain's Bushmen to ≠Khomani San', (BA.Hons. diss. Mount Holyoke College, South Hadley, 2008), 10-12.
16 Now known as the Kgalagadi Transfrontier Park (KTP).
17 Nigel Crawhall, *Written in the Sand: Auditing and Managing Cultural Resources with Displaced Indigenous Peoples: A South African Case Study* (South African San Institute (SASI) in cooperation with UNESCO's office in Windhoek, 2001), 5.
18 Steven Robins, 'NGOs, Bushmen and Double Vision: The ≠Khomani San Land Claim and the Cultural Politics of "Community" and "Development" in the Kalahari', *Journal of Southern African Studies*, 27, 4 (2001): 833-53.

was then called the Department of Environmental Affairs and Tourism (DEAT)[19] assigned 6.5 million Rand to build !Xaus. Many architectural and environmental errors were made in its construction and, as a result, DEAT allocated a further 1.5 million Rand and SANParks another million to finish the lodge.[20] The !Ae!Hai Kalahari Heritage Park Agreement signed by the ≠Khomani Communal Property Association, the Mier Local Municipality, SANParks and the government at Twee Riveren on 29 May 2002, explains that the aim of the lodge is to signify cooperation between the Mier and the ≠Khomani, generate income for these communities and reduce poverty in the region. To aid in this endeavour, a South African company, Transfrontier Parks Destinations (Pty) Ltd (TFPD), signed the !Xaus Lodge contract with the Joint Management Board[21] as the operating party in the agreement[22] in January 2007. At present, both communities benefit from a monthly rental fee paid by the operator and also through the employment of staff working at the lodge and in the re-created cultural homestead. The stakeholders have agreed that after the first ten years of operation, a ≠Khomani and Mier Community Trust will be established to receive a 10% equity stake in !Xaus Lodge's management company.[23]

'The hosts'

Both the Mier and ≠Khomani communities offer cultural experiences at !Xaus Lodge. It is largely the more educated Mier that work at the lodge, attending to the housekeeping, cooking and guests. The cook includes a number of cultural dishes on the !Xaus menu. In comparison the ≠Khomani's cultural offerings include tracking, jewellery making and teaching tourists to shoot with a bow and arrow at the cultural *boma*[24] (about a 5 minute walk away from the lodge). The ≠Khomani at !Xaus Lodge work on a rotational basis; most of the community members live and move between Witdraai,[25] Andriesvale (both about 60 kilometres from the Twee Rivieren gate) and Welkom (a small town just outside the gate to the KTP). The ≠Khomani employees at

19 This is now known as the National Department of Tourism (NDT).
20 Glynn O'Leary, interview at !Xaus Lodge, 13 July 2007.
21 'A Joint Management Board (JMB) was established with the principal parties. These include the ≠Khomani CPA acting on behalf of the ≠Khomani community, the Mier Local Municipality acting on behalf of the Mier community, and South African National Parks (SANParks). The JMB serves as a forum where representatives of the principal parties may discuss and take decisions on a basis of sufficient consensus on aspects subject to the powers and functions of the JMB. The JMB may approve or amend a management plan only with the consent of each principal party' (see footnote 22 for reference).
22 L. Dyll-Myklebust,'Lodge-ical Thinking and Development Communication: !Xaus Lodge as a Public-Private Partnership for Community Development in Tourism', (PhD diss., University of KwaZulu-Natal), 26.
23 !Xaus Lodge. www.xauslodge.co.za (accessed 7 October 2009).
24 A fenced enclosure.
25 A reconstituted farm.

7.1 Oom *(Uncle)*
Gert Swartz making
crafts at the boma
(© Lauren Dyll)

the lodge are part of a sub-group known as the *traditionalists*, who predominantly embrace the romantic 'Bushman' archetype.[26]

The ≠Khomani *boma* also includes a 'traditionally' thatched hut where tourists are received. The lodge management does not impose a dress code on the ≠Khomani; it is their choice to wear traditional outfits if they so wish.[27] Tourists are encouraged to buy crafts, chat to the ≠Khomani if they are familiar with Afrikaans (at times the lodge's host will facilitate communication between Afrikaans and

26 The other sub-group of ≠Khomani, known as the *westerse mense*, are more aligned with the Mier community than with the traditionalists, as both the *westerse mense* and the Mier are farmers and many live in small towns.
27 Glynn O'Leary, e-mail message to authors, 30 January 2009.

English) and are sometimes taught to shoot with a bow and arrow. The wilderness walks are usually led by an ex-SAN Parks ranger aided by a ≠Khomani tracker. While there are accomplished trackers in this community, most of the younger ≠Khomani employees are in training with the ex-ranger, as their knowledge of the bush is not as deep. This is due to the loss of traditional knowledge over time. Furthermore, difficulties with the English language prevent these trackers from conversing freely with the tourists on the wilderness walks. At the time of writing !Xaus Lodge had enrolled two of its ≠Khomani employees (Elvis Swartz and Andot Malgas) at a Western Cape initiative, !Khwa tuu. Both men will be trained as tour guides and trackers at this San Culture and Education Centre.

In the early days of the lodge, the distinction between the Mier and the ≠Khomani was exaggerated by the spatial separation of the two groups: the Mier occupied the staff quarters and attended to the lodge itself while the ≠Khomani remained at the homestead – even living there while working at !Xaus. The Mier were thus afforded more interaction with the tourists while the ≠Khomani's was limited to wilderness walks and time spent at the cultural homestead. Perhaps these disparities amplified the tensions between the two communities. For example, a Mier staff member distanced herself from the ≠Khomani community and told one of the authors in 2007 that the ≠Khomani's drinking habits would have to be closely monitored. This situation, however, is changing; ≠Khomani are slowly being integrated into the lodge itself.

The 'tourist'

When tourists to !Xaus in 2008 and 2009 were interviewed, few made mention of the cultural offerings of the Mier; their comments mainly revolved around the ≠Khomani. The cultural offerings at the *boma* and the guided walk which includes tracking were produced for the benefit of the tourists interested in ≠Khomani 'traditional' culture. These activities help to attract tourists to the lodge. The ≠Khomani also make a profit from selling their jewellery at the cultural homestead and through the lodge's store.

The stakeholders (owners and operators) of !Xaus Lodge are aware of the benefits of 'first people' cultural tourism as seen in the representation of the ≠Khomani in their promotional materials which state that !Xaus draws one into 'the fascinating rituals, traditions and historical culture of these remarkable people, the first people of Southern Africa.'[28] A visitor commented: 'Our decision to visit the lodge was based on the specific promotion of being able to walk with the San people and to learn about their tracking capabilities as

28 !Xaus Lodge 2008 brochure

well as their knowledge of the plant and animal life.'[29] Many visitors are excited at meeting these highly publicised people. The notion of encountering the 'other' is more recently promoted in !Xaus's 2009 website through the use of 'traditionally' stylised San drawings and romantic photographs of ≠Khomani employees. This website is often visited by guests before their arrival at the lodge.[30]

A number of visitors to the lodge referred to the 'Sanness' of the illustrations on the !Xaus website. The majority of respondents enjoyed the 'traditional' aesthetics of these depictions,[31] for these figures fall in with the romantic myth[32] of a Stone Age people who are still physically representative of their forefathers. At !Xaus the majority of the ≠Khomani traditionalists retain these stereotypical features (see Figure 7.2). There are other groups, however, who classify themselves as 'Bushmen' and who do not have 'traditionally' stereotypical features; for example, the CCMS research partners, the !Xoo of Botswana who have integrated with the local Bakgalagadi,[33] and the Duma of the Kamberg.[34]

The drawings of figures with bows and arrows further refer to notions of a hunter-gathering society that is mythically associated with an inherent understanding of nature: that they can read and live off the land.[35] The photographs of ≠Khomani employees in !Xaus's promotional materials are similarly timeless. Topi(es) Kruiper, Elvis Swartz and Shaun Witbooi are shown wearing a !Xai,[36] shooting bows and arrows, while in another photograph taken over the bare shoulder of Kruiper, lions walk languidly through the cultural homestead. There is a facial close-up of Stienie Swartz and Kruiper and a picture of Agarop Rooi in a !Xaus uniform making crafts. These photographs are symbolically representative of a community

7.2 Website drawings, 2009
(© Transfrontier Parks Destinations)

29   E-mail message to authors, 20 November 2008.
30   K. Finlay, 'The Un/changing Face of the ≠Khomani: Representation through Promotional Media' (Master's diss., University of KwaZulu-Natal, 2009), 135-6.
31   Ibid., 136.
32   We mention myths in a semiotic sense, where they are defined as culturally conceptualised dominant connotations of an ahistorical nature. See Maria Camargo Heck, 'The Ideological Dimension of Media Messages', in Stuart Hall, ed., *Culture, Media, Language: Working Papers in Cultural Studies*, 1972-79 (London: Unwin Hyman, 1980).
33   'Bakgalagadi is the name given to a people living on the fringes of the Kgalagadi Desert in Botswana', Botswana Embassy, 'History', http://www.botswanaembassy.or.jp/gene_info/index2.html. (Accessed 2 November 2009).
34   For more information see: M. Francis, 'Explorations of Ethnicity and Social Change among Zulu–speaking San Descendents of the Drakensberg Mountains, KwaZulu-Natal', (PhD diss., University of KwaZulu-Natal, 2007).
35   There have been developmental cultural projects implemented in order to retain 'traditional' knowledge. *Adults in the Park*, a project sponsored by the food store chain Pick 'n Pay, is implemented once a year and offers the elders from the local ≠Khomani and Mier communities a chance to visit the KTP. These recipients stay for a day or two and learn about the environment. It is hoped that this project will aid in the passing down of knowledge, traditions and folklore to the next generation. See Bertus De Villiers, 'Kgalagadi Transfrontier Park', in *People and Parks: Sharing the Benefits* (Johannesburgh: Konrad-Adenauer-Stiftung, 2008). Another project in the pipeline is that of an art and *veld* (wilderness) school which will be led by the Kruipers, a prominent traditionalist ≠Khomani family, and that will encourage the acquisition of creative and environmental knowledge (Belinda Kruiper, e-mail message to authors, 16 January 2009).
36   A loincloth made of skins.

7.3 Website photo-graph, 2009
(© Transfrontier Parks Destinations)

whose traditions have been little affected by time. The 'reality' is that a 'traditional' hunter-gatherer lifestyle has long been impossible as a result of the privatisation of land through European expansion in the 19th and 20th centuries, the creation of the KTP[37] in 1931, and the segregated land policies of apartheid.[38] While the ≠Khomani still retain 'traditional' hunter-gatherer knowledge, it is important to note that much of their oral culture has been lost over the years, due to matters such as

> The expansion of certain dominant world cultures and languages, improvements in telecommunications and transport, the impact of worsening poverty, and in some cases, disregard of the human and civil rights of vulnerable sectors of society. These factors, mostly man-made, lead to a breakdown of intergenerational learning within indigenous societies.[39]

Romantic primitivism & its effect on development

The development at !Xaus is specific to cultural tourism. We are aware that there are many other forms of sustainable development endeavours for indigenous communities;[40] moreover various arguments posit that cultural tourism ventures are detrimental to indigenous communities.[41] !Xaus Lodge, however, is different from many other cultural tourism ventures in that the ≠Khomani and Mier are

37 Then known as the Kalahari Gemsbok Park.
38 M. C. Schenck 'Land, Water, Truth, and Love, Visions of Identity and Land Access: From Bain's Bushmen to ≠Khomani San' (BA Hons. diss. Mount Holyoke College, 2008).
Now known as the Kgalagadi Transfrontier Park (KTP).
39 Nigel Crawhall, *Written in the Sand: Auditing and Managing Cultural Resources with Displaced Indigenous Peoples: A South African Case Study* (South African San Institute (SASI) in co-operation with UNESCO's office in Windhoek, 2001), 2.
40 B. Mhlanga, 'Community Radio as Dialogic and Participatory: A critical analysis of governance, control and community participation, a case study of XK FM radio', (MA diss., University of KwaZulu-Natal, 2006).
Brilliant Mhlanga. 'The Community in Community Radio: A Case Study of XK FM, Interrogating Issues of Community Participation, Governance, and Control', *Ecquid Novi AJS*, 30,1 (2009): 58-72.
41 Melanie Smith. *Issues in Cultural Tourism Studies*, (Oxford: Routledge, 2003), 78.
Milena Ivanovic, *Cultural Tourism*, (Cape Town: Juta, 2008), 22

part owners of the lodge and the aim is that both communities will eventually take responsibility for its operation.

Development potential for indigenous communities has traditionally been marred by a romantic, primitivist perspective.[42] The notion of 'romantic primitivism' is that indigenous communities need to be 'preserved', and their 'primitive' culture kept safe from the harm of modernisation. It involves the inclination of governments towards affording their indigenous communities a significant degree of self government in an effort to preserve their culture and timeless traditions.[43] This is an extension of the 'noble savage' image which implies that Western modes of life work to defile 'Bushman' culture. The 'self government' afforded the ≠Khomani was no more than the South African government handing over land and then leaving the community to fend for itself. Without the skills to manage the land, most of what was once farmland has turned into arid bush and the people remain poverty stricken and perpetually hungry. Roger Sandall maintains that this perspective has brought no good to these communities but has aided in their demise, making them victims of anti-assimilationist policies.[44] Thus, the choice to live a traditionalist lifestyle seems no choice at all. Furthermore, when traditionalists interact with tourists, they become for the latter a representation of a past from which, for the most part, they have been long cut off. There are, of course, multiple viewpoints as to how romantic primitivism affects the contemporary San.

The guests at !Xaus are taken out to meet with the ≠Khomani at the *boma*; after the visit many guests come away with varied opinions of the indigene. Some respondents seem convinced – after their interactions with the San – about their retained 'traditional' knowledge. One visitor said that 'meeting with the San shows their manual skills and their knowledge of their environment.'[45] Many past visitors make it clear that they are aware that the ≠Khomani are part of the modern world and do not live as primitive hunter-gatherers. Visitors mention issues such as the ≠Khomani's drug and alcohol abuse (information that could be obtained from the manager's talk) and discuss past versus present beliefs and culture. Even so, the majority of the past visitors want a 'traditional' representation and to be offered a number of 'cultural' activities. They understand that what they are viewing is a performance of 'primitivity' and they enjoy this cultural experience. For example, one visitor stated that his

---

42 S. Barnabas. '"I Paint therefore I am?" An Exploration of Contemporary Bushmen Art and its Development Potential' ,(MA diss., University of KwaZulu-Natal, 2009). K. Finlay, 'The Un/changing Face of the ≠Khomani: Representation through Promotional Media' (MA diss., University of KwaZulu-Natal, 2009). K. Finlay, 'The Un/changing Face of the ≠Khomani: Representation through Promotional Media' (MA diss., University of KwaZulu-Natal, 2009).
43 Roger Sandall, *The Culture Cult: Designer Tribalism and Other Essays* (Oxford: Westview Press, 2001).
44 Ibid., 14.
45 E-mail message to authors, 10 February 2009.

favourite part of the cultural tourism at the lodge was the bow and arrow shooting.[46] His suggestion that the ≠Khomani guides be sent to other lodges to learn more about storytelling and interacting with guests illustrated his awareness that these cultural offerings were a 'performance'.

The San are part of their own romantic primitivising; it has been argued that the reason this is so is because 'we' (the Same) have displaced 'their' (the Other's) precolonial images of their forefathers and themselves, and have imposed on them our image of what they should be.[47] Sandal decries this as 'Western sentimentalism fashionable among spoiled, white, discontent urbanites'. A further concern he highlights is the ease with which indigenes are 'caught up in the fantasizing of their media admirers and academic friends'.[48] In an interview with two SASI employees, Tomaselli relates his own encounter with Gao, the lead actor in the *Gods Must be Crazy*[49] films:

> ...he [Gao] told us how particularly German tourists spend days driving out there, and some kind of guide will say, 'there's Gao!' There's Gao sitting in his overalls outside his four-bedroom house with a tin roof. The tourists get very angry because they've spent all this time and money getting there and this guy doesn't even exist like he does in the film.[50]

It seems that the San have been persuaded that it is in their own interests to retain timeless representations and, as a result of their severely limited opportunities, they willingly reproduce this notion.[51] Conversely, the ≠Khomani, with emphasis on the leading traditionalist family, the Kruipers, have constructed their authenticity in relation to the romantic myth.[52] This enables them to 'sell these myths to the West (tourists) in terms of discourses of indigeneity (politics), authenticity (owners of original knowledge), of tourism (marketing) and in terms of poverty-alleviation (aid/begging)'.[53] It is thus apparent that while the reiteration of the romantic myth is viewed as reproduced subordination to some, to others, it is a show of the San's own entrepreneurial flair.

In 2007, shortly after we arrived at Molopo Lodge (about 60 kilometres from the KTP and across the road from Witdraai) we headed

46   E-mail message to authors, 21 August 2008
47   Don Kulick and Margaret Wilson, 'Echoing Images: The Construction of Savagery among Papua New Guinea Villagers', *Visual Anthropology* 5, 2 (1992): 143-52.
David J. Lewis-Williams and David G Pearce, *San Spirituality: Roots, Expression and Social Consequences* (Walnut Creek: AltaMira, 2004).
48   Roger Sandall, op. cit., x.
49   Jamie Uys. *The Gods Must be Crazy* (I & II). (Mimosa Films, Botswana, 1980, 1989).
50   Keyan Gray Tomaselli and Anthea Simões, interview with Betta Syen and Lizelle Kleynhans, July 2001.
51   Barbara Buntman, 'Bushman Images in South African Tourist Advertising: The Case of Kagga Kamma', in Pippa Skotnes, ed., *Miscast* (Cape Town: University of Cape Town Press, 1996), 279.
52   Keyan G. Tomaselli, 'The !Xaus Lodge Experience: Issues Arising' (Unpublished report, 2007).
53   While this is so, Tomaselli also states that the ≠Khomani show resentment towards the circuit of dependency in which they have placed themselves: ibid., 12.

out to meet the locals. We came across ≠Khomani craftspeople on the side of the road. When one of the men spotted us coming towards him, he whipped off his blue overalls and donned his !Xai (skins). We could see that he was very cold; it was winter and while we stood in our jackets and scarves this man made the choice to discomfort himself in the hope that seeing him in his skins would encourage us to buy his crafts. This 'marketing' strategy no doubt helps in selling his wares to passing tourists, and judging by how cold it was this was no light decision.

An amalgam of past and present

The crucial point, as Nicholas Thomas states, is that 'indigenous cultures are simultaneously "traditional" and "contemporary"... "traditional" in the sense that distinctive views of the world remain alive, [and] "contemporary" in the sense that they belong in the present'[54]. They could thus be called an amalgam of past and present as they have been 'neither fully absorbed by, nor excluded from, modernity'[55]. This is at the root of the fragmentation these communities feel; they remain in a kind of limbo between past and present, and because they are not fluent with the terms and conditions of the present they look to the past as a kind of salvation. This in turn feeds into the romantic myth already held by 'us' looking at 'them'. Sandall scathingly remarks that, what is created out of this is a tragic people who are '[i]lliterate, vocationally disabled, [and] unpresentable outside the ethnographic zoos they live in.'[56] Preservation, it seems, comes at a price.

When visiting !Xaus in July 2008 we met with a young ≠Khomani employee by the name of Corné Witbooi. Corné told us that he had finished his schooling not too long ago, but that this achievement did not inspire much hope in him. He said that even though he had had more opportunity than many older ≠Khomani this was of little help to him as there were no other employment opportunities in that particular area of the Northern Cape for him other than cultural tourism initiatives. In light of this it is no wonder that the ≠Khomani traditionalists often consciously sell themselves as a culturally 'preserved' community. Conversely, as the ≠Khomani leader, Dawid Kruiper, said of his group's primordial hunter-gatherer representation at the Kagga Kamma Lodge[57], 'I am an animal of nature. I want people

54 Nicholas Thomas, *Possessions: Indigenous Art/ Colonial Culture* (London: Thames and Hudson, 1987), 17.
55 Ibid.
56 Ibid.
57 The Kagga Kamma Nature Reserve in South Africa's Western Cape Province played host to many San in the 1990s, 'A total of forty-nine Bushmen had lived at Kagga Kamma [in the cultural village] by the end of 1991'; they were all 'patrilateral kin of Dawid Kriuper'. The 'San experience' at Kagga Kamma was far more extensive than it is at !Xaus. The general idea, however, was

to see me and know who I am. The only way our tradition and way of life can survive is to live in the memory of the people who see us.'[58] This highlights a way in which these groups are appropriating this representation to their own ends.

!Xaus Lodge and the nostaligic vs modern debate

While the ≠Khomani at !Xaus are being integrated into the business of running the lodge, their cultural representation within it remains nostalgic, evoking imagery of the 'wild Bushmen', in that the employees rely on their 'traditional knowledge' of tracking, shooting with a bow and arrow and the making of crafts. In contrast to the romantic features of the 2009 website, however, (and arguably the representation of the ≠Khomani at the re-created homestead), the then manager of !Xaus Lodge, Pieter Retief, gave a talk to the tourists about the history of the southern African San and the realities of the ≠Khomani's life today. This took place before the visit to the *boma;* Retief was adamant that the *boma* is not a cultural village but a place to interact with the ≠Khomani.

Some tourists feel that the cultural tourism at !Xaus is 'weak'. One visitor stated, 'I felt it was a little forced especially when we saw the "Bushman" group walking back dressed in worn out western clothing.'[59] The general feeling of past visitors is that they expect a performance of primitivity from the employees at this recreated homestead. Furthermore, they want to take part in 'traditional' activities.[60] Two past visitors made suggestions of activities which they felt could be offered at the lodge:

San stories in the *boma* [own italics] round the fire with a translator. (This is done at some camps in Botswana.) Teaching visitors on the walk how to make fire, bird traps. Ending the walk with a dance demonstration. Digging up pre-buried ostrich eggs filled with water. Allowing the San to put on traditional clothing for the activities. (All these things are also done at a few other lodges outside SA.)[61]

Interaction with the Bushmen is limited to a visit to the cultural village where one is left feeling more like an observer than a participant. Buying crafts is nice, but the experience would be richer if visitors could be taught to make – and actually make – their own. Sitting around the *boma* [own italics] was nice, and Pieter [the manager] was a wonderful and informed

the same; tourists were brought into the cultural village by the 'white' tour guide who would give a talk about San history. The tourists were then encouraged to engage with the San. Male tourists were 'instructed in tracking skills' while the female tourists observed the San women in beadwork and craft making. See Hylton White, *In the Tradition of the Forefathers*: Bushman *Traditionality at Kagga Kamma* (Cape Town: University of Cape Town Press, 1995), 9, 12.

58 Ibid, 17.
59 E-mail message to authors, 25 July 2008.
60 K. Finlay, 'The Un/changing Face of the ≠Khomani: Representation through Promotional Media', (Master's diss., University of KwaZulu-Natal, 2009), 125.
61 E-mail message to authors, 27 July 2008.

host, but the stories he told of the Bushmen would have been better received had they actually come from a Bushman.[62]

Although it can be argued that such timeless portrayals lead to a representation of the San as a people who are 'forever not-quite-yet fully modern',[63] we think this can be avoided by both management and ≠Khomani employees through a discussion of their representation with visitors. Through such case studies, performers can be made more aware of what to expect regarding tourist expectations and deal with them accordingly. The 'traditional' representations do not necessarily lead to or support notions of a 'modernizing'[64] people, as long as any timeless concepts are challenged in the process. For example, when I (Finlay) visited Shakaland[65] on 4 August 2007, a guide led us around the reconstructed Zulu village. Instead of telling the audience that this is the reality of Zulu life today, he told us that this was a historical depiction. Furthermore, he made a joke about paying *lobola*[66] with cars instead of cattle and other jokes which reminded the audience that our Zulu guide was most certainly a man of the modern South Africa. If the management and ≠Khomani employees at !Xaus were to use such strategies,[67] it would help in contesting the romantic representation of the San.

The majority of tourists who visit !Xaus do not wish to see a 'museum exhibition' but to interact further with the ≠Khomani[68]. One visitor explained the cultural experience at the homestead:

> The Bushmen in the cultural village were wearing up-market fashionable clothing. We expected something more primitive and some seats to sit on, or mats to calmly sit and chat, even though they spoke only a little English. Language is an issue. The operation lacks one special, passionate, unique guide to spark the other guides and give guests a memorable experience.[69]

The implication of the above arguments is that the ≠Khomani should speak a dominant western language.[70] In the economic and social context of the ≠Khomani today it would be difficult to find an employee who does speak fluent English. The assumption that the ≠Khomani should learn the first language of tourists in order to converse with

62 E-mail message to authors, 1 October 2008.
63 Garland, Elizabeth and Gordon, Robert J. 'The Authentic (In)Authentic: Bushman Anthro-Tourism', *Visual Anthropology* 12 (1999): 267.
64 Ibid., 267-87.
65 Available at: http://www.shakaland.co.za/ for more information.
66 *Lobola* is the payment a man's family must give to the bride's family in order to marry. *Lobola* recognises the bride's family's contribution in raising her and offers compensation for their loss of a daughter (after the marriage she lives with her husband's family). Zolani Ngwane, *Zulu* (New York: The Rosen Publishing Group, 1997), 23.
67 Even if the ≠Khomani do not speak English but use a translator to communicate with guests, this is still possible.
68 E-mail message to authors, 1 October 2008.
69 E-mail message to authors, 21 August 2008.
70 A past visitor to the Lodge in July 2008 writes that: 'Our interaction with the four occupants of the village was extremely limited. None of us speak Afrikaans so we didn't understand what they were saying' (e-mail message to authors, 12 August 2008).

visitors seems naive and even conceited in terms of power relations related to hegemonically dominant languages. Nevertheless, in the future the likelihood of this one-on-one interaction in a western language will probably become more likely if ≠Khomani children gain economic access to schools in the area. Furthermore, as already mentioned, !Xaus Lodge has sent two of its ≠Khomani employees to !Kwa ttu for further training. Perhaps this will assist in their grasp of English.

Conclusion

The case study of !Xaus Lodge illustrates how ≠Khomani representation is a difficult terrain to be navigated by contemporary 'Bushmen' as well as those involved in sharing this representation with the world. The main issues that !Xaus and other similar cultural lodges need to take into consideration is the extent to which these romantic notions of the San should be challenged. If !Xaus Lodge does away with their romantic marketing and the mythologies expressed by the cultural homestead what would this mean for the ≠Khomani who are dependent on such cultural tourism endeavours for their livelihood? The opinions and suggestions expressed by the tourists confirm that they are generally aware of the romantic myth but are not deterred by it. While they understand the myth to be inauthentic and incongruous with the contemporary San, they want to view the portrayal of this myth from a lived experience. When asked if she would expect a 'traditional' representation, a focus group respondent[71] replied: 'Ja, because that is what I would be paying for.' Ultimately, it may be argued that these San present a 'fictive identity', in that:

> While they may indeed be descended from southern Kalahari Bushmen who practiced a foraging mode of existence at some point in the past... they are neither pristine hunters and gatherers nor are they isolated from the industrialized world. Producers of curio commodities and performers of services for tourists' consumption, they are instead integrated participants in a global cash economy.[72]

Yet this is not 'economically motivated fraud'; neither is it 'a primordial essence'; on the contrary, 'the traditional hunter-gatherer self-representation... is a socially significant identity forged in strategic response to a variety of past experiences.'[73]

The use of the romantic myth has proved to have positive economic outcomes for the ≠Khomani. They continue to enter into an engagement with tourists fully aware of the visitors' expectations. If the West,

71 We conducted research on the South Africa target market of !Xaus Lodge in 2007 using focus groups.
72 Hylton White, *In the Tradition of the Forefathers: Bushman Traditionality at Kagga Kamma* (Cape Town: University of Cape Town Press, 1995), 25.
73 Ibid., 51.

however, stops exerting pressure on contemporary Bushman groups to re-enact, reproduce and return to the past then perhaps they could begin to create a space for themselves in the current society that does not rely on myth. And if they choose to continue turning to myth, it will at least be their free choice and not our persistent decision.[74]

74 S. Barnabas, ' "I Paint therefore I am?" An Exploration of Contemporary Bushmen Art and its Development Potential' (Master's diss., University of KwaZulu-Natal, 2009), 91.

PRIMARY REFERENCES

Hanekom, Derek. Speech given at ≠Khomani land claim ceremony, March 22, 2009.
O'Leary, Glynn. Interviewed by Kalahari team at !Xaus Lodge, KTP, July 13, 2007.
Tomaselli, Keyan Gray and Simões, Anthea. Interview with Betta Syen and Lizelle Kleynhans (transcripts courtesy of Keyan Tomaselli) July, 2001.

SECONDARY REFERENCES

Barnabas, S. "'I Paint therefore I am?" An Exploration of Contemporary Bushmen Art and its Development Potential', MA diss., University of KwaZulu-Natal, 2009.
Buntman, Barbara. 'Bushman Images in South African Tourist Advertising: The Case of Kagga Kamma', in Pippa Skotnes, ed., *Miscast* (Cape Town: University of Cape Town Press, 1996), 271-80.
Crawhall, Nigel. *Written in the Sand: Auditing and Managing Cultural Resources with Displaced Indigenous Peoples: A South African Case Study.* South African San Institute (SASI) in cooperation with UNESCO's office in Windhoek, 2001.
De Villiers, Bertus. 'Kgalagadi Transfrontier Park', in *People and Parks: Sharing the Benefits* (Johannesburg: Konrad-Adenauer-Stiftung, 2008).
Douglas, S. S. "'...Attractions and Artillerymen, Curiosities and Commandos...'" An ethnographic study of elites and the politics of cultural distinction', MA diss., University of Cape Town, 1996.
Dyll, Lauren. 'Community Development Strategies in the Kalahari – An Expression of Modernisation's Monologue?' in Petri Hottola ed., *Tourism Strategies and Tourism Responses in Southern Africa* (Wallingford: Cabi, 2009), 41-60.
Dyll-Myklebust, L. 'Lodge-ical Thinking and Development Communication: !Xaus Lodge as a Public-Private Partnership for Community Development in Tourism', PhD diss., University of KwaZulu-Natal.
Finlay, Kate. 'The Un/changing Face of the ≠Khomani: Representation through Promotional Media', MA diss., University of KwaZulu-Natal, 2009a.
—— 'The Un/changing Face of the ≠Khomani: Representation through Promotional Media', *Visual Anthropology* 22(4) (2009b): 344-61.
Francis, M. 'Explorations of Ethnicity and Social Change among Zulu-speaking San Descendents of the Drakensberg Mountains, KwaZulu-Natal', PhD diss., University of KwaZulu-Natal, 2007.
Garland, Elizabeth and Gordon, Robert J. 'The Authentic (In)Authentic: Bushman Anthro-Tourism', *Visual Anthropology* 12 (1999): 267-87.

Heck, Maria Camargo. 'The Ideological Dimension of Media Messages', in Stuart Hall, ed., *Culture, Media, Language: Working Papers in Cultural Studies, 1972-79* (London: Unwin Hyman, 1980), 66-72.

Ivanovic, Milena. *Cultural Tourism* (Cape Town: Juta, 2008).

Kulick, Don and Willson, Margaret. 'Echoing Images: The Construction of Savagery among Papua New Guinea Villagers', *Visual Anthropology* 5(2) (1992): 143-52.

Lewis-Williams, J. David and David G. Pearce. *San Spirituality: Roots, Expression and Social Consequences* (Walnut Creek CA: AltaMira, 2004).

Mhlanga, Brilliant. 'Community Radio as Dialogic and Participatory: A critical analysis of governance, control and community participation, a case study of XK FM radio', MA diss., University of KwaZulu-Natal, 2006.

—— 'The Community in Community Radio: A Case Study of XK FM, Interrogating Issues of Community Participation, Governance, and Control', *Ecquid Novi* AJS 30(1) (2009): 58-72.

Ngwane, Zolani. *Zulu* (New York: The Rosen Publishing Group, 1997).

Penn, Nigel. '"Fated to Perish": The Destruction of the Cape San' in Pippa Skotnes, ed., *Miscast: Negotiating the Presence of the Bushmen* (Cape Town: University of Cape Town Press, 1996), 81-91.

Robins, Steven. 'NGOs, Bushmen and Double Vision: The ≠Khomani San Land Claim and the Cultural Politics of "Community" and "Development" in the Kalahari', *Journal of Southern African Studies* 27, 4 (2001): 833-53.

Sandall, Roger. *The Culture Cult: Designer Tribalism and Other Essays* (Oxford: Westview Press, 2001).

Schenck, M. C. 'Land, Water, Truth, and Love, Visions of Identity and Land Access: From Bain's Bushmen to ≠Khomani San'. BA Hons diss., Mount Holyoke College, 2008.

Smith, Melanie. *Issues in Cultural Tourism Studies* (Oxford: Routledge, 2003).

Smith, Andy, Candy Malherbe, Mathias Guenther, and Penny Berens. *The Bushmen of Southern Africa: A Foraging Society in Transition* (Cape Town: David Philip Publishers, 2000).

Swart, Hennie. Background and History of the !Xun and Khwe San Communities: A History of Relocation. (The Schmidtsdrift Chapter and the Platfontein Chapter), unpublished notes by the erstwhile manager of the !Xun and Khwe CPA at Platfontein, 2004.

Thomas, Nicholas. *Possessions: Indigenous Art/ Colonial Culture* (London: Thames and Hudson, 1987).

Tomaselli, Keyan, G. 'Preface: Our Host Communities', in Keyan Tomaselli ed., *Writing in the San/d: Autoethnography Among Indigenous Southern Africans* (Lanham: Altamira Press, 2007a). vii-xii.

—— The !Xaus Lodge Experience: Issues Arising, unpublished report, 2007b.

White, Hylton. In the Tradition of the Forefathers: Bushman Traditionality at Kagga Kamma (Cape Town: University of Cape Town Press, 1995).

FILMOGRAPHY   Uys, Jamie. *The Gods Must be Crazy* I. Botswana: Mimosa Films, 1980.

Uys, Jamie. *The Gods Must be Crazy* II. Botswana: Mimosa Films, 1989.

8 · Treesleeper camp:
A case study of a community tourism project in Tsintsabis, Namibia

Stasja Koot

'Generally, with one or two exceptions, the bushmen photographed are anonymous. They are portrayed as iconic symbols rather than individuals.'[1]

'Modern day Bushmen will greet you from their homes, inquisitive of intruders in their quiet lives.'[2]

Introduction

Tourism in Namibia has a strong focus on nature. 'Cultural tourism' or 'ethnic tourism' is there, but on the margins of nature-based tourism. Wildlife parks and beautiful landscapes are the main attractions here. The Fish River Canyon, the Namib Naukluft Desert and of course Etosha National Park are amongst the highlights of Namiba. It is a country with good infrastructure and there are plenty of high quality guest farms, hunting farms and lodges where tourists can have an 'African experience'. Wildlife is numerous, also outside the parks and in conservation areas. In a comfortable setting, tourists can go trophy hunting or for game drives in the parks, conservation areas and on farms. In a cheaper setting, camping tourism has evolved.

Community Based Tourism (CBT) and Community Based Natural Resource Management (CBNRM) started to evolve already before 1990 and since 1994 it has been possible for many Namibian communities to acquire limited property rights to use and manage wildlife resources. The most important natural resources in these CBNRM projects are wildlife viewing and trophy hunting. In a large country as Namibia (830.000 km²) the population of 1.7 million is mostly rural.[3] Today these local communities sometimes work together with partners from the private sector in so-called joint ventures, such as the Damaraland Camp in the Torra Conservancy.[4] From a cultural tourism point of view, the two most interesting tribes

1 R. J. Gordon, *Picturing Bushmen: The Denver African Expedition of 1925* (Claremont, South Africa: David Philip Publishers (Pty) Ltd., 1997), 69.
2 !Uris Safari Lodge. http://www.urissafarilodge.com
3 J. I. Barnes, 'Community-based Tourism and Natural Resource Management in Namibia: Local and National Economic Impacts', in A. Spenceley, ed., *Responsible Tourism: Critical Issues for Conservation and Development*, (London: Earthscan, 2008), 343-44.
4 M. Salole, 'Merging Two Disparate Worlds in Rural Namibia: Joint Venture Tourism in Torra Conservancy', in R. Butler and T. Hinch, eds., *Tourism and Indigenous Peoples: Issues and Implications*(Amsterdam: Elsevier, 2007).

in Namibia are the Himba and the Bushmen, as being 'exotic' people.[5]

Bushmen (or San), specifically the Hai//om of Etosha, are the focus of this chapter. It looks into the case of Treesleeper Camp, in which a changing culture and community is connected to tourism. Amongst other examples, the Bushmen's traditional and current connection with wildlife is compared to the tourists' connection with wildlife. The Hai//om Bushmen used to hunt and roam in and around the Etosha National Park, the main attraction where tourists go to watch game. Early in the twentieth century the promotion of tourism in Hai//om habitat was already established and the tribe was used to attract tourists. It was hoped that tourism would lead to settlers. Big-game hunting was also part of the attraction.[6] The Hai//om are an example of a culture which has trouble connecting to its own traditions, while at the same time having trouble connecting to modernisation. On the one hand, the tourist's romanticised picture before he goes to Africa has a big influence on the daily life of these marginalised people: indeed, the existence of national parks is partly the cause of marginalisation for Bushmen all over Southern Africa. On the other hand, that same romanticised picture of Africa brings opportunities for (sustainable) tourism development. Bushmen, as part of the tourist's view of Africa, are subject to two contradictory images, and neither of them captures today's reality. Sometimes they represent the image of real, 'pristine' foraging people, leading an 'authentic' life as humanity's ancestors. In other cases, they are seen as marginalised victims because of the apartheid regime and world-wide capitalism.[7]

Methodological note

For methodological clarity I will explain my own position in the Treesleeper project. My connection with Tsintsabis, where Tree-sleeper Camp is based, started in 1999 when I visited the place for the first time and stayed for half a year to do fieldwork for my MA thesis about the resettlement process in Tsintsabis.[8] In those days many people told me they wanted to work with tourism, since many tourists were passing through on the way to Etosha. Therefore, starting community tourism in Tsintsabis had been my own recommendation to the Ministry of Lands, Resettlement and Rehabilitation (MLRR)

5   R.K. Hitchcock, 'Cultural, Economic, and Environmental Impacts of Tourism Among Kalahari Bushmen', in E. Chambers , ed., *Tourism and Culture: An Applied Perspective* (Albany: State University of New York Press, 1997), 97.
6   R. J. Gordon, *Picturing Bushmen: The Denver African Expedition of 1925* (Claremont, South Africa: David Philip Publishers (Pty) Ltd., 1997), 102-3.
7   R. Hitchcock et. al., 'Introduction: Updating the San, Image and Reality of an African People in the Twenty First Century', *Senri Ethnological Studies* 70 (2006): 1.
8   S. Koot, 'Resettlement in Tsintsabis: Namibian Bushmen in a Changing World', MA thesis, University of Utrecht, 2000.

and some NGOs. In 2002/3 I returned to Namibia for six months, visiting the community several times and discussing the idea again (also with NGOs, potential donors, and the MLRR). I also started the Foundation for Sustainable Tourism in Namibia (FSTN), a small Dutch initiative mainly used for fundraising for the project. From January 2004 until June 2007 I lived in Namibia once more, based in Tsintsabis to help the community with founding and building up Treesleeper Camp and to provide trainings to local employees. In that period I did not do any research, and I was probably – and in some ways still am – more closely attached to this project than the average researcher. The methodological consequences of this are that I know the project very well, in detail, but I am probably less objective than an outside observer.

Historical background

For a long time now scientists have agreed that hunting and gathering Bushmen are the aboriginal inhabitants of Southern Africa[9] and the Hai//om are the largest 'subgroup' of Bushmen in Namibia.[10] Hai//om means 'tree-sleeper' and a big part of Etosha belongs to their original habitat. Before the arrival of the Europeans in northern Namibia, the Hai//om lived semi-nomadic in good conditions for foraging, but over more than a century of colonial rule 'the whole pattern of land possession, use and access, was radically reshaped from pre-colonial patterns to a system which was geared to the benefit of white people.'[11] The Hai//om lost their resources much quicker than any other group because they lived in the best farming area of Namibia. The new European farmers brought in a lot of livestock, hunted game and fenced their land. Many Hai//om started living and working on the new settler farms.

Robert J. Gordon analyses how a group of American scientists in 1925 went looking for 'The Most Primitive Race on Earth: The Heikum Bushmen of the Kalahari.'[12] The aim of the expedition was to put these people on photo and film, so that 'the Bushmen were portrayed as the quintessential primeval people "uncontaminated" by "contact".'[13] Already then these images had a strong impact on Bushmen. It sometimes resulted in them having to leave Etosha because they refused to live according to European notions of

9 I. Schapera, *The Khoisan Peoples of South Africa: Bushmen and Hottentots* (London: George Routledge & Sons, Ltd., 1930), 26; A. Barnard, *Hunters and Herders of Southern Africa: A Comparative Ethnography of the Khoisan Peoples* (Cambridge: University Press, 1992), 28.
10 R.J. Gordon and S. S. Douglas, *The Bushman Myth: The Making of a Namibian Underclass* (San Francisco: Westview Press, Inc., 2nd edn, 2000), 7.
11 D. Pankhurst, *A Resolvable Conflict? The Politics of Land in Namibia* (Trowbridge, Wiltshire: Redwood Books, 1996), 15.
12 Hulse cited in R. J. Gordon, *Picturing Bushmen: The Denver African Expedition of 1925* (Claremont, South Africa: David Philip Publishers (Pty) Ltd., 1997), 1.
13 Ibid., 61.

'traditional Bushman custom.' Officials of Etosha would not allow them to own livestock, keep dogs in the 'wrong' way or beg from tourists.[14] Today, the 'pure' Hai//om or Bushmen that the members of the *'Denver African Expedition of 1925'* were searching for cannot be found anymore. By looking for the 'mystified, pure' Bushmen, 'we' have destroyed the purity that we were seeking. The Bushman as so often portrayed in Western culture is a myth, while in reality Bushmen are victimised people. They are looked down on and at the same time they are strongly romanticised as a 'true nature tribe.' This combination can be harmful. For example, Botelle and Rohde found in Eastern Otjozondjupa (the former 'Bushmanland'), that

> there are two views underlying future development of the region: one typified by the colonial attitude of 'preserving the Bushmen'; and the other, opposing image, being based on the premise that 'Bushmen' are poor, underdeveloped and in need of guidance from 'more advanced' outsiders. [...] Both of these views are unjustified: it should not be outsiders determining the direction of developments but rather local residents themselves, in consultation with outsiders [...][15]

Hai//om and Etosha

Bushmen have mostly been portrayed as hunters. Within their traditional diet, meat approximately accounted for 25 to 35 per cent, while bushfood made up the other 65 to 75 per cent. They used to catch a lot of meat with a variety of traps, such as small antelopes, springhare, guinea fowl, and so on. Big game, such as giraffe, kudu and eland, was hunted with bow and (poisonous) arrow. In case of the Hai//om, Etosha National Park and surroundings have always been an important part of their habitat. Etosha is nowadays the biggest tourist attraction in Namibia, while the surroundings are cultivated farmland, camp sites, guest farms and luxurious lodges.

Etosha gained official status in 1907. It has expanded or diminished in size over the past, due to migration routes of certain species, conservation and a 'necessity' for more farmland.[16] When tourists visit the park, either on an organised tour or on a self-drive holiday, most of them drive through the park from the middle southern part in a east-northeastern direction, or vice versa. The main road lies just south of the enormous Etosha Pan, a dry salt pan in the middle of the park. This all used to be part of Hai//om habitat. In 1928 Bushmen

14 Ibid., 119-20.
15 A. Botelle and R. Rohde. *Those who Live on the Land: A Socio-economic Baseline Survey for Land Use Planning in the Communal Areas of Eastern Otjozondjupa* (Windhoek: Ministry of Lands, Resettlement and Rehabilitation, 1995), 175-6.
16 C. Longden, *Undiscovered or Overlooked? The Hai//om of Namibia and their Identity: One of a Series of Books from the WIMSA Regional Oral Testimony Collection Project* (Windhoek: Capital Press, 2004) and A. Schoeman, 'Etosha – after 75 years, a plucked fowl', in A. Schoeman, ed., *Notes on Nature (2002)* (Windhoek: Gamsberg MacMillan Publishers (Pty) Ltd, 1982), 91-3.

were forbidden to possess bows and arrows – their most important weapon for survival – while if other blacks, or settlers, were found with 'Bushmen bows', these bows were considered 'curios'.[17] Dieckmann noticed how the officers of Etosha in 1942 classified and counted the Hai//om as 'Heikum-wild' (staying at waterholes) and 'Heikum-tame' (regularly working at the stations), a practice followed up in subsequent years. Between a few hundred and a few thousand Hai//om then lived in the park, mainly south of the Etosha Pan.[18] Apparently in 1962 between 150 and 200 Hai//om still lived in the park at Namutoni and Okaukuejo; according to a South African official,

> earlier the area which is now the Etosha Game Park was the homeland and hunting grounds of the Heikoms. Since the proclamation of a game park the Bushmen have been gradually 'squeezed out' and about ten years ago the few who were still found at waterholes in the park were rounded up and relocated at Okaukeujo [sic] and Namutoni. Occasionally there is still infiltration of the game park by Bushmen, but such trespassers are quickly tracked down and removed.[19]

A respondent from Tsintsabis who was born in Namutoni, Etosha, told me in 1999 how 'in 1944 we were happy, because we were living on our own. But then we were chased away from Namutoni [...] because the South African government they wanted to make it a game park. But Etosha belonged to the Hai//om. We were living there.'

In the early 1990s, the Hai//om claimed the Etosha Game Park as ancestral land.[20] Former Hai//om leader Willem /Aib said that 'there are about 10.000 Hei-//om in Namibia. Without a place to call their home and some form of socio-cultural structure, our people fear they might lose their cultural identity.'[21] In 1997 there was a demonstration at the gates of Okaukuejo and Namutoni. The idea was to inform tourists, in a peaceful way, that they were entering ancestral Hai//om land by handing over a leaflet. However, the protest went wrong when people made roadblocks, the police arrived and used teargas and rubber bullets to disperse the crowd. 73 people were arrested in the end.[22] However, to this day there are still Hai//om living in the park. In 2000 there were still 339 Hai//om at the 'locations' of the restcamps Okaukuejo, Halali and Namutoni or at the two entrance gates in place at the time.[23]

17 R. J. Gordon, *Picturing Bushmen*, 61.
18 U. Dieckmann, *Hai//om in the Etosha Region* (Windhoek: John Meinert Printing (PTY) Ltd., 2007), 146 and 162.
19 South Africa 1962, 3 cited in R. J. Gordon, *Picturing Bushmen*, 140.
20 B. Karuuombe, 'Land Reform in Namibia', *Land Update* 59 (1997): 7.
21 New Era 1993, 2 cited in J.S. Malan, *Peoples of Namibia* (Pretoria: Rhino Publishers, 1995), 105.
22 C. Maletsky, 'Hai//om Eye Lists Farms', *The Namibian*, June 16, 1997.
23 U. Dieckmann, *Hai//om in the Etosha Region* (Windhoek: John Meinert Printing (PTY) Ltd., 2007), 278.

Tsintsabis resettlement farm

Tsintsabis is a resettlement farm situated 119 kilometres east of Etosha. 'Resettlement' implies that people have been forcibly moved to a different place, but in Tsintsabis this is not the case. Here the Hai//om have to find a new way of living in an area that traditionally 'belonged' to them but of which they have been dispossessed. Bushmen communities have become victims of land reform, especially in Namibia and Botswana. Bushmen groups know the system called *n!ore*, which entails the sharing of natural resources amongst members of a larger Bushmen community in a certain area. This concept is essentially different from that of the right of ownership of the land. Pastoralists and cattle owners have intruded into the *n!ore* of the Bushmen, so that nowadays they have a system of sharing poverty.[24]

The 'village' of Tsintsabis was created when the Germans made a police station to control the area when farmers settled this far out, shortly after 1915. Camels were used for transport and there was plenty of wildlife. In the following years, supervision by the South African police became stronger. From approximately 1982 until 1990 the Namibian war for independence from South Africa was strongly felt in Tsintsabis. Its police station became an army base for the South African Defence Force (SADF). Many Hai//om became trackers (based on their expertise because of their hunting tradition) for the SADF, looking for South West African People's Organisation (SWAPO) soldiers.

Tsintsabis has been a resettlement farm since 1993. The owner of the land is the Namibian government. The people used to get food and supplies then from the MLRR, who gave the people seeds for growing crops and divided small plots of land for the families on which they could become self-sufficient small-scale farmers. Due to a variety of reasons, this only works on and off and many people are still dependent on food aid. However, agriculture is the core business in Tsintsabis for most people, since it is the core business of the government's resettlement scheme. Most people have hardly any other choice: the Hai//om are originally foragers and thus have no tradition of cultivation. There are two small communities of Bushmen living in the nearby 'sub-settlements' of /Gomkhaos (mainly !Xun Bushmen) and !Khosines, a few kilometres away from the centre of Tsintsabis but officially part of it. Other tribes moved into Tsintsabis after independence. Particularly where jobs are concerned, Bushmen are victims of discrimination. A development committee has been set up with the help of the MLRR, but it lacks the skills, expertise and means available to set up development projects and therefore has turned out to be more of an informal 'problem solving' institution

---

24 A. Thoma, 'The Communal Land and Resource Management System of the San', in J. Malan and M.O. Hinz, eds., *Communal Land Administration: 26-28 September 1996, Windhoek* (Tsumeb: Nation Press, 1997), 61.

than a strong legal body with the necessary qualities to work on the broad concept of 'development'. Its social role is important however, since it consists mainly of elders from the village. They hardly speak English (but Hai//om and Afrikaans), which is the official language in Namibia since 1993, and illiteracy is prevalent in the committee.

Development projects, including national parks, can cause resettlement. The resettlement process itself in many cases accounts for the creation of a very new 'community', in which people show a wide range of social responses, develop new relationships and learn new skills.[25] In many cases the resettled population goes through an important phase of identity change and this is clearly the case in Tsintsabis. For the Hai//om their environment is the same as they have always lived in, only they are directed to other sources of income, such as agriculture, labouring or tourism activities, on much less land than before. Today their traditional lifestyle of hunting and gathering is practised on a very limited scale and many other influences have affected their lives. They are 'villagised' because 'development' was introduced in the form of schools, clinics, police stations and so on. Rural resettlement schemes sometimes include planned villagisation. Authorities claim that this makes the scattered rural population easier to reach to distribute central provisions. However, in many cases there have been accusations that the government tries to tighten their grip on the people.[26]

Tourism in Tsintsabis

Since 1993 the development committee has planned to start tourism to increase employment and income in Tsintsabis. They have asked the government and parties within civil society to support them. Commercial 'Bushmen-tourism' already existed in the area of Tsintsabis, set up by a commercial farmer, who is also the tour guide, explaining Bushmen culture to visitors.

In 1999 the community of Tsintsabis, while still keen to develop tourism, wanted to create a community-based campsite to stimulate the small-scale economy and skills development for the young people of the village.[27] Examples of the positive effects of Bushmen tourism already existed by this time. According to Ashley, 'Ju'hoansi tracking skills, which were dying out, are gaining new value for tourist-guiding in former Bushmanland'.[28] Tsintsabis has a reasonably good location

25 A. Pankhurst, *Resettlement and Famine in Ethiopia: The Villagers' Experience* (Manchester: Manchester University Press, 1992), 10-13.
26 NAR. *Migratie en Bilaterale Ontwikkelingssamenwerking* (The Hague: Distributiecentrum DOP, 1991), 21.
27 S. Koot, 'Resettlement in Tsintsabis: Namibian Bushmen in a Changing World', MA thesis, University of Utrecht, 2000, 87-89.
28 C. Ashley, 'Tourism, Communities and National Policy: Namibia's Experience', *Development Policy Review* 16 (1998): 331.

for tourism, due to the proximity of Etosha, which makes it easy for tourists to combine Tsintsabis with a visit to the park. It was thought that tourism would create some employment, motivation for the (young) people and more variety in ways of earning a living. At the time, there were further reasons, on a national level, to think about tourism as an income-generating and educational enterprise for development. Tourism as sustainable development fitted the country's policy as long as local priorities were taken seriously. Besides, Namibian tourism was booming. In 1990 there were approximately 100,000 tourists visiting the country while in 1997 the figure rose to over 500,000 visitors.[29] In the years to follow it would stabilise and for 2006 the number reached a little over 800,000.[30] According to Ashley

> [t]he Namibian experience shows that community tourism can evolve rapidly, and can generate a range of financial, social and livelihood benefits for communities, as well as problems. The impacts vary according to the type of enterprise development, the local context, and the opportunities for local residents to shape tourism to their needs and priorities.[31]

Treesleeper camp

The basics of Treesleeper Camp were built between 2004 and 2007 with assistance from mostly Dutch donors, often via the Foundation for Sustainable Tourism in Namibia (FSTN). Local community involvement became formal when the Tsintsabis Trust was created in 2004 with the help of the NGO the Legal Assistance Centre (LAC). The Tsintsabis Trust is the legal owner of Treesleeper Camp. This has been important for a variety of reasons: first, Tsintsabis needed to have a *formal* community representation and owner for the project. The TT is an official legal body, registered at the Master of the High Court in Windhoek. Second, a bank account could be opened, which is a necessity for a fundraising project aiming to become a business. Third, a piece of land was needed for Treesleeper Camp. Since the resettlement farm of Tsintsabis is owned by the MLRR, they needed to allocate 10 hectares of land for the project to be a legal body. The Deed of Trust of the Tsintsabis Trust states that the objectives are 'to uplift the living standard of the community of Tsintsabis through the community tourism activities by providing funding to the Treesleeper Project in Tsintsabis'.[32]

A borehole was drilled and a solar pump installed in December 2004. This created a lot of optimism in the village and increased

29 UNDP, *Namibia: Human Development Report 1998* (Windhoek: UNDP, 1998), 70.
30 NTB, 'Summary analysis 2006', http://www.namibiatourism.com.na/trade_docs/summary_analysis_2006.pdf
31 C. Ashley, 'Tourism, Communities and National Policy', 349.
32 Tsintsabis Trust, 'Deed of Trust'. Master of the High Court, Windhoek. (Windhoek: LAC, 2004) and U. Dieckmann, *Hai//om in the Etosha Region* Windhoek: John Meinert Printing (PTY) Ltd., 2007), 318.

belief in the project. A popular saying in Tsintsabis is 'Water is Life.' In fact, Treesleeper is situated at a typically Namibian dry riverbed from the //Ghasa River.[33] Tree decks were built; platforms on poles next to big trees where tourists can camp up high between them. The whole camp site has solar-powered hot water. In August 2005 the first group of tourists arrived while building continued. Labour was mostly supplied by community members, with the help of a variety of volunteers. For the younger generation of Tsintsabis, training courses have been organised by the FSTN for tour guiding, hospitality, acquiring a driver's license, a souvenir workshop, a bicycle repair course, marketing and computer courses. Treesleeper Camp was complemented with a cultural centre and a big 'relaxing' tree deck at the riverbed (called the 'Makalani deck') in 2006. In 2007 a new office was built in the village.[34]

Tourists visiting Treesleeper are offered three activities. First, a bushwalk, during which they find out about traditional Bushmen hunting and gathering, second, a village tour showing contemporary life in Tsintsabis, the history of the Etosha people, and the changes the Hai//om are going through and third, a traditional performance in which traditional singing and dancing ceremonies are included.[35]

Occasionally, community problems required solution – most of them based on envy, a lack of knowledge about the project and high expectations. Two of the most influential families of Tsintsabis often blamed each other for taking all the jobs. A cleaning woman at Treesleeper, belonging to one of these families, had been eaves-dropping in the evening from her room, while the other family was talking in the evening at the camp fire:

> They were talking that they will take the camp, and that they will take the jobs for their brothers and sisters. And then we can lose our jobs. But me, I know it is only the trust [Tsintsabis Trust] who can decide, they cannot just take the jobs. They are only jealous, but I don't want them to take the jobs, we want the jobs...

As Foster describes, 'where people have so little, and where life is so uncertain, the good fortune of fellow villagers seems bound to arouse envy.'[36]

The FSTN guided this process of building up the camp and fund-raising until June 2007, when I left Tsintsabis. Voluntary Services Overseas (VSO) Namibia assisted the project for another two years. Since then, the project has been managed entirely by community members.

33 That is the Hai//om name of the river, which runs all the way to Etosha. It means 'The Thirsty One', since it is normally a dry riverbed. The official name is the 'Owambo River'. In early 2006 the rains were so heavy that the river waters came in for the first time in 15 years. In 2008 it flowed again.
34 Later the office was moved to the Cultural Centre.
35 Treesleeper Camp. 'Activities', http://www.treesleeper.org/activities.html
36 G.M. Foster, *Tzintzuntzan: Mexican Peasants in a Changing World* (Illinois: Waveland Press, Inc., 1988), 153.

8.1 *A tree deck at*
Treesleeper Camp,
2006
(© Stasja Koot)

Treesleeper from 2007 to 2011

When I returned to Treesleeper in March and April 2010 there had been a variety of changes. Some staff had left and been replaced by others. The Namibian Community Based Tourism Association (NACOBTA) and the MLRR have used Treesleeper to show other communities or employees how a tourism project should be run and what can be done at a resettlement farm. Moses //Khumûb, the project manager since June 2007, has finished his studies in tourism development and a Namibian tour operator, African Eagle, is now renting one camp site with eleven tents all year round. A representative from African Eagle that I spoke to stated that they worked with three communities, of which Treesleeper was the only reliable one. Furthermore, Treesleeper had been granted funding of approximately N$ 3 million by the Ministry of Environment and Tourism (MET) for a big upgrade of the project, with a guest house or lodge and some more improvements at the current camp. The profit from Treesleeper has been growing every year and several initiatives in Tsintsabis have been supported by the Tsintsabis Trust from the profit of Treesleeper. //Khumûb has been involved with Treesleeper since 2004 and is nowadays the driving force behind the project. He has been asked by the Working Group of Indigenous Minorities in Southern Africa (WIMSA) to study in Germany for a few years but he has not taken the offer because, as he explained, he is against the so-called 'brain drain'. When I asked him about his personal motivation to commit to the project so strongly he explained how he wanted to prove to those people who do not believe in community projects (especially when the communities consist of Bushmen) how wrong they are. He wants to show that Bushmen can achieve things by themselves.

Theft has been a problem with young men from the community, which had led to some arrests. A member of staff was accused of theft, and has later been fired. There have also been a few problems with alcohol abuse. The community of Tsintsabis supports the project, apart from a few individuals, particularly those elder people in relatively important positions who want to gain financially from the project. They turn against the project because they do not get anything out of it on an individual basis. Sometimes the communication between the Tsintsabis Trust and the community has not been good enough and therefore the plan is now to have regular village meetings, about three every year. Clear communication to the overall community can prevent a lot of problems and is one of the most important lessons learnt at Treesleeper.

Positioning Treesleeper within tourism

International tourism has positive and negative impacts on the host countries and populations in economic, socio-cultural and environmental ways. Early studies on tourism were economic in nature and focused on working out monetary flows and benefits from the tourism activities.[37] Boorstin has argued that tourism was an example of a 'pseudo-event', in which Americans cannot experience 'reality'. Pseudo-events are inauthentic and isolated from the local people and the host environment.[38] MacCannell has suggested that tourists are interested in their hosts if their hosts' life differs strongly from their own.[39] The hosts' life takes place in 'back regions', while tourists get to see a 'staged authenticity' ('front regions'), constructed by the hosts. Urry rejects the idea of the search for authenticity as the key motivating factor for tourists. For him, it is the difference between one's normal place of residence/work and the tourism experience, which is a key feature for the organisation of tourism.[40] Tourists move in an 'environmental bubble' which protects them from many features of the host community.[41] Their basic motivation is to experience those things 'in reality' which they have already experienced in their imagination. Tourism therefore involves daydreaming and the anticipation of new or different experiences. Advertising and other messages from the media clearly relate to these expectations.[42]

37 I. Sindiga, *Tourism and African Development: Change and Challenge of Tourism in Kenya* (Leiden: African Studies Centre, 1999), 8-14.

38 D. J. Boorstin, *The Image: A Guide to Pseudo-events in America. 25th Anniversary Edition (1992)* (New York: Vintage Books, 1961) and J. Urry, *The Tourist Gaze* (London: SAGE Publications Ltd, 2nd edn, 2002), 7.

39 D. MacCannell, *The Tourist. A New Theory of the Leisure Class* (Berkeley and Los Angeles, California: University of California Press, 1976).

40 J. Urry, *The Tourist Gaze*, 85.

41 Ibid., 52.

42 Ibid., 13-14.

The image of the Bushman is at least partly created within this 'environmental bubble' of tourism. Sehume mentions in this respect an example of a tourist (calling himself a 'voyager') who appeared not to be satisfied with the way the Bushmen and their lives were presented at Kagga Kamma (a 'cultural theme park' about Bushmen in South Africa). After moving on into the Kalahari to see the 'real' Bushmen he had sent photographs back to the research team. Ironically, one of the photographs appeared to be of an inhabitant of Kagga Kamma. [43]

It is not easy to position Treesleeper Camp as a certain 'type' of tourism. The project overlaps many definitions and ideas. Ethnic tourism is 'marketed to the public in terms of the "quaint" customs of indigenous and often exotic peoples, [...]. Destination activities include visits to native homes and villages, observation of dances and ceremonies, and shopping for primitive wares or curios, [...].'[44] Ethnic tourism strongly overlaps with 'cultural tourism': 'In most instances, the term *ethnic tourism* has been used to refer to activities that engage tourists in the experience of cultural events and situations that are distinct from their own.'[45] Cultural tourism focuses on the vanishing life-styles of peasant culture[46] and the problem with defining this term nowadays is that it has expanded, and so have the meanings attached to it.[47] Smith defines 'environmental tourism' as 'often ancillary to ethnic tourism. [...] Because environmental tourism is primarily geographic, many education-oriented travellers enjoy driving through mountains and countryside to observe man-land relationships.'[48] In 'nature tourism' the presence of humans weakens the concept of nature as magical and renewing, but there is a way to get closer to nature for those who assume 'nature' a bit boring since there is no dialogue. The people of nature, once labelled Peasants or Primitives and considered creatures of instinct, exemplify all that is good in nature herself. Again, the magic is spoiled by the presence of too many other tourists. This approach to nature is, again, ethnic tourism: therefore the latter is a combination of culture and nature tourism.[49]

Nature and host populations are without doubt intertwined and Treesleeper is a clear example of this. In some cases, the host population even *is* nature. According to Chambers, '[t]ravel brochures advertising tours of such places as the Amazon, Southern African game reserves, or the Himalayas regularly juxtapose photographs and descriptions of local flora and fauna with depictions of indigenous

43   J. Sehume, 'Staging Authenticity via Cultural Tourism', http://ccms.ukzn.ac.za/index. php?option=com_content&task=view&id=428&Itemid=100

44   V. Smith, 'Introduction', in V. Smith ed., *Hosts and Guests. The Anthropology of Tourism* (Philadelphia: University of Pennsylvania Press, 2nd edn, 1989), 4.

45   E. Chambers, *Native Tours*, 100.

46   V.L. Smith, 'Introduction',in *Hosts and Guests*, 4-5.

47   G. Richards , 'Introduction: Global Trends in Cultural Tourism', in G. Richards, ed., *Cultural Tourism: Global and Local Perspectives* (New York and London: Routledge, 2007), 2.

48   V. Smith, 'Introduction', 5.

49   N.H.H. Graburn, 'Tourism: The Sacred Journey', in *Hosts and Guests*, 31-2.

people in traditional dress, in effect, naturalizing these subjects for tourist consumption.'[50]

These kinds of tourism activities are sometimes referred to as 'indigenous tourism', which is based on the relation of people to their natural habitats, their heritage, history and handicrafts.[51] Treesleeper covers a lot of these definitions, but to define it as one specific type of tourism would not do justice to reality.

In a wider Southern African context, Hitchcock has identified several problems and lessons, with regard to Bushmen and tourism:[52]

- Social exclusion and/or discrimination within communities and trusts;
- Often certain members of a community feel excluded because their social and economic benefits are less than others, which has led to local conflicts;
- The important goal of poverty alleviation is often not achieved;
- Community Based Natural Resource Management (CBNRM) programs often have not resolved the significant conflicts between conservation and development;
- Different expectations from Northern people and Southern people;
- The majority of benefits from tourism go to safari operators and companies;
- Community-based integrated conservation and development programs are difficult to implement. Often the institutional capacity of community-based organisations is insufficient;
- CBNRM programs should be monitored in a simple way;
- Implementing the time-consuming and labour-intensive CBNRM activities should be done at the rhythm of the communities, who should be allowed to make their own choices;
- The degree to which communities have control over their own land is limited.

The 'Bushman Myth' at Treesleeper Camp

In Tsintsabis, most people live in small brick houses with a tin roof, in an often changing family setting. Sometimes a tin roof is used as the only shelter and people often do not care about building the walls: they use old plastic and grass and wrap it around the supporting iron poles. Apart from this, 'grass/cotton/plastic' traditional huts can be seen, especially in /Gomkhaos. The people in Tsintsabis do not have toilets or showers and even though there is water in

---

50 E. Chambers, *Native Tours.*, 80.
51 Ibid., 80-1.
52 R. K. Hitchcock, 'Natural Resource Management among Kalahari San: Conflict and Co-operation', in R.K. Hitchcock and D. Vinding, eds., *Indigenous Peoples' Rights in Southern Africa*, (Copenhagen: IWGIA Document No. 110, 2004), 221-6.

the village, provision is very unreliable. Installation of electricity supply started in 1999 in Tsintsabis but its use is limited because of power cuts and a lack of money for the bills. When on a village tour, the tourists go to /Gomkhaos from where they walk back to Treesleeper. Here they see how people live, can communicate a bit with translation from the tour guide, and hear stories about the war for independence, Bushman culture changing into agriculture, migrations, diseases, resttlement, and so on. In short, they are being told about life in a small rural African village, while seeing it and being there. Therefore it can be argued that the village tour is the most interesting activity offered at Treesleeper, because it is as close to 'real Africa' and its people as you can get as a tourist. Occasionaly tourists have started to cry, and some have been tempted to offer 'help' to the villagers, during the tour. On other days tourists have a great time with the people and the children and enjoy the general happiness and hospitality.

Tourist accommodation in Africa often looks 'authentically African', with stone of earthen colours, lots of wood and thatched grass roofs. Treesleeper Camp is no exception in this 'architectural staged African authenticity'. The only brick building is the cultural centre, but it has a grass roof, just as all the other buildings (washrooms, reception, the Makalani deck). The walls are made of reed and this 'local building style' does not have a lot to do with traditional Hai//om habitat: The grass and reeds were both brought from a few hundred kilometres away and these materials simply play an important role in making Treesleeper look 'African' and therefore prove attractive for tourists. When doing a bushwalk or watching a traditional performance, a tourist will see the different huts in which the Hai//om and the !Xun were really living and these are very different compared to accommodation at Treesleeper. Apart from Treesleeper looking 'African', it also looks 'eco' with lots of natural building materials and a total number of seven solar panels for power and hot water.

A traditional performance is normally arranged in the evening because of the setting and the atmosphere. A camp fire creates the light and is the centre of the performance. A specific place has been built for it, with traditional !Xun and Hai//om huts and a 'fence' of wooden branches around it. A sandy spot has been cleared and levelled where the dancers perform. The camp managers explain the ceremony in brief and confirm that film and photo cameras may be used. The performers are sometimes a cultural group from the Tsintsabis school, made up of youngsters who are interested in their own traditions. One teacher who is also a trustee at the Tsintsabis Trust, is fond of the traditions and is helping to organise this feature. Sometimes the group goes into the country to perform at cultural festivals. They do not get paid a salary, but Treesleeper pays part of the income from the performance to the school fund so they can cover costs (travelling/accommodation/food) when they go to visit cultural festivals. Often some food is bought for the young performers. In 2006, on such a trip to the north of the country, a 16 year old girl (then the leader of the children's group) was stabbed with a knife and raped. In June 2007 she was still not sure whether she wanted to perform ever again.

Apart from the children's group there are adults who perform and who get paid. When the men are hunting or working on a farm it can be hard to get the group together in time. Both groups dress up in traditional clothing with beads, ostrich egg bracelets, necklaces and so on. A traditional healing is part of the performance. The women clap and sing and a few men, healers, can reach a trance and heal a patient. At other times in Tsintsabis, you can hear this same singing and clapping in the middle of the night. If you go and see such a healing in Tsintsabis you will see two or three healers, dressed up in old T-shirts and worn trousers, walking around a fire while the women and some children are clapping and singing intensely. Some children are sleeping, the women are dressed up in modern dresses. It goes on for hours deep into the night. It is a very different happening from the staged version at Treesleeper.

Dressing up in traditional clothing for tourists is often controversial. I remember how one day I had a talk with the bushwalk guides, asking how they wanted to be dressed during the walk. In these days, we had just bought nice collared shirts for the staff of Treesleeper with the logo and 'Staff' nicely printed on the front. However, a tour operator that visited Treesleeper regularly to do the bushwalk had asked if the guides could do the bushwalk in traditional clothes. The guides decided for themselves that this was fine. After a while one of them stopped dressing up. On his next tour again he ignored the traditional clothing, later explaining:

> I cannot wear these clothes, the people in the village have seen me. They laugh at me when they see me walk around like that. They are now calling me names, they say I am stupid, also the children of my family. It is fine for tourists, I don't care, they can see me like this, they like it and they can make the pictures. They do not laugh at me. But I cannot wear this when my own people see me.

The same tour operator later again explained to //Khumûb that a German tourist had complained that he wanted to see the Bushmen but did not see them at Treesleeper. The staff at Treesleeper discussed the matter again and decided not to do the bushwalk anymore in full traditional clothes. However, at the end of the walk, where the traditional huts are seen, the staff change into these clothes to display them for the tourists. In 2010 only the traditional dancing was performed in 'authentic' dress.

8.2 *Traditional performance at Treesleeper Camp, 2007*
(© Vesa Nuutinen)

8.3 *Traditional healing in Tsintsabis, 2004*
(© Stasja Koot)

Bushmen as well as tourists are connected with wildlife, both in their own way. Wildlife parks and hunting show very different relationships between Bushmen and wildlife on the one hand and tourists and wildlife on the other. Around Tsintsabis there are some hunting farms and lodges (such as La Rochelle on the road to Tsumeb), as in the whole of Namibia. Tourists who visit the area do not only come to watch the animals (as in Etosha National Park); some have come to kill them. Since the 1970s the lucrative market for international recreational trophy hunting on private land has been developed to a very serious level in Namibia. Fomerly, where hunting and guest farms had suitable tourist attractions and if they were big enough, they would be developed into 'pure' game farms. In these cases, land was used mainly for tourism (middle and up-market lodges), livestock production ceased and safari hunting has turned out to be highly profitable.[53] In contrast to this often luxurious style of hunting, when Bushmen killed an animal it was eaten and the remains used for a variety of purposes, such as the skins for clothing or blankets. Hunting by Bushmen was a method of survival. Still today many Hai// om and !Xun in and around Tsintsabis want to hunt. Some of the older men go hunting in the communal area north of Tsintsabis and on the nearby resettlement farm Oerwoud. As a respondent explained there is sometimes a conflict with the farmers; '[t]hey do not like each other, the young boys from the Bushmen and the farmers because of the hunting. They kill the farmers' cows and then the whites and the Hereros blame the Bushmen.'

The bushwalk offered at Treesleeper consists for a large part of explanations about traditional Bushmen hunting methods. Tour guides show the tourists tracking, a variety of traps, the different hunting bows and arrows, digging sticks and so on. Here it is possible to get to know the traditional relationship of human beings with the animals (in fact, with the environment) a bit better. Ironically, the marginalised Bushmen who need wildlife for survival purposes, are limited nowadays in hunting. The relationship between tourists and wildlife is one in which the tourist is in control; it takes place within the environmental bubble. For a tourist, it is merely part of the romanticised, 'adventurous' picture of 'real' Africa. In other places in Namibia, such as Bwabwata National Park (the former West Caprivi Game Reserve) and the Nyae Nyae Conservancy, Bushmen communities *do* benefit financially from trophy hunting. The Hai// om do not profit at all from any such hunting in their traditional habitat and are in that way disadvantaged. The Namibian policy on conservancies, where a community has rights to resources on

---

53 J. Barnes and B. Jones, 'Game Ranching in Namibia', in H. Suich, B. Child and A. Spenceley, eds., *Evolution & Innovation in Wildlife Conservation: Parks and Game Ranches to Transfrontier Conservation Areas* (London: Earthscan, 2009).

the land, therefore does not benefit the Hai//om. The creation of a conservancy for the Hai//om at the southeastern side of Etosha is unlikely to materialise in the near future, due to a variety of reasons. It looks as if the Hai//om will again be left out of benefiting from American funds from the Millennium Challenge Account (MCA) currently aimed at conservancies.

In March 2011 two farms were acquired by the Namibian government and have been handed over to the Hai//om traditional authority with the idea that they would start benefitting from tourism, including hunting safaris and lodges, in addition to other commercial activities such as cultivation and the production of charcoal. Consequently, a total of seven farms has been handed over to the Hai//om chief in the last few years.[54] According to some respondents the government wants to give the people some land so that they will have done their duty to the Hai//om, who will in turn have no more grounds to ask for parts of Etosha to be returned to them. Deputy Prime Minister Hausiku suggested that more adjacent farms should be added to ensure a vast area for all the envisaged projects so that a 'Little Etosha' for the Hai//om would be created.[55]

Bushmen and wildlife parks

Treesleeper, Hai//om and Etosha can be seen in a wider Southern African context. Wildlife parks are the main reason why tourists come to Africa. In Namibia, Botswana and South Africa quite a few of these parks have a story of 'resettled' or 'relocated' Bushmen groups. According to Hitchcock, a serious problem faced by many indigenous peoples in Southern Africa when claiming their resource rights and land is the controversy between nation-states establishing national parks, game reserves, sanctuaries and monuments on the one hand and indigenous peoples' rights to ancestral homelands on the other. This often creates conflicts. People at grassroots level favour a Community Based Conservation (CBC) approach, while policy makers often favour strict preservation of wildlife, habitats and other natural resources.[56]

Recently, Bushmen have benefited from Community Based Natural Resource Management (CBNRM) projects in South Africa, Botswana, Zimbabwe and Namibia. These projects have tourism as an important component. In some cases in South Africa, CBNRM projects are located in the buffer zones around national parks and game reserves, for example around the Kgalagadi Transfrontier Park (the former Kalahari-Gemsbok Park). In Namibia in particular, the

---

54 'Govt hand farms to San', *The Namibian*, 16 March 2011 and 'San get 'Little Etosha', *Namibian Sun*, 28 March 2011.
55 'San get "Little Etosha"', *Namibian Sun*, 28 March 2011
56 R. K. Hitchcock, 'Natural Resource Management among Kalahari San' 204.

Caprivi Strip and the Nyae Nyae region contain reserves and national parks where CBNRM projects have taken place. In Botswana some of the CBNRM related tourism projects can be found around the Okavango Delta. CBNRM is not always associated with protected areas, (such as in the Tsodilo Hills or at /Xai /Xai in Botswana); when related to tourism it often takes place in areas that are ecologically or culturally significant.[57] The main cases of Bushmen resettlement and the creation of national parks can be seen in Table 8.1.

Table 8.1 National parks, game reserves and conservation areas in Southern Africa that resulted in the involuntary resettlement of local Bushmen populations.[58]

Park or Reserve Area, Establishment Date, Size	Country	Comments
Central Kalahari Game Reserve (1961), 52.730 sq km	Botswana	Over 1.100 G/ui, G//ana were resettled outside the reserve in 1997 and 2002
Chobe National Park (1961), 9.980 sq km	Botswana	A few Bushmen were resettled in the Chobe Enclave, where 5 villages are in 3.060 sq km
Moremi Game Reserve (1964), 3.880 sq km	Botswana	Khwe were relocated out of Moremi, one of the first tribal game reserves in the 1960s
Tsodilo Hills (1992, declared a World Heritage Site in 2001), 225 sq km	Botswana	Ju/'hoansi were resettled away from the hills in 1995 but continue to use resources there
Kalahari Gemsbok Park/Kgalagadi Transfrontier Park (1931), 37.991 sq km	South Africa, Botswana	≠Khomani were resettled out of the park in the 1930s, some of whom remained on the peripheries
Etosha National Park (1907), 22.175 sq km	Namibia	Hai//om were resettled outside of the park and sent to freehold farms in 1954
West Caprivi Game Park/Bwabwata National Park (1963), 5.715 sq km	Namibia	Khwe were resettled in the early 1960s and some more in the 1980s
Hwange National Park (1927, 1950), 14.620 sq km	Zimbabwe	Tyua were rounded up and resettled south of Hwange Game Reserve in the late 1920s

57 Ibid., 208-14.
58 R. K. Hitchcock, 'Natural Resource Management among Kalahari San', 207.

Obviously, the Hai//om are not the only Bushmen tribe who have lost their land due to the creation of a national park, but so far they hardly got anything back (e.g., land or natural resources) as have the ≠Khomani in Kgalagadi Transfrontier Park or the Khwe in Bwabwata. It is a bigger Southern African phenomenon, which can partly be explained by historical reasons and the Bushmen's lack of political power. Treesleeper Camp is not part of a broader CBNRM project, but must be positioned as a singular tourism project. The focus on Hai//om culture at Treesleeper Camp means that there is, however, an equal focus on wildlife since it has always played an important role in Bushmen culture. A visit to Treesleeper can make tourists see things very differently when they get to Etosha.

The Schoeman Commission, which was established in 1952, looked at the possibilities of creating a reserve for the Hai//om, adjoining Etosha National Park, where they would have hunting rights. However, this idea was dropped in 1953 for political reasons, while the !Xun Bushmen eventually got the Nyae Nyae Reserve.[59] Since then, the Hai//om have always been a tribe without land of their own. This is the root cause of many of their problems. It is doubtful if the current farms that are bought by the government to create a 'Little Etosha' will seriously change that situation.

Conclusion

Tourism does play a role in the life of Bushmen. Their traditional culture is part of the tourist's picture of Africa, mostly created in the environmental bubble. Treesleeper Camp is an example where the dynamics between Bushmen, wildlife (parks) and tourism are made clear. Both the tourist and the Bushman have a strong relationship with wildlife, but with a very different level of access to it. Tourists have the means to see or even hunt the wildlife, while Bushmen are restricted in hunting, their own tradition. They are allowed to explain and talk about hunting traditions to tourists, but can be put in jail when hunting in the wrong place. So the Bushman's hunting tradition now serves the tourist, when tourists come to gaze at the traditional Bushman's way of life. Obviously, this is a way to generate income for the Bushmen and in that way tourism gives another meaning to the Bushman's traditions. The character of the village tour at Treesleeper is very different, for tourists learn about 'real life' in the village of Tsintsabis. In this tour the *changing of* traditions is the focus, instead of the tradition itself.

The tourists visiting Treesleeper Camp come to see 'Bushmen', according to their expectations of what 'a Bushman' is. They often have a picture of Africa and Bushmen *before* travelling to Africa,

59 C. Longden, *Undiscovered or Overlooked?*, 25.

through access to the internet, travel guides, postcards, the Discovery Channel, *National Geographic*, fellow tourists, and everything else in the tourist's environmental bubble. They come to Africa to fill in the expectation they have of Africa. Only in this bubble does the 'real' Bushman still live. You can meet Bushmen when you go to a place like Treesleeper but you have to pay and they have to dress up so that the tourist can capture the 'reality' of this 'primitive tribe' on camera. It has nothing to do with the daily life of the Bushman in Tsintsabis, but is part of the picture on the tourist's mind when he comes to Africa. The 'Bushman Myth' lives on in tourism and is part of the tourists' broader 'African Myth'.

Treesleeper, as a relatively succesful community development project, is one part of this African Myth. Ideologically it fits well with ideas within civil society, such as a community approach, community ownership and (environmental) sustainability. However, Treesleeper is not situated in a conservation area. The Hai//om in Namibia are the only tribe without land of their own, contrary to promises which have been made in the past by colonial powers. A conservation area for Hai//om people (as possessed by many other tribes in Namibia) so that they can reconnect with their natural resources and wildlife, would be a logical and ethical step forward for this shattered and marginalised community. It would make the area more interesting for the development of tourism, conservation and CBNRM activities. So far Hai//om people have been left out of most of these programmes, and while the first steps to create a conservancy for them have been taken, serious doubts exist if this 'Little Etosha' will become a place of development or a rural slum like most of the resettlement farms in villages such as Tsintsabis.

Before Treesleeper was built tourists never came over to Tsintsabis or /Gomkhaos. It was just a dusty little village on the way to Etosha where they would sometimes stop for a drink. Apart from that, there was 'nothing interesting'. Ironically, the tourists stopping for a drink then were indeed in the middle of 'real Africa' and just moved on. Gordon and Sholto Douglas' Bushman Myth was focused on 'primitiveness' – what the members of the Denver African Expedition were looking for (1992).[60] The comparison with tourism is evident. Tourists look at Bushmen in the same way that they look at wildlife: they are also a part of their 'Africa'. In many ways, tourists look at Bushmen in the same way as the members of the Denver African Expedition in 1925. In 2011, 86 years after the expedition, the Bushman Myth is alive as never before within tourism and is part of a broader African Myth. At Treesleeper Camp both have come together.

---

60 R.J. Gordon and S. S. Douglas, *The Bushman Myth: The Making of a Namibian Underclass* (San Francisco: Westview Press, Inc., 2nd edn, 1992).

REFERENCES   Ashley, C. 'Tourism, Communities and National Policy: Namibia's Experience', *Development Policy Review* 16 (1998): 323-52.

Barnard, A. *Hunters and Herders of Southern Africa: A Comparative
Ethnography of the Khoisan Peoples* (Cambridge: University Press, 1992).

Barnes, J. I. 'Community-based Tourism and Natural Resource Management
in Namibia: Local and National Economic Impacts', in A. Spenceley, ed.,
Responsible Tourism: Critical Issues for Conservation and Development
(London: Earthscan, 2008), 343-57.

Barnes, J. and B. Jones. 'Game Ranching in Namibia', in H. Suich, H. B. Child
and A. Spenceley, eds., *Evolution & Innovation in Wildlife Conservation:
Parks and Game Ranches to Transfrontier Conservation Areas* (London:
Earthscan, 2009), 113-26.

Boorstin, D. J. *The Image: A Guide to Pseudo-events in America. 25th
Anniversary Edition (1992)* (New York: Vintage Books, 1961).

Botelle, A. and R. Rohde. *Those who Live on the Land: A Socio-economic
Baseline Survey for Land Use Planning in the Communal Areas of
Eastern Otjozondjupa* (Windhoek: Ministry of Lands, Resettlement and
Rehabilitation, 1995).

Burns, P. M. *An Introduction to Tourism & Anthropology* (London and New
York: Routledge, 1999).

Chambers, E. *Native Tours. The Anthropology of Travel and Tourism* (Illinois:
Waveland Press, Inc., 2000).

Dieckmann, U. *Hai//om in the Etosha Region* (Windhoek: John Meinert
Printing (PTY) Ltd, 2007).

Foster, G. M. *Tzintzuntzan: Mexican Peasants in a Changing World* (Illinois:
Waveland Press, Inc., 1988).

Gordon, R. J. *Picturing Bushmen: The Denver African Expedition of 1925*
(Claremont, South Africa: David Philip Publishers (Pty) Ltd., 1997).

—— and S. S. Douglas. *The Bushman Myth: The Making of a Namibian
Underclass* (San Francisco CA: Westview Press, Inc., 2nd edn.,1992).

Graburn, N. H. H. 'Tourism: The Sacred Journey' in V. Smith, ed., *Hosts
and Guests. The Anthropology of Tourism. Second edition* (Philadelphia:
University of Pennsylvania Press, 1989), 21-36.

Hitchcock, R. K. 'Cultural, Economic, and Environmental Impacts of Tourism
Among Kalahari Bushmen' in E. Chambers, ed., *Tourism and Culture: An
Applied Perspective* (Albany: State University of New York Press, 1997), 93-
128.

—— 'Natural Resource Management among Kalahari San: Conflict and
Cooperation', in R.K. Hitchcock and D. Vinding, eds, *Indigenous Peoples'
Rights in Southern Africa* (Copenhagen: IWGIA [International Work
Group for Indigenous Affairs] Document, 2004 No. 110).

—— Ikeya, K., Biesele, M., & Lee, R. 'Introduction: Updating the San, Image
and Reality of an African People in the Twenty First Century', *Senri
Ethnological Studies* 70 (2006): 1-42.

Karuuombe, B. 'Land Reform in Namibia', *Land Update* 59 (1997): 6-7.

Koot, S. 'Resettlement in Tsintsabis: Namibian Bushmen in a Changing
World', Utrecht University, MA thesis, 2000.

Longden, C. *Undiscovered or Overlooked? The Hai//om of Namibia and
their Identity: One of a Series of Books from the WIMSA Regional Oral
Testimony Collection Project* (Windhoek: Capital Press, 2004).

MacCannell, D. *The Tourist. A New Theory of the Leisure Class* (Berkeley and Los Angeles, California: University of California Press, 1976).

Malan, J.S. *Peoples of Namibia* (Pretoria: Rhino Publishers, 1995).

Maletsky, C. 'Hai//om Eye List's Farms', *The Namibian*, 16 June 1997.

The Namibian 'Govt hand farms to San', 16 March 2011.

The Namibian Sun, 'San get "Little Etosha"', 28 March 2011.

NAR (Nationale Adviesraad voor Ontwikelingssamenwerking). *Migratie en BilateraleOntwikkelingssamenwerking* (The Hague: Distributiecentrum DOP, 1991).

NTB (Namibia Tourism Board). 'Summary analysis 2006'. http://www.namibia-tourism.com.na/trade_docs/summary_analysis_2006.pdf (accessed 24 September 2009).

Pankhurst, A. *Resettlement and Famine in Ethiopia: The Villagers' Experience* (Manchester: Manchester University Press, 1992).

Pankhurst, D. *A Resolvable Conflict? The Politics of Land in Namibia* (Trowbridge, Wilts.: Redwood Books, 1996).

Richards, G. 'Introduction: Global Trends in Cultural Tourism',. in G. Richards, ed., *Cultural Tourism: Global and Local Perspectives*, (New York and London: Routledge, 2007), 1-24.

Salole, M. 'Merging Two Disparate Worlds in Rural Namibia: Joint Venture Tourism in Torra Conservancy', in R. Butler and T. Hinch, eds., *Tourism and Indigenous Peoples: Issues and Implications* (Amsterdam: Elsevier, 2007), 206-19.

Schapera, I. *The Khoisan Peoples of South Africa: Bushmen and Hottentots* (London: George Routledge & Sons, Ltd, 1930).

Schoeman, A. 'Etosha – after 75 years, a plucked fowl' in A. Schoeman, ed., *Notes on Nature (2002)*, (Windhoek: Gamsberg MacMillan Publishers (Pty) Ltd, 1982), 91-3.

Sehume, J. 'Staging Authenticity via Cultural Tourism', http://ccms.ukzn.ac.za/index.php?option=com_content&task=view&id=428&Itemid=100 (accessed 31 October 2011)

Sindiga, I. *Tourism and African Development: Change and Challenge of Tourism in Kenya* (Leiden: African Studies Centre, 1999).

Smith, V. 'Introduction' in V. Smith, ed., *Hosts and Guests. The Anthropology of Tourism* (Philadelphia: University of Pennsylvania Press, 2nd edn.,1989), 1-17.

Thoma, A. 'The Communal Land and Resource Management System of the San', in J. Malan and M.O. Hinz, eds., *Communal Land Administration: 26-28 September 1996, Windhoek* (Tsumeb: Nation Press, 1997), 61-3.

Treesleeper Camp. 'Activities' , http://www.treesleeper.org/activities.html (accessed 31 October 2011).

Tsintsabis Trust. 'Deed of Trust', Master of the High Court, Windhoek. Windhoek: LAC, 2004.

UNDP (United Nations Development Programme). *Namibia: Human Development Report 1998.* (Windhoek: UNDP, 1998).

!Uris Safari Lodge. Welcome to !Uris Safari Lodge – "in the footsteps of the diggers": A treasurable discovery on your way to Etosha National Park, Namibia'. http://www.urissafarilodge.com (accessed 31 October 2011).

Urry, J. *The Tourist Gaze* (London: SAGE Publications Ltd, 2nd edn, 2002).

9 · 'The lion has become a cow':
The Maasai hunting paradox

Vanessa Wijngaarden

Introduction

I vividly remember the nights around the campfire at an ecotourism camp on the edge of Masai Mara National Reserve, with lions and a resident leopard roaring in the distance while young Maasai men dramatically describe their culture and customs to tourists sipping their sundowners.[1] The men speak confidently in English, but are dressed in Maasai *shukas* and red blankets,[2] wearing sandals and beaded jewellery. Their stories are told with stern, powerful voices, in the theatrical manner that is common to Maasai men speaking in public.

As the tourists gaze in amazement and curiosity at the spears and swords flickering along the belts of these tall, dark-skinned men, they listen to tales about the violence and adventure of Maasai life. The men explain the hierarchy and restrictions that come with ceremonial lion hunts, but when the tourists ask whether they still hunt lions, the Maasai answer in the negative. Explanations are given immediately and in line with the logic of community-based conservation: 'Now that the tourists have come, we have come to realize the value of wildlife; the lion has become a cow.'[3]

Another phrase regularly returning during these campfire sessions is: 'We despise people that hunt and gather, there is no place for that in our society. We eat livestock meat, not wild meat and if we see someone hunting we will spear him.'[4] In contemporary tourism contexts, an image of Romantic harmony between pastoralism and wild animals is often being sketched and local Maasai commonly refer to themselves as the guardians of the Masai Mara's wildlife:

1 Five months of fieldwork were made possible with funding from the Schuurman Schimmel – van Outeren Stichting, Stichting Dr. Hendrik Muller's Vaderlandsch Fonds and the University of Amsterdam Fieldwork Fund, and support from the Kenyan Wildlife Service, Basecamp Masai Mara, Kecobat, International Livestock Research Institute and Koiyaki Guiding School. A special thanks to the local communities, Mannfred Narrida, the Maasai Buffalo Dance and Cultural Change Group and Mara Discovery and Community Empowerment Centre.
2 The anglicised plural of the Swahili word *shuka* is often used to refer to traditional Maasai dress.
3 Maasai traditionally live from their livestock, cows being the most important source of income. In the Mara area big cats, and especially lions, are the most prominent tourist attraction. Hence tourism businesses, governmental actors, NGOs as well as local Maasai use the above phrase, which underlines that wildlife can provide a livelihood. Parallel expressions are 'drinking the milk of the elephant' or 'milking the rhino', which is also the title of a documentary by D.E. Simpson (2008).
4 Talek, July 2007.

being herders they have safeguarded these animals for the people of the world to come and see.

The idea that Maasai have never hunted wildlife to eat the meat, and that they never will, is supported consistently all around the Mara Reserve. During an interview a Maasai man from Ololulunga speaks of the Maasai way of life, telling me the same story I always hear: 'Maasai have a taboo on eating wild meat. We do not use it.' I must say I am surprised when later on, when we get to know each other better, the same person reveals to me that many young Maasai men in the area kill wildlife regularly, eating the meat and bringing home usable products when it suits them. This paradox is largely a result of the influence of tourism on Maasai communities near the Mara Reserve. In order to explain how image and reality have become so diverted I will use the concept of the tourist bubble.

The tourist bubble is the mediating infrastructure that stands between local 'hosts' and visiting 'guests'. The term has evolved from Cohen's idea of the 'environmental bubble',[5] which is inspired by Knebel's concept of the *touristische Eigenwelt* (touristic own or inner world).[6] According to Cohen, during their trip tourists want to 'enjoy the experience of change and novelty only from a strong base of familiarity, which enables them to feel secure enough to enjoy the strangeness of what they experience.'[7] As a result the environmental bubble arises, consisting of the familiar institutions that tourists use as a protective surrounding while abroad.

These days, the term 'tourist bubble' has come to refer to this phenomenon, because the concept of environwelt can be confusing as it signifies such a wide variety of things. The newer term also makes explicit the connotation with tourism. The tourist bubble mediates the interaction between tourists and the local population and generally consists of a sending and a receiving side, including travel agencies in Western countries as well as local guides, tourist attractions and all other institutions that have come into existence as a result of the phenomenon of paying guests.[8] Often it consists of tourist infrastructure or facilities such as hotels, buses, food and souvenir shops, all based on, or adapted to, Western standards. But it also consists of surrounding the tourist with imagery he is familiar with.

Cohen predicted that the development of a tourist establishment would have an enormous impact 'on the culture, style of life, and world view of inhabitants of tourist regions'[9] and would have 'mixed

5 E. Cohen, 'Toward a Sociology of International Tourism', *Social Research* 39, 1 (1972): 164-82.
6 H.J. Knebel, *Soziologische Strukturwandlungen im Modernen Tourismus* (Stuttgart: Ferdinand Enke, 1960).
7 Cohen, 'Toward a sociology', 166.
8 W.E.A. Van Beek, 'Africa and its Tourist Bubble' (Abstract for the AEGIS European Conference on African Studies, African Studies Centre, Leiden, The Netherlands, 11-14 July 2007).
9 Cohen, 'Toward a Sociology', 179.

results for international understanding'.[10] Van Beek however argues that often the tourist bubble does not have such a deep impact on local life at all, because around the bubble life largely continues as usual. The bubble would mainly stress the local culture's central value systems, reinforcing existing definitions of the self.[11]

In this chapter I look at the effect the tourist bubble has on Maasai people living on the edge of one of the world's most famous ecotourism hotspots: the Masai Mara National Reserve in Kenya. I will focus most prominently on the impact the bubble has on these Maasai's relationship with wildlife and use this case study to examine to what extent the bubble generates international understanding. I will start with outlining the research setting. Then I will describe some of the varied economic and social impacts the tourist bubble has had in the Mara area,[12] paying most attention to the (changed) relationship between local Maasai and wildlife. Finally, the implications of the disparities between the Maasai image and their daily practice are discussed. It becomes clear that in order to affirm a definition of self that is in line with existing cultural categories and correlates with certain ideas of outsiders, Maasai understate less prominent, more ambiguous aspects of their identity.

Masai Mara: the ecotourism heaven

The Masai Mara National Reserve is the prototype of an area that has been set aside for tourist use. Initially only comprising the Mara Triangle, the Masai Mara Game Reserve was extended to encompass the plains east of the Mara River in 1961, and has excluded settlement and grazing since it was redesignated the Masai Mara National Reserve in 1976.[13] Today, only vehicles are allowed to pass through the gates, and most Maasai have never been inside the National Reserve or seen any of the large predators that tourists come to observe.

With the adjoining Serengeti in Tanzania, the Masai Mara National Reserve forms

a natural ecosystem containing the largest concentration of wildlife anywhere in Africa and accommodating the greatest land migration

10 Ibid., 181.
11 W.E.A. Van Beek, 'African Tourist Encounters: Effects of Tourism on two West African Societies', *Africa* 73, 2 (2003): 251-89; W.E.A. van Beek, 'Approaching African Tourism: Paradigms and Paradoxes', in P. Chabal, U. Engel and L. de Haan, eds., *African Alternatives* (Leiden: Brill, 2007), 145-72.
12 In this research the Mara area is defined as all group ranches surrounding the Masai Mara National Reserve in Kenya, not including the protected areas of the Reserve and the Mara Triangle. Data for this paper are based predominantly on a combination of ethnographic observations and 67 semi-structured interviews carried out in this area from July until September 2007.
13 R.H. Lamprey and R.S. Reid, 'Expansion of human settlement in Kenya's Maasai Mara: What future for pastoralism and wildlife?' *Journal of Biogeography* 31 (2004): 997-1032.

of animals anywhere in the world.[14] Possibly the most filmed and photographed area of Africa, the Mara's typical savannah vegetation as well as its famous migration of wildebeest have actually developed only several decades ago, after the thorough intervention of Maasai grazing, fire and rinderpest vaccination campaigns by the colonial government.[15] The importance of these relatively recent human interventions, however, does not stop the area from being a symbol of timeless and pristine wilderness for many all over the world.

The Mara area is often considered to harbour the first ecotourism experiments in Africa. Ecotourism is defined as 'responsible travel to natural areas that conserves the environment and improves the well-being of local people'[16] and is currently one of the fastest growing industries in Sub-Saharan Africa.[17] Until the 1977 hunting ban, most income in the Mara area came from rich whites shooting game, something which many might not easily perceive as a form of ecotourism. However, the money earned did add to local well-being: already in 1961 the Masai Mara Game Reserve's management was granted to Narok County Council, which used the income for community projects. By 1990, when wildlife viewing had long taken over as the most important tourist activity, the area was regarded as 'Africa's most sustained success in incorporating local communities in conservation.'[18] These days the borders of the Mara Reserve are dotted with tourist camps that strongly advertise a green tourism image and community support activities.

The Maasai, who are the Mara Reserve's closest neighbours, consist of approximately 850,000 Maa speaking people of Nilotic origin, who can be divided into different sections, traditionally almost all pastoralists. Although their lands were far more widespread before colonial times, they are now concentrated in the border region of Kenya and Tanzania due to forced resettlements. The people living near the Mara Reserve are mostly Maasai, belonging to the il-Purko section. I want to underline that the Mara area is not a representative example of the influence tourism has on daily Maasai life. This area is such an extremely popular tourist destination that the influence of the industry is magnified. This might clearly demonstrate the effects of tourism, but slightly different dynamics may be at play than in areas where the industry is less prominent. Even though most tourists

14 M. Honey, *Ecotourism and Sustainable Development: Who owns Paradise?* (Washington DC: Island Press, 1999), 201.

15 Before, the Mara area was mainly covered in woodlands, and the modest wildebeest migration in Tanzania did not reach here till 1969, as the population was limited by rinderpest. Lamprey and Reid, 'Expansion of Human Settlement'; P.D. Little, 'Pastoralism, Biodiversity, and the Shaping of Savanna Landscapes in East Africa', *Africa* 66, 1 (1996): 37-50.

16 This is the International Ecotourism Society (TIES) definition of ecotourism, http://www.ecotourism.org/site/c.orLQKXPCLmF/b.4835303/k.BEB9/What_is_Ecotourism__The_International_Ecotourism_Society.htm (accessed 31 October 2011).

17 M.E.M. Rutten, 'Partnerships in Community-based Ecotourism Projects: Experiences from the Maasai Region, Kenya: Volume 1', *ASC Working Paper* 57 (Leiden: African Studies Centre, 2004).

18 Honey, *Ecotourism and Sustainable Development*, 201.

visit the Mara area primarily to see wildlife, and interaction between Maasai people and tourists is limited as well as regulated, the tourist bubble's influence on local life is considerable, and probably more intense than in other places. As the tourism industry in developing countries is expected to continue to expand, the Mara area is a good location to determine what effects this can have.

Does tourism generate development?

Even though the tourist bubble brings in money, the income for the host country and local population are often overestimated. The main venues to profit from foreign visitors are tourist bubbles themselves.[19] Especially in Africa, the infrastructure that mediates tourist encounters is generally foreign, and an estimated 70 per cent of the income of tourism businesses in Kenya goes straight to the overseas multinationals which are co-owners or act as intermediaries to local organisations.[20] For Kenya, tourism is a major economic sector and source of foreign direct investment and state revenue. However, the costs of leaving land such as the Mara undeveloped by setting it aside for conservation have been calculated to be much higher than the income from wildlife and tourism.[21] The reason that Kenya is so focused on conservation and tourism is largely because of pressure exerted by international donors and the advantages it brings the governing elite. Conservation efforts secure the elite's position, personal income and control over the rural areas, and can be seen as a component of a repressive international political structure. However, conservation efforts, donor funding and tourism do also positively contribute to relative national stability.[22]

In the Mara area most tourism venues present themselves as ecotourism businesses. However, as in other places, the idea that therefore they would act responsible or even beneficial environmentally and socio-culturally is generally inaccurate.[23] The concept of ecotourism has been adopted, popularised and watered-down by the tourism industry and is now often used simply as a marketing tool to describe anything related to nature. Large tourism players exchange ecotourism awards between themselves and make use of symbols such as the Green Globe, which are not connected to any actual

---

19   Van Beek, 'Approaching African Tourism', 145-72.
20   Van Beek, 'African Tourist Encounters', 251-89.
21   L. Emerton, 'The Nature of Benefits and the Benefits of Nature: Why Wildlife Conservation Has Not Economically Benefitted Communities in Africa', *Community Conservation Research in Africa: Working Papers* 5 (Manchester: Institute for Development Policy and Management, University of Manchester, 1998); M. Norton-Griffiths and C. Southey, 'The Opportunity Costs of Biodiversity Conservation in Kenya', *Ecological Economics* 12 (1995): 125-39.
22   V. Wijngaarden, *'Blessings and Burdens of Charismatic Mega-fauna: How Taita and Maasai Communities Deal with Wildlife Protection in Kenya'* (MA thesis, University of Amsterdam, 2008).
23   J. G. Carrier and D.V.L. Macleod, 'Bursting the Bubble: The Socio-Cultural Context of Ecotourism', *Journal of the Royal Anthropological Institute* 11 (2005): 315-34.

changes but can simply be purchased. With sophisticated advertising and the travel press acting as an in-house public relations arm, the travel industry often appears 'green' without making fundamental or costly reforms.[24]

For the people of the Mara the costs of (eco)tourism are high. Conservation has a negative influence on communities' abilities to meet their most pressing daily needs, such as food, water and physical safety, because access to resources such as grazing land and drinking water have to be shared with wildlife. Purchasing power is low in the area neighbouring the Masai Mara National Reserve: about half of the local Maasai live on an income less than a US dollar (Ksh 70[25]) a day.[26] Roads and public transportation are in very poor condition. Health facilities, even on the edge of the park, have no clean water and necessary operations are performed with a torch as there is no electricity.

The latest publication of the Kenya Human Development Index (HDI) of 2004 calculates the overall score for Narok, which is the district that harbours the Masai Mara National Reserve, to be below the Kenyan average. The Human Poverty Index (HPI) of the same year states that in Narok district 22.5 per cent of the children below five years are underweight, 52.5 per cent of the people do not have access to safe drinking water and 71 per cent live with poor access to a qualified doctor, again all performances worse than the Kenyan average.[27]

Still, in the Mara area the tourist bubble has produced more local benefits than in other tourist areas in Kenya, such as the Tsavo National Parks region.[28] However, the money is divided highly unequally, with only the county council and a small Maasai elite benefiting considerably.[29] The foreign (eco)tourism businesses – such as tourist camps – benefit only a handful of local landowners and employees, while (eco)tourism projects which more truly involve considerable sections of the community – such as community wildlife sanctuaries – regularly develop division and conflicts over who forms the community that should benefit.[30] As the elite representing the board often benefits highly personally, the Mara's community-based

24 Honey, *Ecotourism and Sustainable Development*; P. Wight, 'Ecotourism: Ethics or Eco-Sell?' *Journal of Travel Research* 31, 3 (1993): 3-9.
25 The 2007 average exchange rates were US$1 to 67Ksh. Central Bank of Kenya, 'Indicative exchange rates', http://www.centralbank.go.ke/forex/default.aspx (accessed 22 May 22 2008).
26 R.S. Reid et al., *People, Wildlife and Livestock in the Mara Ecosystem: The Mara Count 2002* (Nairobi: International Livestock Research Institute, 2003), 17.
27 UNDP, *Linking Industrialisation with Human Development* (Nairobi: UNDP, 2005), 44-45, 48-49.
28 Wijngaarden, *Blessings and Burdens*.
29 Lamprey and Reid, 'Expansion of Human Settlement'.
30 The Maasai secretary of Koiyaki Landowners Conservation Association and secretary of the Narok Wildlife Forum for instance tells that 70 per cent of the people in Koiyaki-Lemek (the biggest group-ranch neighbouring the Mara) are not benefiting directly from game viewing fees, because they have no land inside the conservancy. However, sometimes they do have a lot of problems as a result of the wildlife on their land. Interview in Olkimitare, August 2007.

wildlife associations have split into fractions time and again, becoming completely splintered.

Within the county council as well as within the community, large sums of tourism money are pocketed and illegal transactions of land for tourism projects take place, leading to division.[31] Maasai do get increasing job opportunities at the county council as rangers and clerks, even the senior warden of Masai Mara National Reserve being Maasai. However, the 19 per cent of park fees that is supposed to go to the Reserve's surrounding group ranches, has effectively only been 10 per cent, which again largely ends up in the pockets of a small elite instead of the construction of public facilities. Many locals state that for the past years the money has not even been accounted for at all.

Other effects of the tourist bubble are land-use changes. As the value of people's land increases under the influence of its tourism potential, communally owned group-ranches are being subdivided at a fast rate. During subdivision of land, conflicts arise over the allocation of plots that are most attractive for tourism, because these are very valuable. Many Maasai who compare their situation to those making money in tourism have taken up farming on their plot because it provides a better income than pastoralism.[32] However, their crops are raided constantly by wildlife. As many young Maasai want to work in tourism, payment is not very high and employment is insecure, depending on the considerable fluctuations in the tourism market, something locals have become painfully aware of again during the 2007-2008 post-election violence as well as the current global financial crisis.

The promise of an income, however, continues to attract Maasai and non-Maasai families, who migrate into the Mara area. The commercial centres that have developed at the gates of Masai Mara National Reserve have practically no garbage disposal or sewerage. The newcomers have set up shops and small eating venues, but up to half of the towns' buildings are bars where people quickly come to spend the money they have made in tourism. Smoking, improper dressing, loss of traditions, and especially excessive drinking and prostitution are considered problems by locals from within and outside these shantytowns.

Nevertheless, the tourist bubble also channels local-tourist interactions towards support for schools, medical dispensaries,

---

31 See also Honey, *Ecotourism and Sustainable Development*; Rutten, 'Partnerships in Community-based Ecotourism'; D.M. Thompson, 'Better Policy and Management Options for Pastoral Lands: Valuing Land use Options in the Maasai Mara', in *Report of the 2004 Socio-Economic Survey*, ILRI (2006).

32 For the Mara area 'agricultural returns overwhelm those from either livestock or wildlife'. M. Norton-Griffiths et al., 'Land Use Economics in the Mara Area of the Serengeti Ecosystem', in A.R.E. Sinclair et al., eds., *Serengeti III: Human impacts on ecosystem dynamics*, (Chicago: University of Chicago Press, 2008) 379-416. According to calculations in Lamprey and Reid's 'Expansion of Human Settlement' income from livestock in the Mara area is about US$ 5-13 per ha per year, tourism generates US$ 10 per ha for the local people each year, while small scale cultivation would produce a yearly income of US$ 50-120 per ha, or more.

waterpoints and other community projects, especially if the tourism business is involved in ecotourism. In addition, local people use their own money, made in the tourism industry, in projects. An example is the group of mothers who has started a primary school in Talek. However, it must be noted that this social infrastructure generally does not provide subsistence, income or a secure livelihood to most community members and that these services are basic amenities that should actually be provided by the state,[33] as they are still under national average quality in this area.

Gender related effects of the tourist bubble are contradictory. Women might loose influence in the villages because men now make money, which makes them less dependent upon women's labour. However, many Maasai women also see themselves as more economically independent as a result of tourism. In Kenya, as is the case more generally, tourists like to buy handicrafts as souvenirs. Maasai sell weapons such as clubs and spears (often specially adapted to the tourism market, for instance by making them collapsible for transportation) but most popular is Maasai beadwork, which is generally a domain of women. These days, a range of beaded products is being sold: from 'traditional' necklaces and bracelets to Western items as beaded napkin rings, coasters and wine baskets.[34] The beads for these 'traditional crafts' are generally imported from Czech Republic and much 'Maasai' beadwork is produced and sold by Kikuyu people. Nevertheless, in the Mara area many women have come to make their own money by selling jewellery, which they either buy from Nairobi through middlemen or make themselves. Selling these items to tourists -for instance at the gates of the Mara Reserve- provides them with cash, which many invest in clothing and food for their children.

The relationship between the old and the young has also changed. Youngsters are more likely to go to school, although the possibility of finding a job in tourism also pulls them out early. To the regret of many elders, the dress and ambitions of young Maasai have changed. They can sometimes be heard speaking in high pitched voices imitating the tourists whose immense wealth they have seen or heard of, and youngsters as well as many elders desire to 'live like an American'.[35] The contrast they perceive between their own situation and the wealth of the tourists only adds to the local idea that 'tourism makes a lot of money, yet we do not see that money.'[36]

---

33   Emerton, 'Nature of Benefits'; J. Otuoma, 'The Effects of Wildlife-Livestock-Human Interactions on Habitat in the Meru Conservation Area, Kenya', *Land Use Change Impacts and Dynamics (LUCID) Project Working Paper* 39 (Nairobi: International Livestock Research Institute, 2004).

34   Even those ornaments resembling traditional designs are almost always (slightly) adapted to make them suitable for commercial use.

35   Interviews in Koiyaki Lemek Wildlife Trust, August 2007.

36   Interview, 43 year old Maasai man from Oltorotwa, August 2007.

The image of the Maasai that is spread worldwide as a component of the tourist bubble is one of people who live far away from the money culture, outside the realm of development. Maasai have been produced and reproduced according to 'the ideal mental conceptualisation of the Western European idea of an African "noble savage"'.[37] They represent 'a global image of African tribesmen'[38] and are often seen as the symbol of an Africa that has remained static and devoid of civilization. In the Garden of Eden, as Africa has been approached since colonial times, the Maasai is the 'untouched African primitive'[39] who simply blends into the landscape. These days, texts and images that present Maasai as noble savages can be found in almost every brochure advertising travel to Africa.

Tourists primarily come to the Mara area to see Kenya's charismatic mega-fauna, which are large mammals that attract international revenue, such as lions, leopards and elephants. However, as a tourist attraction, Maasai now take a close second place.[40] As is the case with the savannah wildlife, Maasai images are constantly used in advertising Eastern Africa as a tourist destination. An encounter with the Maasai 'is an adventure. It is exciting. It is similar to the excitement of the safari game run in the parks.'[41] In the Mara area, Maasai joke that tourists now come to see the 'Big Six', the Maasai being the latest addition to the animal series that every visitor comes to shoot pictures of.

Maasai culture, as well as African wildlife, is presented as belonging to the untouched, natural, unchanging, authentic, wild, and harmonious world that has been lost by overseas tourists. But again there is a gap between reality and the image projected by the tourism industry. Firstly, Maasai living in the Mara area have not done so for eternity. Their ancestors moved south from the Southern Sudan during the first millennium AD, arriving in the Rift Valley and moving towards Tanzania between the sixteenth and seventeenth century.[42] During colonial times many Maasai have been relocated and the people from the il-Purko section were moved to the Mara area from Laikipia by the colonial authorities in 1913.[43] Secondly, the National Reserve is not as natural, authentic and harmonious as it is

37 B.K. Ole Kantai, Foreword to S.S. Ole Sankan, *The Maasai* (Nairobi: East African Literature Bureau, 1971), vii.

38 E.M. Bruner, 'The Maasai and the Lion King: Authenticity, Nationalism and Globalization in African Tourism', *American Ethnologist* 28, no. 4 (2001): 893.

39 Ibid., 889.

40 Bruner, ibid.; I. Sindiga, *Tourism and African Development: Change and Challenge of Tourism in Kenya*.(Aldershot: Ashgate Publishing, 1999).

41 E.M. Bruner and B. Kirshenblatt-Gimblett, 'Maasai on the Lawn: Tourism Realism in East Africa', *Cultural Anthropology* 9, 4 (1994): 455.

42 T. Spear and R. Waller, eds., *Being Maasai: Ethnicity and Identity in East Africa.* (London: James Currey, 1993).

43 Lamprey and Reid, 'Expansion of Human Settlement': 1002.

often depicted. This protected area is there largely for the tourists, not for animals.[44] Although some wild animals are well adapted to being followed around by cars,[45] others have trouble feeding their young as a result of the constant proximity to humans.[46] Pollution, disturbance and erosion make clear that even ecotourism degrades the area considerably.[47]

There is another discrepancy between the image of Maasai as noble savages and local reality. [As] '"our primitive ancestors" who have not yet eaten of the tree of knowledge that is "modern civilizations" ... the Maasai [are characterised as] shepherds whose flocks live in harmony

9.1 Inside Masai Mara National Reserve. Cheetahs in eco-tourism paradise? 2007
(© Vanessa Wijngaarden)

44 The National Reserve was originally a hunting ground for white hunters and has become a restricted area as such. These days many animals rather stay in the community areas due to the positive influence of pastoralism on biodiversity, as is described by Little, 'Pastoralism, biodiversity and savanna'. Reid et al.'s large scale research in the Mara area even concludes that '[c]onservation policy that excludes low to moderate levels of traditional pastoral use may inadvertently impoverish the very lands it was instituted to protect' (*People, Wildlife and Livestock*,13). However, grazing is prohibited in the Masai Mara National Reserve and many of the surrounding conservancies because tourists want to see wildlife, not cows.
45 Some lions use cars as a cover while stalking their prey, while some cheetahs use them as a look-out post.
46 Interview Daniel Konchella, deputy district warden KWS, Wasongiro, July 2008. See also Basecamp Explorer, 'Mara Cheetah Conservation', http://www.basecampexplorer.co.uk/mara-cheetah-conservation/p_117/ (accessed 25 May 2009).
47 R. Duffy, *A Trip too Far: Ecotourism, Politics and Exploitation* (London: Earthscan Publications, 2002); Honey, *Ecotourism and Sustainable Development*; Kenyan Wildlife Service, *Wildlife–Human Conflicts in Kenya: Report of the Five-Person Review Group* (Nairobi: KWS, 1994); Wijngaarden, *Blessings and Burdens*.

with their predators.'[48] However, in truth, relations between Maasai and wildlife have always been complex and ambivalent. Furthermore, their interaction seems to have become more troublesome lately, as a consequence of the influence of the tourist bubble.

Wildlife: burdens and blessings

Maasai compete with wildlife for land and water, and this situation has intensified due to the increased pressure on these resources as a result of tourism. Alongside the Masai Mara National Reserve, many other areas have been reserved exclusively for animals and/or tourists. In addition, considerable amounts of livestock and crops are lost to wildlife, to the point that many Maasai have given up planting and the hope for a more beneficial food source for their families.[49]

The competition for grass between wildebeest and Maasai livestock can be so fierce that whole herds of cows starve. Wildebeest also infect livestock with malignant catarrh. In addition, cows as well as sheep and goats are regularly killed by predators such as lions, leopards and occasionally a cheetah, and it is not unusual for people to lose a hundred animals a year. Hyenas form an extraordinary threat and regularly kill dozens of small stock in one night, eating only a few, while leaving the rest to die from their wounds.[50] People are also considerably restricted in their movements, especially between dusk and dawn. Elephants, buffalo, rhino, hippo, lions, leopards and hyenas regularly attack, injure and sometimes kill people, mostly when it is dark, but sometimes even during the day.

Remarkable was an incident that took place July 2007 at Kekero village, where a young boy as well as his father – who tried to save his son when he heard his cries – were killed by hyenas. Two other sons trying to rescue their father and brother from being ripped apart were treated in Tenwek hospital, having lost part of their faces and buttocks. Daniel ole Taki, health officer at the Maasai dispensary on the edge of Masai Mara, estimates that on average two to three people per week come to the dispensary with injuries caused by wildlife.

It comes as no surprise that Maasai defend their livelihoods and themselves. They use fenceprickly bushes, cow-dung, old tyres, fires and torches, and bang their pans to keep the animals away. When necessary they use their swords and spears or resort to trapping, snaring or poisoning. However, overall, people do not feel bitter about wildlife. When asked whether wildlife and people could ever live

48 Bruner and Kirshenblatt-Gimblett, 'Maasai on the Lawn', 438.
49 Thompson, 'Better Policy and Management'; Wijngaarden, *Blessings and Burdens*.
50 In general in Kenya, the presence of wildlife reduces livestock returns by 30 per cent according to M. Norton-Griffiths and B. Butt, 'The Economics of Land Use Change Loitoktok Division, Kajiado District, Kenya', *Land Use Change Impacts and Dynamics (LUCID) Project Working Paper* 34 (Nairobi: International Livestock Research Institute 2003).

9.2 Use of wildebeest skin to tie a calf while milking, 2007
(© Vanessa Wijngaarden)

9.3 Cows and wildebeest grazing together, 2007
(© Vanessa Wijngaarden)

9.4 Small stock and zebra grazing together, 2007
(© Vanessa Wijngaarden)

peacefully together, a Maasai widow living on the edge of the Mara Reserve simply says: 'They cannot be separated.'[51] The wild animals are so integrated into daily life that people generally cannot imagine a life without them.

Wild animals provide a range of goods and services. I name only a few examples here: traditionally buffalo hide and horns were used to make sandals, shields and plates. In mythology, elephants are seen as the servants of women as they fell trees, and they still provide them with firewood today. Furthermore, when they forage at the river, the elephants keep predators away. Every morning and evening during milking time, local Maasai tie their calves with wildebeest skin, which is softer and more supple around a calf's neck than rope.

Gazelle, wildebeest and especially zebra are often seen grazing together with livestock or close to the *boma*,[52] their elevated alertness diminishing the threat of an unseen predator approaching and killing one of the cows.

Lions, colobus monkeys, crocodiles, ostrich and other birds provide men with traditional ornaments[53] which are still worn on special occasions, and the long twisted horn of the kudu is played during ceremonies.[54] Wildlife also provides medication. Drinking the fat of a lion is supposed to cure internal injuries and is considered generally good for the body. Although some locals dispute its workings, others – even young Maasai with good jobs in the tourism industry – still mix soaked and filtered elephant dung with milk and give it to their babies to prevent them from getting measles.

Now I come back to the hunting paradox I referred to at the start of this chapter: Maasai generally claim not to hunt wild animals for food, as they are herders, and often pose it is taboo to eat meat from wild animals.[55] However, in the past, eating wild meat was fairly common[56] and when the subject is broached in confidence it becomes clear that even these days almost every Maasai man of this area has eaten wildlife, and that hunting still takes place Buffalo and eland are

---

51 Interview in Talek, July 2007.
52 The word *boma* (pl. *maboma*) means cattle-pen in Swahili and is commonly used to refer to Maasai homesteads, where several houses are built in a circle around the central livestock pen. The Anglicised plural *bomas* is often used.
53 T. Ole Saitoti, and C. Beckwith, *Maasai* (New York: Harry N. Abrams, 1980), 96-97, 126-127, 149-153, 157.
54 Interviews with and performances attended of the Maasai Buffalo Dancers Cultural Group, July-September 2007. See pictures in S.S. Ole Sankan, *The Maasai* (Nairobi: East African Literature Bureau, 1971); Ole Saitoti and Beckwith, *Maasai*, 121, 156, 158.
55 See also D.K. Ndagala, *Territory, Pastoralists, and Livestock: Resource Control among the Kisongo Maasai* (Uppsala: Acta Universitatis Upsaliensis, 1992); Ole Sankan, *The Maasai*. The only Maasai that eat wild animals would be the Dorobo, a Maa speaking hunter-gatherer group that has become assimilated with the Maasai community but who are looked down upon because of their non-herding heritage. The word Dorobo means 'poor', as those without cattle are considered poor. On the perception of Dorobo see also N. Kipury, *Oral Literature of the Maasai* (Nairobi: East African Educational Publishers, 1983); Ndagala, *Territory, Pastoralists and Livestock*. However, during my fieldwork it became clear that non-Dorobo Maasai consume wildlife too.
56 D. Reid and P. Chapman, *Maasai tot in de dood* (Amsterdam: Uitgeverij Vijfplus, 1997).

9.5 Spear, sword, bow and arrows, Maasai weapons are still used to hunt wild animals, 2007
(© Vanessa Wijngaarden)

9.6 Maasai arrows, not poisoned, 2007
(© Vanessa Wijngaarden)

the most common and undisputed sources of wild meat, as they are considered to resemble cows. However, giraffe is generally considered the tastiest animal, but bushbuck, topi, gazelle and dikdik, and even hares are sometimes eaten, although the last are despised.

Most young men hunt wild animals while herding, especially when they have not yet been circumcised.[57] They do this as a form of sport, to practice skills and test strength, to compete and prove who is brave and who is faint-hearted, but also simply to cook and eat the meat. It can be part of adventure or to provide food in-between meals at home, especially when herders stay in the bush for a long time. Wild animals are eaten to prevent sacrificing the wealth of the family, for the taste or simply when an exceptionally fat animal crosses one's path.

Wildlife's symbolic significance

Contrary to what these hunting practices might incite, to these Maasai, the connection between wild animals and people is much deeper than simply material: wild animals have widespread symbolic significance. Children grow up with mythological stories, riddles, proverbs and figures of speech in which wild animals play a central role. Most prominent are narratives in which wild animals are the main actors. They have the bodily features of animals but speak and behave like human beings. These stories often involve a trickster aspect and are entertaining, but under the surface they provide life lessons. They are told to teach youngsters about history, culture and social interaction and can be used to comment upon events within the community, reflect upon one's own position and actions, or comment upon social activities of others. Elders often tell these stories to 'ridicule and scorn any unbecoming behaviour without having to point a finger at any individuals.'[58]

Moreover, Maasai social structure has historically been regulated by an age-set system and a categorisation into clans, which are both deeply connected to wildlife. In mythology the age-set system came into being as a result of the interaction young boys had with a leopard and a python that were send by God.[59] Each of the clans has a totemic connection to a wild animal which symbolises certain personal qualities. The people of the clan of the elephant (*ilmoleleian*) for instance, have leadership qualities and are good speakers, while the people of the clan of the hyena (*iltarlosero*) are greedy, and those of the buffalo selfish and unpredictable. The clan

---

57 Ole Saitoti and Beckwith state that animals are hunted to obtain materials for ceremonies, but that most hunting is done by young men to prove that they are ready to be circumcised (*Maasai*, 58, 97,114). My informants spoke of more casual and day-to-day hunting activities.
58 Kipury, *Oral Literature*, 19. An example told to me several times is the story of the lion and the ostrich, in which the lion tries to claim the children of the ostrich. With rhetoric and a cunning trick involving a termite mound, a small mongoose defeats the powerful lion's plans.
59 Ole Sankan, *The Maasai*.

of the rhino (*ilaiser*) is split into two sections, one part providing the best warriors (*lemusere*), the other providing magicians (*lekitui*).[60]

In addition, Maasai make use of wildlife in their ceremonies and believes. Some examples are that in times of disease the skin of the eland and wildebeest is used to protect or cure livestock. In 1998 in the Mara area, during the last epidemic affecting cows, locals tied eland skin around the neck of a black heifer (or if not available, any bull) to protect their herd. During the yearly returning threat of malignant catarrh, Maasai from the clan of the rhino provide charms and hang strips of the skin of baby wildebeest at the entrances of the *boma*. When the cows pass through they will be touched by the skin and not become ill if they happen to graze in an area infected by the wildebeest's calving. As a result an animal like the wildebeest is not only a bringer of disease but, when properly used, can also be a means to ward it off.

Perhaps most striking is that the complex interaction between Maasai and wildlife already begins when Maasai are small children and does not end with death. Traditionally, the bodies of those who had died were put outside the *boma*.[61] If they were eaten by the lions, that meant the family was being blessed; if they were eaten by hyenas it meant the opposite. Maasai in the Mara area state that they only started burying their dead five to ten years ago, and some still do not want anything other than to be put outside when their time comes.

A changed relationship

The interaction between wildlife and Maasai of the Mara can best be described as a lifelong and complex entanglement that is sometimes exploitative but also shows aspects of symbiosis. It is striking that currently, local Maasai (as well as locals of other regions in Kenya) report that staying with the animals has become increasingly difficult, while research shows that wildlife populations in Kenya have generally dropped, around 50 per cent over the last 25 years.[62] It has been reported that the Mara area even lost 70 per cent of its wildlife between 1976 and 1996[63] and overall numbers have continued to

---

60   Naomi Kipury in *Oral Literature* (40) has a slightly different classification and spelling of the clans' names, speaking of the Ilmolelian, Aiser and Iltaarrosereo. Reid and Chapman also report on how wild 'animals are relatives of the clans' (*Maasai tot in de dood*, 179, my translation). That this relationship is not just symbolic, concerning mythical icons of the animals, but also concerns the real animals in flesh and blood becomes clear with the story of a killed cobra, which was related to the clan of the *loitayo* (ibid. 180).
61   Reid and Chapman, *Maasai tot in de dood*.
62   D.J. Campbell et al., 'Interactions between People and Wildlife in Southeast Kajiado District, Kenya', *Land Use Change Impacts and Dynamics (LUCID) Project Working Paper* 18 (Nairobi: International Livestock Research Institute, 2003); M. Norton-Griffiths, 'Wildlife Losses in Kenya: An Analysis of Conservation Policy', *Natural Resource Modeling* 13, no. 1 (2000): 13-34.
63   Lamprey and Reid, 'Expansion of Human Settlement'; Reid et al., *People, Wildlife and Livestock*.

diminish.[64] How is it possible that the inhabitants of the Mara area often have the feeling that there are more animals and definitely more problems with animals now than several decades ago?

The increase in human–wildlife conflict that also has been recorded by other researchers and the KWS[65] is probably the result of several changes which I have all linked to the influence of the tourism bubble. Firstly, the population of some animals that cause problems, such as the hyena, has grown locally.[66] This is probably the result of conservation efforts. Secondly, and more importantly, the human population in the Mara area has also grown considerably.[67] In addition, more land is used for farming, which local people as well as researchers, the government, KWS and NGOs all agree is less compatible with wildlife.[68] Therefore, less space is left for animals and people to share, and in these places, human –wildlife conflict has become aggravated.

Another explanation for this feeling is based on interviews with informants in the Mara area, where locals report a change in the attitude of wildlife towards them. An old Maasai lady from Eluai voices the general feeling as follows: 'Compared to the old days [the] animals have become very many now. They also were not aggressive a long time ago, but now they are.'[69] Local Maasai link the increased aggression of wild animals to their protected status. A Maasai sub-chief in the Mara area states that when poaching was prohibited 'people became very shy and the animals multiplied.'[70] A Maasai lady in her seventies from Oltorotwa clarifies:

> Now the animals are more aggressive than before as now they are being protected. Before, if an elephant kills someone, it is being killed. Now people are afraid to kill it. People used to form a group to go after it. The animals were fearsome [afraid].... In the future animals will be [even] more protected and they will become very proud just moving around here [points to the area directly surrounding the compound]. People and livestock will not be comfortable.[71]

In the eyes of the locals, the strict conservation efforts that are fuelled by tourism have disturbed the hierarchy between animals

64 J.O. Ogutu et al., 'Dynamics of Mara-Serengeti Ungulates in Relation to Land-use Changes', *Journal of Zoology* 278, no. 1 (2009): 1-14.
65 Campbell et al., 'Interactions in Kajiado District'; Kenyan Wildlife Service, *Wildlife-Human Conflicts.*
66 Campbell et al., 'Interactions in Kajiado District'.
67 Lamprey and Reid, 'Expansion of Human Settlement'; Reid et al., *People, Wildlife and Livestock.*
68 Kenyan Wildlife Service, *Wildlife-Human Conflicts*; Norton-Griffiths et al., 'Land Use Economics'; Otuoma, 'Effects of Wildlife-Livestock-Human Interactions'.
69 Interview in Eluai, August 2007. The same trend is affirmed for these as well as other areas by Campbell et al., 'Interactions in Kajiado District' 7; Otuoma, 'Effects of Wildlife-Livestock-Human Interactions'; Wijngaarden, *Blessings and Burdens*; and the KWS itself: Kenyan Wildlife Service, *Wildlife-Human Conflicts.*
70 Interview in Koiyaki-Lemek Wildlife Trust, August 2007.
71 Interview in Oltorotwa, August 2007.

and people.[72] As a consequence, the animals do not know their place any more. Local people feel that as a result of their protected status, wildlife has become arrogant.

Why Maasai say they do not hunt

Maasai hunting and use of wild animals is generally no threat to wildlife numbers. Recent surveys have concluded that in the Mara area, wildlife is actually more numerous in community areas where Maasai live than in protected areas such as the National Reserve.[73] Grazers like the fresh grass growing on deserted Maasai cow pens, and make use of the added protection of Maasai homesteads, in turn attracting predators. As a result of these habits of the Maasai's domestic animals, the environment becomes more diverse and useful for wild species than if left alone. Likewise, the Maasai practice of burning parts of the savannah produces short and nutritious grass. As a result, many species are more numerous on community land.[74]

Reid and his co-authors conclude that 'there appears to be a density of bomas ideal for promoting abundant species-rich wildlife; any increase or reduction in the number of bomas may decrease the number of wildlife.'[75] The density of *bomas* was at an optimum at the time of research in 2002, which suggests that despite population growth, the Maasai living around the Mara have at least up till the early years of the new millennium mostly supported and facilitated the animal population in their vicinity, even when they were using them and competing with them.

However, Maasai have obvious reasons not to speak of their complex coexistence with and use of wild animals. In the first place, Maasai are often suspected of diminishing wildlife numbers by overgrazing the land[76] and killing the wild animals. Hunters have to be careful, as all wildlife is anxiously protected by Kenyan law, and rangers – often operating in military style – track, catch, abuse, and sometimes even

---

72   Although it might be aware of the problem, the Kenyan government fears that relaxing the strict protective rules would damage its image towards tourists and thus its income. David Western's 1996 draft wildlife policy and the 2007 draft wildlife bill both proposed the partial lifting of the hunting ban, one proposing sports hunting for some species, the other the limited use of wildlife resources. The 1996 draft was never implemented because income from tourism stagnated at the time (Honey, *Ecotourism and Sustainable Development*). The 2007 draft was shelved by the Tourism and Wildlife Minister Dzoro 'because of vested interests among key players in the wildlife industry'. See G. Gathura, 'Draft Bill seeks right of way for wildlife', *Daily Nation*, 30 May 2009.

73   Ogutu et al., 'Dynamics of Mara-Serengeti ungulates'; Reid et al., *People, Wildlife and Livestock*. This is also known by experienced driver-guides, who often take their clients for game drives in the community areas instead of into the Reserve, although the entrance fee has already been paid. Personal observation and communication with driver-guides, July 2007.

74   Interviews with Dickson Kaelo, a local Maasai and researcher for the International Livestock Research Institute (ILRI), Koiyaki group ranch, August 2007; Little, 'Pastoralism, Biodiversity and Savanna'.

75   Reid et al., *People, Wildlife and Livestock*, 130.

76   This accusation is contradicted by Little in 'Pastoralism, Biodiversity and Savanna'.

kill offenders.[77] Again the influence of the tourist bubble can be seen: wildlife is an important source of income for the Kenyan state and the Kenyan elite.[78] The image of black poachers who threaten nature, has been created in colonial times and still stands strong.[79] As a result of paying visitors, this image is continuously recreated because it attracts donations for saving wildlife, urges visitors to come and see the animals 'while they are still there' and encourages the spread of tourism which supposedly finance wildlife's continued existence.

The real threats to wildlife that can be associated with Maasai people come from further increases in population pressure and changes in land-use systems. Under the influence of the tourist bubble, local incomes and the quality of medical facilities have risen, but only slightly so. This results in a fall in mortality rates, but not in birth numbers. Consequently the population is growing fast. In addition, the tourist bubble leads to migration into the area. The urge for development and land subdivisions stimulated by the flow of money that the tourist bubble generates, leads to an increase in agriculture and other businesses. This is at the cost of the pastoralist way of life, which – as explained earlier – is far more compatible with sustaining wildlife.[80]

The second reason that Maasai do not speak of their intimate relationships with wildlife is because historically they have an ideal of pastoralism, which they are underlining again due to the imagery produced by the tourism bubble. Although it may also have existed in the Neolithic period, the ideal of Maasai as pure pastoralists is mostly a modern phenomenon. It is closely linked not only to Maasai self-conceptions, but also to historical and ethnographic literature where Maa-speaking people who were not living off livestock were not regarded as 'real' Maasai.[81]

However, 'the "pure pastoral" tradition has not been the only one in Maasailand nor, in the long term, has it necessarily been the dominant mode.'[82] Maasai have systematically relied on the products of farmers and hunters and assimilated with these communities and their modes of production, especially in times of need. In fact, Maasai only practised pure pastoralism during a short period of time in the eighteenth and nineteenth centuries, while before and after

77 Kenyan Wildlife Service, *Wildlife-Human Conflicts*; N. Kithi and J. Otieno, '3 KWS rangers and 4 poachers shot dead', *Sunday Nation*, 20 May 2007; R.P. Neumann, 'Disciplining Peasants in Tanzania: From State Violence to Self-Surveillance in Wildlife Conservation', in N. L. Peluso and M. Watts, eds., *Violent Environments*, (New York: Cornell University Press, 2001), 305-327.
78 Wijngaarden, 'Blessings and Burdens'.
79 E. Steinhart, *Black Poachers, White Hunters: A Social History of Hunting in Colonial Kenya*, (Oxford: James Currey, 2006).
80 To the north of Masai Mara National Reserve there has been an enormous growth of commercial wheat cultivation. At the shantytown-like commercial centres that have evolved at the Reserve's gates, populations have risen so much that the former coexistence between wildlife and people has begun to break down. See also J.O. Ogutu et al., 'Dynamics of Mara-Serengeti Ungulates'.
81 Spear and Waller, *Being Maasai*.
82 R. Waller, 'Conclusions', in Spear and Waller, op cit, 292.

this period many Maasai were directly engaged in non-pastoralist modes of production, such as hunting.[83] However, with the modern revival of the 'pure pastoral' ideal under the influence of tourism from the twentieth century on, hunting – especially when practised as the major form of subsistence – has remained a sign of poverty and is associated with an uncultured, unrestrained existence in the wilderness.

The Mara's wildlife guardians

The Mara area's Maasai firmly present themselves as guardians of wildlife in reaction to their widespread image as noble savages, natural beings living devoid of development and in harmony with wild animals. As is the case in other areas, when tourists visit, locals stage the 'authentic' image that Western people have of the destination, reflecting back the imagery that is projected on to them.[84] By presenting themselves as guardians of wildlife, Maasai give tourists what they come for: a utopia of natural harmony. However, in so doing, they also underline their agency in their historical and current dealings with wildlife. I will explain both points in the following paragraphs.

These days, more and more Maasai become self-employed as guides or set up their own tourism businesses, such as cultural *manyattas*, campsites and small travel agencies.[85] They are slowly but increasingly taking the production of Maasai people as a tourist attraction into their own hands, but largely go along with the existing imagery that the bubble has produced in order to achieve success. As a result, another paradox develops: the tourist bubble that incentivises development[86] is at the same time an obstacle to its achievement. It seems that one of the reasons that public facilities in the Mara area are below average, is because the Kenyan states' concern to comply with the images that tourists expect. I will give two examples: a bad infrastructure severely limits personal mobility and business opportunities, especially for small businesses. However, there are only dirt roads (that are regularly washed away) connecting the Mara area to the rest of Kenya, because

83 Spear and Waller, *Being Maasai*.
84 K.M. Adams, 'Come to Tana Toraja, "Land of Heavenly Kings": Travel Agents as Brokers in Ethnicity', *Annals of Tourism Research* 11 (1984): 469-85; D. MacCannell, 'Staged Authenticity: Arrangement of Social Space in Tourist Settings', *American Journal of Sociology* 79 (1973): 586-603.
85 Cultural *manyattas* are villages built for tourists to visit in order to experience Maasai life. The word is the anglicised plural of the Maa word *e-mányátá*, which means ceremonial home, and originally refers to the ceremonial village where Maasai men of the same age-set used to reside during most of their warriorhood. Examples of Maasai-owned tourism businesses are Topi Trackers Safari campsite, Experience Mara, Oldarpoi Mara Camp and Saltsprings Mara Camp and The Mara Discovery and Community Empowerment Centre.
86 Maasai use the Swahili word *maendeleo* in this context, which is the plural of the Swahili *endeleo*, which means progress, development or improvement. It is used to refer to Maasai tourism businesses (such as a campsite, or beadwork enterprise) as well as the movement towards a higher living standard.

asphalt would undermine the tourist's authentic experience of African wilderness. For the same reason, the state prohibits locals in several parts of the Mara area from building houses that do not look traditional, even if this has health consequences for the population.[87]

Local Maasai do not simply accept all aspects of the imagery projected onto them. By portraying themselves as wildlife guardians, they contradict ideas of absolute primitivism historically attributed to them, internationally as well as nationally. For a long time, Maasai have been looked down upon as savages, first by the English colonisers, later by the Kenyan and Tanzanian state, as well as by other ethnic groups and this continues till today.[88] The image of the ignoble, dangerous, low, raw savage is the reverse side of that of the noble savage. This negative imagery has been used historically in the oppression, forced relocation and denial of infrastructure, schooling and medical facilities that Maasai people have experienced and still deal with today.

By underlining the positive aspects of the imagery the tourist bubble produces, Maasai elevate themselves above this history. As the people who have safeguarded the wildlife treasure of East Africa, Maasai become people with a culture and partners in conservation, instead of cruel poachers living in the bush without rule or constraint. However, they cannot completely escape their portrayal as savages. In order to be an attractive object of tourism and achieve a higher standard of living through this industry, a certain amount of primitivism has to be put on stage.[89]

Conclusion

While sitting around the campfire with tourists, Maasai of the Mara area underline their distant but harmonious relationship with wildlife. In truth, their coexistence with wild animals is much more intimate and complex. This discrepancy is the result of the growing influence that the tourist bubble has on daily life around the Masai Mara National Reserve. Today, encouraged by the state, tourism industry and conservation NGOs, some locals say that 'the lion has become a cow': wildlife has become a source of income. Nevertheless

---

87 Traditional houses are small, often leak, and produce health problems because the smoke cannot escape. Western-style houses with iron roofs solve these problems and save the women from collecting dirty river water to drink and cook with because they make it possible to collect rain water. However, as they would clash with the 'genuine' experience of the Maasai world that tourists come to see, the government prevents the building of any other than traditional houses at places where tourists often pass by. Interview in Ekeju-Emutukaa, August 2007.

88 L. Schneider, 'The Maasai's New Clothes: A Developmentalist Modernity and its Exclusions', *Africa Today* 53, 1(2006): 101-31; A. Talle, 'Pastoralists at the Border: Maasai Poverty and the Development Discourse in Tanzania', in D. M. Anderson and V. Broch-Due, eds., *The Poor Are Not Us: Poverty and Pastoralism in Eastern Africa* (Oxford: James Currey, 1999), 106-24.

89 V. Wijngaarden, 'Cosmopolitan Savages: The Challenging Art of Selling African Culture to Tourists', *Etnofoor* 22, 2 (2010): 98-125.

the revenue that wild animals produce still largely bypasses local Maasai people, while simultaneously conservation continues to impose negative effects on them; not only because it limits their use of resources, but also because the wildlife – enjoying the strict protection of the law – has become more destructive and arrogant, and increasingly difficult to live with.

As a result of the phenomenon of paying guests, Maasai of the Mara area have become increasingly aware of their actual and relative position of poverty. As neither lions nor cows bring in enough personal revenue, a move to combine or replace these livelihoods with agriculture takes place. Since ecotourism has left its promise of benefiting local people largely unfulfilled, it is questionable how long Maasai will want to remain guardians of wild animals.

The history of their complex, sometimes even symbiotic relationship with wildlife is an important reason for Maasai to continue to put up with them. However, as this relationship is often misunderstood by NGOs, conservationists and tourists, and matches the international images of the ignoble savage poacher rather than the noble savage living peacefully within nature, it cannot be part of the dialogue with tourists or (inter)national wildlife organisations. This has resulted in a paradox, combining a strong non-hunting rhetoric with relatively common hunting practices. As Cohen predicted, international understanding has not simply advanced as a result of increased contact through tourism: a widening gap has developed between the internationally popular image of the untouched Maasai living harmoniously with wildlife and Maasai people's concrete urge for development and daily struggle with wild animals.

In line with Van Beek's argument, important aspects of Maasai traditions and practices are solidified and hardened, 'reinforc[ing] dominant strains of identity construction.'[90] Pastoralism is underlined as a dominant aspect of Maasai identity. However, it would be interesting to explore to what extent this is mere rhetoric, as pastoralism stands in contrast with many locals' desires for wage-labour and changes in land use towards agriculture. In order to affirm a definition of self that is in line with existing cultural categories and correlates with certain ideas of outsiders, Maasai understate some less prominent, more ambiguous aspects of their identity.

Maasai have their reasons to reinforce the image that exists of them. They embrace and stage these outside ideas in order to acquire the basic amenities and wealth they long for. They also embrace the particular imagery of the peaceful herder because it elevates them above the level of primitive people, living without culture or constraints. However, this image in itself can also be an obstacle when trying to achieve a better life, because it obscures the often symbiotic relationship Maasai and wildlife still have and denies local people's

---

90   Van Beek, 'African Tourist Encounters', 286.

desires for development. This results in a loss of opportunities as well as a lack of realism, which can limit the advance or continued existence of forms of development – in the tourism sector or not – which benefit nature as well as local communities.

REFERENCES   Adams, K.M. 'Come to Tana Toraja, "Land of Heavenly Kings": Travel agents as brokers in ethnicity', *Annals of Tourism Research* 11 (1984): 469-85.

Bruner, E.M. 'The Maasai and the Lion King: Authenticity, Nationalism and Globalization in African Tourism', *American Ethnologist* 28, 4 (2001): 881-908.

——and B. Kirshenblatt-Gimblett. 'Maasai on the Lawn: Tourism Realism in East Africa', *Cultural Anthropology* 9, 4 (1994): 435-70.

Campbell, D.J., H. Gichohi, R. Reid, A. Mwangi, L. Chege and T. Sawin. 'Interactions between People and Wildlife in Southeast Kajiado District, Kenya', *Land Use Change Impacts and Dynamics (LUCID) Project Working Paper* 18, Nairobi: International Livestock Research Institute (September 2003), http://www.lucideastafrica.org/publications/Campbell_LUCID_WP18.pdf

Carrier, J.G. and D.V.L. Macleod. 'Bursting the Bubble: The Socio-Cultural Context of Ecotourism', *Journal of the Royal Anthropological Institute* 11 (2005): 315-34.

Cohen, E. 'Toward a sociology of international tourism', *Social Research* 39, 1 (1972): 164-82.

Duffy, R. *A Trip to Far: Ecotourism, Politics and Exploitation* (London: Earthscan Publications, 2002).

Emerton, L. 'The Nature of Benefits and the Benefits of Nature: Why Wildlife Conservation Has Not Economically Benefitted Communities in Africa', *Community Conservation Research in Africa: Working Papers* 5, Manchester: Institute for Development Policy and Management, University of Manchester (May 1998), http://www.sed.manchester.ac.uk/idpm/research/publications/archive/cc/cc_wp05.pdf

Gathura, G. 'Draft Bill seeks right of way for wildlife', *Daily Nation* 30 May 2009. http://www.nation.co.ke/News/-/1056/604684/-/ujpwt7/-/index.html (accessed 31 October 2011).

Honey, M. *Ecotourism and Sustainable Development: Who owns Paradise?* (Washington DC: Island Press, 1999).

Kenyan Wildlife Service. *Wildlife-Human Conflicts in Kenya: Report of the Five-Person Review Group* (Nairobi: KWS, 1994).

Kipury, N. *Oral Literature of the Maasai* (Nairobi: East African Educational Publishers, 1983).

Kithi, N. and J. Otieno. '3 KWS rangers and 4 poachers shot dead', *Sunday Nation* 20 May 2007.

Knebel, H.J. *Soziologische Strukturwandlungen im Modernen Tourismus* (Stuttgart: Ferdinand Enke, 1960).

Lamprey, R.H. and R.S. Reid. 'Expansion of human settlement in Kenya's Maasai Mara: What future for pastoralism and wildlife?' *Journal of Biogeography* 31 (2004): 997-1032.

Little, P.D. 'Pastoralism, biodiversity, and the shaping of savanna landscapes in East Africa', *Africa* 66, 1 (1996): 37-50.

MacCannell, D. 'Staged Authenticity: Arrangement of social space in tourist settings', *American Journal of Sociology* 79 (1973): 586-603.

Ndagala, D.K. *Territory, Pastoralists, and Livestock: Resource Control among the Kisongo Maasai* (Uppsala: Acta Universitatis Upsaliensis, 1992).

Neumann, R.P. 'Disciplining Peasants in Tanzania: From State Violence to Self-Surveillance in Wildlife Conservation', in N. L. Peluso and M. Watts (eds.), *Violent Environments* (New York: Cornell University Press, 2001) 305-27.

Norton-Griffiths, M. 'Wildlife losses in Kenya: An analysis of conservation policy', *Natural Resource Modeling* 13, 1 (2000): 13-34.

—— M.Y. Said, S. Serneels, D.S. Kaelo, M. Coughenour, R.H. Lamprey, D.M. Thompson & R.S. Reid, 'Land Use Economics in the Mara Area of the Serengeti Ecosystem', in A.R.E. Sinclair, C. Packer, S.A.R. Mduma, J.M. Fryxell, eds., *Serengeti III: Human impacts on ecosystem dynamics* (Chicago: University of Chicago Press, 2008), 379-416.

——and B. Butt. 'The economics of land use change Loitoktok Division, Kajiado District, Kenya', *Land Use Change Impacts and Dynamics (LUCID) Project Working Paper* 34. Nairobi: International Livestock Research Institute (2003), http://www.lucideastafrica.org/publications. htm

——and C. Southey. 'The opportunity costs of biodiversity conservation in Kenya', *Ecological Economics* 12 (1995): 125-39.

Ogutu, J.O., H.P. Phiepo, H.T. Dublin, N. Bhola and R.S. Reid. 'Dynamics of Mara-Serengeti ungulates in relation to land-use changes', *Journal of Zoology* 278, 1 (2009): 1-14.

Ole Sankan, S.S. *The Maasai* (Nairobi: East African Literature Bureau, 1971).

Ole Saitoti, T. and C. Beckwith. *Maasai* (New York: Harry N. Abrams, 1980).

Otuoma, J. 'The Effects of Wildlife-Livestock-Human Interactions on Habitat in the Meru Conservation Area, Kenya', *Land Use Change Impacts and Dynamics (LUCID) Project Working Paper* 39. Nairobi: International Livestock Research Institute (January 2004), http://www.lucideastafrica. org/publications/Otuoma_LUCID_WP39.pdf

Reid, D. and P. Chapman. *Maasai tot in de dood* (Amsterdam: Uitgeverij Vijfplus, 1997). Originally published as *Waters of the Sanjan* (Nairobi: Read, 1982).

Reid, R.S., M.E. Rainy, J. Ogutu, R.L. Kruska, K. Kimani, M. Nyabenge, M. McCartney, M. Kshatriya, J.S. Worden, L. Ng'ang'a, J. Owuoar, J. Kinoti, E. Njuguna, C.J. Wilson and R.H. Lamprey, *People, Wildlife and Livestock in the Mara Ecosystem: The Mara Count 2002* (Nairobi: International Livestock Research Institute, 2003). Also available from http://www. maasaimaracount.org/downloads.html

Rutten, M.E.M. 'Partnerships in Community-based Ecotourism Projects: Experiences from the Maasai Region, Kenya: Volume 1' *ASC Working Paper* 57 (Leiden: African Studies Centre, 2004). Also available from https://openaccess.leidenuniv.nl/handle/1887/9459

Schneider, L. 'The Maasai's new clothes: A developmentalist modernity and its exclusions', *Africa Today* 53, 1 (2006): 101-31.

Sindiga, I. *Tourism and African Development: Change and Challenge of Tourism in Kenya* (Aldershot: Ashgate Publishing, 1999).

Spear, T. and R. Waller, eds. *Being Maasai: Ethnicity and Identity in East*

Africa (London: James Currey, 1993).

Steinhart, E. *Black Poachers, White Hunters: A Social History of Hunting in Colonial Kenya* (Oxford: James Currey, 2006).

Talle, A. 'Pastoralists at the border: Maasai poverty and the development discourse in Tanzania', in D. M. Anderson and V. Broch-Due, eds., *The poor are Not Us: Poverty and Pastoralism in Eastern Africa* (Oxford: James Currey, 1999) 106-24.

Thompson D.M. 'Better Policy and Management Options for Pastoral Lands: Valuing Land use Options in the Maasai Mara', in *Report of the 2004 Socio-Economic Survey* by ILRI, 2006.

UNDP. *Linking Industrialisation with Human Development*, Nairobi: UNDP, 2005.

Van Beek, W.E.A. 'African Tourist Encounters: Effects of Tourism on two West African Societies', *Africa* 73, 2 (2003): 251-89.

—— 'Approaching African Tourism: Paradigms and Paradoxes', in P. Chabal, U. Engel and L. de Haan, eds., *African Alternatives* (Leiden: Brill, 2007), 145-72.

—— 'Africa and its Tourist Bubble', Abstract for the AEGIS European Conference on African Studies, African Studies Centre, Leiden, The Netherlands, 11-14 July 2007.

Waller, R. 'Conclusions', in T. Spear and R. Waller eds., *Being Maasai: Ethnicity and Identity in East Africa* (London: James Currey, 1993), 290-302.

Wight, P. 'Ecotourism: Ethics or Eco-Sell?' *Journal of Travel Research* 31, 3 (1993): 3-9.

Wijngaarden, V. *Blessings and Burdens of Charismatic Mega-fauna: How Taita and Maasai Communities Deal with Wildlife Protection in Kenya* (München: Martin Meidenbauer Verlagsbuchhandlung, 2010).

—— 'Cosmopolitan Savages: The Challenging Art of Selling African Culture to Tourists', *Etnofoor* 22, 2 (2010): 98-125.

10 • The organization of hypocrisy? Juxtaposing tourists & farm dwellers in game farming in South Africa

Shirley Brooks, Marja Spierenburg & Harry Wels

Charles is a landowner in an area of KwaZulu-Natal province known locally as the Midlands. Over the past decades he has built up a profitable business as a cattle breeder. Now however, there is pressure for him to participate in a land-use change fuelled by the tourism industry: the conversion of some sixteen privately owned farms in the area into an upmarket wildlife-based lifestyle development called the Gongolo Wildlife Reserve (GWR). Charles's farm is located inside the area that would constitute the proposed GWR, so he finds himself in a difficult position as the only 'hold-out' against the move to a tourism-oriented wildlife-based future.

Charles has reluctantly agreed to participate in the venture, but worries about the future of the people who currently live and work on his land. Resulting from a complex agrarian history in which African families have lived, worked and kept cattle on white-owned farms in the region for generations, Charles has a total of twenty-five *imizi* (homesteads) located on his land. Currently they are continuing to do what Charles says they have done for three generations: looking after his cattle when they move down to the 'thornveld' grazing during the summer, and for the remainder of the year maintaining fences and tending to their own cattle. These people will however have to move if and when the GWR becomes a reality. The farm dwellers' current homes will be in the middle of a 'Big Five'[1] game reserve populated by dangerous wild animals – it would no longer be safe to live there and they would be unable to keep cattle. Some landowners in the area have already introduced white rhino and buffalo on their parts of the proposed GWR, and signs warn, 'No trespassing' in English and isiZulu. The question of where the farm dwellers would go is unresolved.[2]

This chapter sets out to examine the phenomenon of private game farming in South Africa in light of the broad concept of 'organised hypocrisy'; an idea first developed in organisational sociology by Nils

---

1 The term 'Big Five' refers to the large African animals conventionally considered most dangerous and therefore most exciting for tourists to see: lion, leopard, elephant, rhinoceros and buffalo.
2 For Charles's story, see Lot van Brakel, 'Who is winning (from) the game?' (M.Sc. diss., VU University, Amsterdam, 2008), 44-5, 53-4.

Brunsson[3] and later extended to a wider arena by political scientist Stephen Krasner.[4] In the last decade, the concept of organised hypocrisy has been applied in a variety of contexts, from analysis of the functioning of large institutions or organisations such as the World Bank;[5] to the workings of citizenship regimes through the regulation of migration;[6] to the way governments propound particular ideologies whilst actually practising something different (for example, proclaiming nuclear non-proliferation while at the same time maintaining a nuclear arsenal).[7] To our knowledge, the concept has not been widely applied in the field of tourism studies. Yet the tourism industry does have the effect of drawing actors into regulatory regimes involving – perhaps even premised on – a certain degree of 'organised' or structural hypocrisy.

The chapter considers the usefulness of the concept of organised hypocrisy for understanding changes in a landscape that is being reshaped in particular ways for tourism. In South Africa, a 'wilderness' landscape is being brought into being on private land in the interests of catering to the perceived requirements of (often overseas) tourists. This has serious implications for poor farm dwellers or so-called 'labour tenants' such as those living on Charles's farm. At the same time, in the contemporary South African context it is important for developers and private business people to demonstrate social responsibility – to show that private game reserves and wildlife-based lifestyle developments like the Gongolo Wildlife Reserve are also beneficial for the poor. The result is an uneasy fit between an essentially capitalist venture in wilderness tourism, and the developmental rhetoric of job creation, partnership, and even community-based natural resource management (CBNRM). This is a situation that arguably involves both host and visitor in a situation of structured or organised hypocrisy.

Organised hypocrisy and the tourism industry

There is much debate in the literature about the meanings and key characteristics of organised hypocrisy. Brunsson initially employed the term in the context of formal institutions such as government bureaucracies.[8] His argument was that, when a complex organisation

3 Nils Brunsson, *The Organization of Hypocrisy: Talk, Decisions and Actions in Organizations* (New York: Wiley, 1989).
4 Stephen Krasner, *Sovereignty: Organized Hypocrisy* (Princeton NJ: Princeton University Press, 1999).
5 Catherine Weaver, *Hypocrisy Trap: The World Bank and the Poverty of Reform* (Princeton NJ: Princeton University Press, 2008).
6 Horng-luen Wang, 'Regulating transnational flows of people: An institutional analysis of passports and visas as a regime of mobility', *Identities* 11, 3 (2004): 351-76.
7 Michael Lipson, 'Organized hypocrisy and the NPT' (paper presented at the annual meeting of the American Political Science Association, Washington DC, 1-4 September 2005).
8 Brunsson, *The Organization of Hypocrisy*.

is confronted with a situation where it has to conform to conflicting imperatives, some level of 'organised hypocrisy' – understood as a gap of greater or lesser magnitude between the organisation's stated objectives, and its actual practices – develops because it is functional in ensuring the organisation's survival. The concept of organised hypocrisy draws our attention to the 'difference between words and deeds, the eventuality that organisations may talk in one way, decide in another and act in a third.'[9] Robert Whipple, CEO of a consultancy firm training leaders in the United States, speaks of 'neon hypocrisy' in situations where the top brass of an organisation sets standards that are hardly ever executed in the day to day operations of the organisation, for instance the often used slogan 'people are our most important asset.' 'It is in the daily actions of managers and leaders at all levels that the hypocrisy of the statement shines like a *neon* sign to everyone who works in the company. Most managers simply do not act as if they believe people are the most important asset.'[10]

While this can of course be damaging for the organisation if the gap becomes too evident or if too much attention is drawn to it (for example by the media or other critics), maintaining a certain level of ambiguity can be very useful. Brunsson has noted that organised hypocrisy can even have a morally good outcome, because the maintenance of a gap between words and deeds may protect an organisation against too rigid an application of some passing ideological fad or the fanatical ideas of a powerful leader.[11] Fineman goes further: 'Without such hypocrisy it would be very difficult, if not impossible, to achieve a viable working order, either for everyday social communication and relationships, or for producing the goods and services that we have come to appreciate.'[12]

Krasner imported the term 'organised hypocrisy' into political science, thus taking it beyond the realm of organisational sociology and applying it to less formal regimes or institutions, in particular regimes of global governance.[13] In thinking through the international community's attitude to nuclear non-proliferation, for example,[14] or the Iraq war[15] and UN peacekeeping operations,[16] the concept provides a useful perspective. It sheds light on the way leaders of a particular state espouse the principles of democracy in order to gain membership of a group of democratic nations, while violating

9 Brunsson, Introduction to *The Organization of Hypocrisy: Talk, Decisions and Actions in Organizations* (Copenhagen: Copenhagen Business School Press, 2nd edn 2002), xiii.
10 http://thetrustambassador.com/2011/03/19/neon-hypocrisy/ (accessed 26 September 2011). Italics added.
11 Brunsson, *The Organization of Hypocrisy:* 2nd edn.
12 Stephen Fineman, *Understanding Emotion at Work* (London, New Delhi: Sage, 2003), 20.
13 Krasner, *Sovereignty.*
14 Lipson, 'Organized hypocrisy and the NPT'.
15 Amitav Acharya, 'State sovereignty after 9/11: Disorganized hypocrisy', *Political Studies* 55 (2007): 274-96.
16 Michael Lipson, 'Peacekeeping: Organized hypocrisy?' *European Journal of International Relations* 13, 1 (2007): 5-34.

these principles at home. It helps explain why a set of long-standing internationally accepted governance norms – such as non-intervention in the affairs of a sovereign state – may be ignored, with the blessing of the international community, for the sake of some 'higher principle'.[17] Krasner has however attracted criticism for decoupling the concept of organised hypocrisy from the actual workings of organisations. By focusing too narrowly on the intentions of leaders or 'rulers', who are assumed to be rational actors making a conscious choice to adopt a hypocritical stance, 'hypocrisy' in this instance can come across as overt and intentional, rather than (as in the Brunssonian sense) the almost inevitable outcome of organisational change, reflected in the gap between rhetorical claims and the everyday practices of workers in complex organisations such as bureaucracies.[18]

It is important to acknowledge that the word 'hypocrisy' is a strong one and, in everyday language, carries a considerable charge of moral opprobrium. It must be noted that the point of the theoretical concept of organised hypocrisy is not to assign moral blame in this sense, and certainly not to blame individual actors. Rather it is to gain a better understanding of the structural context within which everyday practices and idealistic visions or rhetoric fail to coincide. In this chapter, we are particularly interested in the insight that 'organised hypocrisy' is often a response to what Lipson and Weaver call the 'authorizing environment' in which a particular organisation or set of actors must operate.[19] This is because organisations 'must signal conformity with societal norms and rules in order to obtain the legitimacy necessary to demonstrate social worthiness and mobilize resources'.[20] The theory alerts us to the fact that actors 'satisfy contradictory demands from their external environment through inconsistent rhetoric and behaviour'.[21]

In maintaining a more neutral stance towards hypocrisy, we are able to see that the notion of organised hypocrisy is useful in 'helping us understand organisational behaviour [rather than] formulating general prescriptions for the way organisations should behave'.[22] At the same time, we are reluctant to abandon the normative altogether. When the gap between rhetorical claims and everyday practice acts to reinforce the unequal power relations that exist in particular power-laden contexts, it is surely appropriate to argue that ways should be found not only to expose but also to narrow that gap. It is perhaps allowable, in contexts where rhetoric and daily practice have become widely separated, to question whether conscious misrepresentation

17 Acharya, 'State sovereignty after 9/11'.
18 Michael Lipson and Catherine Weaver, 'Varieties of organized hypocrisy', Paper presented at the annual meeting of the International Studies Association, San Francisco CA, 25-29 March 2008).
19 Lipson and Weaver, 'Varieties of organized hypocrisy', 7.
20 Ibid., 8.
21 Lipson, 'Organized hypocrisy and the NPT', Abstract.
22 Brunsson, Introduction to *The Organization of Hypocrisy*, 2nd edn, xvii.

and even outright lying about daily practices might exist. In such a case, the concept of 'organised hypocrisy' remains useful only up to a point: moral judgement cannot be suspended indefinitely.

It is perhaps surprising that the tourism industry has not attracted scholarly attention as a site of organised hypocrisy. The tourism industry is not a formal institution. However, in some parts of the developing world, it can be thought of as an informal governance regime prescribing particular kinds of outcomes while drawing individual actors into relations characterised by just the sorts of tensions discussed above. Critical tourism scholars have identified elements of structured hypocrisy in the way the tourism industry is organised and the tourism 'product' delivered – it is just that they may not have adopted a Brunssonian framework to do so.

Most famously, following MacCannell, attention has been drawn to the 'tourist bubble' in which consumers of tourism products are often forced to exist.[23] Rather than being offered wider choices to experience the messy reality of everyday life in a particular host country, it is assumed by actors in the industry that tourists need and expect to be protected from precisely this reality. The resulting tourist bubble can take numerous forms, from the organised coach tour in which visitors travel through their host country observing it from the safety of a hermetically sealed environmental bubble, to the luxurious coastal resort from which tourists are not encouraged (or even allowed) to move on their own, so that they see nothing of the world of poverty and violence outside. Immersed in the tourist bubble, visitors' awareness is limited to the artificial environment that has been constructed for them. Cushioned from the shock of the real, managed twenty-four hours a day and carefully insulated from any unpleasantness, the tourist's entire experience – what John Urry famously termed the tourist 'gaze'– is in this sense premised on hypocrisy.[24]

A second arena in which critical scholars of tourism have identified a strong element of hypocrisy is in the managed cultural encounters between tourists and hosts, notably in presentations of so-called 'primitive' or 'tribal' cultures. These encounters have been extensively analysed in terms of the notion of 'staged authenticity'. Again following MacCannell[25] (who in turn drew on Goffman),[26] scholars have attempted to unpack the relationship between 'front stage' spaces – designed to facilitate the performance or staging of culture for tourists – and 'backstage' spaces, to which tourists are usually not admitted. As Tomaselli notes, most cultural tourism

23   Dean MacCannell, 'Staged authenticity: Arrangements of social space in tourist settings', *American Journal of Sociology* 79, 3 (1973): 589-603.
24   John Urry, *The Tourist Gaze: Leisure and Travel in Contemporary Societies* (London: Sage, 1990).
25   MacCannell, 'Staged authenticity'.
26   Erving Goffman, *The Presentation of Self in Everyday Life* (New York: Doubleday, 1959).

takes place 'front stage, in the public spaces where the meeting of hosts and guests/tourists is designed to occur. Back stage is where the hosts and performers live, retire, and conduct their own social, leisure and symbolic lives.'[27] The question of who actually controls these exercises in cultural entrepreneurship, i.e. where the profits are made and how they are (re)distributed, is crucial. All too often in tourism ventures featuring so-called 'indigenous people', it is not the performers who control the benefit stream, but rather the manager or owner of the business who remains offstage, paying the performers a pittance for their efforts. In these cases, tourist encounters fail to shift – and indeed act to reinforce – a powerful dynamic of marginalisation and exploitation that is deeply entrenched in many post-colonial societies.

Implicit in this critique is a necessary engagement with the problematic power relations resulting from a history of imperialism and colonialism. As Hammet and Jayawardane argue in their analysis of the tourist experience offered at Nyoni's Kraal in Cape Town – one of many southern African 'cultural villages' where, as the authors put it, the effect is to create spaces of interaction featuring 'theatrical versions of the primitive' – this form of cultural tourism replicates rather than challenges colonial relations.[28] Equally, while alternative forms of tourism such as 'ecotourism' are supposed to provide a better and more responsible form of engagement with both communities and the environments in which they live, in reality the 'ecotourist bubble' can often be a similarly protected sphere in which tourists exist and within which their experiences are shaped and framed.[29] Wilderness safaris and campfire cultural performances, we argue, raise identical questions about the structured relations of hypocrisy implicit in the tourism experience, particularly in a post-colonial context such as Africa. For Hammet and Jayawardane, neither hosts nor tourists are absolved of responsibility for this situation: both are 'complicit in the fashioning of these venues and the imageries produced and consumed therein.'[30] Armed with these theoretical insights, the next section turns to the spaces and imaginaries being constructed in the context of private game farming and private game reserves in South Africa.

27 Keyan G. Tomaselli, 'The semiotics of anthropological authenticity: The film apparatus and cultural accommodation', *Visual Anthropology* 14, 2 (2001): 176. There is a large literature on this topic which cannot be fully reviewed here. For recent contributions, see John L. Comaroff and Jean Comaroff, *Ethnicity Inc.* (Chicago and Pietermaritzburg: University of Chicago Press and University of KwaZulu-Natal Press, 2009); Chris Ryan and Michelle Aicken, eds., *Indigenous Tourism: The Commodification and Management of Culture* (Oxford: Elsevier, 2005).
28 Daniel Hammet and Neelika Jayawardane, 'Performing the primitive in the postcolony: Nyoni's Kraal in Cape Town', *Urban Forum* 20, 2 (2009): 215.
29 James G. Carrier and Donald V.L. Macleod, 'Bursting the bubble: The socio-cultural context of ecotourism', *Journal of the Royal Anthropological Institute* 11 (2005): 315-34.
30 Hammet and Jayawardane, 'Performing the primitive', 231.

A noticeable phenomenon in Southern Africa's agrarian landscape, especially since the early 1990s, has been the emergence of private 'wilderness' spaces which are marketed to tourists as part of an African wilderness or ecotourism experience. In many parts of South Africa, especially those areas where agriculture requires substantial technological and financial inputs, landowners have come to the conclusion that without state subsidies, conventional farming is no longer profitable. Many have either sold their land, thus making way for private conservation initiatives, or have taken the decision to themselves shift to a wildlife- and tourism-based livelihood. The result is the mushrooming of private game reserves or game farms, offering products ranging from weekend hunting packages to luxury safari experiences for the very wealthy. Most private wildlife initiatives start on a single farm. From this basis, landowners often continue linking up, or buying up, other farms adjacent to the original farm in order to create economies of scale, allowing for the introduction of more wildlife – especially the 'charismatic megafauna' such as elephants and rhinoceros that tourists allegedly associate with Africa – and for cost-sharing in matters of security such as fencing and game guards.[31] Still, the establishment of private wilderness areas requires major financial investments.

Ted Steyn provides an early example of such a venture.[32] In his memoirs of the Northern Tuli (Private) Game Reserve in Botswana, Steyn introduces the reader to an impressive list of shareholders in the various properties that jointly constitute this private wildlife conservancy. In 1964 the list included:

> ... well-known business personalities such as ... the Vosloo brothers Piet and Thys (well-known property developers who controlled JSE quoted companies Moncor and Mondorp) ... Mr C.S. (Punch) Barlow ... for many years chairman of the Voelcke Trust, which finances and sponsors the continual updating and improvement of Roberts' Bird Book ... [and] The Barlow Group [which] held the Southern African agency for Caterpillar equipment ...[33]

Dave Varty, who together with his brother John established the highly successful Londolozi Private Game Reserve near the Kruger National Park in the 1970s, also recently published his memoirs.[34] The original market-based philosophy is summed up in a pithy quote from John Varty: 'If I can eat it, if I can hunt it, if I can photograph it, that is what

---

31 Harry Wels, *Private Wildlife Conservation in Zimbabwe. Joint Ventures and Reciprocity*, (Leiden: Brill, 2003).

32 Ted Steyn, *Northern Tuli Game Reserve. Memories of the Founding of a Major Private Game Reserve*, (Kelvin: E & R Steyn, 2004).

33 Ibid., 24-5.

34 Dave Varty and Molly Buchanan, *The Full Circle: To Londolozi and Back Again, A Family's Journey*, (Johannesburg: Penguin, 2008).

I will do. I will make money out of wildlife.'[35]

Two key points need to be made about these multiplying land-scapes. First, they are 'constructed' landscapes in both the physical and discursive sense – a fact that is often obscured for tourists and others by their new status as 'wilderness', as if these are 'pristine' areas untouched by humans.[36] Second, these spaces must succeed in the marketplace: private wildlife production bets on international and relatively rich nature tourists coming to South(ern) Africa to enjoy an unforgettable wilderness experience. As a result, the relations between hosts and guests on private game reserves/game farms are largely shaped by the (perceived) demands of the market. From the point of view of the landowner or 'host' – for whom wildlife-based development is now a crucial source of capital generation – the wildlife and wilderness experience provided must live up to the expectations of the tourist and the market-based images to which they have been exposed. Just what tourists will see, hear, smell and experience is carefully moulded to deliver the anticipated outcome: the 'wilderness experience', the 'real Africa'. This involves the discursive repositioning of farms through tourist marketing, as well as, in most cases, physical and spatial alterations to the landscape.[37] In the resulting 'ecotourist bubble', the hosts' constructions need to match tourists' expectations, thus ensuring that they are willing to pay for the services provided.

The belief that overseas or urban-based tourists prefer to visit 'pristine' wilderness areas, devoid of human habitation, is a key assumption on which the marketing of these wilderness experiences is based.[38] African wilderness appears to hold a particular mystique: one expressed, for example, by Ted Steyn in his description of the landscape of the Northern Tuli Private Game Reserve as constituting 'vast vistas of savannah ... with clean horizons and *no sign of human habitation or encroachment*'.[39] It is this kind of empty landscape, populated only by wildlife that constitutes the essence of the tourism-driven African wilderness construct. It is rarely that the social history of these landscapes is considered, especially by tourists. Yet game farms and private reserves such as these are of course premised on colonial histories of land (dis)possession and, in particular, private or freehold land ownership. In the case of the Tuli block for example, the

35   John Varty, cited in Varty and Buchanan, *The Full Circle*, 35.
36   Shirley Brooks, Marja Spierenburg, Lot van Brakel, Annemarie Kolk and Khethabakhe B. Lukhozi, 'Creating a commodified wilderness: Tourism, private game farming, and "third nature" landscapes in KwaZulu-Natal', *Tijdschrift voor Ekonomische en Sociale Geografie* 102, 3 (2011), 260-74.
37   Ibid.
38   William Wolmer, *From Wilderness Vision to Farm Invasions: Conservation and Development in Zimbabwe's South-east Lowveld* (Oxford and Harare: James Currey and Weaver Press, 2007). See also Jonathan S. Adams and Thomas O. McShane, *The Myth of Wild Africa: Conservation without Illusion* (London, New York: Norton, 1992).
39   Steyn, *Northern Tuli Game Reserve*, 21, emphasis added.

land was held by Cecil John Rhodes's British South Africa Company[40] and then sold off to white farmers in the 1920s. Other parts of the southern African region have different agrarian histories.

We began this chapter by introducing the reader to Charles, a landowner and cattle farmer located in the Midlands region of the KwaZulu-Natal province of South Africa. The Midlands region has a particular history of private land ownership dating back to the nineteenth century.[41] Few 'native reserves' or communal land areas were designated in the western part of the Natal Colony, with the result that from the 1870s, black people in the region needed to find places to live on white-owned farms. Informal (verbal) contracts were negotiated between farm owners and the heads of local Zulu-speaking households, in which the homestead head undertook to ensure that the members of his household performed labour for the farmer. In exchange, the homestead head gained access to grazing land for cattle and a place to establish his homestead or *umuzi*.

This social arrangement, known as labour tenancy, became the dominant relation in this part of the Natal Colony. Over time, a characteristic way of life for Natal's labour tenants emerged in which young male dependents of homestead heads would spend six months working on the farm and the other six months working elsewhere in order to earn money for hut taxes and other obligations. This was referred to as the *isithupa*, or six-month, system. In the nineteenth century, *isithupa* offered a degree of reciprocity and a relative freedom of movement. However, this way of life was increasingly squeezed as harsher state controls were imposed in the period after 1910.[42] Finally, in the late 1960s, the state intervened to ban the practice of labour tenancy – a measure that led to large-scale forced removals from farms in the Natal Midlands area and great hardship for labour tenants.[43] Those who managed to stay on farms during this difficult period fifty years ago, are now understandably reluctant to leave privately owned land that the owners want to use for wildlife production or game farming – land which they, the former labour tenants or farm dwellers, may not own, but to which they do have a historical claim.

In our fieldwork,[44] we paid particular attention to the way space

40 Alan C.G. Best, 'Gaberone: Problems and Prospects of a New Capital', *Geographical Review* 60, 1 (1970), 3.
41 Shirley Brooks, 'An historical overview of the KwaZulu-Natal Pilot Land Reform District, 1800-1996', (Status quo report, KwaZulu-Natal Pilot Land Reform Programme. Pietermaritzburg: Department of Land Affairs, 1996).
42 Thomas McClendon, *Genders and Generations Apart: Labour Tenants and Customary Law in Segregation-Era South Africa, 1920s to 1940s* (Portsmouth, Oxford and Cape Town: Heinemann, James Currey and David Philip, 2007). See also John Lambert, *Betrayed Trust: Africans and the State in Colonial Natal* (Pietermaritzburg: University of Natal Press, 1995).
43 Brooks, 'An historical overview'.
44 The research team, including graduate students and led by Shirley Brooks and Marja Spierenburg, has worked in both KwaZulu-Natal and the Eastern Cape. In the KwaZulu-Natal Midlands area, research was conducted on fifteen game farms in total. This research was supported by the South Africa-Netherlands Partnership for Alternative Development (SANPAD). In the Eastern Cape, interviews have focused on game farms in the Cradock area. The Eastern Cape extension of the project is funded by NWO-WOTRO.

is being (re)shaped by the landowners or hosts – generally white, well resourced and relatively sophisticated in terms of understanding the niche market to which they are appealing – in an effort to fit in with tourists' perceived expectations. Our research shows that the presence of farm dwellers is widely regarded as standing in the way of the hosts' aim to offer tourists a sanitised wilderness landscape: i.e. to many landowners, the production of wilderness on game farms is considered incompatible with the continuing presence of the former labour tenants.[45] The turn to wilderness production in the interests of international tourists, appears particularly unfortunate for farm dwellers who do not fit into the idealised picture that tourists are presumed to have of a wild African landscape.

In developing forms of wildlife-based production on private land, the fact is often overlooked that each of these farms is home to resident farm labourers and (former) labour tenants, generally poor and ill-educated but with their own particular histories on the land and claims to it. The position of these people on the farms – we refer to them collectively in this chapter as 'farm dwellers' – is severely impacted by the expansion of private wildlife initiatives.[46] Established agrarian relationships such as those existing between Charles and the black farm occupants of his land, are being challenged, restructured, and in many cases broken.

When research was conducted on Charles's large Midlands farm in 2007, the farm was occupied by the members of twenty-five *imizi* (homesteads) who have long histories on the land.[47] In the move to private game farming – here in the form of the proposed Gongolo Wildlife Reserve (GWR) – the land will be sold off to developers. The GWR is conceived as an upmarket wildlife-based lifestyle development encompassing a large area of about sixteen existing farms. At its core will be a 'Big Five' game reserve and the most exclusive properties would be for sale there. As described on the website of the proposed GWR:

> The Gongolo Wildlife Reserve (GWR) is a 40,000+ Ha [hectare] project which is in the process of being developed by the farmers and landowners who have contractually contributed their land to a company in exchange for shares in that company, in order to create a 'big five' game reserve and certain lifestyle activity projects in association with it.[48]

45 See Brooks and Spierenburg, 'Creating a commodified wilderness'.
46 See AFRA (Association for Rural Advancement), 'Investigation of the effects of conservation and tourism on land tenure and ownership patterns in KwaZulu-Natal', Phase 1 Report (Pietermaritzburg: McIntosh Xaba & Associates, 2003); Kelly Luck and Zweliyanyikima Vena, 'Contested rights: Impacts of game farming on farm workers in the Bushmans River Area', in eds. A. Watson and J. Sproull , eds., *Science and Stewardship to Protect and Sustain Wilderness Values: Proceedings of the Seventh World Wilderness Congress Symposium*, (Rocky Mountain Research Station: United States Department of Agriculture), 85-9.
47 Van Brakel, 'Who is winning (from) the game?', 53. Several interviews with Charles were conducted during the period March to May 2007.
48 Gongolo Wildlife Reserve Limited, 'Gongolo Wildlife Reserve: A Lifestyle Activity Project for KZN', http://gongolo.net/about.html (accessed 22 November 2009).

Charles is especially concerned about the members of those home-steads which at the time of the interviews in 2007 were still located in the low-lying 'thornveld' section of his farm. These former labour tenants do not want to leave their homes. Charles has been assured that the Gongolo development has reserved a site for thornveld farm dwellers, but this is some distance away and in a different tribal authority area. There is also the promise of jobs for these people (discussed in more detail in the next section).[49] However, their livelihood is cattle-based: will they be able to take their cattle with them to the resettlement area? Can longstanding lifestyles, ecologies, and relationships between land and cattle, easily be replicated somewhere else? Certainly the non-material aspects of home – sense of place, easy access to ancestors' graves, and family history – will be lost, and livelihoods will have to be reconstructed. Charles expressed the hope that when the game reserve development comes into effect, he will be able to retain the same relationship with his workers that he had at the time of the interview.[50] This will be difficult, however, in the case of the thornveld farm dwellers: they will have to move and will no longer be working for Charles.

In other cases, the disruption appears less extreme, but still significant. We end this section with a telling example of the 'erasure' of the farm dweller presence on private game farms in the Midlands region, in the interests of wilderness tourism. In examples such as this one, farm dwellers are not entirely dispossessed but are spatially confined to the edges of the farms. Although allowed to remain on the land after its conversion to game farming, assumptions about how much and what kind of contact tourists desire with farm dwellers strongly influence decisions about the space now allocated to them.

The owner of another game farm in the KwaZulu-Natal Midlands explained that, in setting up his game farm, he had managed to persuade the farm dwellers living on the farm to move away from their existing dwellings. He had first offered them housing close to the new lodges that were being built to accommodate tourists. The farm dwellers had been allowed to take their small stock with them to the new housing. But after a while, the owner decided that the sight of families living with their goats and chickens 'was not good for the lodge'. In an attempt to solve the 'problem', he constructed a bamboo screen in order 'to keep them out of sight of the tourists'. This, he said, did not work because the people 'were still making too much noise'. The farmer finally decided to move the families to the edge of the farm, where he constructed dwellings for them as well as providing a water reservoir and a fenced field where they could grow crops for their own consumption and for sale to the lodge. The farm dwellers' cattle were not mentioned in the interview.[51]

49 Van Brakel, 'Who is winning (from) the game?', 53-4.
50 Ibid., 54.
51 Interview with game farmer, Paul. Van Brakel, 'Who is winning (from) the game?', 42-3.

This example speaks to the issue of front- and backstage presentations, as well as to the notion of the 'tourist bubble'. There is an obvious disjuncture here between the 'front stage' presentation constructed for tourists, and the backstage relationships that are hidden from them. What is missing in the story presented to the potential 'guests' by these 'hosts' is an understanding of the agrarian history of the region in the form of other presences on the (former farm) land that the tourists are currently consuming as a commoditised wilderness. As far as the host can ensure it, the tourists exist in an 'ecotourist bubble'. As noted above, the disparity between 'front stage' and 'backstage' presentations has been well documented in the case of cultural tourism in postcolonial contexts. Our research suggests that similar forces are in operation in the case of private wilderness and wildlife tourism, and that this disparity requires closer attention from critical scholars of tourism.

Demonstrating social worthiness:
Private game farming and the rhetoric of social responsibility

It is at this point that we return to the notion of 'organised hypocrisy'. While few private game reserves engage directly, in their public statements and marketing strategies, with the fate of former labour tenants or farm dwellers on their land, there is a strong awareness that the presence of poor people in South Africa makes it morally unacceptable (and bad for business) for developers and other entrepreneurs in the post-apartheid climate not to show that they are also engaging in some way with the issue of poverty. In the context of post-apartheid South Africa, it is important to demonstrate that one is socially aware and that wildlife-based enterprises are not contributing to the creation of poverty,[52] but rather are doing the opposite – improving living conditions for poor people.

This is close to the explanation given by Lipton and Weaver of why organisations or sets of actors may engage in structured hypocrisy: such behaviour serves to favourably locate the actors in a given 'authorizing environment' by signalling 'conformity with societal norms and rules'.[53] These actions are necessary in order 'to obtain the legitimacy necessary to demonstrate social worthiness and mobilize resources'.[54] We suggest that, in the case of wildlife-based production on private land, the rhetoric of social responsibility is designed to show that private game reserves and upmarket wildlife-based developments are not simply intended to make money for landowners and developers, but that they also contribute to improving the lives of the poor. Two main components of this rhetoric can be identified: first

52 See Vigdis Broch-Due and Richard A. Schroeder, eds., *Producing Nature and Poverty in Africa* (Stockholm: Nordisk Afrikainstitutet, 2000).
53 Lipson and Weaver, 'Varieties of Organised Hypocrisy', 7-8.
54 Ibid., 7.

the promise of job creation – a common feature of the marketing of these spaces – and second, claims by many private game reserves that they are involved in social upliftment programmes and thus actively contributing to poverty alleviation in the country.

First, the argument that private wildlife enterprises provide increased job opportunities plays an important role in the promotional narrative of private game farms. In the popular press and in some of the existing studies, conversions from conventional farming to wildlife-based production are often presented by the owners and managers of private wildlife reserves as win-win strategies that foster both the conservation of biodiversity and local socio-economic development through job creation. Two much-cited studies, based on an internet survey questionnaire administered to managers of private game reserves in the Eastern Cape,[55] argue that the demand for labour actually increases after conversion to game farming and that wages increase as well. Job creation benefits are reported from private game reserves all over the country. For example, Newsome and colleagues describe the job opportunities offered by Sabi Sabi Private Game Reserve in Mpumalanga province:

> Sabi Sabi employs 190 [local] Shangaan people ranging from unskilled labour in training to professionally trained rangers, trackers and training managers. With the ratio in the rural areas of breadwinners to dependants 10 to 1, Sabi Sabi supports over 1800 rural inhabitants.[56]

The promotional website of the proposed Gongolo Wildlife Reserve, into which Charles's farm will be incorporated, joins in with the chorus celebrating farm conversions as a win-win strategy for everyone, and specifically talks about job creation. Indeed, an important rationale given for the establishment of the GWR is that 'there is a decline in their [the landowners'] livestock grazing and cropping, and ... this has resulted in scores of people becoming unemployed.'[57] The new project will, it is claimed, turn this trend around:

> The proposed development lies in a commercially depressed area and the communities in the towns of Estcourt, Mooi River and Weenen have little scope for finding jobs in their area. These Town Councils and their Mayors recognize and acknowledge that the *GWR is the single largest potential project in the area*, and that it will *substantially improve the expectations of their communities*.[58]

55   J.A. Langholz and G.I.H. Kerley, 'Combining conservation and development on private lands: An assessment of ecotourism-based private game reserves in the Eastern Cape', Centre for African Conservation Ecology Report No. 56. (Port Elizabeth: Nelson Mandela Metropolitan University, 2006); R. Sims-Castley, et al., 'Socio-economic significance of ecotourism-based private game reserves in South Africa's Eastern Cape Province', *Parks* 15, 2 (2005): 6-18.
56   David Newsome, Ross Dowling and Susan Moore, *Wildlife tourism*, (Clevedon, UK: Channel View, 2005), 130.
57   Gongolo Wildlife Reserve Limited, 'Gongolo Wildlife Reserve: A Lifestyle Activity Project for KZN', http://gongolo.net/about.html (accessed 22 November 2009).
58   Ibid.: emphasis added.

The relocation of farm dwellers is not seen as a problem, and is indeed presented on the website as a positive outcome for these people. Provided that a particular former labour tenant family has been recognised by the GWR as having a legitimate claim, its members are to be accommodated in the following way: they will be 'given title deed to their own land adjacent to the reserve', 'provided with certain services' and 'guaranteed *inter alia* jobs in the reserve'.[59] The website goes so far as to claim: 'GWR believe[s] that these people would, as a result of their relocation [,] have achieved greatly enhanced lifestyles.'[60]

The rhetoric of job creation thus performs a crucial function in legitimising the game farming industry and demonstrating its social worthiness. In a power-laden context such as this, however, it needs to be subjected to careful scrutiny, particularly in the case of promised jobs for farm workers and farm dwellers. The nature of jobs that become available on game ranches and private wildlife reserves is very different from those in conventional agriculture; the skills required to function effectively at this level are not likely to be possessed by uneducated farm dwellers whose main interests are usually their cattle and land. In the upmarket ecotourism industry, many of the new jobs created through wildlife-based production, especially the most lucrative ones, are not available to the farm dwellers. Most farm dwellers have very little formal training, and may have difficulty expressing themselves in English. Taking this limited skills base into account, relocation from farms appears an even riskier option for farm dwellers, as it will inevitably require additional investments to restore previous livelihoods. Already marginalised, and unable to function effectively in the new ecotourism 'bubble', such people can easily end up in abject poverty.

What local people *can* offer to upmarket tourism ventures is the performance of an authentic ethnicity, one that takes place 'front stage' with the tourist spectators remaining firmly within the confines of the ecotourism bubble. The Shangaan trackers at Sabi Sabi mentioned above are such performers. So are the people enlisted as performers in spaces such as the Thanda Private Game Reserve, located in northern KwaZulu-Natal. As the Thanda website informs us, Zulu dancing is a feature of the experience tourists can expect at the game reserve:

Thanda has employed and trained some 58 local men and women as performing dancers at Vula Zulu. These dancers live at home in the surrounding communities and come to work each day where they work in

---

59 Ibid.
60 Ibid. Interestingly, realisation of the GWR vision has been disrupted by a strong counter-narrative about land claims. Few of the affected labour tenants are in fact 'enthusiastic supporters of the project': they have used the land reform legislation introduced in post-apartheid South Africa to file claims for the restitution of about 18,000 hectares of the proposed Gongolo Reserve. This has seriously delayed the project. While the GWR website refers to these claimants rather dismissively as 'local people with certain tribal affiliations', the ongoing land claim issue is one of the main stumbling blocks to realising the GWR corporate dream.

the Vula Zulu theatrical showcase and Zulu Cultural Centre. By living at home minimal disruption occurs to their social lives and they are able to continue providing for their families on a daily basis.[61]

The word 'showcase' is telling here: this performance of staged ethnicity is controlled and managed by the private game reserve and the 'back-stage' lives of the performers are clearly of little interest either to the reserve or to the tourists. We will return to Thanda Private Game Reserve below.

The notion of 'organised hypocrisy' does, we feel, speak to the justificatory narrative of job creation adopted by many private game reserves. More probing questions need to be asked about the nature of the jobs created; further research needs to be undertaken to follow the actual life histories of farm dwellers after the farms on which they live have been converted to game farms. In the Eastern Cape studies mentioned above,[62] the survey samples and methodologies were limited and the studies directed only at one sub-sector of wildlife-based production (upmarket ecotourism), leaving out the game farms engaged in hunting and venison production. In addition, there was little analysis of who was in fact getting the new jobs. Reported positive outcomes such as these, have been contradicted by more worrying reports emanating from rural advocacy NGOs such as AFRA and the South African Human Rights Commission, warning of a significant increase in evictions of farm dwellers as a result of farm conversions to wildlife production.[63]

In the research interviews conducted with game farmers in both KwaZulu-Natal and the Eastern Cape province, the indications were that wildlife-based production appealed to the landowners at least partly because it is less labour intensive. As one farmer in the Eastern Cape described the impact of minimum-wage regulations:

> Government is pushing up the costs of labour through the minimum wages, not just in farming, but also in the service industries, so the farmer also pays more for petrol, for fixing his vehicles etc., all these labour costs in these other sectors also weigh on him. And the prices for the products don't go up at the same rate ... you cannot have wage increases of six to seven percent each year when your product prices don't increase.[64]

On the other hand, when asked whether the farm conversion had entailed actual retrenchments of farm labourers or removals of farm dwellers, few if any respondents admitted to having fired any labourers. On the contrary, they said they had hired more staff to

---

61 Thanda Private Game Reserve, 'Social Responsibility: Community-Based Natural Resource Management', http://www.thanda.com/social-responsibility.html (accessed 2 June 2010).
62 Langholz and Kerley, 'Combining conservation and development on private lands'; Sims-Castley, Kerley, Geach and Langholz, 'Socio-economic significance of ecotourism-based private game reserves'.
63 AFRA, 'Investigation of the effects of conservation and tourism'; SAHRC, 'Final report on the inquiry into human rights violations'. See also Luck and Vena, 'Contested rights'.
64 Interview with game farmer A, Cradock area, Eastern Cape, 23 March 2009.

cater for their clients – apparently confirming the studies conducted by Langholz and Kerley.[65]

The contradiction may be partially explained by the fact that most farms undergo significant expansion in the process of conversion to game farms. The majority of the Eastern Cape game ranchers interviewed had expanded their landholding by buying land from neighbours who had opted out of farming.[66] Most game farms in this region resulted from the incorporation of between four and ten farms; over the years, one farmer had added fourteen farms to his original property. If one takes the farm incorporations into account, the job creation picture changes. A respondent who is involved in the wildlife related service industry remarked:

> Game farming does not require that much labour, in fact, hardly any at all. Look at [name of a game rancher]. He has got a big operation; he bought 15 farms, at about 4 labourers per farm, that would be 60 labourers. Does he have 60 labourers? No! He has about 15 I would say.[67]

Where have the people gone? When questioned directly about the farm dwellers on the incorporated former farms, most Eastern Cape game farm owners replied that the farm dwellers had moved together with the owners who sold the farms. Some respondents said that occasionally farm dwellers stay behind when land owners sell their land, and in some cases they were incorporated into the labour force. However in other cases, the new landowner 'just waited for them to leave' when they got tired of waiting for work on the game farm.[68] There are clearly many questions to be asked about the depth and nature of the 'job creation' story.

In addition to the job creation narrative, another important aspect of the rhetoric of social responsibility is a broader discourse about community engagement and the social upliftment of neighbouring poverty-stricken communities. Like the job creation narrative, this is important to the discursive positioning of private game farms in the post-apartheid context, where the construction of a private wilderness landscape needs to be accompanied by specific justifications and claims to social responsibility. A number of private game reserves have invested in 'social responsibility' projects, arguing that they are making an impact in reducing poverty in the region. Despite the repeated use of the term 'partnership', this can be a paternalistic discourse that again leaves untouched the structural relations of post-colonial land (dis)possession, perhaps mainly acting as a salve to the possible social consciences of visitors to upmarket private game reserves.

In northern KwaZulu-Natal, for example, an area known histori-

---

65 Langholz and Kerley, 'Combining Conservation and Development on Private Lands.'
66 See also Langholz and Kerley, 'Combining Conservation and Development on Private Lands', p. 4.
67 Interview with game farmer A, Cradock area, Eastern Cape, 23 March 2009.
68 Interview with game farmer B, Cradock area, Eastern Cape, 25 March 2009.

cally as Zululand, privately owned land is surrounded by large areas of communal land or former 'native reserves', where most people live in poverty. Thanda Private Game Reserve, a former cattle farm, has been transformed in the last decade into an exclusive private wilderness owned by a wealthy Swedish businessman. According to the *Mail and Guardian* newspaper, a single night's stay at Thanda costs R47,500 (or around 4000 Euros) and the reserve recently won an award as the 'World's Leading Luxury Lodge'.[69] The 'royal suite' where a controversial but politically well-connected KwaZulu-Natal businessmen recently stayed – a man currently out of jail on medical parole after having been convicted of fraud – is described as '1000 square metres of sheer unadulterated luxury ... equipped with a private boma, library, cellar, business room with internet connectivity, games room, heated swimming pool and a magnificent viewing deck that looks out over a water hole'.[70] The journalist investigating the story about the medical parolee's visit was told that no information could be given due to 'the exclusive ethos of Thanda Private Game Reserve, the fact that it is a private and access-controlled environment, and our privacy policy obligations to our clients'.[71] This is one of the most expensive of the private game reserves and the very epitome of the 'ecotourism bubble'.

This reserve however advertises on its website an extensive engagement with 'social responsibility' concerns.[72] Here the somewhat startling claim is made that the reserve is committed to the practice of community-based natural resource management. Thanda Private Game Reserve views itself as:

> ... a private enterprise partner that believes in this philosophy and is willing and committed to embrace the principles of CBNRM [,] and to participate wherever possible in the economic and social upliftment and development of neighbouring communities.[73]

In addition to the 'Vula Zulu theatrical showcase and Zulu Cultural Centre', already mentioned, Thanda also aims to raise funds 'to involve such communities in education programmes centred on biodiversity and community based natural resource management'.[74] The Thanda Foundation co-ordinates the reserve's 'social responsibility' agenda and has set up a number of (wildlife-based) projects, for example the establishment of a 'community game reserve' in a neighbouring tribal area.

It is unclear how these projects objectively contribute to poverty alleviation. One could be forgiven for wondering just who is the dominant partner in such projects: they appear to reflect Thanda's

69 Yolandi Groenewald, 'Shabir Shaik's Parole Paradise', *Mail and Guardian* online, 8 January 2010. http://www.mg.co.za/article/2010-01-08-schabir-shaiks-parole-paradise.
70 Ibid.
71 Ibid.
72 Thanda Private Game Reserve, 'Social Responsibility: Community-Based Natural Resource Management', http://www.thanda.com/social-responsibility.html (accessed 2 June 2010).
73 Ibid.
74 Ibid.

conservation priorities rather than the concerns of local people about improving their livelihoods. The fact that communities are considered to be in need of education on biodiversity and *community*-based natural resource management [sic], too, suggests that communities' visions regarding nature and conservation are of little or no importance.[75] The education theme is popular: HIV-AIDS education is another focus of Thanda's social upliftment agenda, in the form of the JAC programme (the acronym stands for Jobs, Aids, Conservation).

The above-mentioned initiative has been leveraged to create JAC Entrepreneur (Pty) Ltd (JAC-E), a company formed 'with the objective of promoting business links between South African and Swedish entrepreneurs in order to pursue broad-based Black Economic Empowerment (BEE) opportunities in South Africa.'[76] The website further informs us that the Thanda Foundation has sponsored

> ... national projects such as the Nelson Mandela Statue erected at the Nelson Mandela Square in Sandton and the Hector Pieterson Memorial Statue erected at the Maponya Mall in Soweto. Both projects were undertaken in partnership with local black leaders as a joint token of goodwill between Sweden and South Africa.[77]

Questions can be raised about the relevance of these grand gestures and money-making initiatives – clearly intended to form lucrative partnerships not with ordinary local people but with the powerful in post-apartheid South African society – to the lives of the Zululand poor. Do BEE-based deals with a politically well-connected black middle class really constitute community development?

Most private game reserves include information about their 'community engagement' or social upliftment initiatives on their websites. Prospective guests may not give such websites a very close reading; it is apparently sufficient that the good intentions of these hosts have been proclaimed, so the holiday can proceed in good conscience. The opportunity is there for tourists to feel magnanimous about participating in the preservation of Africa's wildlife and support-ing initiatives to improve the lot of poverty-stricken neighbouring communities, whilst sipping their evening cocktail on the viewing deck and gazing out over a 'pristine' African bushveld.

We do not doubt for a second that many reserves engage in these initiatives with great sincerity and put significant resources into building relationships with impoverished neighbours. This sincere belief may even be considered one of the key characteristics of 'organised hypocrisy'. That is not the point: the aim here is not

---

75 See also Malcolm Draper, Marja Spierenburg and Harry Wels, 'African dreams of cohesion: Elite pacting and community development in Transfrontier Conservation Areas in southern Africa', *Culture and Organization* 10, 4 (2004): 341-51.

76 Thanda Private Game Reserve, 'Social Responsibility: Community-Based Natural Resource Management', http://www.thanda.com/social-responsibility.html (accessed 2 June 2010).

77 Ibid.

to pinpoint individual private game farms and assess the sincerity or otherwise of their intentions. Rather, this chapter has drawn attention to the ways in which, in the current South African context, an essentially capitalist venture in wilderness tourism benefits from being presented in conjunction with the developmental rhetoric of job creation, partnership, poverty alleviation, and even community-based natural resource management. The latter is, of course, a fundamental contradiction in terms, as the natural resources in private game reserves are by definition privately owned and managed, and 'the community' is only able to engage with the benefits generated by such enterprise in a limited way and on terms dictated by the private game reserve. Contradictory demands such as those outlined above constitute fertile ground for an evolving 'organised hypocrisy'.

Conclusion

We have attempted to draw together the literature on organised hypocrisy and critical studies of tourism in order to cast a fresh light on the emergence of private wilderness spaces – game farms and private game reserves – in southern Africa, and post-apartheid South Africa in particular. The chapter draws attention to what is an inherent or structural contradiction in the relationship between hosts and visitors, when the hosts are the owners of these private wilderness areas. These game reserves may be viewed as an 'ecotourist bubble' within which visitors are shielded from the deeper issues which play out 'backstage', away from the spotlight illuminating the 'front stage' performance of pristine wilderness – a drama in which local trackers and, in some cases, performers of a staged ethnicity are briefly visible. These spaces are a constructed wilderness, and their construction has inevitably involved impacts for people like the farm dwellers described here – impacts intentionally rendered invisible to the visitor. If, as is the case in regions like the KwaZulu-Natal Midlands, such farm dwellers have long-standing histories on the farms, these are brushed aside and the people involved placated with promises of jobs and community projects.

We have suggested that the theory of organised hypocrisy, in its morally neutral conceptualisation, helps to explain some of the social and socio-cultural processes at work here. In the context of post-apartheid South Africa, it is important for private enterprise to demonstrate its willingness to contribute to poverty alleviation and improving the plight of the poor. Private game reserves are effectively a capitalist venture that need to make money by attracting wealthy tourists to spend their money in these 'wilderness' spaces. The key imperative is to make money, and with private land ownership of these spaces, there are few obvious impediments. At another level, however, private game farms need to signal to their potential consumers as well as to South African society their good intentions with regard to poor people: to, as Lipson and Weaver put it, demonstrate willingness to conform to 'societal norms and rules' in addition to the primary money-making objective.[78] In this case, the narratives of job creation, and social responsibility more broadly, function to enable this industry to 'obtain the legitimacy necessary to demonstrate social worthiness and mobilize resources'[79] in the context of contemporary South Africa.

Can and should we remain unmoved by this? When Brunsson urges us to retain a neutral perspective, he is able to do so himself because he does not relate the performance of organised hypocrisy to the extremely unbalanced power relations that might occur in certain organisations, contexts and configurations – such as those between land owners/wildlife tourism operators and farm dwellers (and other poor people) in South Africa. The imbalance can be conceptualised in terms of 'organised hypocrisy'; but it also seems to beg for greater moral sensitivity than is envisioned by Brunsson in his use of the concept. Can one in fact have tourism in postcolonial contexts like these without a structural element of hypocrisy being introduced into the relations between hosts and visitors? The business strategy employed in this case is based on ideas about a 'pristine' wilderness vision that have a long history in Western culture and are widely shared, while their impacts on poor people are largely hidden. In order to legitimise the creation of a commodified (and lucrative) wilderness on private land, the industry is at pains to display its 'social conscience'. One might argue that, in simply accepting this imaginary – along with its complex outcomes described in this chapter – we all become complicit in a form of 'organised hypocrisy'.

78 Lipson and Weaver, 'Varieties of Organised Hypocrisy', 8.
79 Ibid.

REFERENCES

Adams, Jonathan S. and Thomas O. McShane. *The Myth of Wild Africa: Conservation without Illusion* (London, New York: Norton 1992).

Acharya, Amitav. 'State Sovereignty after 9/11: Disorganized Hypocrisy', *Political Studies* 55 (2007): 274-96.

AFRA (Association for Rural Advancement). 'Investigation of the Effects of Conservation and Tourism on Land Tenure and Ownership Patterns in KwaZulu-Natal. Phase 1 Report' (Pietermaritzburg: McIntosh Xaba & Associates, 2003).

Best, Alan C.G. 'Gaberone: Problems and Prospects of a New Capital', *Geographical Review* 60 (1970) 1: 1-14.

Broch-Due, Vigdis and Richard A. Schroeder, eds. *Producing Nature and Poverty in Africa* (Stockholm: Nordisk Afrikainstitutet, 2000).

Brooks, Shirley. 'An Historical Overview of the KwaZulu-Natal Pilot Land Reform District, 1800-1996. Status quo report, KwaZulu-Natal Pilot Land Reform Programme' (Pietermaritzburg: Department of Land Affairs, 1996).

—— and Marja Spierenburg, Lot van Brakel, Annemarie Kolk and Khethabakhe B. Lukhozi. 'Creating a Commodified Wilderness: Tourism, Private Game Farming, and "Third Nature" Landscapes in KwaZulu-Natal', *Tijdschrift voor Ekonomische en Sociale Geografie* 102 (2011) 3: 260-74.

Brunsson, Nils. *The Organization of Hypocrisy: Talk, Decisions and Actions in Organizations* (New York: Wiley, 1989).

—— *The Organization of Hypocrisy: Talk, Decisions and Actions in Organizations* (Copenhagen: Copenhagen Business School Press, 2nd edn 2002).

Carrier, James G. and Donald V.L. Macleod. 'Bursting the Bubble: The Socio-Cultural Context of Ecotourism' *Journal of the Royal Anthropological Institute* 1 (2005): 315-34.

Comaroff, John L. and Jean Comaroff. *Ethnicity Inc.* (Chicago and Pieter-maritzburg: University of Chicago Press and University of KwaZulu-Natal Press, 2009).

Draper, Malcolm, Marja Spierenburg and Harry Wels. African Dreams Of Cohesion: Elite Pacting and Community Development in Transfrontier Conservation Areas in southern Africa. *Culture and Organization* 10 (2004) 4: 341-51.

Fineman, Stephen. *Understanding Emotion at Work* (London, New Delhi: Sage 2008).

Goffman, Erving. *The Presentation of Self in Everyday Life* (New York: Doubleday, 1959).

Hammet, Daniel and Neelika Jayawardane. 'Performing the Primitive in the Postcolony: Nyoni's Kraal in Cape Town', *Urban Forum* 20 (2009) 2: 215-33.

Krasner, Stephen. *Sovereignty: Organized Hypocrisy* (Princeton, NJ: Princeton University Press, 1999).

Lambert, John. *Betrayed Trust: Africans and the State in Colonial Natal* (Pietermaritzburg: University of Natal Press, 1995).

Langholz, J.A. and G.I.H. Kerley. 'Combining Conservation and Development on Private Lands: An Assessment of Ecotourism-Based Private Game Reserves in the Eastern Cape' (Centre for African Conservation Ecology, Report No. 56. Port Elizabeth: Nelson Mandela Metropolitan University 1959).

Lipson, Michael. 'Organized Hypocrisy and the NPT', Paper presented at the annual meeting of the American Political Science Association, 1-4 September 2005, Washington DC.

Lipson, Michael. 'Peacekeeping: Organized Hypocrisy?' *European Journal of International Relations*, 13 (2007) 1: 5-34.

Lipson, Michael and Catherine Weaver. 'Varieties of Organized Hypocrisy', Paper presented at the annual meeting of the International Studies Association, 25-29 March 2008, San Francisco, CA.

Luck, Kelly and Zweliyanyikima Vena. 'Contested Rights: Impacts of Game Farming On Farm Workers in the Bushmans River Area', in A. Watson and J. Sproull, eds., *Science and Stewardship to Protect and Sustain Wilderness Values: Proceedings of the Seventh World Wilderness Congress Symposium* (Rocky Mountain Research Station: United States Department of Agriculture 2003), 85-9.

MacCannell, Dean. 'Staged Authenticity: Arrangements of Social Space in Tourist Settings', *American Journal of Sociology* 79 (1973) 3: 589-603.

McClendon, Thomas. *Genders and Generations Apart: Labour Tenants and Customary Law in Segregation-Era South Africa, 1920s to 1940s* (Portsmouth, Oxford and Cape Town: Heinemann, James Currey and David Philip, 2007).

Newsome, David, Ross Dowling and Susan Moore. *Wildlife Tourism* (Clevedon, UK: Channel View, 2005).

Ryan, Chris and Michelle Aicken, eds. *Indigenous Tourism: The Commodification and Management of Culture* (Oxford: Elsevier, 2005).

SAHRC (South African Human Rights Commission). 'Final Report on The Enquiry into Human Rights Violations in Farming Communities' (Johannesburg: South African Human Rights Commission, 2003).

Sims-Castley, R., G.I.H. Kerley, B. Geach and J. Langholz. 'Socio-economic Significance of Ecotourism-Based Private Game Reserves in South Africa's Eastern Cape Province', *Parks* 15 (2003), 2: 6-18.

Steyn, Ted. *Northern Tuli Game Reserve. Memories of the Founding of a Major Private Game Reserve* (Kelvin: E & R Steyn, 2004).

Tomaselli, Keyan G. 'The Semiotics of Anthropological Authenticity: The Film Apparatus and Cultural Accommodation', *Visual Anthropology* 14 (2001), 2: 173-83.

Urry, John. *The Tourist Gaze: Leisure and Travel in Contemporary Societies* (London: Sage, 1990).

Van Brakel, Lot. 'Who is Winning (from) the Game?' M.Sc. diss., VU University, Amsterdam, 2008.

Varty, Dave and Molly Buchanan. *The Full Circle: To Londolozi and Back Again, A Family's Journey* (Johannesburg: Penguin, 2008).

Wang, Horng-luen. 'RegulatingTransnational Flows of People: An Institutional Analysis of Passports and Visas as a Regime of Mobility', *Identities* 11 (2004) 3: 351-76.

Weaver, Catherine. *Hypocrisy Trap: The World Bank and the Poverty of Reform* (Princeton, NJ: Princeton University Press, 2008).

Wels, Harry. *Private Wildlife Conservation in Zimbabwe. Joint Ventures and Reciprocity* (Leiden: Brill, 2003).

Wolmer, William. *From Wilderness Vision to Farm Invasions: Conservation and Development in Zimbabwe's South-east Lowveld* (Oxford and Harare: James Currey and Weaver Press, 2007).

PART III
Intensive Contact

11 · Backpacking in Africa

Ton von Egmond

Introduction

Backpacker tourism is a recent phenomenon that originated in the 1960s and 1970s and expanded exponentially in the 1990s. The emergence of backpacking as a large-scale contemporary tourism phenomenon is related to certain distinctive traits in Western societies and the position of youth in them. In the early days, Cohen[1] differentiated between non-institutionalised tourists and their institutionalised counterparts. The latter complied with the conventional features of mass tourism, particularly in their preference for being confined to the Western 'environmental bubble' or 'tourist bubble', while the former were referred to as 'drifters' or 'nomads'.[2] A variety of names have been used in the literature since then to describe the drifter or nomad-style traveller, but studies in recent years have tended to refer to them as 'backpackers'. Pearce is thought to have coined the term.[3]

Most definitions of backpackers refer to 'form-related' attributes of tourism, as opposed to 'type-related ones'.[4] Forms refer to visible institutional arrangements and practices by which tourists organise their journey: the length of the trip, the flexibility of the itinerary, the destinations and attractions to be visited, the means of transportation and accommodation, and contact with local people.[5] A frequently used, predominantly form-related definition is offered by Loker-Murphy & Pearce[6] who see backpackers as young and budget-minded tourists who exhibit a preference for inexpensive accommodation, place an emphasis on meeting other people (locals and outsiders), have indep endently organised and flexible itineraries, take longer rather than brief vacations, and stress informal and participatory recreational activities.

1 Eric Cohen, 'Towards a Sociology of International Tourism', *Social Research* 39 (1972) 1: 164-182
2 'drifters': see Erik Cohen, 'Nomads from Affluence: Notes on the Phenomenon of Drifter Tourism', *International Journal of Comparative Sociology* 14, (1973): 89-103.
3 Pearce, P.L., *The Backpacker Phenomenon: Preliminary Answers to Basic Questions* (Townsville: James Cook University of North Queensland, 1990.)
4 N. Uriely, Y. Yonay & D. Simchai, 'Backpacking Experiences. A Type and Form Analysis', *Annals of Tourism Research* 2, 2 (2002): 520-38.
5 Ibid., 521.
6 L. Loker-Murphy & P. Pearce, 'Young Budget Travelers: Backpackers in Australia', *Annals of Tourism Research* 22 (1995): 819-43.

Type-related attributes are less tangible psychological issues, such as tourists' attitudes towards the fundamental values of their own society, their motivation for travel and the meanings they assign to their experiences.[7] This chapter on backpackers' relationships with their hosts focuses on types rather than forms.

In Europe, the hitchhikers of the 1950s were followed a decade later by the travelling hippie or drifter. While the majority of young travellers restricted their journeys to Europe, quite a few began to travel to more remote locations. Soon North Africa, Morocco in particular, East Africa and the Middle East (including Egypt) became part of the itinerary of many young Europeans, while others followed an emerging route through South and South East Asia to Australia. Young Westerners from the US and Canada followed the trend pioneered by their European peers, not only criss-crossing their own countries and Europe but also extending their scope to less developed countries in Central and South America (Cohen 1973: 92). During the late 1960s, thousands of young Westerners travelled to Asia on the Hippie Trail, the overland route from Europe via Iran and Afghanistan to India and Nepal.[8]

By the year 2000, backpacking had undergone a transformation from alternative tourism to mass tourism and then to an increasingly mainstream form of tourism or an institutionalised form in Cohen's terms. According to UNWTO[9] estimates, the proportion of all international tourist trips undertaken by young travellers grew from 14.6 per cent in 1980 to more than 25 per cent by 2008. In absolute numbers of arrivals, this meant 42 million in 1980 and over 230 million in 2008. How many of these can be identified as backpackers is uncertain because, on the one hand, there is no generally accepted definition of backpackers and, on the other hand, most destination statistics do not make a clear distinction between the age or type of inbound tourists. Young tourists who fit the broad definition[10] make up a considerable proportion of the 230 million youth arrivals. Backpackers travel more frequently within their own world region than to other regions, which is consistent with the travel market as a whole. However as their experience grows, they travel increasingly further afield. Australia is the destination many European backpackers aim for on their first long-haul trip. In the hierarchy of long-haul destinations Australia is at the top, with an increase of backpacker arrivals from 272,320 in 1995 to half a million ten years later.[11] A rough estimate of the number of young travellers heading for Asia, Latin America or Africa would

7 Uriely et al., 'Backpacking Experiences', 521
8 K. Westerhausen, *Beyond the Beach. An Ethnography of Modern Travellers in Asia* (Studies in Asian Tourism 2, Bangkok: White Lotus, 2002), 22.
9 United Nations World Tourism Organization (www.unwto.org).
10 Loker-Murphy & Pearce, 'Young Budget Travelers'. Greg Richards and Judie Wilson, eds. *The Global Nomad. Backpackers Travel in Theory and Practice* (Clevedon: Channel View Publications, 2004).
11 http://www.tourism.australia.com/Research.asp?sub=0297&al=2424

be 10 to 15 million. Thailand is the top destination in the developing world. Other Asian countries such as China, Vietnam and Cambodia are rising rapidly in the hierarchy of backpacker destinations. Most African countries have a modest position in this hierarchy although South Africa, as one of the most popular destinations in Africa, noticed an increase in backpacker arrivals from virtually zero in 1994 to some 90,000 in 2005.[12] Consequently, backpacker arrivals in African countries will range from almost none in politically unsafe countries to several hundreds or thousands in less popular countries and several tens of thousands in the more popular ones.

The backpacker phenomenon

Present-day backpackers are different from the drifters or nomads of the 1960s and 1970s. The drifters Cohen[13] observed in the early 1970s were almost exclusively drawn from the countercultures in society and appeared to have made a commitment to an alternative (escapist, anarchist and hedonistic) lifestyle prior to departure. In Cohen's view, they were severely alienated from their home societies. The long-term travellers of the 1980s, as described by Riley,[14] were no longer primarily recruited from the countercultures but from a far wider section of Western society. They were not hippies, deviants or anarchistic hedonists but were overwhelmingly middle-class, educated, European, single and obsessively budget-conscious. Backpacker tourism today involves much less of a counterculture than in the early days. As Westerhausen[15] noted: 'Even though a significant proportion of the counterculture continues to engage in subcultural travel abroad, the majority of today's travellers have little commitment to its values before leaving home. Few appear to be substantially alienated by life in the West prior to their departure.' In general, they are the (future) pillars of society but on temporary leave from affluence and with clear and unwavering intentions of returning to 'normal' life. Almost all have a fixed return date, typically defined by their airline ticket[16]

Cohen[17] concluded in 2004 that the overall degree of backpackers' alienation has decreased over time. 'Few see in travel an alternative to a "normal" career or seek an "elective centre" abroad. Within this limited period, they primarily desire the achievement of unlimited freedom to do their own thing, which may include the unrestricted

12 http://www.dti.gov.za/publications/Backpackingpublication.pdf.

13 Eric Cohen, 'Towards a Sociology of International Tourism, *Social Research* 39, 1 (1972): 164-82; Cohen, 'Nomads from Affluence'.

14 P. J. Riley, 'Road Culture of Long-Term Budget Travellers', *Annals of Tourism Research* 15 (1988): 313-28.

15 K. Westerhausen, *Beyond the Beach. An Ethnography of Modern Travellers in Asia* (Studies in Asian Tourism 2, Bangkok: White Lotus, 2002), 159.

16 A. Sörensen, 'Backpacker Ethnography', *Annals of Tourism Research* 30, 4 (2003): 847-67; 852.

17 Cohen, 'Backpacking', 51.

hedonistic quest of enjoyment and fun.' According to van Egmond[18] backpacker travel perfectly reflects the modern consumer culture that prevails in Western countries nowadays. Firstly, consumers in these countries have learned to 'want' holidays and have come to think of them as essential for their psychological well-being. Rather than being a departure from the routines and practices of everyday life, holidaying is now an integral part of contemporary modern lifestyles. Secondly, a characteristic of today's consumer culture is a generalised curiosity and restless drive to have interesting and exciting experiences. In explaining the global nomad, Richards and Wilson[19] point to the 'experience hunger' of modern backpackers who seem to be driven to the far corners of the globe in their restless search for ever-new experiences. 'Once they have consumed the experiences offered by one place, they need to move on to find new ones. Just like traditional nomadic peoples, the global nomad constantly moves from place to place.' Destinations are not places of specific interest but objects of generalised curiosity. Although they constitute a hierarchical order with the most popular ones at the top and the least popular at the bottom, destinations are chosen arbitrarily and are easily interchanged.

From the very beginning, backpackers have been young, predominantly male members of Europe's middle classes. 'Europe' is limited here to the United Kingdom, Germany, the Netherlands, Scandinavia, Switzerland, Austria and, to a lesser extent, France. Southern and Eastern European countries generate few backpackers. The backpacker-generating European countries not only have a fully fledged consumer culture but also have a high score on *individualism* in Hofstede's[20] terms, as opposed to *collectivism*. Other backpacker-generating countries, such as Australia, Canada, New Zealand and the US, also have a strong bias towards individualism. Consequently, looking for individual rather than group experiences is the norm among backpackers from these countries.

Backpackers on average have a high level of education. Most are students or former students: undergraduates, graduates, temporary quitters, drop-outs or students-to-be. They all have, at least potentially, a high level of cultural capital in terms of Bourdieu's[21] embodied state (i.e., cultivation and education), and many have a high cultural capital in the institutionalised state (i.e., academic qualifications). Their economic capital is limited although they can afford to travel for months on a low-budget basis. Most, however, anticipate having

18 Ton van Egmond, *Understanding Western Tourists in Developing Countries* (Wallingford: CABI, 2007.)
19 G. Richards & J. Wilson, *The Global Nomad. Backpacker Travel in Theory and Practice* (Clevedon: Channel View Publications, 2004), 5.
20 Gerard Hofstede, *Cultures and Organizations. Software of the Mind* (New York: McGraw-Hill International, 1991.)
21 Pierre Bourdieu, 'The Forms of Capital', in J. Richardson ed., *Handbook of Theory and Research for the Sociology of Education,* (New York: Greenwood Press, 1986), 241-58.

high, personal economic capital in the future and have the academic qualifications required tofind well-paid jobs. Social capital varies according to the individual, but the ability to interact with fellow backpackers and especially with local people is highly valued.

According to van Beek[22] and van Egmond, Romanticism appears to be an extremely important concept in explaining the long-haul travel of Westerners to developing countries, or West-South travel. The European countries mentioned witnessed a Romantic movement during the late-eighteenth and nineteenth centuries. And the second half of the twentieth century, and the 1990s in particular, exhibited a new wave of Romanticism in terms of interest in pristine nature and unspoilt communities that were uncontaminated by the achievements of the modern consumer state. This is reflected in Urry's *Tourist Gaze*.[23] National parks and wildlife but also the simplicity and non-modernism of exotic communities have become major selling points for tour operators across the Western sphere of influence. This 'Romantic gaze' is common among backpackers, particularly those in Africa (see Table 11.1, p. 232).

Along with this new romantic wave today, the perception of exotic communities has shifted from primitiveness and underdevelopment to simplicity, naturalness and authenticity. Exotic destinations are thus commonly presented by both the travel industry and the travel literature as paradises or idyllic communities where life is unspoilt, simple and natural, reflecting an idealisation of 'the other' and of difference. Recurring themes are: exotic, timeless, authentic, paradise, unspoilt, mystical and erotic.[24] Ironically, for many of the communities visited, 'paradise' is in fact to be found in the very countries that generate their visitors.

Authenticity is becoming a key word among Western travellers in developing countries, while 'tourist traps' refer to staged authenticity, i.e. the adaptation of local culture to visitors' tastes. Having seen 'the real thing' rather than 'the tourist version' is highly valued by contemporary travellers. As a matter of fact, many aspects of real life in poor countries do not appeal to most tourists at all. Grinding poverty, disabled beggars and dirty and smelly streets without sewer systems represent forms of authenticity that most tourists are definitely *not* searching for.[25]

In addition to an individualistic lifestyle and a 'Romantic gaze', many backpackers from Northern and Western European countries show a tendency towards temporarily renouncing luxury in favour of an ascetic lifestyle. Low spending patterns, living the hard way, eating in a 'street

22 Walter E.A. van Beek, 'Approaching African Tourism; Paradigms and Paradoxes', in P. Chabal, U. Engel & L. de Haan, eds., *African Alternatives* (Leiden, Brill, 2007), 145-172. Egmond *Understanding*.
23 J. Urry, *The Tourist Gaze* (London: Sage, 1990, 2002.)
24 C.M. Echtner, 'The Content of Third World Tourism Marketing: A 4A Approach', *International Journal of Tourism Research* 4, (2002): 416.
25 van Egmond *Understanding*.

smart' manner at the cheapest food stalls or even 'suffering like the local people' contribute to road status, reflecting the traditional Protestant values in their home countries, two features discussed below.

Backpacker culture

Negative attitudes towards mass tourism or conventional tourists who are 'led' or 'herded' rather than travelling freely form the glue of the backpacker community. These anti-tourist sentiments are much more prominent among medium- and long-term travellers than among short-term travellers. In the words of Welk[26], 'despite the scene's own increasing resemblance to conventional tourism in recent years, anti-tourist attitudes are an important ingredient in the construction of backpacker identities.' Backpacking as a form of tourism may not differ much from the mainstream but the backpacker as a type of tourist does constitute a distinct identity. Backpacking, and long-term travelling in particular, is a way of life.[27]

Characteristic of backpacker culture,[28] subculture[29] or community[30] is an informal system of norms, values, social hierarchies and codes of conduct that are transmitted from experienced backpackers to newcomers, even without fixed or permanent social institutions to facilitate the process. These norms and values, however, are continuously negotiated, challenged, manipulated and changed through social interaction. The opportunity for this is enhanced by the combination of the continuous replacement of backpackers within the community on the one hand, and a near absence of institutions that can hold and transfer meaning over time, on the other.[31]

An important element of backpacker (sub)culture is 'road status'. This refers to an informal status hierarchy among backpackers in terms of travel experience. Interaction with local people, having authentic experiences, travelling off the beaten track, getting the best deal, low spending patterns, long-term travel, risk taking and independence but also disease and deprivation contribute to road status. Guidebooks, such as the *Lonely Planet*, are much scorned and seen as symbols of the lesser traveller. 'Real' travellers have left the *Lonely Planet* behind. Among non-verbal expressions, equipment and clothes play an important role. To dress properly means to dress down rather than up. Worn, ripped clothes tell a story of rough living and adventure.

26 P. Welk, P., 'The Beaten Track: Anti-Tourism as an Element of Backpacker Identity Construction', in G. Richards & J. Wilson, eds., *The Global Nomad. Backpacker Travel in Theory and Practice* (Clevedon: Channel View Publications, 2004), 90.
27 Westerhausen, *Beyond the Beach*.
28 Sörensen, 'Backpacker Ethnography'.
29 Westerhausen, *Beyond the Beach*.
30 Welk 'The Beaten Track'.
31 Sörensen 'Backpacker Ethnography', 855.

Interaction with local people, indigenous people in particular, contributes greatly to road status. There is a clear hierarchy in interaction, in which observing local life is basic but 'living with locals' is the most favoured type of interaction. Most travellers, however, experience local society as interested observers rather than as active participants interacting with locals on their own level, although travellers are able to access a far wider spectrum of local society than conventional tourists, and exhibit a greater readiness to talk with anyone willing to talk to them.[32]

'Living with the locals', having authentic experiences and travelling off the beaten track are highly valued experiences among backpackers, especially among long-term travellers. Although some are actually live with local people for some time, the vast majority do not, in spite of the social desirability of doing so. Contacts are basically restricted to an English-speaking minority employed in the low-budget tourism sector. For most backpackers there is a discrepancy between their intentions and reality. In Cohen's words, 'the actual practice of most backpackers is at considerable variance with the predominant image of the young traveller who roams far off places all alone.'[33]. One way of reducing the discrepancy between the model and actual behaviour is to create experiences in backpacker narratives.

Classification of backpackers

Although backpackers can be distinguished from other types of tourists, they are not a homogeneous category of tourists or travellers. Van Egmond[34] roughly classifies backpackers in four categories ranging from pure 'hedonists' to mere 'pioneers' (see Figure 1). This classification is based on backpackers' interests, their preference for interaction and connection with residents in the places they visit, their attitude regarding authenticity as well as their readiness to renounce luxury and comfort.

'Hedonists' and 'pioneers' do not have much in common. They have different, often opposite, needs and expectations and thus define the quality of their experiences in different terms. From left to right in Table 11.1, needs are increasingly specific, willingness to renounce comfort grows, and the desire to learn and connect with local people becomes more urgent. The more backpackers tend to be dedicated (to real life) or even pioneer, the less tolerant they are of the staging of authenticity, specific tourist things, and coming across other tourists. Obviously, 'dedicated' backpackers and 'pioneers' consider themselves 'travellers' rather than 'tourists'.

The concentration of backpackers varies greatly per category. In the

32 Westerhausen *Beyond the Beach*: 88-90
33 Cohen 'Backpacking', 48
34 Egmond, *Understanding*.

Table 11.1 A classification of backpackers

'Hedonists'	Mainstream Backpackers	'Dedicated' Backpackers	'Pioneers'
• Seek places 'where the action is' (parties) • Seek fun/ excitement /drugs/sex • Go to 'famous' places • Not prepared to renounce comfort • Have no desire to learn or connect • Are not or are hardly interested in interaction • Are indifferent to 'authenticity' • Have no experiences of culture or nature • Numbers depend on destination • Short-term backpackers	• Stay on the beaten backpacker track • Exhibit a generalised curiosity • Visit places described in the travel literature • Renounce comfort to a certain extent • Express a real desire to learn and connect • Actual learning and interaction are very limited • 'Authenticity' is important but highly negotiable • Have either shallow or 'deep' experiences • Largest numbers • Both short-term and long-term backpackers	• Try to go off the beaten track • Exhibit a generalised curiosity • Go beyond 'must-see' places • Renounce comfort to a certain extent • Express a real desire to learn and connect • Actual learning and interaction are comparatively great • 'Authenticity is important and hardly negotiable • Claim to have 'deep' experiences • Small numbers • Mostly long-term backpackers	• Get off the backpacker circuit • Exhibit a generalised curiosity • Avoid touristy places • Temporarily renounce comfort completely • Express a real desire to learn and connect • Actual learning and interaction greatest of all categories • 'Authenticity' is important and not negotiable • Claim to have 'deep' experiences • Very small numbers • Long-term backpackers

Source: van Egmond, *Understanding*.

first decade of the 21st century, many places in their home continents, in Australia and in the coastal areas of Thailand were the places to be for 'hedonists'. And the unprecedented disaster of the tsunami in December 2004 had only a temporary impact on backpacker numbers in Thailand. By definition, mainstream backpackers are concentrated in tourist areas around the highlights of the country of destination and in backpacker enclaves. 'Dedicated' tourists prefer to go off the beaten track, but they still visit the highlights. 'Pioneers' are the most dispersed backpackers, consciously avoiding the tourist circuit and their numbers are often negligible in tourist areas.

Host–guest relationships in Africa

Research among backpackers in African countries has been very limited and studies concerning the interaction between backpackers and local residents or 'hosts' are almost non-existent. While a lot of researchers have focused on backpacker tourism in Australia and New Zealand[35] and Asia[36], backpackers in Africa constitute a field ready for further exploration. South Africa is an exception to the rule.[37] In Rogerson's survey of international backpackers in South Africa,[38] more than half were drawn from Western European countries, about 30 per cent from Australasia and a further 14 per cent from North America. Domestic backpackers are unusual in South Africa, and in other African countries they are virtually absent. The decision to visit South Africa is one that is exclusive to only 56 per cent. For the remainder, South Africa is part of a wider pattern of international (Sub-Saharan or Southern African) travel. The most significant African destinations visited by international backpackers are Swaziland, Mozambique, Botswana and Namibia. Although they tend to visit the well-known South African icons and highlights and do 'typical tourist things' such as game viewing and safaris, surfing and wine tours, many criticise cultural villages that represent staged rather than real experiences. The cultural villages that are appreciated and rated positively are those that function as communities and where tourism is one aspect of the village rather than its very reason for existence.[39]

As most African countries have a (very) modest position in the hierarchy of international backpacker destinations, the assumption seems justified that backpackers in most Sub-Saharan countries tend to be 'dedicated' and 'pioneer-like' travellers rather than 'hedonistic' or 'mainstream' travellers. Scanning travel blogs, travelogues or

35 E.g. Richard & Wilson, *The Global Nomad*.
36 E.g. Westerhausen, *Beyond the Beach*.
37 G. Visser, 'The Developmental Impact of Backpacker Tourism in South Africa', *GeoJournal* 60, (2004): 283-99. C.M. Rogerson, 'Backpacker Tourism in South Africa: Challenges and Strategic Opportunities', *South African Geographical Journal* 89, 2 (2007): 161-71.
38 Ibid.
39 Ibid.,168

travel journals on the Internet, however, clearly reveals that the interests of individual travellers in Africa – not all of them can be labelled backpackers – are much more 'icon-oriented' and 'fellow-traveller-oriented' than 'host-oriented'. In other words, it seems to be mainstream tourists rather than travellers who go off the beaten track. The narratives in weblogs are about famous places to visit, such as Egypt's pyramids, the Kruger Park, Mount Kilimanjaro, Victoria Falls, Table Mountain; the famous cities in North Africa (Cairo, Alexandria, Marrakech, Casablanca) and South Africa (Cape Town, Pretoria, Johannesburg); activities such as safaris, gorilla watching, diving, trekking, rafting; spectacular scenery (particularly deserts); and tourist attractions such as cheetah, crocodile and ostrich farms. Numerous references are made to accidental or planned meetings with other travellers, many of whom are compatriots.

The Best Backpacker Destinations in Africa[40] refer to 'remote' or 'picturesque' beaches, 'the cheapest place in the world', bars and restaurants where one can 'chill out', 'taking a rest from the rigors of East African travel', 'a great place to unwind and wash off the dirt and grime accumulated from some hard travelling', 'stunning nature/scenery/desert', as well as 'diving, snorkelling, fishing, hiking / trekking and surfing'.

Interaction with local people and the inhabitants of the destinations visited is only mentioned incidentally in the weblogs, travelogues and diaries of individual travellers in Africa. Some references are negative in terms of 'not being harassed by hustlers or bombers', 'the children were very annoying over there, begging for candy or money all the time', 'people were not so pushy, we could easily walk around', and 'the locals were nice, they took no notice of us'. Or, more positively, 'the guys played a game of soccer with some kids', 'we walked into the area to get the real Africa feeling. Every now and then we talked to locals just by body language' or with locals who speak 'quite a bit of English'. Local markets that are frequented by residents are popular spots for a stop, allowing the tourist to smell the *couleur locale*. They are popular precisely because they are not set up for tourists and allow interaction without personal involvement or commitment.

Some blogs mention positive or negative interaction with police officers, local repairmen, guest-house owners, waiters and barkeepers. A few talk about visits to schools, development projects, missionary posts and orphanages. Narratives on visits to African villages and interaction with local chiefs or families are virtually absent. Quotes such as 'there was a smile and openness from everyone we met. I was introduced to the chief's first wife, a lovely woman in her 70s, and even though we could hardly communicate, I felt an instant connection with her' and 'We sat in their home and had a chance to ask each other questions. The oldest son wanted to know what country we

40 http://goafrica.about.com/od/africatraveltips/tp/topbackpackerplaces.htm

were from, our ages, if we had any children and what we liked to eat. We wanted to know what they did for fun – "dance" and if they knew anything about the US or England – "no"' are infrequent.

So a quick scan of weblogs suggests that the dedicated and pioneer-like travellers either do not write weblogs or they are virtually non-existent in Africa. Few references were found to going beyond 'must-see' places or even avoiding 'touristy' places, being prepared to renounce comfort temporarily, having a great desire to connect with the local people, wanting to see 'real life' or being allergic to any staging of authenticity. Although backpackers in Africa are presumed to share negative attitudes and sentiments towards conventional tourists, they tend to exhibit typical tourist interests, according to their weblogs, demonstrating that backpacking as a form of tourism may not, in fact, differ much from mainstream tourism.

This conclusion is consistent with my [41] findings among Western tourists in developing countries who, in spite of their expressed desire to connect with local people, show a considerable discrepancy between social desirability and social practice. Moscardo and Pearce[42] who studied tourism in Aboriginal communities in Australia, refer to an approach-avoidance conflict, where the stimulus to interact is strong but unidentified fears prevent tourists from actually interacting. The nature of these fears has not yet been explored. Is this because interaction is difficult? Is it because tourists feel embarrassed about demonstrating their wealth? Is it because tourists do not know how to bridge the difference between obviously distinct life-worlds? Or is it because tourists are afraid that the romantic images they cherish will be affected by direct contact?

This conclusion confirms Cohen's[43] and van Beek's statements that 'the actual practice of most backpackers is at considerable variance with the predominant image of the young traveller who roams far off places all alone' and that 'Africa is for tourists the continent of "the wild", of "pristine nature" and "authentic cultures", admired but feared, gazed at but not participated in.' It is also consistent with Rogerson's findings that backpackers are critical of staged instead of real experiences while travelling around South Africa's well-known icons and highlights.

While host-guest interaction is limited as far as individual travellers in Africa are concerned, one might wonder whether tourism is indeed the powerful tool for developing a better understanding between peoples, as UNTWO claims it to be. According to its Secretary General, 'tourism and peace are inseparable' and 'tourism is a harbinger of peace'. Are backpackers such harbingers? Many weblogs of backpackers in Africa refer to the 'Africa feeling', an intangible

---

41 Van Egmond, *Understanding*.
42 G. Moscardo & P.l. Pearce, 'Understanding Ethnic Tourists', *Annals of Tourism Research* 26, 2 (1999): 416-35.
43 Cohen 'Backpacking', 48; van Beek 'Approaching African Tourism'.

11.1 Dutch back-packers among the Himba in Namibia
(© W. van Beek)

but enchanting mixture of smells, colours and light, and even more so of relaxed and charming people. The values and interests of travellers, however, might be fundamentally different from those of the residents in most of the areas visited. Travelling individually, not having any social or family obligations, renouncing Western comfort, being interested in poor local life, romanticising local life ('these people are poor but happy'), hiking and camping in rural areas, and being concerned about protecting the environment and preserving local culture are among the features that are seen by local residents as wholly alien. A lot of mutual personal investment is required for both parties to understand each other. Only a few backpackers are able and/or prepared to do so, as most tend to travel on a backpackers' circuit and invest more in social interaction with fellow travellers than with local people.

Conclusion

There are very few academic studies on the interaction of backpackers with local residents or 'hosts' in Africa. However many travellers have recently started to publish their personal experiences and stories on the internet, and weblogs and travelogues are a valuable source of information nowadays. A quick scan of these personal expressions reveals that individual travellers in Africa are not the 'dedicated' and 'pioneer-like' travellers many of them profess to be. Rather than experiencing 'real' African life, the vast majority travel the normal tourist routes and stay on the beaten track. The assumption that backpackers in most Sub-Saharan countries are anything other than hedonistic or mainstream tourists seems to be premature. However, the validity and possible biases of these personal expressions on the internet have not yet been studied. Is it possible that writing weblogs is perceived by 'real travellers' as a typical tourist thing? Is it possible that dedicated and pioneer-like travellers do not want to share their experiences with a large audience and/or want to keep them for future novels or professional travel reports? Host-guest relationships in Africa offer a productive field for further academic research.

REFERENCES

Bourdieu, Pierre. *The Forms of Capital*, in John Richardson ed. *Handbook of Theory and Research for the Sociology of Education* (New York: Greenwood Press 1986), 241-258.
Cohen, Erik. 'Towards a Sociology of International Tourism.' *Social Research* 39 (1972) 1: 164-182.
Cohen, Erik. 'Nomads from Affluence: Notes on the Phenomenon of Drifter Tourism.' *International Journal of Comparative Sociology* 14 (1973): 89-103.
Cohen, Erik (2004) *Backpacking: Diversity and Change*, in Greg Richards and Judie Wilson, eds. *The Global Nomad. Backpacker Travel in Theory and Practice* (Clevedon: Channel View Publications, 2004), 43-59.
Doxey, G.V. *A Causation Theory of Visitor-resident Irritants; Methodology and Research Inferences*, in Peter E. Murphy ed. *Tourism, A Community Approach* (New York, Methuen, 1985).
Echtner, Charlotte M. 'The Content of Third World Tourism Marketing: a 4A Approach,' *International Journal of Tourism Research* 4 (2002): 413-434.
Egmond, Ton van. *Understanding Western Tourists in Developing Countries* (Wallingford: CABI, 2007).
Egmond, Ton van. *The Tourism Phenomenon. Past, Present, Future* (Leiden: ToerBoek, 2001).

Hofstede, Geert. *Cultures and Organizations. Software of the Mind* (McGraw-Hill International, 1991).

Loker-Murphy, Laurie, and Pearce, Philip. 'Young Budget Travelers: Backpackers in Australia'. *Annals of Tourism Research* 22 (1995): 819-843.

Moscardo, Gianna, and Pearce, Philip L. 'Understanding Ethnic Tourists'. *Annals of Tourism Research* 26 (1999) 2: 416-435.

Pearce, Philip L. *The Backpacker Phenomenon: Preliminary Answers to Basic Questions* (Townsville: James Cook University of North Queensland, 1990).

Richards, Greg, and Wilson, Julie. *The Global Nomad. Backpacker Travel in Theory and Practice* (Clevedon: Channel View Publications, 2004).

Riley, Pamela J. 'Road Culture of Long-Term Budget Travellers'. *Annals of Tourism Research* 15 (1988): 313-328.

Rogerson, Christian M. 'Backpacker Tourism in South Africa: Challenges and Strategic Opportunities'. *South African Geographical Journal* 89 (2007) 2: 161-171.

Sörensen, Anders. 'Backpacker Ethnography'. *Annals of Tourism Research* 30 (2003) 4: 847-867.

Uriely, Natan, Yonay, Yuval, and Simchai, Dalit. 'Backpacking Experiences. A Type and Form Analysis'. *Annals of Tourism Research* 29 (2002) 2: 520-538.

Urry, John. *The Tourist Gaze* (London: Sage,1990, 2002).

Welk, Peter. *The Beaten Track: Anti-Tourism as an Element of Backpacker Identity Construction*, in Greg Richards and Judy Wilson eds. *The Global Nomad. Backpacker Travel in Theory and Practice* (Clevedon: Channel View Publications, 2004), 77-91.

Van Beek, Walter E.A. van. *Approaching African Tourism: Paradigms and Paradoxes* (Leiden/Boston: Brill, 2006).

Visser, G. 'The Developmental Impact of Backpacker Tourism in South Africa', *GeoJournal,* 60 (2004): 283-299.

Westerhausen, Klaus. *Beyond the Beach. An Ethnography of Modern Travellers in Asia* (Studies in Asian Tourism No.2, Bangkok: White Lotus, 2002).

12 • 'I'm not a tourist. I'm a volunteer': Tourism, development and international volunteerism in Ghana

Eileadh Swan

The bustling town of Ho in Ghana is not a typical tourist destination, those places where buses filled with camera-wielding tourists have become an everyday occurrence. Ho is the administrative capital of the Volta Region in the mainly Ewe speaking South East of the country, where the few luxury hotels located there are used primarily by Ghanaian and foreign governmental and non-governmental organisations for meetings, conferences and workshops. Nonetheless, some tourists do come to stay in Ho for a few days at a time, making it a base from which to explore the famous waterfalls, mountains and monkey sanctuaries within the region. In addition, the annual Yam Festival which lasts for the month of September attracts a number of tourists keen to witness local culture and to get a glimpse of chiefs in their ceremonial splendour. Tourism is rarely out of public and political debate for long; there is ongoing discussion concerning how tourism in Ghana should be promoted and how tourism might encourage and facilitate economic growth and development for the country. One of the main sources of income generated from tourism in Ghana at present comes from what is often described in the anthropology of tourism literature as 'roots tourism'. Every year, thousands of African Americans travel to Ghana and its slave forts, especially at Elmina and Cape Coast, to connect with their ancestral heritage.[1] However, as Katharina Schramm has stressed, in this context the word tourism is rarely used and the visits made by African Americans are rather framed as 'homecomings'. Ghana is represented as an ancestral home and the African American visitors as long separated but now returning relatives.[2] Interestingly then, Ghana's main source of tourist revenue comes from visitors who see themselves essentially as non-tourists. However, not only African American visitors to Ghana resist being classified as tourists. International volunteers; the group of visitors to Ghana, the focus of this chapter, also describe themselves specifically as non-tourists, albeit for very different reasons.

Ho, like many other towns and villages throughout Ghana, has in recent years become host to a constantly growing number of

---

1 Edward M Bruner, 'Tourism in Ghana: The Representation of Slavery and the Return of the Black Diaspora', *American Anthropologist* 98 (1996): 290-304. See also Chapter 4, this volume.
2 Katharina Schramm, 'You Have your Own History. Keep your Hands off Ours: On Being Rejected in the Field', *Social Anthropology* 13 (2005): 171-83.

mainly white European and American volunteers, who pay thousands of pounds or dollars to British and American organisers for the opportunity to 'help' Africans while at the same time being 'immersed' in a different culture. Challenging traditional distinctions between tourism and development as modes of travel, international volunteering is emerging as an increasingly popular travel option for individuals looking for an 'authentic' and 'hands-on' cross-cultural experience without the professional experience, training and time commitment demanded by older volunteering organisations such as Volunteer Service Oversees (VSO) and the Peace Corps.[3] Indeed, it is the great flexibility, choice and support offered to volunteers that characterises the newer volunteering organisations, rather than their ability to match volunteer skills with the needs of the recipient communities.[4] As such, the movement has been described by various travel journalists as 'Peace Corps Light', 'meaningful travel', 'volunteer vacationing' and 'volun-tourism'. Its flexibility appeals primarily to Gap Year students, but also to people taking career breaks, the retired, and the typical modern traveller for whom every experience, including the holiday, becomes an opportunity for self creation and development.

Within tourism studies and development studies, international volunteerism is a little studied phenomenon, perhaps in part reflecting its confused identity, the great variance within the movement itself and its relatively recent growth.[5] What has emerged clearly, though, is the idea that it both can and should have a positive impact upon its host community.[6] However, like other forms of cultural or ethnic tourism in Africa, international volunteerism's emphasis on experiencing different cultures requires that there are recognisably different cultures to be experienced as such. As Stan Frankland has argued, it is the perceived basic Otherness and difference of the people being visited that makes them attractive in the first place.[7] Stephen Wearing

3 Volunteer Service Abroad (VSO) and the Peace Corps have been active since the late 1950s and early 1960s respectively. They demand that volunteers can work for at least one year but in the majority of cases, two. Another very important difference is that while volunteering with the Peace Corps or VSO demands that volunteers demonstrate the skills, qualifications and experience which they intend to bring to the country, and undergo a thorough selection process, most of the newer organisations make no such demands, much to the frustration of 'host' communities. The monetary aspect also differs: VSO is funded by the taxpayer and pays its volunteers a local salary, meets expenses for flights, medical insurance and accommodation (www.vso.org.uk). This is in contrast to the more recently established organisations that demand up to £4,000 in fees from volunteers for a twelve week programme. Volunteers must also pay for their own flights, medical expenses and usually travel insurance.

4 For examples of such volunteering organisations see: www.madventure.com; www.projects abroad.co.uk; www.crossculturalsolutions.org; www.i-i.com .

5 However, for a good overview of the existing research and writing on international volunteerism, see Wearing, Stephen and Jess Ponting, 'Breaking Down the System: How Volunteer Tourism Contributes to New Ways of Viewing Commodified Tourism', in Tazim Jamal and Mike Robinson, eds., *The Sage Handbook of Tourism Studies* (London: Sage Publications Ltd, 2009).

6 Harng Luh Sin, "Volunteer Tourism: 'Involve Me and I will Learn'", *Annals of Tourism Research.* 36 (2009): 481.

7 Stan Frankland, 'The Bulimic Consumption of Pygmies: Regurgitating an Image of Otherness', in Mike Robinson and David Picard, eds., *The Framed World: Tourism, Tourists and Photography*

and Jess Ponting have noted that the economic power of tourism marketers has given them representational power and the freedom to commoditise and package their own ideas of Otherness in the developing world, in ways that do not always have a positive impact on those Others. However, they propose that it may be through some forms of volunteer tourism that this Otherness can be experienced as difference without inferiorisation.[8] Invoking Homi Bhabha's 'third space', the authors suggest that volunteer tourism be considered as a positive form of cross-cultural engagement and interaction, one through which identities can be negotiated and in which both tourists and hosts can learn from one another. In this context, they argue, the tourist destination is a space for interaction, learning and reflexivity; tourism here does not damage or destroy the culture of the host community but rather adds value and benefits both the volunteers and their hosts.[9]

Nevertheless, juggling volunteers' desires to experience a 'different' culture while also 'helping' its members is no easy task, given the Western tendency to impute a correlation between material improvements in the lives of Africans with the loss of their cultural authenticity. Advertising volunteering programmes therefore involves choosing words and descriptions carefully so that the potential volunteer is assured that they can in fact help Africans without 'destroying' their culture. Avoiding the word 'development' is key here. As Kate Simpson has pointed out, most organisations do not use the word 'development' in their advertising campaigns, with many preferring to talk instead about 'making a difference', 'sustainable community initiatives', 'building futures' and 'alleviating poverty and hunger'.[10] While specific mention of development tends to be avoided, tourism is used frequently throughout the websites of volunteering organisations in a negative sense to reassure potential volunteers that even if what volunteerism *is* left slightly unclear, it is definitely *not* tourism. Potential volunteers are told that their experience of life in a 'different culture' will be something that a tourist could never experience. One popular organisation called 'i-to-i' claims on its website: 'You'll become part of the local community and have the kind of authentic cultural experiences that backpackers and package tourists daren't even dream about.' Quite a claim.

The focus of this chapter will be the particular position international volunteerism holds in relation to tourism and development and how this position is often viewed differently by volunteering organisations, volunteers and their 'host' communities. I intend to show that the majority of volunteers I worked alongside, in line with the organisation's

(Surrey: Ashgate Publishing Limited, 2009).
8 Wearing and Ponting. 'Breaking Down the System', 256.
9 Ibid., 263.
10 Kate Simpson, 'Doing Development: The Gap Year, Volunteer-Tourists and a Popular Practice of Development', *Journal of International Development*. 16 (2004): 681-92.

rhetoric, maintained that they were definitely not tourists. However, when some volunteers became disillusioned and angered when there was no volunteering work for them to do, they began to suggest that perhaps they were not so different from package tourists; in being prevented from 'helping', they had not received the product they had paid for. It was these volunteers who suggested that the vagaries of volunteerism's position as somewhere in-between tourism and development, might make it morally questionable. The chapter also questions whether 'host' communities always acknowledge the distinctions between tourists, volunteers and development workers that are often emphasised so emphatically by the volunteering organisations and the volunteers themselves. In Ho, such distinctions were not always made by local people, and interviews and discussions revealed that the 'hosts' and their 'guests' were often at odds over the very nature and purpose of international volunteerism itself. One of my main arguments, however, is that before Ewe hosts considered the distinctions between tourists, development workers and volunteers, the presence of volunteers in their town reminded them first of other differences: those between being a Westerner and being a Ghanaian, being rich and being poor, differences which immediately divided the 'guests' from their 'hosts' as relatively undifferentiated groups. That is, the differences that matter may not always be the same for African 'hosts' and their 'guests'.

Volunteer perspectives

The American-run organisation I volunteered with in Ho, Cultural Exchange International (CEI) housed volunteers together rather than placing them with local families.[11] We lived in what was called the 'home base', a relatively modest bungalow by local standards with shared rooms and bunk beds. Meals were provided for us and consisted mostly of western foods with the occasional watered down

11 Cultural Exchange International (name has been changed) is an international organisation that sends volunteers all around the world. They had a base in Ho for around ten years until 2008 before moving their base to another town. The study cannot represent all volunteering organisations, whose policies and organisation often differ significantly in terms of whether they offer family home stays or not and the emphasis they put on working time in relation to free time. The research upon which this chapter is based was carried out in the town of Ho over a period of four months in 2005-6, for a further eighteen months between 2007 and 2008, and two months in 2009. During the first period of research I was a volunteer with the organisation, conducting research at the same time. A few months after I returned in 2007 to conduct further research, the organisation relocated to another town. The later periods of research have therefore provided me primarily with further insights into the perceptions and experiences of the 'host' side; indeed, many people were even more forthcoming in their comments during this and the later period of research because the organisation was no longer present in their town and, no doubt, because I was no longer a volunteer. While there were a number of other volunteering organisations that had recently opened in Ho, arguably similar in many ways to the one I was involved with, Cultural Exchange International (CEI) had been the first of such organisations in the town and, having operated for over ten years, it was the one most people invoked in their discussions about volunteering with me.

Ghanaian dish. There was a constant supply of refrigerated bottled water and we were all warned never to drink the tap water, despite the fact that it was perfectly safe. From Monday to Friday there was a mini bus that took us to our placements in the morning and picked us up at the end of our working day, three or four hours later. As the website had explained, the volunteering aspect only constituted a third of the programme, with the other two parts comprised of cultural immersion and free time. We were free to do as we pleased every day from noon onwards and at weekends, tours around the country were offered at additional cost. Upon our arrival and on the kitchen noticeboard we were reminded that we should not give any individual or organisation money; we were here to give our time and through such an endeavour, generate cross-cultural respect and understanding. Giving money would result in a relationship of dependence and create problems for future volunteers. We were also discouraged from inviting local visitors to the home base and if we did wish to do so we had to have permission from the staff. Our 'bubble' was safe, comfortable and secure.[12] Almost all of the volunteers made comments similar to this one: 'It is just such a relief to be able to come home to other volunteers at the end of the day. Sometimes the town is just so stressful with people shouting '*yevo*'[13] and asking for money and it is nice to be living with people who understand.' For the volunteers then, the home base was an enclave of familiarity in a strange place and a space in which the day's experiences could safely be shared.

However, the volunteers did not feel that existing and working through this 'bubble' made them tourists or detracted from the 'authenticity' of their experience. One volunteer told me: '...volunteering is completely different from being a tourist because we live and work for an extended time in another culture. You are not just an observer passing through so you understand and learn more.' It was the fleeting nature of the tourist experience and its lack of depth that volunteers argued made their own experience so different. Another explained to me that 'as a tourist you just get to see the surface and you are always looking in from outside. Living here as a volunteer enables you to experience the real stuff: everyday life, people, cooking, eating, visiting each other and things.' The idea was that while tourists watch, volunteers 'experience'. Not only did volunteers buy into the notion that there existed a general travel hierarchy in which they as volunteers

12 Valene Smith, ed., *Hosts and Guests: The Anthropology of Tourism* (University of Pennsylvania Press, 1977).
13 The Ewe word for white person, usually taken to refer to all Westerners, irrespective of their skin colour. In some areas the word used is *yevu* rather that *yevo*. There are a number of explanations of the meaning and origins of the words themselves. Some people told me that *yevu* means 'crafty dog', a reference both to the crafty nature of white people in their early dealings and trade with the Ewe people and their tendency to get angry and 'snap' very quickly, just as dogs do. The word *yevo*, on the other hand, literally combines craftiness (*aye*) with freedom (*vo*), and people told me of their belief that it was the craftiness of white people that had always guaranteed their freedom.

were situated on a higher level than tourists, they also constructed an internal hierarchy within the volunteer group, one which was based on how long volunteers had or were planning to stay. The few people who stayed for the maximum time (between nine and twelve weeks) took it upon themselves to act as guides for the incoming groups and often privately mocked the volunteers who had only come for three weeks, saying that they would only be able to scratch the surface like tourists. Occasionally some of the 'long timers' started to eat food with their hands and some even began to drink the tap water instead of the provided bottled water, eliciting shock and awe from the newly arrived volunteers who exclaimed: 'Wow! You're like soooo local!'. These shows of 'cultural competence' and attempts to demonstrate that they could survive outside the organisational 'bubble' were put on despite the fact that only a few weeks earlier, I had watched the same volunteers arrive feeling excited, afraid and completely unsure of how things were going to work out, just as I had done.[14]

In addition to claims about the 'authenticity' of their experience and the length and depth of their stay, it was the meaningfulness of their presence in Africa that volunteers used to distinguish themselves most from what they called 'traditional tourists'. As one volunteer put it: 'It is different because I am here for a reason and not just to spend time looking at things'. While all the volunteers I spoke with mentioned that they had volunteered so that they could learn about a 'different' culture, they also stressed that they wanted to do something to help others. Some volunteers put more weight on the former than the latter but everyone mentioned both. One young woman said: 'I wanted to volunteer so that I could learn more about Ghanaian culture and also to help others and become more humble.' And another told me: 'I was hoping to make a small difference in the lives of the kids I was teaching but mainly, I wanted the experience of living somewhere so different.' A volunteer who worked in the local hospital and was a nurse in America said: 'My aim was to experience another culture and gain insight into a different health system. Mainly though, I wanted to be accepted into a different community.' For many people, the most important thing was to undergo a personal transformation and to develop the Self through an engagement with the Other. As one volunteer put it: 'I wanted to learn about the lifestyle and culture of Ghanaians. I wanted to go back to the US with a better understanding of myself and a new perspective on the world by working with local organisations and people.' One man simply told me: 'I just wanted to see and experience a totally different culture. We get to see and experience a totally strange way of life and in exchange they get to see and touch living, breathing yevos!' Such comments suggested that the volunteering experience was not always able to challenge the negative

14 Interestingly, my presence in 2007 appeared to unnerve some of the self-proclaimed 'long timers' because I had already volunteered in 2005 and was now staying in Ho for eighteen months, this time living with a local family.

stereotypes Westerners had about Africa, as the organisation hoped.

Challenging stereotypes of the West and Africa was indeed one of the main aims of the CEI. The idea was that by working with local schools and organisations and interacting with people in the community, there would be a genuine exchange of ideas and knowledge between the volunteers and their Ghanaian hosts. Through genuine interaction and service, the stereotypes that Ghanaians and Westerners held about each other would be challenged. When I asked volunteers towards the end of their stay what they had learnt and how their perspectives had changed, in addition to saying that they felt 'lucky' to be American, many expressed that they had realised that money was not the most important thing in life but that it was the small things that really counted, 'like holding the hand of a sick child and seeing her smile'. One young woman explained: 'In terms of money they don't have much here but they have a lot of culture and they seem happy enough.' As we shall see when we turn to the 'host' perspectives though, such sentim.ents were resented by many local people who told me that volunteers had no business telling their friends and family at home that Ghanaians were happy being poor: 'We are just trying to maintain some dignity, that's all'. The 'poor but happy' interpretation is a common one within international volunteerism and one that Kate Simpson has discussed. She notes that volunteer organisations often end up teaching that all difference, including economic difference, can be explained through 'culture'. Organisations' claims to neutrality often end up denying both history and politics to the extent that 'questions of material inequality can be ignored under the panacea-justifying cloak of 'culture'.[15]

However, other volunteers were not satisfied with making the occasional sick child smile and learning something about Ewe 'culture'. Their strong desire to 'help', coupled with the very light volunteering workload and excessive free time resulted in many of the volunteers complaining to me that the exchange was not equal and that they were receiving too much but not giving enough. In some sense, they had realised that volunteering projects always work within a context of inequality and that '(T)he processes that allow young westerners to access the financial resources, and moral imperatives, necessary to travel and volunteer in a "third world country", are the same as the ones that make the reverse process almost impossible.'[16] One woman complained to me: 'We are supposed to be on an exchange; I am learning about Ghanaian culture and trying to help the people here but I am the one here. How many of my new friends will ever see and get to experience my American life? This is not a real exchange at all.' On the last night of her stay, one of my friends expressed similar

15 Kate Simpson, 'Doing Development': 689. See also James Ferguson, *Global Shadows: Africa in the Neoliberal World Order* (Durham and London: Duke University Press, 2006).
16 Simpson, 'Doing Development', 690.

sentiments, this time stressing not the unequal physical exchange but rather the exchange of cultural knowledge and help: 'The cross-cultural exchange seemed very one sided in that I have been offered extraordinary opportunities to expose myself to Ghanaian ways of life and culture but I felt that I was not giving anything at my end of the exchange.' However, other volunteers were even more angry and one man told me:

> If other companies are like this one, then any impact volunteering can make is small. I would never recommend this one to someone who wanted to do serious volunteering work. This one is basically to help volunteers understand the place they visit so they can impress their family and friends because they have survived the 'wilds' of Africa. Their family will never know the luxury they really experienced.

What is most interesting about the above comment is that the volunteer described the volunteering organisation as a 'company'. On the numerous occasions when volunteers became frustrated and angry, discussions turned to money and the fact that they had 'paid for their experience' and 'paid to help'. This was something that the organisation staff disagreed with and during interviews with them they always insisted that volunteers did not pay for their experience as such and that cross-cultural exchanges simply could not be conceived of in monetary terms; they were connecting humans across the world and indeed working towards making the world a better place. Certainly, during my formal interviews with volunteers while their activities were running smoothly and according to their expectations, volunteers maintained the organisation's rhetoric. The large sums of money that had been paid were almost never discussed. Given that both the organisation's rhetoric and the volunteers' own perceptions of their experience was that they were definitely not tourists, this was quite understandable. However, when things began to go wrong for volunteers, their approach changed and they began to talk about the fact that they had indeed paid for their experience and so had every right to complain when the product did not meet the 'company's' description. I recall vividly the first evening that money entered into our conversation and it became clear to me then how much it had previously been avoided because it might threaten the 'authenticity' of their experience as non-tourists. Some volunteers stressed that they had paid over the odds to volunteer with CEI precisely because they had assumed the higher price would ensure better organisation and services. Complaints about the 'service' ranged from inadequate and poor quality food, the lack of washing machines, having to share bedrooms, the poor quality of the road leading up to the house and having to pay extra 'tourist' fees for the weekend trips visiting tourist sites around the country. One of my friends went so far as to say that he felt he had been 'conned'. He said:

> Can't you see? We paid the money months ago in the States. They think

that out here, they can just put us in some falling apart house and give us bad food but that because we are in Africa we'll forget we've paid! Someone in New York is sitting on a big pile of my money.

However, while such complaints certainly reveal numerous similarities between 'traditional' or package tourists and volunteers and thus question their insistence on the distinction, volunteers' main reasons for complaints highlight the tension I raised in an earlier section on volunteering's position in relation to international development. While on the organisations' websites this tension can be subtly side-stepped through the avoidance of the word 'development' and the focus is instead on 'building futures' and 'making a difference', on the ground in Ghana, these vagaries began to cause problems. A common complaint was that there was not enough volunteering or that volunteers had not been allocated to the placements that they had been assured of getting. Many of us, myself included, had stated prior to arrival that we did not want to work teaching in schools. We were subsequently guaranteed other placements that reflected the skills and interests that we had written on our application forms. Despite such guarantees, we were almost all placed in private schools and nurseries. I was placed in a small private nursery that already had three teachers to thirty pupils and my presence allowed them time to sleep or read the Bible. My fellow volunteers experienced similar situations and became increasingly frustrated when they walked past other schools, orphanages and organisations where they felt their 'skills' could have been better utilised. This was only made worse when other teachers or workers at the orphanage asked volunteers for their assistance and volunteers were forced to refuse. As a result, many volunteers complained that the organisation did not take the volunteering component seriously enough.

This feeling was only compounded when the schools went on Christmas holidays for three weeks and no other placements were arranged for volunteers, with many of them complaining that there was little to do but lounge around reading novels or go swimming at the local hotel. Admittedly, because I was there primarily to conduct research, the lack of volunteering was a point of interest rather than a source of distress for me. But for the majority of the volunteers, and especially the Americans, it constituted a good enough reason to insult and threaten local staff, often saying that that they would ask for their money back. Occasionally, volunteers even called the office in New York to complain and I heard of a previous volunteer who had demanded to go home. As one angry volunteer put it:

> First, I didn't ask to teach. I don't do children and I have skills in other areas that the community actually needs. Second, I am only here for five weeks and now the school I am teaching at has gone on holiday for three of them. This is just a joke! As soon as I get back, I am going straight to the New York office to demand my money back.

For the volunteers at the point of utter frustration the issue was quite simple. Despite the rhetoric and advertising campaigns of the volunteering organisation that volunteers were definitely not tourists, volunteers had paid the American organisers for the opportunity to 'help' Ghanaians and the organisation had now failed to deliver. It was during these outbursts which often occurred in the home base during the evening while volunteers shared their daily experiences that I began to question some of the statements that they made during our interviews about the distinctions between tourism and volunteerism. While expressing their frustrations to each other and complaining to local staff, they spoke as though they had travelled with the very tourist companies that they had previously criticised for only offering 'meaningless' travel. The illusion of the tourist/volunteer distinction had begun to fall away and volunteers rendered themselves paying customers just like the tourists they usually tended to look down upon. The fact that they had paid to 'help' only made the position of volunteerism, situated as somewhere in-between tourism and development, look increasingly fraught and untenable. Many volunteers realised that perhaps they were not so different from package tourists and that in being prevented from 'helping', they had not received the product they had paid for.

Host perspectives

What about the inhabitants of Ho who were interacting with the volunteers? Did the 'host' community acknowledge the distinctions between tourists and volunteers that were emphasised in many contexts by the volunteering organisation and the volunteers themselves? My answer is twofold. Certainly, on some grounds and in particular contexts, people in Ho did make qualitative distinctions between volunteers and tourists. However, their ideas about the nature and identity of volunteers and the purpose of international volunteerism usually still remained at variance with volunteers' self-perceptions. While the volunteers generally saw themselves as significantly different from both tourists *and* international NGO and development workers, the majority of people I spoke to in Ho, often including the teachers and leaders with whom the volunteers were 'placed', had different conceptions and contrasting views about the differences and distinctions that mattered to them. Before the people of Ho considered the potential distinctions between tourists and volunteers, they said that the presence of volunteers in their town tended to remind them of other differences; those between black and white and rich and poor, differences which immediately divided the 'guests' from their 'hosts' as relatively undifferentiated groups. The fact that tourists, volunteers, NGO workers and missionaries all had the freedom and money to travel to and live in Ghana was recognised by local people as doing more to unite than differentiate them. As we shall see below, this immediate fact of 'whiteness' elicited different types of responses and invoked a variety of memories, desires and ideas about 'self' and 'other'. In Ho, the presence of volunteers often reminded Ewes of their own subject positions as Africans within a globalised but increasingly unequal world, heightening their sense of 'abjection'.[17]

In addition, the presence of the *yevo* made local people revalue themselves and their positions from an imagined 'white perspective', an argument Ira Bashkow has made with reference to their work in Papua New Guinea. As Bashkow has recently argued, while the 'whiteman' may be a universal category, the meanings attributed to it are varied and can tell us a great deal about a particular people. He argues that through globalisation (and I would stress through a much longer historical engagement), the West has had a material effect on the lives of people all around the world and white people play a role simply in instantiating categories such as 'European', 'Westerner', or 'American', categories through which we constitute an other that exerts a powerful force around the world.[18] In a similar vein, I argue that while today it is tourism, development and – somewhere between – international volunteering that structures the kinds of relationships Ewe people have with Westerners, Ewe peoples' interpretation and evaluation of volunteers has to be seen within a much broader set of Ewe meanings and understandings of 'whiteness'. This involves acknowledging the variety of historical contexts such as the transatlantic slave trade, colonialism, missionisation, and globalisation that have generated particular understandings of who and what the *yevo* is.

Throughout my research in Ho, and with the typical embarrassment of the anthropologist well schooled in anti-colonial sentiments, I found that the *yevo* was almost always encountered by people as someone who was clever, rich and free. However, differences soon began to emerge in terms of how the younger and the older generation evaluated and interpreted this initial fact, revealing that Ewe ideas about the *yevo* could be used as a window through which to consider Ewe generational consciousness and intergenerational relations. Anthropology has seen a recent surge in literature that focuses on the experiences of young Africans in an increasingly globalised but ever more restricted world.[19]

17 James Ferguson, *Global Shadows: Africa in the Neoliberal World Order* (Durham and London: Duke University Press, 2006).
18 Ira Bashkow, *The Meaning of Whitemen: Race and Modernity in the Orokaiva Cultural World* (Chicago and London: University of Chicago Press, 2006), 2.
19 David Berliner, 'An "impossible" Transmission: Youth Religious Memories in Guinea-Conakry', *American Ethnologist* 32 (2005). See also Jennifer Cole, 'Fresh Contact in Tamatave, Madagascar: Sex, Money, and Intergenerational Transformation', *American Ethnologist* 31 (2004); Filip De Boeck and Alcinda Honwana, *Makers and Breakers: Children and Youth in Postcolonial Africa* (Oxford: James Currey, 2005); Mamadou Diouf, 'Engaging Postcolonial Cultures: African Youth and Public Space', *African Studies Review* 46 (2003); Deborah Durham, 'Youth and the Social Imagination in Africa: Introduction to Parts 1 and 2', *Anthropological*

It is argued that young Africans, more acutely than anyone else, experience globalisation as a process through which 'many are called but few are chosen'[20] and one where at best there is a globalisation of dreams. And the more the West battens down its borders, the more valuable white facilitators and potential 'middle-men' become.[21] This was certainly the case in Ho, where volunteers were often perceived both as potential vehicles for, and obstacles to, a better life in the West. Being perceived in such a way frustrated volunteers, who explained to me that they had come to 'help' but did not want to be treated like 'walking wallets'. Moreover, young Ewes' desires to escape to America and their approval of all things Western often made volunteers feel uncomfortable because, in the words of many volunteers: 'It's not very authentic' or 'We didn't come all the way to Ghana to see people dressed up like the rap stars back home'. This discomfort can be seen as part of a much more widely shared 'embarrassment' felt by white people – including anthropologists - faced with 'Westernised Africans' who refuse their own supposed authenticity and alterity and make claims to similarity rather than difference.[22]

However, most of the older Ewes I spoke with *did* complain that the youth were just copying the West blindly and that this was leading to disrespect and indiscipline within the town. While elders stressed that *yevonya* (white/western knowledge and practices) had its benefits, they argued that it should always be blended with *afeme nunya* (home/traditional knowledge and practices). The two systems were described to me as being potentially complementary. However, the current problem was that young people were embracing only *yevonya* and dismissing *afeme nunya* as 'archaic' and contrary to the demands of modernity. Allusions were often made by elders to the slave trade and colonialism and the youth were sometimes described as slaves to the West once again. Within this context, then, volunteers were not always viewed in the same positive light that young people viewed them because older Ewes' memories and perceptions of 'whiteness' and the *yevo* were not drawn so much from television programmes and global media but rather from past experiences of and stories about white people during colonialism and during the early years of independence. More so, the elders complained that because the

Quarterly 73 (2000); Eric Gable, 'The Culture Development Club: Youth, Neo-Tradition, and the Construction of Society in Guinea-Bissau', *Anthropological Quarterly* 73 (2000); Francis Nyamnjoh, '"For many are called but few are chosen": Globalisation and Popular Disenchantment in Africa', *African Sociological Review* 4 (2000); Brad Weiss, 'Thug Realism: Inhabiting Fantasy in Urban Tanzania', *Cultural Anthropology* 17 (2002); Brad Weiss, 'The Barber in Pain: Consciousness, Affliction and Alterity in Urban East Africa', in Filip De Boeck and Alcinda Honwana, eds., *Makers and Breakers: Children and Youth in Postcolonial Africa* (Oxford: James Currey, 2005).

20 Nyamnjoh, 'For many are called but few are chosen'.

21 Francis Nyamnjoh and Ben Page, 'Whiteman Kontri and the enduring Allure of Modernity among Cameroonian Youth', *African Affairs* 101 (2002): 612.

22 James Ferguson, *Global Shadows: Africa in the Neoliberal World Order* (Durham and London: Duke University Press, 2006). See also Eric Gable, 'The Funeral and Modernity in Manjaco', *Cultural Anthropology* 21 (2006).

youth were just seeing and speaking to the volunteers while they were on 'holiday' in Ghana, young people still remained ignorant of the real troubles and hard work they would have to endure if they ever managed to travel to the West: 'They might be friendly because we are independent now, but wait till you get to their country under their control. Then you will know suffering.' As such, the often unrestrained adoration of volunteers by younger Ewes was matched by careful yet friendly reservation on the part of the elders. Yes, *yevos* were rich and free individuals, but for many of the elders with whom I spoke, such a status could only be achieved through a certain amount of selfishness and by sacrificing one's responsibilities to the extended family and community, something that elders felt was working to break down rather than reproduce 'good' and 'respectful' social relations within the town.

It was the fact that volunteers were first and foremost *yevos*, and not whether they were tourists, volunteers, or NGO workers that framed the kinds of immediate perceptions and interactions local people had with volunteers. However, throughout my interviews with local people, it became clear that further distinctions were sometimes made between different *yevos* and, in particular, between tourists and volunteers. Many of my Ghanaian interviewees, in line with the arguments made by volunteers, cited length of stay and depth of interactions as reasons why volunteering was quite different from tourism. One teacher explained: 'Tourists don't get so close and they don't interact with the people so much because they don't have the time – they are always on the move and they just come, see and then go. Volunteers get closer and stay for longer so they can be speaking to the people.' Another woman, who had accepted volunteers to work with her NGO in the past said: 'The intentions of tourists and volunteers are different but they both want to see the culture. Volunteers come to study our culture and to see it for themselves but also to help us develop.' Nonetheless, many of the people with whom volunteers worked complained that their stay was not long enough: 'The main problem is the short time they stay – what can a person do in two weeks? Even two months is not enough because by the time they leave they are only getting used to the system. Then we have to get to know another person and so on.' And almost everyone complained that the volunteers did not stay with local families but rather in a volunteer 'homebase' that was itself situated beyond the main part of the town. As one old man put it:

> The home is where everything happens here – it is the centre of our life so if the volunteers don't come to live with us then I don't know what they can really know. When we want to insult people here we tell them that they don't come from any home.

What is interesting then is that while people from the town understood that there was supposed to be a difference between volunteers and tourists, they often stressed that in the end, they were not so different. One angry teacher complained to me that she was considering severing her link with the organisation because she was becoming frustrated with the broken promises of volunteers. She said:

> They always promise to stay in contact but they never do. So in some ways they are no different from the tourists who come and go except they stay a bit longer before they go. But they never continue the relationship – once they have had the experience they came for, they just sort of disappear. So they have not really learnt anything about our culture at all because the most important thing to us is to cherish and nourish relationships with each other.

Many teachers also complained to me that when they agreed to host volunteer teachers in their schools, they had assumed that the volunteers could actually teach and had received some prior teacher training. When they realised that CEI had placed completely untrained volunteers in schools and that the children were no longer learning the correct syllabus, the teachers began to complain. One of the head teachers asked me: 'Would you let a Ghanaian or even a British person who had not been to teacher training to come and teach in your Schools? I do not believe you would.' Such comments return us to the issue of 'whiteness' and Nyamnjoh's argument that Africans have been forced to realise that with white skin comes all kinds of advantages; 'whiteness' has come to symbolise power, status and 'the good life even for the most fragile or the most mediocre of whites' (Nyamnjoh 2000:7). The assumption that simply because they were white, volunteers could work in any field angered many of the Ewes with whom I spoke. One retired teacher said:

> You see, this is still our problem. We say we are independent but we are still favouring useless whites over trained blacks to teach our children. When will we ever learn? All this talk of cross-cultural learning or whatever is a nonsense; every time an untrained volunteer comes to teach, our children are still seeing that white is best. It is just neo-colonialism.

The older generation especially, simply did not buy into the organisation's liberal rhetoric that argued volunteerism facilitated a cross-cultural understanding that would benefit everyone in the 'global village'. For them, the kinds of race and power relationships that international volunteerism facilitated and perpetuated were often of the same type that colonialism had introduced and in this sense, it was just colonialism in a different guise. As one man put it, somewhat bluntly: 'Just because some smiley Yank is playing with our children doesn't mean that she has any respect for our elders.'

Further problems also arose because people often assumed that volunteers were international aid or development workers with projects and resources and did not fully grasp that volunteers were giving only their time. There has been a recent upsurge in small, locally run NGOs in Ho and their staff are ever on the lookout to make connections with larger international NGOs, something which has become increasingly difficult because of corruption and dishonesty within the small NGO sector in Ghana. Therefore, the 'genuine' NGOs have to work even harder to persuade western funding bodies of their legitimacy. Within this framework, volunteers were often encountered and engaged with as representatives of international NGOs and their help was often sought. However, they were often left disappointed and confused with the response that the organisation told volunteers to offer to any local person requesting money or international connections: 'I am just a volunteer. I am only here to give my time.' Understandably, the issue was made all the more confusing when people found out the amounts of money that volunteers had paid to organisers in New York for their Ghanaian experience. From the local perspective, if it was the case that volunteers were not like other international NGO and development workers because they were not offering money but only time, then why was it that they had to pay up to $7,000 to the American organisers for the chance to help out in a Ghanaian school for three hours a day? Even the teachers and local organisations who accepted volunteers to work alongside them often complained that they had not been properly informed of what international volunteerism was. One teacher said: 'At the introductory seminar, they told us not to expect any money from volunteers but not much else.' And during one of my interviews, an old school headmaster said: 'We really appreciate the volunteers helping out with classes but what we actually need is a bus so that the children from the villages can get to school more easily.' Perhaps somewhat ironically then, both the volunteers and the local people often felt that volunteers were not responding to the real needs of the community. As Sarah Pink has noted, 'helping' is not a universally fixed category and we should always be mindful of local understandings about what constitutes 'help'.[23] While local people appreciated the value of cross-cultural interaction, they tended to feel that there were more pressing projects that volunteers could work on and to which they could contribute a portion of their large volunteering fee. After all, it was the volunteers who were receiving the genuine cross-cultural experience, so what was the benefit to the local community?

Conclusion

I hope what has become clear throughout this chapter is that even if we take international volunteerism as a mode of travel situated somewhere between tourism and development, such a position is by no means a stable or easily defined one. Organisations have used their websites and literature to persuade potential volunteers that even as they are being asked to pay for the pleasure of helping

23 Pink, Sarah, 'The White "Helpers": Anthropologists, Development Workers and Local Imaginations', *Anthropology Today* 14 (1998): 9.

Africans, they will be acting neither as tourists nor development workers. Volunteers are told that they differ from tourists because their experience will be authentic and involve 'deep immersion' into another culture. In addition, they will be able to 'make a difference', work towards securing 'better futures' for Africans and contribute to 'community led initiatives', but can do so in three weeks and without any professional qualifications, experience of or employment within the field of international development. However, as we have seen through my discussion, international volunteerism's rather vague position in relation to both tourism and development was easier to maintain on websites than in reality. The fact that volunteers had paid to 'help' Africans but felt that even that service had not been rendered to them, only made the whole project of international volunteerism appear increasingly fraught and even morally questionable.

In addition, and from the perspectives of their Ewe hosts, volunteers were not always instantly sub-divided in line with our own much loved and hierarchically ordered categories of tourists, volunteers, development workers and finally anthropologists! As my examples have shown, volunteers were often encountered first and foremost as Westerners and only in particular instances as a group of guests whose intentions and actions differentiated them from traditional tourists or development workers. We must therefore become more cognizant of the wider, unifying frameworks and power relations through which such Western 'guests' are understood. Whatever name or description this recent volunteering movement is given, and while particular 'host' communities do often acknowledge some benefits, the volunteering companies exist first and foremost for themselves and their customers. Their primary aim is self perpetuation rather than global poverty reduction. And as long as the prevailing logic behind international volunteerism is that 'Africans might be poor but at least they're happy', things are unlikely to change soon. Returning then to the article by Wearing and Ponting, which posits certain types of volunteer tourism as positive and an example of real cross-cultural interaction and exchange, I can only agree with their comment that this alternative model of tourism may, in some senses, be idealised and that ultimately it depends upon 'considerable shifts in power between Western and host societies'[24] – shifts which would perhaps work towards making the exchange a more equal one, for the African 'hosts' as much as their 'guests'.

24 Wearing and Ponting. "Breaking Down the System': 263.

REFERENCES

Bashkow, Ira. *The Meaning of Whitemen: Race and Modernity in the Orokaiva Cultural World* (Chicago and London: University of Chicago Press, 2006).

Berliner, David. 'An "impossible" Transmission: Youth Religious Memories in Guinea-Conakry', *American Ethnologist* 32: 4 (2005): 576-92.

Bruner, Edward. M. 'Tourism in Ghana: The Representation of Slavery and the Return of the Black Diaspora', *American Anthropologist* 98: 2 (1996): 290-304.

Cole, Jennifer. 'Fresh Contact in Tamatave, Madagascar: Sex, Money, and Intergenerational Transformation', *American Ethnologist* 31: 4 (2004): 573-88.

Diouf, Mamadou. 'Engaging Postcolonial Cultures: African Youth and Public Space', *African Studies Review* 46: 2 (2003): 1-12.

Durham, Deborah. 'Youth and the Social Imagination in Africa: Introduction to Parts 1 and 2', *Anthropological Quarterly* 73:3 (2000): 113-120.

Ferguson, James. *Global Shadows: Africa in the Neoliberal World Order* (Durham and London: Duke University Press, 2006).

Frankland, Stan. 'The Bulimic Consumption of Pygmies: Regurgitating an Image of Otherness', in Mike Robinson and David Picard, eds., *The Framed World: Tourism, Tourists and Photography* (Surrey: Ashgate Publishing Limited, 2009), 95-116.

Gable, Eric. 'The Funeral and Modernity in Manjaco', *Cultural Anthropology* 21:3 (2006): 385-415.

—— 'The Culture Development Club: Youth, Neo-Tradition, and the Construction of Society in Guinea-Bissau', *Anthropological Quarterly* 73:4 (2000): 195-203.

Honwana, Alcinda and De Boeck, Filip. *Makers and Breakers: Children and Youth in Postcolonial Africa*, Oxford: James Currey, 2005.

Nyamnjoh, Francis. '"For many are called but few are chosen": Globalisation and Popular Disenchantment in Africa', *African Sociological Review* 4:2 (2000): 1-45.

Nyamnjoh, Francis and Ben Page. 'Whiteman Kontri and the Enduring Allure of Modernity among Cameroonian Youth', *African Affairs* 101 (2002): 607-34.

Pink, Sarah. 'The White "Helpers": Anthropologists, Development Workers and Local Imaginations', *Anthropology Today* 14:6 (1998): 9-14.

Schramm, Katharina. '"You Have your own History. Keep your Hands Off Ours": On being rejected in the field', *Social Anthropology* 13:2 (2005): 171-83.

Simpson, Kate. 'Doing development: The Gap Year, Volunteer-Tourists and a Popular Practice of Development', *Journal of International Development.* 16:5 (2004): 681-92.

Sin, Harng Lu. 'Volunteer Tourism: "Involve Me and I Will Learn"', *Annals of Tourism Research.* 36 (2009): 480-501.

Smith, Valene, (ed.). *Hosts and Guests: The Anthropology of Tourism* (University of Pennsylvania Press, 1977).

Wearing, Stephen and Jess Ponting. '"Breaking Down the System": How Volunteer Tourism contributes to New Ways of Viewing Commodified Tourism', in Tazim Jamal and Mike Robinson, eds., *The Sage Handbook of Tourism Studies* (London: Sage Publications Ltd, 2009), 254-68.

Weiss, Brad. 'Thug Realism: Inhabiting Fantasy in Urban Tanzania', *Cultural Anthropology.* 17:1 (2002): 93-124.

—— 'The Barber in Pain: Consciousness, Affliction and Alterity in Urban East Africa', in Filip De Boeck and Alcinda Honwana, eds., *Makers and Breakers: Children and Youth in Postcolonial Africa* (Oxford: James Currey, 2005), 103-19.

13 • Becoming
'real African kings & queens':
Chieftaincy, culture, & tourism in Ghana

Marijke Steegstra

Home to quite possibly the friendliest and most welcoming people on the planet, most people travel to Ghana to experience its rich and diverse culture.[1]

The Institution of Chieftaincy is the kingpin of Ghanaian traditional culture, and its contemporary relevance is generally recognised.[2]

A British couple yesterday became Africa's first white chief and queen. John Lawler – already chief of the village of Shia, Ghana – saw his new wife Elaine made queen in front of thousands of well-wishers. The ceremony was just 24 hours after their marriage was blessed in front of chiefs and elders from across Ghana. John, 31, was made chief Togbui Mottey I eight years ago after helping set up a secondary school during a gap year. The village's main chief decided to bestow the title on Elaine, 33, after travelling to Newcastle to meet her. Elaine, of Gateshead, Tyne and Wear, will be now known as Mama Amenyo Nyowu Sika. She said: 'It was totally overwhelming but the people were so friendly and it was a wonderful privilege.' John, who runs a gap year travel company, added: 'She looked a real African queen.' (The Sun Online, July 11, 2006)

Ghanaians are often called the friendliest people in Africa in tourist guides and on tourist websites. They indeed have quite an over-whelming way of dealing with foreign guests. As stated in the excerpt above, John Lawler was even installed a chief after he had spent a gap year as a teacher in the Volta Region in Ghana. After further visits to Ghana, he established a travel company called 'Madventurer' which organises 'expeditions that encompass adventure and development work in developing countries'. No doubt some of the adventurer volunteers participating in his programme have also been made chiefs or queens in Ghana by now. Since the early 1990s, dozens of tourists, volunteers, expats and other visitors have received the honour of a chiefly title. Examples such as that of John Lawler and his wife Elaine have become rather common. Calling them 'Africa's first white chief and queen' therefore makes no sense and should be understood as part of the Western imagination of untouched African culture.

The foreign chiefs are also imagined to 'rule as kings over African tribes'. This misunderstanding is partly caused by the fact that in the English language there is no distinction made in the title 'chief', but

1 http://www.madventurer.com/page/Ghana.
2 'The Cultural Policy of Ghana', (National Commission on Culture, 2004).

in the local languages the different titles used designate the different hierarchical positions and functions. The actual title the foreigners usually receive is that of what in English is called a 'development chief' or 'development queen mother'. The original Akan title is 'Nkosuohene' (fem.: 'Nkosuohemaa'). Nkosuo means 'development' or 'progress' (-hene is the designation for a chief). Some of the foreigners hold different titles, but it is merely a variation on the same theme. Contrary to the traditional chiefly positions, this position is not based on descent i.e., not hereditary. It is an honorary position bestowed on commoners and foreigners in order to commend and secure their contribution to local development efforts. It does not imply any political or traditional power, despite what some popular Western media try to make us believe. The function of Nkosuohene was created by the late Asantehene, Otumfuo Opoku Ware II, in the course of the 1985 Golden Jubilee celebrating the 50th anniversary of the restoration of the Asante Confederacy.[3] Before long some foreigners were given the position, at first mostly African-Americans were installed, mainly along the coast, as many of them come to visit Ghana's former slave castles as roots tourists, but then also expatriate Dutch, German and British nationals familiar with the particular community through working there as doctors, businessmen or otherwise. Very soon non-Akan speaking communities in mostly southern Ghana started to copy the phenomenon and used their own terms to designate very similar positions, such as that of John Lawler's, who became a so-called Ngoryifia (Ngoryi means 'development' or 'progress' and -fia is an Ewe designation for a chief). The number of foreign development chiefs is now mushrooming.

The phenomenon of the development chief has brought up a lot of debate in Ghana. Critics fear that the installation of foreigners as chiefs will have a negative impact on Ghanaian culture and will lead to an erosion of chieftaincy. One Dutch development chief threw in the towel himself, because he felt that other Dutch chiefs are behaving like 'carnival prince[s]' and that 'white chiefs' are degrading traditional chieftaincy. This former export-manager of Dutch Heineken beer and later Dutch schnapps for Henkes-Bols was installed as chief of Oguaa-Effutu near Cape Coast in 1992, but took off his traditional sandals and now calls himself a 'retired chief'.[4] This view echoes the initial anthropological approach on the negative effects of outsiders in the form of tourism, viewing it as a major disruption of local cultures and as a dismaying commoditisation of culture.[5] Such a view does not explain the local popularity of the practice and denies any agency to the Ghanaians involved. This chapter explores the interplay of chieftaincy, culture, and tourism, and discusses some aspects of

3 Pieter R. van Dijk and Kuntu Jackson, *The Golden Age of Development and Progress* (Kumasi: 2002).
4 Taking off one's traditional sandals or having them removed is a traditional way of designating one's abdication from the 'stool' ('throne').
5 Valene Smith, ed., *Hosts and Guests: The Anthropology of Tourism* (Oxford: Blackwell, 1978).

what happens in the interaction between foreign visitors in Ghana who are installed as so-called development chiefs and queen mothers, and their hosts, in order to assess the impact of this practice on local culture. It argues that although the proliferation of development chiefs contributes to an erosion of the title itself, it does not weaken the position of the Ghanaian hereditary ruler and his office. Rather, the advisory foreign development chiefs add to the grandeur of his court and offer one of several modern means to strive for development.

There are no official records of *Nkosuo* stools.[6] So far, through newspaper clippings and electronic sources, I was able to trace the names of about seventy non-Ghanaians who were given a chiefly title, men and women, and I interviewed eleven of them, three women and eight men, all white Western Europeans and one white Canadian. Unfortunately, I did not get the chance to interview any of the Africans of the Diaspora who received a chiefly position. Bob-Milliar may have a point when he argues that the honour of a *Nkosuohene/hemaa* title has a different and far more spiritual meaning for diasporan Africans than for white Westerners.[7] For this and other reasons it may be justified to treat them as different groups, although I doubt whether Ghanaians always make the same distinctions and whether members of each group always behave very differently. In this chapter I concentrate on white Westerners. I further conducted fieldwork in various communities in southern Ghana where white development chiefs were installed during six months between 2004 and 2005.[8] In this chapter I will first sketch a brief background of tourism in Ghana. Then I will investigate the 'installation bubble' as part of the 'tourist bubble', and ask what happens during the rites of installation: what meanings do both parties, 'hosts' and 'guests', attribute to these performances?[9] I will then ask what the effect is on Ghanaian chieftaincy, and end with a short conclusion.

Tourism in Ghana

The Ghanaian state tries to promote tourism from the West to

6 A chiefly 'stool' symbolises authority and the power of the ancestors. A chief 'occupies a stool', which refers to his influence sphere. It also is an actual wooden seat. During the installation ('enstoolment') the new chief or queen is ceremonially seated on his or her stool. The inherited stools are considered far more sacred than non-hereditary stools.
7 George M. Bob-Milliar, 'Chieftaincy, Diaspora, and Development: the Institution of Nkosuohene in Ghana', *African Affairs* 108/433 (2009), 555. For information about African-American development chiefs and queen mothers in particular see: Susan Benson, 'Connecting with the Past, Building the Future: African Americans and Chieftaincy in Southern Ghana', *Ghana Studies* 6 (2003).
8 The research took place in the context of my post-doctoral research project 'The cultural construction of development: the installation of "white" chiefs in Ghana'. It was financially made possible by the Netherlands Foundation for Tropical Research (WOTRO) and the Radboud University Nijmegen.
9 W.E.A. van Beek, 'Approaching African Tourism; Paradigms and Paradoxes', in P Chabal, U Engel, and L de Haan, eds., *African Alternatives* (Leiden: Brill, 2007).

Ghana as it is thought to benefit the economy. There is a growing awareness, stimulated by international organisations such as the UNESCO that want to safeguard 'traditional culture' and folklore, that Ghana's cultural heritage can be used to promote national development, in particular with regard to tourism. Tourism is thus one area where the aims of preservation of 'culture' and at the same time development and progress come together. The Cultural Policy of Ghana says that:

> Tourism in Ghana is recognized as a major industry that depends on the buoyancy and attractiveness of the unique expressions of our culture. Ghana shall therefore recognize Tourism as a means by which the wealth of cultural products and values are shared with the rest of the world towards the promotion of our common humanity and global understanding.[10]

Being one of those 'unique expressions of culture', the Ghanaian state promotes chieftaincy for tourism. For innocent Western visitors, it may even seem as if chiefs are simply one of the attractions travel agencies put on their programme for them, therefore they are part of folklore. The website of the Ministry of Tourism opens with various pictures of chiefs, including that of the most famous of them all, the Asantehene (Asante king). In 1993, a special Ministry of Chieftaincy and Culture was even created, in the words of its minister in 2006, Mr. S.K. Boafo, '[to] give meaning to the Ghanaian tradition and cultural heritage'.[11] This Ministry works closely together with the National Commission on Culture.

According to the World Tourism Barometer, Ghana belonged to the 'World's Top Emerging Destinations' over the period of 1995 to 2004, when an average annual growth of 8.3 per cent occurred. In 2004 Ghana had 584,000 international tourist arrivals.[12] Many of the visitors coming in on tourist visas include exchange students and volunteers such as those who participate in the programmes on offer from the Madventurer company, which combine study or development work with travel. Therefore the claimed difference between international volunteerism and traditional tourism should be questioned. Still today, Ghana is not a mass-tourism destination. Therefore, the Ghanaian tourism sector puts great emphasis on establishing long-term connections with visitors. This happens mostly through the institutionalisation of pilgrimage tourism to the slave sites, which explains the relatively large number of African-American and other Diasporan visitors (see Chapter 4 this volume). With the government change in December 2008, the Ministry of Tourism, which had been the 'Ministry of Tourism and the Modernization of

10 'The Cultural Policy of Ghana'.
11 http://www.ghanaculture.gov.gh/index1.php?linkid=65&adate=26/07/2006&archiveid=212 &page=1; http://www.ghana.gov.gh/index.php?option=com_content&view=article&id=339:m inistry-of-culture-a-chieftaincy&catid=74:ministries&Itemid=224
12 World Tourism Organization (UNWTO): http://unwto.org/facts/eng/inbound.htm. No new figures are available yet.

the Capital City' under the former (NPP) government, has now even changed its name to the Ministry of Tourism and Diasporan Relations. But this establishing of long-term connections also happens 'from below': Ghanaian communities establish 'life-long' connections with foreigners by installing them as 'development chiefs' and 'development queen mothers' through elaborate ceremonies, as will be described in the next section. In this 'installation bubble' it becomes clear that the foreigners have a different understanding of what is happening from the Ghanaians involved.

Staged installations

Ghanaian chieftaincy is very appealing: it is very colourful and impressive, with a lot of pomp and pageantry. The way chiefs and queens appear at gatherings and durbars, dressed fully in *kente* and other precious African cloths, surrounded by horn blowers, sword and umbrella carriers, wearing golden ornaments or glass beads, makes it tempting to see them as evidence of timeless traditions. Even though most of the development chiefs and queens claim or aim 'to do good', many first of all seem to be fascinated with the 'authentic' traditions of chieftaincy and to become a 'real' chief or queen mother. Most of those whom I met personally, proudly showed me the chiefly regalia they were given at their installation as 'signs of traditional authority', such as ceremonial stools, swords, or clothes. Various chiefs even appear in chiefly dress in public in the West. Ghanaian chiefs are often more than willing to meet their expectations, especially when installing them. Many people in Ghana feel very proud of their chieftaincy culture and of course the interest of Westerners boosts their confidence. The *Agogohemaa* (paramount Queen Mother of Agogo in the Ashanti Region), for example, recognised foreigners' interest in participating in Ghanaian 'traditional culture' when she told me:

> When they [the foreigners] come down and help, the community sees an installation as something to motivate them and show their appreciation. Over here a chieftaincy title is not just given on a silver platter, so it is a big honour for foreigners to be installed. So when they take it up over there [abroad], there it means they can show that they were here and they did something beneficial. Chieftaincy is the most respected institution in Ghana. Here we respect our chiefs more than any others. The foreigners like you are interested in our culture; when they snap pictures and so forth they get happy and show it at home and they learn something about our culture. Some of them request that we write the records and send them with them to be taken home. So it is a two-way affair. (Interview with Nana Abena Serwaa, Agogo, 19 January 2005)

Another chief that installed the Austrian woman Christine Rafael as a queen mother, (described below), also emphasised the interest of both parties in the matter:

> The world is becoming a global village and we should be part of it. We can import expertise and money and we can also export our culture and other things we have available. Making Christine a queen mother is giving her a better understanding of how our system works. You know she feels part of us. When she comes she does not feel like she is a foreigner. We accept her and we treat her just like one of us. So she feels welcome here and if she can mobilise help for us, all the better! (Interview with Nana Offei Kwasi Agyeman, Accra, 3 November 2004)

Below I will discuss different aspects of the installation of two different foreign queen mothers and three chiefs. An installation ceremony can be quite a spectacular happening and many would-be development chiefs and queens bring their friends and sometimes family or even members of the media along to enjoy and record the show. In October 2004, I witnessed the elaborate installation of the Austrian woman mentioned above as *Nkosuohemaa* in a rural town in the Eastern Region, to encourage her to continue and expand the work with her NGO there. She had brought a group of friends and acquaintances with her to witness the ceremony. They all took photos and filmed the event:

> On the first day of the ceremony, a Tuesday, Christine was dressed in dark clothes, to signify that she was still a person 'in between'. Her followers, a group of Austrians who are members of her NGO, were all wearing the same white cloth for this joyful event. In her 'family house', the linguist explained that because Christine has been hard working and helping the community, the elders and the family had decided to elevate her position (from an advisor to the chief, in this case the *Krontihene*) to a queen mother for development (*Nkosuohemaa*). The family women tied pieces of white calico around everybody's head or neck. Then Christine was seated on a wooden stool thrice. A white sheep was brought in and after a long pouring of libation with schnapps by the linguist and young men representing the chief's house, it was slaughtered, and the bright red blood was made to flow over Christine's bare feet. In the meantime, one of the women was pouring white talcum powder on everybody around 'as a sign of victory and joy'. After that, a small crowd of her countrymen and people from the house followed Christine outside through the streets of the town. The women cheered and waved with pieces of white calico towards her and poured more powder around. We arrived at the *Krontihene*'s palace where he and his elders and some of his queen mothers sat waiting on the veranda and Christine was presented to them. The *Krontihene* told us that Christine would have to come to do the swearing of an oath to him on the following Thursday. Crates of drinks were presented to him and Christine went round to greet the chief and the elders. After that, it was time for refreshments.
>
> The next Thursday Christine herself was also dressed in light coloured clothes, to signify that now she had 'come out' and become a queen mother. There was dancing and drumming, in which Christine took part,

before she swore a short oath in English to her chief, which was translated into Twi. She said literally that whether in the night or during the day, she would come when she was called upon. Again, she went round after that to shake hands with the *Krontihene* and elders, and she sat on the chief's lap as part of the ceremony. After that, there was another presentation of drinks to the chief and his followers, who sat across the inner courtyard on the veranda, opposite Christine and her group. Then different people danced, and two of the women present took Christine to dance in front of her chief. From Christine's side some money donations and the offering of the ceremonial bottle of schnapps to the various elders and the chief followed. During the whole ceremony, I noticed how Christine was asked several times to bring money to 'pay' for different rituals being performed. The *Krontihene* gave a short speech in which he recalled that Christine came the first time about six years ago (1998). Since then, she had returned every year and 'done something'. He enumerated her good deeds, of which the building of a computer school was praised the most. He said that her name 'Nana Odoso II' was given to her, because 'Odoso' is the name of his (Ghanaian) queen mother's mother. He said: 'It demonstrates how important you are.' Everything ended with another libation.

The following day Christine proudly sat 'in state' among the many chiefs and queens who were present at the grand durbar for the annual Odwira Festival. She was not the only white queen mother among them. I saw two other foreign white queen mothers and a white chief among the huge crowd (Research notes, 5 and 7 October 2004).

This installation resembles an installation of an Akan or any Southern Ghanaian chief or queen mother that I have witnessed several times before. The installation of a queen mother, however, is usually much less elaborate than that of a chief and installation ceremonies in general vary from area to area in Ghana, as chieftaincy has been shaped by values of very different cultural traditions and consequently carries sharply different meanings from area to area.[13] Even though installations always vary, some elements in Christine's installation can still easily be recognised as a substitute, like the talcum powder that replaces the usual sacred white clay, while pouring the blood of a slaughtered sheep on the feet of a would-be queen mother is rather *not* common in the installation ceremony of any queen mother. It is a ritual performed in some areas for higher ranking chiefs as a purification ritual, but even chiefs, because they are often Christians, usually refuse to have blood poured on their feet and make alternative arrangements. Another important element in legitimising authority is: *who* is performing the rituals? In the case of a hereditary chief, the stool priest for example will perform some crucial rites, not some young boys or a lawyer as in the case described below. Before going into the meaning of the installation of foreign development chiefs and queens further, let us look at a few more examples of foreigners' installations.

13 Richard Rathbone, *Nkrumah and the Chiefs. The Politics of Chieftaincy in Ghana 1951-1960* (Accra: F Reimmer/ Athens: Ohio University Press/ Oxford: James Currey, 2000), 4.

13.1 Christine's
installation as a
development queen
mother, 2004
(© Marijke Steegstra)

Whereas pouring blood on one's feet is also not part of the installation ceremony for Ewe queen mothers in the Volta Region, the German Cornelia Von Wülfing, an 'importer of healing plants and supporter of development projects', claims to have become the paramount queen (sic!) of a town called Alavanyo and describes in her book, entitled *My Life as a Queen in Ghana* how she had to walk through the blood of a slaughtered sheep 'to make her strong'.[14] When

14 Cornelia von Wülfing, *Mein Leben Als Königin in Ghana* (Berlin, München: Ullstein Verlag, 2003), 47.

I asked her paramount chief why this was done, he indeed answered that: 'She is a foreigner and we were bestowing a lot of work on her. This blood is a sign that she must be brave (...) She was coming to spearhead development here, she needed to be very brave.' Both Wülfing and her Ghanaian chief seem to present the ritual as a test of endurance.

One particular German chief's romanticised story seems to fascinate the German media the most. Fritz Pawelzik, a former expat who used to work for the YMCA, has told the story of his 'kingship' in Konongo (Ashanti region) to many journalists and in presentations for schools. He gave me a CD of his 'listening book', in which he narrates the fantastic, romanticised story of his installation in 1991, thereby appealing to western fantasies of 'Dark Africa'. He recounts how he was captured and did not know what was going to happen when he was taken far into the jungle, where he was undressed in a hut and for a moment thought that the large cooking pot in the middle was meant for him... He goes on to describe how animal blood was poured over him 'from head to toe'. The story of thirty-six wives that were then 'given' to him has often been recounted in the western media, even though he makes clear that they are nominal wives. He claims the people of Konongo told him that he was now their king, and that they also made him their highest priest, warlord and judge. The Ghanaian chief (*ohene*) of Konongo who installed Pawelzik, had fond memories of the event and his development chief, but remembered the installation as a 'one day of merrymaking', with another day of church-going. According to him, they approached the German about this matter in 1991, and he accepted, then they 'went ahead to enstool him in 1992.' Pawelzik used to visit Ghana more often, but is now an old man in his eighties, and does not travel such distances anymore.

Another attempt to make the installation of foreign chiefs look authentic and legitimate to outsiders is to suggest a link with the local ancestors or a certain predecessor. The ones who install the foreigner may explain the chosen title with the extension 'II' ('second') as due to the fact that the installed person, although a foreigner, resembles a dead ancestral chief or queen mother. One of the two Dutch chiefs who have drawn much media attention in the Netherlands but also worldwide, Henk Otte, told me that the people in Mepe (Volta Region) explained to him that he resembled his Ghanaian wife's dead grandfather who supposedly was also a chief. A diviner was even said to have revealed that Otte is the reincarnation of the grandfather, and thus was named *Togbe* Korsi Ferdinand Gakpetor II ('the second'). Even though he did not believe in his own reincarnation, the Dutchman told me, the claim convinced him that the people of Mepe wanted him, a 'common man', as their chief. When I visited Mepe myself, the wife's relatives and Mepe chiefs put the story in perspective and said that the link with the dead grandfather was only a symbolic one. But they could not foresee that the western media would pick it up and spread the news through the internet from Japan to the USA that an 'unemployed ex-builder from Amsterdam has been crowned King Togbe Korsi Ferdinand Gakpetor II following the discovery that he is the reincarnation of the last great warrior king of the 250,000-strong Ewe tribe in Ghana'.[15] There was even a film made about Otte, called 'Togbe', (the Ewe reference for a chief) with 'the incredible true story of how an ordinary man became a king', by some American film makers.[16] In Ghana a lot of uproar followed the foreign 'news' that an 'unemployed white man' ruled as a monarch in Ghana.

Whereas Henk Otte himself denied being or striving to be above his paramount chief, another Dutch chief who has often appeared in his national media, Arthur Paes, also feeds the story with exotic representations of 'kingship' in Africa by calling himself 'King of Somey' in the coastal area of the Volta Region, where he is a development chief. So far, Dutch journalists have been very uncritical of his claims. For example, the well-known Dutch presenter Ivo Niehe devoted a television show to Paes on 27 February 2009, in which he presented him admiringly as a mineworker's son who has worked his way up to a real estate millionaire and king of Somey. Paes' website opens with the pretentious headline 'King of Somey, Togbui Ngoryifia Kofi Arthur Paes Dunenyo I'.[17] Noteworthy is that 'King' Paes' Ghanaian title clearly indicates his position as a development chief. Both 'Ngoryi-fia' and 'Dunenyo' mean 'development'. According to this millionaire, the people in Somey 'handed over the power to him' and made him a 'king' and not a 'chief'. When I asked him what the difference was, he answered that he has 'the final responsibility for development', and that everything was discussed and confirmed by a lawyer (brought by him) during the installation. Although Paes pretended not to know the exact meaning of his title when asked, according to him being the 'boss of development' is more significant than anything anyway. Moreover, other chiefs in the area are less important than he is, he claimed, 'because they do not have money'. The paramount chief (sic!) by whom he was installed, Togbega Hor II, did not deny that he had received a car from Paes at the time of the installation. Whereas some sort of bribery may more often than not be involved in obtaining desirable chieftaincy positions in Ghana, it is clear that simply paying money or bringing a western-style lawyer to the scene are not the

15 'Jobless white builder rules as African king. Dutchman is declared reincarnation of monarch', *Sunday Telegraph*, 2000.

16 Copyright Reel Films, 2001. For more details, see: Marijke Steegstra, 'Development Encounters: Westerners and Chieftaincy in Southern Ghana', in Jan Abbink and André van Dokkum, eds., *Dilemmas of Development: Conflicts of Interest and Their Resolutions in Modernizing Africa, African Studies Collection, Vol. 10* (Leiden: African Studies Centre, 2008).

17 http://www.somey.nl/pagina/king_somey/index.html. 'Togbe' or 'Togbui' is the Ewe reference for a chief, just like the additive '-fia'. But 'Togbui' is also used in the south of the Volta Region for 'any old person' and is also the title of reference for native priests and is not translated as 'king'. The title 'Togbega' would refer to a paramount chief, the highest in rank. Whilst in this particular area two different paramountcies exist side by side, due to particular migration histories, the paramount chief under whose authority Paes was installed is Togbega Hor II.

traditional ways of making an installation legitimate. Photos on the website of his installation show more examples of how Paes created his own symbols of chieftaincy. In one photo for instance he is seated on a huge wooden chair with carved lions in the armrests; it seems quite a unique chair, certainly not one commonly used in chief's ceremonies.

What makes Arthur Paes stand out from most of the other white chiefs, who, despite the fantastic stories from some sources, usually behave more in line with the spirit of the title they have been awarded, i.e., 'lesser chief', is that he and not others proclaims to be 'the king of the area'. He seems to have learned the distinction from the man who introduced him to the Somey area and showed him the way to chieftaincy through money, his friend Céphas Bansah. This Ghanaian, German-based development chief has a conflict with his own paramount chief, as I will describe below. What Paes does have in common with many of the other white chiefs and queen mothers is that they do not understand their position well, and often do not even mobilise the community to undertake projects as they are expected to. Paes' own paramount chief complained to me that the Dutchman had not yet lived up to the expectations of 'development' in his area.

As stated earlier, installation ceremonies of chiefs vary from area to area in Ghana. However, in every area, the installation of 'real' Ghanaian chiefs and queen mothers is taken very seriously. There are some secret and sacred parts of the installation ceremonies, such as the period of confinement (during which certain ceremonies take place) that are very crucial. They will indicate something about the power and importance of the particular chief or queen installed. The particular procedure and naming indicates the rank of the chief or queen in the strong hierarchical system of chieftaincy. If the installation of a powerful chief is not done in the 'proper way', or s/he was not the right person, in other words, s/he was not from the right descent, serious trouble may follow. I once witnessed the installation of a high-ranking chief in the Krobo area, who died suddenly not long afterwards. Rumour had it that he had been the wrong person to be put on the particular stool, in other words, that fact had been the cause of his death. A hereditary chiefly title has a sacred dimension and comes with a so-called 'black stool' (i.e. consecrated stool), which is imbued with ancestral power. A black stool is kept in the 'stool house', which is only accessible to a limited number of people, and it is cleansed yearly with an animal (in past times human) sacrifice.

The installations discussed above can be understood as what MacCannell has described as 'staged authenticity': what is generated through the tourists' quest for authenticity.[18] They are performances that will be accepted by the visitors as authentic or at least a reasonable

---

18 D. MacCannell, *The Tourist* (New York: Schocken, 1989).

imitation of the 'normal' performance. Ghanaians are aware of foreigners' fascination for the traditions of chieftaincy and gladly tap into their performative cultural repertoire to make the foreigners part of an 'authentic' experience. The installations of Westerners as development chiefs does not so much reflect their position in the chiefly hierarchy, but varies according to resources, region and creativity. These events can be characterised as local inventions of tradition, as there usually are no previous examples available. They do not follow customary regulations and are not subject to political or sacred considerations like those of customary chiefs. The position and title remains honorary. Therefore it does not really matter which rituals are used to install the foreigners. Who is eligible to become a 'real' Ghanaian chief is often a contested matter too, as numerous succession disputes in Ghana demonstrate. But foreigners who do not share a blood relation as a general rule remain in the position of an (appreciated) outsider and their installation is an imitation of old ceremony.

13.2 The Dutch development chief Mauritz Verhagen at a school opening in the Brong Ahafo Region, 2005
(© Marijke Steegstra)

An erosion of chieftaincy?

The fact that hardly any of the foreign chiefs speak the local language, have a clue about what is going on during their installation, and are in complete ignorance of the power dynamics of the social relationships in which the chieftaincy practices are embedded, underlines the bubble. Although Paes rather brought in western elements such as a lawyer to confirm his leadership, in his own fashion, he shares the western image of the exotic African king ruling as some sort of benevolent dictator and sees his own position in this line. The slaughtering of live animals and other rituals involving blood, as well as practices involving polygyny, diviners and ancestors described in the other ceremonies, all contribute to the image of Africa as the continent of strange, colourful cultures and rituals.

Most foreign development chiefs do not stay with 'their' community, not even for the installation. Some arrive in the town for their installation and will go and stay in a hotel afterwards. Others do stay in a local house for the occasion, but on later visits stay in a guesthouse or hotel. Some of the foreign development chiefs never return to the community after their installation, even though some long-distance contact may continue for some time. Paes visits the area of Somey a few times per year, but arrives in his private air-conditioned four-wheel drive, to return to his four star hotel in Accra the same day. Another Dutch chief visits 'his' community in the Brong-Ahafo Region every year, bringing supporters of his NGO along, and stays with them in the guesthouse that the NGO built for income-generating purposes. The permeability of the walls of the bubble differs, but the bubble is always there.

The development chiefs may sometimes sit in state during durbars (gatherings) and contribute to 'development' of the local community, but they have no influence whatsoever on the day-to-day chiefly practice. For example, one German chief and his wife who used to visit 'their' town in the Brong Ahafo Region almost every year felt close with the local people, but finally left the place out of frustration about the effects of large-scale gold mining in the area, on which they could exert no influence. The man recalled how, as the development chief, he advised against allowing a big South African mining company to search for gold in the area. While he felt it would only benefit a few people and bring about many unwanted side effects, such as harming the health of people over time, he complained that the other chiefs saw the exploitation of gold in the area as an opportunity for self-enrichment and would not listen to him.

In general, my impression is that Ghanaian chiefs find it convenient that foreign chiefs are ignorant of chieftaincy affairs. Although Ghanaian development chiefs are also honorary chiefs and have a specific function, there is always the danger that through their affluence they try to 'outperform' other chiefs in the way they dress or the projects they can accomplish. One clear example was given to me by the present paramount chief of Gbi Hohoe Traditional Area, Togbega Gabusu VI, who instigated the installation of Céphas Bansah as a development chief in 1992. He told me that before Bansah was installed as an Ngoryifia, he had already donated some equipment from Germany to the local hospital, at a time when Ghana was in serious economic crisis and short of medications. People also noticed the cars he brought down for his brothers and saw that too as a sign of development. By installing Bansah who resides in Germany and has white friends, people in Hohoe hoped to get access to more development. After his installation, Bansah, amongst others, constructed a foot-bridge, helped pay school fees for needy children, and brought used ambulances and a bus for the traditional council. Even though Bansah is the development chief, Togbega Gabusu sees himself as the instigator of development, as he was the one who initiated the installation of a development chief in the area. But Togbega Gabusu regrets that he chose Bansah for the position. These days, Bansah does not consult him and the elders anymore about projects needed, and operates on his own. For example, he presented a generator each to the Hohoe Police and the Hohoe Evangelical Presbyterian Secondary School, but Togbega Gabusu was not informed.[19] 'He cannot decide what our problems are', Togbega said. 'We are putting up a traditional council office. We want his assistance and others. But it is not coming.' Now Togbega Gabusu is frustrated about the fact that some people even seem to think that Bansah is above him, as he calls himself 'King (König) Bansah' in Germany, and 'because he has a few euros' and 'is able to buy things people in Ghana cannot buy.'[20] He called poverty 'a disease', and sees it as the main reason why Bansah has influence and why so many white people are also installed as development chiefs, implying that some people can easily be bought.

Even though Togbega Gabusu regrets Bansah's installation, he touches on some important reasons for installing foreigners or those residing abroad as development chiefs. The installation of a development chief rubs off on the paramount chief himself. Creating foreign alliances conveys status, because in the popular imagination of Ghanaian society, 'abrokyere' ('abroad') is the source of innovation, opportunity and material success.[21] By attracting external funding for projects and forming alliances with foreigners, chiefs can acquire social and symbolic capital that might yield economic or other opportunities and thus raise the status of their

19 In the national newspaper, the *Daily Graphic* at the time, it was reported that Céphas Bansah, the 'ngoryifia of Hohoe' and 'executive director of CEBAF (Céphas Bansah and Friends Development Foundation)', donated the generators (*Daily Graphic*, 20 September 2004).
20 http://koenig.matoma.de/mcms.php
21 Jenna Burrell, '"I Have Great Desires to Look Beyond My World": Trajectories of Information and Communication Technology Use among Ghanaians Living Abroad', *105th AAA Annual Meeting* (San Jose CA, USA: 2006). Karen Tranberg Hansen, 'Second-Hand Clothing Encounters in Zambia: Global Discourses, Western Commodities and Local Histories', in Richard Fardon, Wim van Binsbergen, and Rijk van Dijk, eds., *Modernity on a Shoestring. Dimensions of Globalization, Consumption and Development in Africa and Beyond* (Leiden and London: EIDOS in association with the African Studies Centre Leiden and the Centre of African Studies London, 1999), 219.

town or village, including their own reputation. Many chiefs in Ghana are highly educated: some hold a PhD, MBA or MA title from (prestigious) universities in the UK, America or elsewhere. They have lived abroad before, and now travel regularly to the West, and some, including Togbega Gabusu, are often invited to be present and speak at conferences or other events. They are already part of global interaction. Installing foreigners as their development chiefs adds to their grandeur. Some chiefs even have several foreigners with a chiefly title among their entourage.

I will briefly describe one chief who can serve as an example here. He has installed many foreigners as chiefs, both African-Americans and (white) Europeans. Nana Akuoku Sarpong is the Paramount Chief of Agogo in the Ashanti Region. He is a lawyer by profession and operates a firm as a 'legal and cultural consultant' in Accra. He is also the former presidential advisor on chieftaincy affairs and the former president of the National Commission on Culture. He is quite an affluent man. He drives a nice car and has built a large palace in Agogo where peacocks wander about in the garden just like at the Asantehene's place. He often flies to the USA where he has connections with members of African-American communities in New Jersey, New York, and Philadelphia, amongst others with one particular society whose members trace their roots to Egypt and claim royal African roots. Nana Sarpong has appointed at least eight foreigners as chiefs, both African-Americans and (white) Europeans, for whom he has created different positions. For example, one man from Switzerland was given the title *Papayehene*, meaning: 'benefactor'. Together with other former expats, this man works with the Ernst Beyer Foundation which has mainly contributed resources to the Agogo hospital. One successful African-American received the particular *Nkabom* stool and is 'Nkabomhene', meaning: chief for unity. The mere ability of Nana Sarpong to bring in Westerners as development chiefs raises his status. Nana Sarpong exploits the aesthetic symbolism of having a foreign development chief to the maximum, by creating different positions with different titles for foreigners.

Conclusion

Although the way white Westerners view *Nkosuo* stools from their cultural perspective may sometimes conflict with how Ghanaian chiefs see them – principally as development initiators – Ghanaians involved in chieftaincy and development are drawing on some pretty contentious ideas about the exoticism and primitivism of African culture in their 'romanticisation' of ritual in the installation of development chiefs. They quench the foreign visitors' thirst for authenticity and 'African culture' by giving them an 'authentic' instal- lation as development chiefs and queens. Do the reinforcement of exoticism or even primitivism, and the installation of foreigners as such, have a negative impact on Ghanaian chieftaincy?

The ease with which a title is given these days could be interpreted as a degradation of the development chief's title. With so many foreigners installed as 'real African kings and queens', it is not a unique gift anymore and there is the risk of installing people of dubious reputation. However, it does not mean an erosion of chieftaincy as such. The installation of westerners as development chiefs and queens can be considered as staged authenticity and part of a 'tourist bubble'. With the exception of a few people, they do not speak the language, do not live in the area, and do not have a good idea of what the concept of chieftaincy entails. Giving them an 'authentic' installation and dressing the 'bubble' in a grandiose way, is very convenient for the local chiefs. The development chiefs thus have no influence on the daily chieftaincy practice. Where there is always the danger with Ghanaian development chiefs – who are often insiders – that they might outperform the paramount chief due to their affluence, western development chiefs are mostly considered harmless and can only add to the grandeur of a Ghanaian chief. By attracting external funding for projects and forming alliances with foreigners, chiefs can thus acquire social and symbolic capital that might yield economic or other opportunities and thus raise the status of their town or village, including their own reputation. Rather than leading to an erosion of chieftaincy, an increasing number of western development chiefs and queens also strengthens the western interest in, and thereby the importance and culture of, Ghanaian chieftaincy.

REFERENCES

Beek, W.E.A. van. 'Approaching African Tourism; Paradigms and Paradoxes' in P. Chabal, U. Engel and L. de Haan, eds., *African Alternatives* (Leiden: Brill, 2007),145-72.

Benson, Susan. 'Connecting with the Past, Building the Future: African Americans and Chieftaincy in Southern Ghana', *Ghana Studies* 6 (2003): 109-33.

Bob-Milliar, George M. 'Chieftaincy, Diaspora, and Development: the Institution of Nkosuohene in Ghana', *African Affairs* 108/433 (2009): 541-58.

Burrell, Jenna. "'I Have Great Desires to Look Beyond My World": Trajectories of Information and Communication Technology Use among Ghanaians Living Abroad', in 105th AAA Annual Meeting (San Jose, CA, 2006).

Dijk, Pieter R. van, and Kuntu Jackson, 'The Golden Age of Development and Progress' (Kumasi: 2002).

Hansen, Karen Tranberg. 'Second-Hand Clothing Encounters in Zambia: Global Discourses, Western Commodities and Local Histories', in Richard Fardon, Wim van Binsbergen and Rijk van Dijk, eds., *Modernity on a Shoestring. Dimensions of Globalization, Consumption and Development in Africa and Beyond* (Leiden and London: EIDOS in association with the

African Studies Centre Leiden and the Centre of African Studies London, 1999), 207-26.

MacCannell, D. *The Tourist* (New York: Schocken, 1989).

National Commission on Culture. 'The Cultural Policy of Ghana' (2004).

Rathbone, Richard. *Nkrumah and the Chiefs. The Politics of Chieftaincy in Ghana 1852-1960* (Accra, Athens, Oxford: F. Reimmer, Ohio University Press, James Currey, 2000).

Smith, Valene L., ed. *Hosts and Guests: The Anthropology of Tourism* (Oxford: Blackwell, 1978).

Steegstra, Marijke. 'Development Encounters: Westerners and Chieftaincy in Southern Ghana', in Jan Abbink and André van Dokkum, eds., *Dilemmas of Development: Conflicts of Interest and Their Resolutions in Modernizing Africa* (Leiden: African Studies Centre, 2008), 228-41.

Wülfing, Cornelia von. *Mein Leben Als Königin in Ghana* (Berlin, München: Ullstein Verlag, 2003).

14 • Sex trade & tourism in Kenya: Close encounters between the hosts & the hosted

Wanjohi Kibicho

The purpose of this chapter is to highlight the interaction between hosts and guests in romance-oriented tourism, demonstrating how local people's views on sex (trade)-oriented tourism vary according to their interest and experience. In order to illustrate the nexus between the tourism industry and the sex profession, I draw on the data from a leading tourism destination area in the country – Malindi, (see map) where local residents view tourism as a creator of sex trade. Further, the interactions between the tourists and the host community has challenged behavioural patterns in Kenya, as the one-time or long-term relationships in the sex trade have become an integral part of the local tourist bubble. The trade has offered new roles for local men and women, exposing weaknesses within the norms of local social spheres. For instance, it has highlighted the vulnerability of local attitudes as local men increasingly take up relationships with female tourists who are willing to enter into casual sexual relationships. Thus, sex-oriented tourism entails the willingness of (foreign) tourists to engage with the 'Other', resulting in a profound involvement with contrasting cultures, to some degree, on their own terms.

Currently, tourism is the second largest contributor to national revenues after agriculture.[1] From a general point of view, the national tourism industry has experienced a spectacular growth especially during the post-independent era, a potential already recognised in the first independent National Development Plan (1966/67-1972/73). The setting up of the Kenya Tourist Development Corporation in 1965 marked this recognition, institutionalised by the establishment of the Ministry of Tourism a year later. Successive economic development plans since 1972/73 have laid emphasis on the industry as an engine for socio-economic development of the country.

From the mid to the late 1970s, Kenya's tourism industry changed from small-scale public and private businesses to mega-scale investments funded by overseas multinational companies and investors.

* The author thanks Ahmed Juma, Edith Mwihaki, Josephine Kasichana, and the MWA's Secretary for their assistance during the lengthy data collection period.

1 *Kenya Economic Survey*. (Nairobi: Government Printers, 2007, 2008); Wanjohi Kibicho, 'Community-based tourism: a factor-cluster segmentation approach', *Journal of Sustainable Tourism*. 16, 2 (2008): 211-31; Wanjohi Kibicho, *Sex Tourism in Africa: Kenya's Booming Industry* (Leiden & London: Ashgate Publishing, 2009).

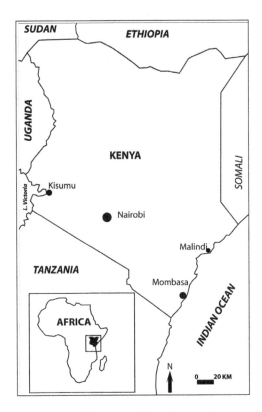

14.1 Map of Kenya showing location of Malindi

Tourism policy was thus directed towards large-scale investments in cooperation with transnational enterprises. It was an era of 'tourism industrialisation' where the tour operator controlled the whole of the tourist product production process including chartered flights, accommodation and transport in the visited destination. During this period, the demand side of the tourism industry largely exceeded that of the supply. Consequently, the tourism resource base (both natural and cultural) was overwhelmed by uncoordinated tourism development largely governed by a *laissez-faire* policy. This created the institutional vacuum for an upsurge of sex (trade)-related tourism within the leading tourism destination areas.[2]

Kenya's tourism industry can be divided into four major sectors: beach, safari, business/conference and culture. In this chapter we are on the beach, and for an examination of the marriage between tourism and the sex business we look at tourism development in Malindi.

Tourism and the Malindi economy

The development of modern tourism in Malindi dates back to 1931 when an 18-bed hotel was built as the base for deep-sea fishing off

2 Gitonga, A. and Anyangu, S. 2008. 'More than 1,000 Women Trafficked to Germany', *East African Standard*, (http://www.eastandard.net/): II (Accessed 20 November 2008).

Malindi Bay.[3] Here the world-famous writer, Ernest Hemingway stayed for several weeks in 1934, in a hotel by the name *The Blue Marlin*, now classified as three-star. In the same year, in 1934, the tourism industry was formerly launched by the then District Commissioner, Sir Leo Lawford, who later built a *makuti* (coconut palm fronds) hotel in 1935 under the name Lawford's Hotel.[4] The hotel still stands as a four-star establishment. From the local people's viewpoint, Lawford is considered a visionary for the type of planning he used for Malindi's development. It was based on a semi-master plan that included the establishment of three fundamental commitments – strict control of land use, development of recreational areas, and preservation of two square kilometres of marine reserve – currently known as Malindi Marine National Park. Lawford's goal was to maintain the area's natural beauty by developing tourism in such a way that the destination's natural attributes would be enhanced rather than being destroyed.[5]

However, with an ever-increasing (mass) tourism development, it was difficult to maintain the high quality set by Lawford. By 1968, for instance, the resort had almost tripled its bed capacity to about one thousand.[6] On account of its pristine beaches and the influx of foreign investors, particularly from Italy, Malindi has experienced a tourism boom especially in terms of hotel bed capacity. The study area has a total of 5,700 beds, 42 star-rated restaurants, 28 tour operators and 517 beach operators.[7] It is estimated that there are 3,500 beds in private villas and homes used by tourists. At the same time, from 1995 to 2000, the total number of tourists to Malindi increased by almost 70 per cent, or from 121,000 to 206,000 visitors.[8] Today, Malindi is a concentration of various types of tourist facilities, ranging from curio shops, cheap restaurants, bars, guesthouses, villas to luxurious hotels of international standard. As a result the area has become a mass tourism destination, largely due to its attractions of sand, sun, sea and (to some extent) sex.[9] Today, tourism generates majority of the employment opportunities in Malindi. These jobs are mainly in the service-oriented sectors of the local economy – retail, catering, transport and security.

A quick look at the development of local business in Malindi from

3 Peake, R. 'Tourism and Swahili Identity in Malindi Old Town, Kenyan coast', *Africa*, 59, 2 (1989): 209-20; Kibicho, W., 'A Critical Evaluation of How Tourism Influences the Commercial Sex Workers' Operations in Malindi Area, Kenya', *Annals of Leisure Studies* 7, 3-4 (2004): 188-201;
4 Kibicho, W., 'Tourism and the Sex Trade: Roles Male Sex Workers Play in Malindi, Kenya', *Tourism Review International* 7, 3-4 (2004): 129-141; Kibicho, 'A Critical Evaluation'
5 Peake, 'Tourism and Swahili identity'; Kibicho, 'Service quality in Malindi's tourism industry: a study of tourist perceptions', *ASEAN Journal on Hospitality & Tourism Research*. 12, 3 (2006): 218-31.
6 PTLC 1998.
7 *Malindi District Development Plan: 2002-2008*. Nairobi: Government Printers; Kibicho, 'Impacts of tourism'.
8 The figures are from Kenya 2002-2009.
9 *Kenya Economic Survey*, 2008.

1990 to 2005 demonstrates a heavy dependency on tourism. In 1990 there were 226 big and small businesses recorded.[10] One hundred and ten (49 per cent) of these are fully dependent on tourism – hotels, tour operators, sport-fishing companies, casinos, motorbike hire shops, jewellery boutiques, and curio shops. Another 108 (47 per cent) are dependent for up to four-fifths of their custom on domestic and international tourists – supermarket outlets, taxis, bars and restaurants, discotheques, massage parlours, postcard shops, bait-and-tackle shops, car-hire businesses, internet cafes, butchers, news-agents, foreign currency exchange bureaux, fast food cafes, curio workshop, fresh-produce retail market, the national marine park, crocodile farms, animal sanctuaries, barber shops, gymnasiums among others. The remaining eight businesses (4 per cent) – hardware shops, electrical, bakeries, video shops, banks etc –, are not primarily dependent on the tourism industry but they certainly benefit through the demand – a multiplier effect. In short, a full-blown tourist bubble dominates the Malindi economy.

In 1990, 70 per cent of the business that absolutely relied on the tourism industry was owned and operated by foreigners. By September 2005, this percentage had increased to 91 per cent (Italians 69; Germans 6; British 4, and others including Kenyans 4 per cent). Similarly, foreigners dominated the second category of business. This was due to closing down of almost 43 per cent of locally owned businesses by the end of 1997.[11] So the trend towards foreign-owned and operated businesses is clear in Malindi with a steady expansion of Italian operations.[12] In total, the number of businesses operating in Malindi in 2005 was 441 compared to 216 in 1990, a significant rise of 70 per cent. The unaltered foreign ownership of businesses has lessened local peoples' control of the tourist bubble and increased leakage.

This phenomenon has left many local residents with only one option: trading in small-scale businesses in the informal sector of the tourism industry. They include but are not limited to curio selling on the beach, Malindi city tour guiding, the making and selling of artefacts of all kinds, and clandestine work like drug dealing, illegal money changing and trading in sex. Accordingly, some residents feel that these massive capital foreign investments do not help the local economy.[13] 'Greg', a local restaurateur captures the foregoing in the following words:

> ...we will end up nowhere with this kind of tourism development. Tourists come here on all-inclusive tour packages. They pay rent to hotel owners, eat in foreign-owned large restaurants, their local transport is pre-paid

10 PTLC 1998.
11 Ibid.: 49.
12 *Kenya Economic Survey.* 2007. Nairobi: Government Printers.
13 Cf. also Kibicho, 'Impacts of Tourism in Malindi'. Note that in all interviews quoted in this chapter, pseudonyms have been used, indicated by inverted commas.

in their home countries, with profits going back to the tourist generating countries. They [tourists] are raping our resources, our community and most sickening they are stealing our women… Tourism has stolen our pride. Our identity is gone *kabisa* [for ever].

Malindi's tourism and the sex profession

The tourism-oriented sex trade is too diverse, complex and multi-faceted to be adequately covered in any detail in one chapter,[14] so here we focus on the nexus between sex (trade) and tourism, both in quantitative and qualitative terms.

From an established African perspective, wealth was the all-important factor.[15] A wealthy man could rise above others: wealth freed one from the obligation to serve others. This feeling still prevails with many locals who see wealth as the key social differentiation factor – those who control and those who serve.[16] With the intention to accumulate wealth, therefore, many Kenyans participate in the tourism industry at different levels, serving in various capacities. After all, the tourism industry did create new roles in its major destination areas in the country.

As the Kenya report [17] mentions, however, '…whilst the new jobs in the tourism industry offer opportunities to the local residents, they have also created some side effects.' At the coastal region for instance, the old primary industries, particularly fishing and agriculture, have been superseded in popularity as employment areas by tourism and its related sectors of the local economy[18]. Many local men, for instance, have abandoned fishing, preferring to work in the tourism-oriented service industry. Of course, this trend cannot wholly be blamed on tourism, but the industry does provide job options, thereby encouraging a displacement of the workforce.[19] Tour and hotel operations, bar and restaurant work, tour guiding, safari selling and taxi driving provide an extra form of income for many families. Probably the most controversial impact of tourism-related work crossovers has been the expansion of the sex trade both for men and women.[20] 'Ed', a veteran fisherman in Malindi, complains:

14 The subject has been examined extensively elsewhere, for example Wanjohi Kibicho, *Sex Tourism in Africa: Kenya's Booming Industry* (Leiden & London: Ashgate Publishing 2009); J. Belliveau, *Romance on the Road: Travelling Women who Love Foreign Men* (Baltimore MD: Beau Monde Press, 2006).

15 J. Mensah, *Black Canadians: History, Experiences, Social Conditions* (Winnipeg: Fernwood Publishing, 2005).

16 Gitonga, A. and Anyangu, S., 'More than 1,000 Women Trafficked to Germany', *East African Standard*. (http://www.eastandard.net/): II. Accessed 20 November 2008.

17 Malindi District Development Plan: 2002-2008. Nairobi: Government Printers.

18 *Kenya Economic Survey*. Nairobi: Government Printers, 2004-2008.

19 *Kenya Survey 2002; 2007*; Kibicho, 'Impacts of Tourism' 2005.

20 A comparable case is found in Eric Cohen, 'Thailand Girls and Farang Men: The Edge of Ambiguity', *Annals of Tourism Research*. 19, 3 (1982): 403-28.

Tourism has destroyed our youngsters. You can no longer teach them how to fish. Today, they want easy and fast cash; they want the tourists' lifestyles. They prefer working in disco clubs and bars. When not working, they are in the beer-bars during the day and in the nightclubs during the night. To fish you need to be in the deep-sea by five o'clock in the morning. At this time these youths are still drunk... They do not want to be bothered. As long as tourism is in our midst and tourists are intermingling with our youths, then we are in a big mess, insurmountable trouble. We need to go back to the basics – the spirit of our forefathers... the spirit of hard work [he concludes with a sense of disappointment].

'Lady Carol' – (who insists on being addressed as such), a retired high school geography teacher, further dismisses the argument that Malindi's tourism is beneficial to the local people and their economy. She observes that the industry has increased drug usage and trafficking, alcohol consumption, permissive sexual activities, increased materialism and phonographic tendencies [sic] amongst our youth.

However, as a number of commentators on socio-cultural effects of tourism note, the association between tourism growth and (juvenile) delinquency is not easy to differentiate from general trends in changing social behaviour.[21] Nevertheless, it is undeniable that tourism has introduced radically different ways of behaviour that, at times, blatantly contravene local codes of conduct, especially in gender relations, sexual conduct and codes of dress.

Interestingly, some local people in Malindi do not blame tourism development for the growth of sex business. They shift the burden to the sex workers themselves, blaming them for tarnishing the image of a 'good economic undertaking – tourism' (as 'Emma', a 38-year-old local businesswoman reports). She further notes:

Sex workers create demand for commercial sexual services. They make the first move, by dressing in a sexually provocative fashion. If they can be removed from the streets, from our beaches, then no tourist will come knocking by our doors asking for sexual services. The whole whore thing is anti-African. It puts us as a community to shame. I wish I had the means; I would lock all of them in jail and then throw the keys into the deep waters of Indian Ocean... We need tourists, our economy needs tourism, but we do not need sex trade. It dents Malindi's image as an international tourism destination.

Many within the local community echo Emma's sentiments. This strong feeling can be linked to Malindi's strategic and positional entity, or simply social entity. Local residents often regard a sex worker as a fool, a bitch, someone with loose morals and someone who should be avoided. They are infamous and mocked in their presence and/or absence both privately and publicly. Numerous sanction mechanisms are used to deal with those engaged in sex business in Kenya, one of the

21 See, for example, S. Agarwal, 'Social Exclusion'; S. Page and J. Connell, *Tourism: A Modern Synthesis* (UK: Cengage Learning, 2nd edn 2006).

most 'effective' being that of isolation whereby those who transgress social norms are ignored. In this case, local people avoid known sex workers, a social sanction extended to any person who knowingly or unknowingly associates with the person being isolated. Thus, the isolation process ranges from the simple interpersonal level between one-time friends to the more general, as the entire society isolates one of its members, which may lead to psychological instability for the person concerned. To deal with this social punishment, most of the sex workers shift their operation bases to areas where they have no relatives and where few people know them. In their new territories, female sex workers freely approach men, tourists or non-tourists, defining the encounter much more as a meeting of equals with 'something' to share. The mass media, education system and of course tourism do play a role in all this, as they separately and cumulatively impinge, at a growing rate, on local gender roles, especially among the younger generation.[22]

In Malindi society, a man and a woman who are not married are not expected to socialise. As in the Canary Islands, Spain, 'it is often assumed that when a man and a woman are seen together there is no obvious alternative, sexual relations are the objective.'[23] This assumption is reinforced by the fact that local gender role construction portrays men as sexual predators, the 'hunters' in the 'game' of sexual encounters. Consequently, Kenyan masculinity is defined largely by sexual prowess that includes predatory instincts and the ability to 'satisfy' women. Thus, local men are expected to exhibit their sexual prowess by sexually conquering their female counterparts.[24]

On the other hand, throughout the socialisation process, women are conditioned to wait for men to make sexual advances and never the opposite. Consequently, local women expect 'real men' to make an advance if conditions are 'favourable', so (ultra) macho behaviour predominates amongst young men in Malindi. Further, a man who allows his wife to socialise with other men is teased by both men and women folks. Thus, social pressure and Malindi's culture, which has a heavy Islamic influence, curtail the possibility of having men-women friendships.[25] This also affects the friendships between locals and domestic or international visitors. For example, local girls are warned against getting involved with male tourists. They are criticised and regarded as *maraya* (Kiswahili for whores) if they befriend them. Further, daughters in Malindi and in Kenya in general are usually not allowed to venture out of the confines of their homes after seven o'clock in the evening until the age of eighteen. However, it is certain

22 For a comparison see G. Gmelch, *Behind the Smile: Working Lives of Caribbean Tourism*, (IN: Indiana University Press, 2003).

23 D. Macleod, *Tourism and Cultural Change: An Island Community Perspective* (Bristol: Channel View Publications, 2004), 83.

24 Cf. for example, Gmelch, *Behind the Smile*.

25 S. Migot-Adhola, S., *Towards Alternative Tourism in Kenya* (Kenya: University of Nairobi Press, 1990).

that parents cannot restrict them from contact with friends or tourists if they so desire, as parents are unable to control their activities when they leave home for studies or work – but to be chaste is implicit. This is further complicated by the total lack of sexual education at school, while talking about sex at home is still a taboo, in Malindi as in many African contemporary societies.[26]

In contrast, female sex workers feel free to pursue any available tourists as clients, contradicting the African traditional social behaviour regarding relations between men and women. Thus, it is fair to say that any local woman is vulnerable to stigmatisation as a whore because of her life experience, sexist abuse, or ill fortune. Female sex workers' vulnerability to stigmatisation rests on their relatively poor power position, and at the same time, if it is effective, reinforces their overall subordination and makes it more difficult for them to achieve desired goals. Thus, stigmatisation becomes self-propelling or snowballing in its impact. Additionally, this results in a negative perception of the tourism industry as some locals see this behaviour as anathema to their traditions and (Islamic) religion. Local boys, however, are free to 'hook' female tourists, most preferably financially stable Europeans and North Americans, with their age being inconsequential. Thus, Malindi's socially determined link between sex trade and immorality punishes the (female) sex worker and shows how the local people feel offended as the whole community becomes tarnished.

Local residents and the expanding sex (trade)-oriented tourism

Local communities form an integral component of the tourist product [27] as local people's perceptions play an influential role in the success or failure of the tourism industry. During the past decade, local people's perception of the tourism has become a major preoccupation for tourism practitioners, policy-makers and academics. The concept of community-based tourism, the leitmotif of this book, points to the fact that host communities' involvement strives to reconcile existing conflicts between goals of economic development and social well-being. This eventually alters the local residents' perception of the tourism industry and its related activities[28].

If the local community do not support tourism development policies, then programmes are most likely to be ineffective in their implementation, so overall, development should be compatible with the local community's norms. This insight demands an exhaustive

26 I. Sindiga. *Tourism and African Development: Change and Challenge Of Tourism in Kenya* (Leiden and London: ASC & Ashgate, 1999).

27 S. McCool and R. Moisey, 'Tourism, Recreation And Sustainability: Linking Culture and the Environment', in S. McCool and R. Moisey eds., *Society, Recreation and Sustainable Tourism* (Wallingford, Oxon: Cabi Publishing, 2001), 133-35.

28 Macleod, D. *Tourism and Cultural Change*, 2004.

analysis of (inter)relationships within a tourist host community before the implementation of a tourism project. There is a potential backlash for tourism-development projects that fail to take into account the external relationships of the community. The latter's internal power structures could lead to an anti-growth movement by members of the local community who feel that tourism is harmful to it. General economic theory contends that an interest in economic growth forms the overriding common interest within a community. The idea is that any resident who is part of the growing sector will seek to influence the rest of his community members as after all growth is to be desired and is economically beneficial to everyone. In some cases there may be an altruistic, surplus effect, which leads individuals to recognise the communal good derived from such an undertaking, and therefore lessens opposition to tourism development, even among those who may not benefit directly. But the reverse may hold as well, and irrespective of the locals' perception of the tourism development, the expansion of sex-related tourism leads to deep local ambivalence about the tourist bubble in Malindi.

Through the wall of the tourist bubble?

Certainly, international tourists are hosted by a travel-generating culture, a tourist bubble, envisaged in this book as spatial-cultural and functional differentiation. Thus, the visitors are physically 'in' the hosts' culture while socially 'outside' it, when culture is understood as place-bound. Yet a good percentage of tourists intend to learn about contemporary foreign cultures during their holidays. Tourists are aware of this bubble, and try to breach its walls in order to get a 'first-hand' experience of the host culture. It appears that the realm of 'pleasure', through sex-related tourism, has become one crucial mechanism to penetrate the bubble wall, as the majority of sex tourists are willing to engage with the 'Other' in such a profound involvement, even if only momentarily. That means sex is often on the initial agenda, and indeed I found that 64 per cent of the (sex) tourists ($n = 104$) had the intention to engage in sex with local men at their destination even before departure from their home country,[29] and that 79 per cent of the total respondents had already entered into one or more sexual relationships with local men while on holiday in Kenya. Although 58 per cent of the respondents admitted to economic elements to their liaisons, they did not perceive their encounters as *sex worker-client* transactions, nor did they view their partners as sex workers.

In addition, none of them would accept to be labelled sex tourists. 'Jarngerd', a 44- years-old Norwegian female (sex) tourist sums it in the following words:

---

29 See Kibicho, *Sex Tourism in Africa* for the research methodology and details.

To be honest with you… it all started at the beach. This guy [referring to her sex partner] sold me a souvenir then proposed a 'cheap' safari to Tsavo West National Park. We spent the following day in the park together. Since then, we have become [sex] partners … Definitely, this cannot be called sex tourism. We are simply helping one another. He helps me to 'see' and 'discover' Kenya [sic] while I help him with some pocket money as a sign of appreciation. Having sex with him is just a side thing … to keep ourselves busy at night. Of course, I enjoy it. I am a normal woman … with normal sexual feelings. But, I am not a sex tourist. I am against sex tourism. It degrades the local people. It is disrespectful to local cultures [she concludes].

Further, 40 per cent of the total tourists who admitted coming to Malindi for sex believe that they are helping their local partners, and thus the local economy, by giving them money and gifts.

Host versus guest: points of difference

In his analysis of tourism effects Cazes (1992) writes of tourists' search for 'reality' and 'authenticity' in the visited destinations. Based on my interviews, this search of 'authenticity' is a major part of the driving force behind sexually motivated (female) visitors to Kenya's coastal region. They often spoke of the regulated and culturally restricted life in terms of constraints in time and moral expectations back home and the apparently relaxed lifestyles of the members of the tourist host community. Thus, many women from the North are today travelling to tourism destinations in the South away from their culture for either a quick sex fix or a more sustained relationship,[30] and for them this door 'out of the tourist bubble' is opened before the (sex) tourists leave their homes. However, from their side, the sex workers themselves are in fact part of that very tourist bubble, forming an infrastructure at the service of the tourists. So, despite the intensive contact, the tourists do not really leave the bubble.

By constructing Kenya's coastal region as a place somehow 'un-modern', travelling to Malindi fulfils the desire to 'escape' – albeit momentarily – from hectic modernity: as MacLeod comments: '… they are also escaping the reality of life in an urban metropolis, with its authentic pressures.'[31] Contrastingly, some local residents feel that sex workers, in their endeavour to please their clients/tourists, transgress their own social norms. 'Emma', the businesswoman mentioned earlier on, states: 'They are just acting. They do not represent the reality. At least not my community's reality and hence the [sex] tourists' experience is inauthentic.' Thus, 'authentic' and 'reality' become terms subject to personal expectation and experience. As a consequence,

30 See for example C. Ryan & M. Hall 2001, *Sex Tourism, Marginal People and Liminalities*; Kibicho 2004b.
31 D. Macleod, D. 2004. *Tourism and Cultural Change*, 79.

one is tempted to argue that like visitors, the visited indulge in non-ordinary (sexual) activities like flirting in public.

A key difference between the hosts/local people in Malindi and their visitors/tourists is the general attitude towards public nudity. The literature reveals that international tourists are unself-conscious about nudity in public settings such as beaches.[32] In contrast, Malindi's residents abhor public (near) nudity, so that local women who exhibit their bodies are automatically labelled as *maraya* (sex workers). Yet, there is a reaction gap towards female tourists who flaunt their sexuality by wearing less clothing or sunbathing topless. Local young men often pursue such women regarding them as sexually available, looking upon them as objects of desire.

Generally however, there has been a gradual relaxation of attitudes towards nakedness and immodest beachwear over time. This relaxation can be attributed to local people's realisation of the financial rewards from tourism. In early 1990s for instance, local people resented topless sunbathing and tourists were reprimanded, their near nudity considered a public nuisance. However, today there is a gradual tolerance amongst local residents who have become more accommodating and often turn a blind eye, accepting topless and at times nude bathers to continue with their activities, with little acrimony. Moreover, 88 per cent of the respondents fully support the growth of Malindi's tourism although they regret the socio-cultural effects of the industry, especially its role in the expansion of the sex profession.[33] Additionally, if given the opportunity to participate in a tourism undertaking, such as home-stay, cultural performances or restaurant operation, all participants indicated that they would like to be involved. This example illustrates how tourism development does influence local ideas of social behaviour and introduces new norms. Needless to say, there will be further changes within the social norm spectrum as the visited and the visitor cultures interact, and as more local residents themselves enter the tourist bubble.

Cultural stereotypes

Stereotypic attitudes help the agent to interpret the unknown through his/her own system of logic, his/her own set of meanings, in a situation where specific characteristics are emphasised and persistently used to describe members of different communities.[34] In this section, we start our discussion with an examination of local commercial sex workers [CSW] attitudes towards their tourist-clients followed by how the residents conceive the tourists, and then visitors' views on their hosts.

32 D. Pruitt, and S. LaFont, 'For Love and Money: Romance Tourism in Jamaica', *Annals of Tourism Research*. 22, 2 (1995): 367-84.
33 Kibicho, 'Impacts of Tourism'.
34 Macleod, *Tourism and Cultural Change*.

Sex workers in Malindi have divided 'tourists' into different stereotypic categories. German female (sex) tourists, for instance, are reported to be friendlier and more generous with the local men than tourists from other countries. Experience has taught sex workers that there is a hierarchy of willingness among (sex) tourists ranging from Germans ('the most cooperative') to British ('the least cooperative'). To validate the foregoing, 'Jones', a male sex worker in Malindi observes:

> It is much easier to get [sic] a German (sex) partner ... Germans are very good, understanding, accommodating, out-going and friendly than other *wazungu* [Kiswahili word for white people]. They do not care whether you speak German language. They adore the 'African banana' [male sex organ]... they are warm. However, you have to be a performer [meaning one has to be sexually active] as they are like 'empty bottles', which never get filled up. Yeah, they are like empty vessels waiting to be filled with the men's milky' stuff [Jones jokingly elucidates]. They are sexually starved [he concludes with a contagious smile].

On the contrary, British (sex) tourists are referred to as uncoopera-tive, narrow-minded, inflexible, sexually inactive, authoritarian and exhibiting a colonial mentality. 'Jones' completes the description by saying:

> British women are the worst ... they are bullies. Even if you speak English [language] like Shakespeare, you will end up nowhere with them. Their relationships with us [male sex workers] are like 'hit-and-run' sex affairs. You sleep with one, but when you meet with her the following day; she pretends that she has never seen you. They rarely cooperate with us ... they are too mechanical [sic].

They are yet to discover the 'African sex magic'... they are sexually cold, in fact inactive. One day, a Briton paid me a whopping 250 US dollars for a night. After the first round – if you know what I mean [he smiles], she placidly requested me to cover her when I am through with the rest of the business [he concludes with an infectious laugh].

(Sex) tourists of Italian origin are said to be noisy, messy, self-possessed, defensive, too critical and sexually demanding. On the other hand, female sex workers describe local domestic male (sex) tourists as aggressive, unreasonable in their sexual demands, stingy, free-riding and mean with their money. This implies that not only is there a potential for friction between sex workers and their clients but that the former are not prejudicial against other nationalities in terms of their criticism. By extension, this finding suggests that the eventual entry into the tourist bubble by the host community through sex trade may depend on the (sex) tourists' nationality.

Further, nationality of clients plays a crucial role during the selection of the clients, as 'there is a strong link between the country of origin and generosity...' as 'Jones' notes. Clients of Italian origin are ranked immediately after the Germans in the CSWs' 'generosity-scale'. However, they are reported to have a higher tendency towards violence, and thus, just like the Britons are avoided by the CSWs as much as possible. Any avoidance, however, is also influenced by the economic needs of the sex worker, for the higher the economic need, the less selective the sex worker is. In all cases however, pecuniary considerations take precedence over sexual ones. Both male and female sex workers in Malindi, for example, often decline to stay with clients who are 'sexually gratifying' but fail to offer 'sufficient' amounts of money. They choose their 'suitors' by financial capacity and calmly reject those they consider below their economic needs.[35]

Local people conceive tourists as visitors of a particular type and not as individuals. They are grouped in terms of their 'perceived' motives for visiting, and thus are divided into sex tourists, beach tourists, cultural tourists and safari tourists. After all, neither party ever meets on relatively equal footing, living in separate realities on both sides of the bubble wall. Language barriers further aggravate this problem. From a general standpoint, the locals describe the tourists as morally depraved and sexually deprived.

For their part, tourists themselves have some negative and stereotypical opinions about the local people. They are strongly influenced by images and stereotypes in their attitudes regarding their hosts, viewing the locals as noble savages, backward, uncivilised, untrustworthy and hyper-sexualised. These were certainly the images perpetrated by western publications during the colonial era, aimed at justifying colonialism in Africa.[36] In addition, some tour operators and travel agents in the tourist-generating countries contribute to this scenario. 'Birgitte', the female tourist from Uppsala, Sweden, confirms this: 'I was advised to be constantly vigilant about local people by my travel agent back at home. I was told that the locals are violent and thievish [sic]'. When asked what her principal motivation in visiting visit Malindi was, Birgitte non-hesitatingly responded:

> Love [she smiles]. I am looking [sic] for good and lasting romance. My women friends back home told me that Africans are sexually endowed – you know, their 'rods' [referring to male's sex organs] are of the right sizes... better than those of our white folks. Sizes any 'sensible' woman would not resist – you get my gist? [She asks this author with a hearty laugh].

To complete this stereotyping discourse on African male's sex organ, 'Tom', a male sex worker who spent three months touring North America, a trip paid for by his (sex) tourist turned 'girlfriend' noted: 'When I was in Canada, one (white) woman came right up to me and asked me if it is true that we have bigger dicks. I told her I wouldn't know because I don't walk around examining dicks. Besides,

---

35 For a detailed discussion of the categorisation of (sex) tourists in Malindi and Kenya in general, see Kibicho, *Sex Tourism in Africa*.
36 Cf. for example G. Cazes, *Tourisme et tiers-monde, un bilan contraversé: les nouvelles colonies de vacances* (Paris: L'Harmattan, 1992).

I haven't seen many white dicks'.[37] Of course, residents dislike this condescension meted out to them by their visitors. Stereotypes are dangerous, as they may lead to distorted visions of the self and the other, with negative stereotypic attitudes based on inaccurate or lack of information and may result in hatred – even more so when the fantasies are not satisfied. This eventually '… destroys one's sense of values and his/her objectivity causing him/her to describe the beautiful as ugly and ugly as beautiful, and to confuse the true with the false and the false with the true', as Martin Luther King Jnr stated in a televised sermon. In the absence of these stereotypical tendencies, strong relationships may develop between the visitors and the visited, sex workers and their tourist-clients. Ideas can be exchanged, and indeed marriages may result. This would have innumerable consequences for the tourist host society at large. Many local families might have their social networks expanded to include foreign friends and relatives living in the tourist-sending countries. Tourists might gain an opportunity to learn about their hosts' cultures and traditions, resulting in a general process of socio-cultural communication. It would be a win-win situation for both parties – hosts/visited and guests/visitors. Both would have the opportunity not only to glimpse the Other's culture but also to reflect on their own culture through the culture of Others.[38]

Inevitably, the question of imperialism is likely to crop up at the back of our minds when considering tourism's far-reaching effects, borne out of local resident-tourist encounters. This is more so when we consider global-system theory and the exploitation of the South by the North in areas of export economy. The *Oxford Dictionary* defines imperialism as the 'expansion of a society's influence abroad'. The clear development of a foreign society's interests – a tourist-generating society – in Malindi, makes this description applicable, (as also in the case of Botswana[39]). This postcolonialism is compounded by the all-inclusive tour packages and political interest groups which have rapidly changed the tourism equation in this destination. Powerful multinational companies are now controlling (almost) all aspects of the tourism industry in Malindi and Kenya at large.[40] They define, design, own and sell tourist products in Kenya, and in much of Africa. Locally owned small-scale tourism enterprises are no longer viable compared to the big businesses that enjoy full exploitation of local resources. In the meantime, trading in sex remains one of the surest alternatives for small-scale enterprise, as well as for direct and close encounters between the hosts and their guests. Of course, exit from the vicious circle of poverty through (longterm) financial gains and

37 Gmelch, *Behind the Smile*, 127.
38 Cf. for example D. Wilson, 'Paradoxes of Tourism in Gao', *Annals of Tourism Research*, 24, 2 (1997): 52-7.
39 See Mbaiwa, this volume.
40 Cf. Peake, 'Tourism and Swahili Identity'.

memorable experiences are the key motivating factors for both the locals and the tourists. Intransigent poverty and the need for unique tourist experiences help in creating a separate section of the bubble by putting visitors and their hosts in the same 'world', which rarely realises its potential to break down the tourist bubble.

Conclusion

My main purpose has been to offer a descriptive rather than prescriptive analysis. But as the local residents in Malindi view tourism as a creator of sex trade and react accordingly, any realistic approach for future tourism development programmes has to be holistic, seeking integration rather than disintegration. Unfortunately, current national strategies in Kenya and Africa in general are dominated by individual interests, with priorities determined accordingly. Evidently, establishing tourism guidelines on how to deal with the undesirable effects of sex tourism is important, yet to undertake this without reference to broader issues may be folly. At the same time, to regard hosts' and visitors' cultures in isolation is to ignore the exchange element in this tourism, as the two groups display similar demands: the hosts need tourists' dollars, while the tourists need satisfaction from the products/services they pay for.

The interactions between the visitors/tourists and the visited/tourist host community and especially through the tourism-related sex trade has challenged behavioural patterns in Malindi and in other principal destinations in Kenya. It has offered new roles for local men and women but exposed weaknesses within the norms of their social spheres. It has offered them a greater diversity of options, even for those who may not be looking for an alternative. These issues aside, the industry has highlighted the vulnerability of local attitudes as men increasingly focus on female tourists who are more willing to enter casual sexual relationships. This leads to heightened competition as far as local women are concerned, with consequent resentments. In some cases, individual men acquire reputations that hinder their chances with local women. All in all, this study is a testimony to the fact that the tourist bubble itself changes the tourist destinations, with the visitors' attitudes as one major factor. Sex-oriented tourism is thus one major way to construct the 'local' in response to the 'different', even inside an ongoing production of the 'universal', which is, in the end, what the bubble aims at.

Finally, as policy-makers strategise how to deal with sex trade, they should keep in mind that the local community is not a homogenous group of social or politically like-minded people but a conglomeration of individuals with differing opinions, interests and aspirations. Their affiliations may intersect or clash on numerous socio-cultural, economic and political planes, and only with a thorough consideration of the community's aspirations may a tourism destination avoid an anti-growth backlash from locals who feel that the project is not being carried out in accordance with their profound, developmental needs.

REFERENCES

Agarwal, S. 'Social Exclusion and English Seaside Resorts', *Tourism Management*, 27, 4 (2006): 351-72.

Belliveau, J. *Romance on the Road: Travelling Women Who Love Foreign Men* (US: Beau Monde Press, 2006).

Cazes, G. *Tourisme et tiers-monde, un bilan contraversé: les nouvelles colonies de vacances* (Paris: L'Harmattan, 1992).

Cohen, E. 'Thailand Girls and Farang Men: The Edge of Ambiguity', *Annals of Tourism Research.* l9 (3) : (1982): 403-28.

—— 'Authenticity and Commoditization in Tourism', *Annals of Tourism Research* 15 (3) 1988): 371- 86.

Gitonga, A. and Anyangu, S. 2008. 'More than 1,000 Women Trafficked to Germany', *East African Standard.* (http://www.eastandard.net/): II (Accessed 20 November 2008).

Gmelch, G. 2003. *Behind the Smile: Working Lives of Caribbean Tourism* (ID: Indiana University Press).

Kenya Economic Survey (Nairobi: Government Printers, 2004-2008).

Kibicho, W. 'Tourism and the Sex Trade: Roles Male Sex Workers Play in Malindi, Kenya', *Tourism Review International* 7, 3/4 (2004): 129-41.

—— 'A critical evaluation of how tourism influences the commercial sex workers' operations in Malindi Area, Kenya', *Annals of Leisure Studies*, 7, 3-4 (2004): 188-201.

—— 'Impacts of Tourism In Malindi: An Analysis Of Gender Differences In Perception', *ASEAN Journal on Tourism and Hospitality* 4, 1 (2005): 83-96.

—— 'Service Quality in Malindi's Tourism Industry: a Study of Tourist Perceptions', *ASEAN Journal on Hospitality & Tourism Research* 12, 3 (2006): 218-31.

—— 'Community-based Tourism: A Factor-Cluster Segmentation Approach', *Journal of Sustainable Tourism* 16, 2 (2008): 211-31.

—— *Sex Tourism In Africa: Kenya's Booming Industry* (Leiden & London: Ashgate, 2009).

Macleod, D. *Tourism and Cultural Change: An Island Community Perspective* (UK: Channel View Publications, 2004).

McCool, S. and Moisey, R. 'Tourism, Recreation and Sustainability: Linking Culture and the Environment', in S. McCool and R. Moisey, eds., *Society, Recreation And Sustainable Tourism* (UK: Cabi Publishing, 2001), 133-5.

Malindi District Development Plan: 2002-2008 (Nairobi, Government Printers, 2002).

Mensah, J. *Black Canadians: History, Experiences, Social Conditions* (Winnipeg: Fernwood Publishing, 2005).

Migot-Adhola, S. *Towards Alternative Tourism in Kenya* (Kenya: University of Nairobi Press, 1990).

Page, S. and Connell, J. *Tourism: a Modern Synthesis* (UK: Cengage Learning, 2nd edn, 2006).

Peake, R. 'Tourism and Swahili Identity in Malindi Old Town, Kenyan Coast', *Africa* 59, 2 (1989): 209-20.

Pruitt, D. and LaFont, S. 'For Love And Money: Romance Tourism in Jamaica', *Annals of Tourism Research* 22, 2 (1995): 367-84.

Ryan, C. and Hall, M. *Sex Tourism: Marginal People and Liminalities* (London: Routledge, 2001).

Sinclair, M. *Tourism Development in Kenya* (Washington, DC: World Bank, 1990).

Sindiga, I. *Tourism and African Development: Change and Challenge of Tourism in Kenya* (Leiden & London: Ashgate, 1999).

Wilson, D. 'Paradoxes of Tourism in Gao', *Annals of Tourism Research* 2, 2 (1997): 52-7.

15 • Host-guest encounters in a Gambian 'love' bubble

Lucy McCombes

Introduction

Romance tourism involves a very direct kind of host-guest encounter,[1] popularly brushed aside as an unsavoury means for young men and women in a destination to 'get rich quick' from love-struck or lusting tourists. Drawing on my research on factors that affect the nature of the interaction between package tourists and 'bumsters' (i.e. beach boys) in The Gambia,[2] this chapter illustrates different perspectives of the nature of the host-guest encounters involved in romance tourism. The history, context, and characteristics of these encounters are considered and the concept of the tourist bubble applied to reflect how these encounters are affected by intermediaries and the tourism infrastructure. These encounters are then further examined in terms of their impact on relations with the host community, and on The Gambia as a holiday destination. The intention is to highlight some of the complexities of 'romantic' host-guest encounters in The Gambia, to add depth with the voices of bumsters, tourists and tourism industry stakeholders to the existing popular debate about whether they are about money or love. I argue that upon closer inspection such host-guest encounters are not as 'black or white' as they might seem, but rather they represent a complex social phenomenon which is unlikely to stop.

By hovering above the tourist bubble mediating between these 'romantic' host-guest encounters, and reflecting on the characteristics of these encounters, I aim to show how they are shaped by a number of different variables and intermediary organisations which enable tourists to stay within that home-like culture i.e. the tourist bubble.[3] This concept is used here to refer to

> those infrastructural arrangements that permit the professional reception of guests – such as hotels, lodges, personnel, logistics – plus those arrangements making the travel of tourists possible; travel agencies in the sending as well as the host countries, transport facilities and a massive internet

---

1 Note the term 'host' and 'guest' are used here in an ironic sense since the special rules that apply to willing hosts receiving invited guests in their home are suspended when the transaction becomes a commercial one.

2 L. McCombes, 'Ingredients for Positive Tourist-Host Encounters: A Study to Investigate the Factors that Affect the Nature of the Tourist-Host Encounter Between Tourists And "Bumsters" in Kololi and Kotu, The Gambia', (MSc Diss., University of Greenwich, 2007).

3 K.S. Jacobsen, 'The Tourist Bubble and the Europeanisation of Holiday Travel', *Journal of Tourism and Cultural Change*, 1, 1 (2003): 71-86.

information business. This 'bubble' is where the tourist travels, arrives and is housed, this bubble protects the visitor from the unfortunate aspects of a destination while permitting some view to the outside. It is this bubble that interacts with the guest society, and so this bubble stands central in the dynamics of the tourist encounter.[4]

Who or what is a bumster?

Broadly speaking, 'bumsters', as they are referred to locally, are the Gambian equivalent of beach boys common in many other tourist destinations. To paint a portrait and remind us of the human face behind this phenomenon, they are typically young men who have left school early and are without formal employment although commonly engaged in informal income generating activities such as farm work, carpentry, selling crafts and fishing, in particular out of the tourist season. Few don traditional Gambian clothing but rather they adopt either a Rasta appearance with dreadlocks and clothing associated with that image, or casual, modern western dress. Most originate from rural and urban Gambia but there is an increasing number from neighbouring African countries.

The popular stereotype of bumsters is that they aim to 'sleep their way out of The Gambia with old White women'[5] and seek relations with tourists that are not about romance but rather about sex tourism and prostitution, generating negative impacts for The Gambia as a destination. This common negative attitude was reflected in my content analysis of local media in which bumsters were labelled variously as 'menaces', 'scroungers', 'aggressive', 'sleazy', 'hasslers', 'gigolos', or 'wheeler-dealers'. Interestingly, the tourists' and tourism industry's responsibility for the existence of such relations received less attention.

Sexual relations are actually only one of a range of services that bumsters today may offer, and the young men are by no means uniform in their approach to interacting with tourists. For example, my survey of package tourists showed that 69 per cent of a total sample of 52 tourists interviewed had used bumsters for one or more of a list of activities, including assistance with arranging trips (67 per cent), help with shopping or going to the market (47 per cent), 'friendship' (44 per cent), showing them the nightlife (28 per cent), help with business (6 per cent) and 'other' activities (19 per cent).

My research in The Gambia also found that there are many different perspectives and explanations of 'who' or 'what' a bumster is. Some bumsters and others from the informal sector argued that a bumster is anyone who solicits assistance from a tourist either formally or

---

4 Walter van Beek & Annette Schmidt, this volume; see also W.E.A. Van Beek, 'African Tourist Encounters: Effects of Tourism on two West African Societies', *Africa. Journal of the International African Institute*, 73, 2 (2003): 251-98.

5 T. Gupta, *Sugar Mummies* (Royal Court Theatre, London, 2006).

informally, in other words, almost all tourism stakeholders. On the other hand, the majority of key informants described bumsters as generally unemployed young men[6] operating illegally/unlicensed in the Tourism Development Area (TDA) who approach tourists to establish a relationship for some kind of personal reward. However, they commonly differentiated between 'good' or 'civilised' bumsters who provide a useful service or who are entrepreneurs such as informal guides, and 'bad' or 'uncivilised' ones who 'don't take no for an answer' and 'want something for nothing'.

Romance and sex tourism in The Gambia

The Gambia has had a low-key reputation as a 'sex destination' since the 1960s, largely as a result of the practice of older European women looking for holiday romance with young Gambian men, many of whom are bumsters. This has also been accompanied by an increasing number of young Gambian women looking for western husbands. This type of 'romance tourism', well documented in other destinations such as Barbados, Jamaica, and Dominican Republic, is disputably used to describe a form of female sex tourism based on the appearance that relationships focus more on romance than on sex for money.[7]

This phenomenon was researched by Nyanzi et al. who carried out ethnographic fieldwork[8] with eight 'toubab-bumster'[9] couples, and forty bumsters, of whom thirty-eight had had a sexual relationship with a white tourist. This research found that 'bumsters variously indulge in a complex web of sexual activity ranging from commercial to non-commercial, voluntary to socially-imposed, individual to peer-driven, heterosexual to homosexual, casual to regular, particularly with foreign tourists'.[10] The findings also showed that most bumsters

6 It was also recognised that female bumsters do exist but in much smaller numbers, and that their characteristics and methods may differ from their male counterparts. Those informants who mentioned female bumsters described them as typically experienced sex workers who have gone beyond the point of prostitution to adopt a more subtle approach to make gains from tourists through sexual or intimate relationships, business ventures, and sponsorship.

7 K. de Albuquerque, 'Sex, Beach Boys, and Female Tourists in the Caribbean', *Sexuality and Culture* 2 (1998) 87-111. T. Bauer & B. McKercher, *Sex and Tourism: Journeys of Romance, Love, and Lust*, (The Haworth Hospitality Press, London, 2003). Pruitt, D. and S. LaFont, 'Romance Tourism: Gender, Race and Power in Jamaica' in Sharon Bohn Gmelch (ed.) *Tourists and Tourism: A Reader* (Waveland Press, Inc., 2004); D. Pruitt & S. LaFont, 'For Love and Money: Romance Tourism in Jamaica', *Annals of Tourism Research* 22,2 (1995): 422-40.

8 The research team consisted of two black Africans, a Gambian ex-bumster with partial residence in Europe, and a local Gambian, which facilitated a multi-perspective analysis and researcher triangulation.

9 The term *toubab* evolved from the localisation of the English slang 'two bob', the equivalent of the cash that foreigners paid their African servants in the 1960s. However, the term *toubab* is now sometimes extended to cover wealthy black foreigners, thereby having some social or economic class implications (UNICEF, CPA and Terres des Hommes, 2003). Thus its meaning is now commonly understood as describing a rich or powerful person.

10 S. Nyanzi, O. Rosenberg-Jallow & O. Bah, 'Bumsters, Big Black Organs And Old White Gold: Embodied Racial Myths In Sexual Relationships Of Gambian Beach Boys', *Culture, Health & Sexuality* (Health Policy Unit, London School of Hygiene and Tropical Medicine, London, 2007), 557.

reported having regular relationships with older white women since they reasoned that they had the advantage of having larger savings, more independence, are more in need of a young man to boost their self image, and are unable to conceive.

Such sexual encounters between tourists and bumsters typically have different characteristics to prostitute-client transactions in the West which account for its description as 'romance tourism'. Firstly, in Western countries prostitution is typically organised as a narrowly contractual commodity exchange where 'x' sexual services are provided for 'y' sum of money and time. In comparison, in the prostitute-client relationship between some bumsters and tourists, the exchange is often more open-ended and loosely specified. Prices and limits are not always negotiated in advance and bumsters/prostitutes may spend a long time with their clients as well as carry out non-sexual labour. Secondly, in contrast to western prostitution, bumsters are independent and will often act in ways with their western clients which can be taken to signify genuine affection, for example holding hands and kissing.

Such characteristics of 'romance tourism' make it easy to see how many tourists will interpret the experience as confirming a mutual attraction and courtship, like a holiday romance, and will thus construct the act of giving money to the bumster/prostitute not as payment for services rendered, but as a gesture of friendship or generosity. O'Connell Davidson refers to such sex tourists as 'situational prostitute users' which are defined as a 'subgroup of sex tourists (men and women) who do not subjectively perceive themselves as prostitute users'. She argues that they are able to deceive themselves about the true nature of their sexual interaction with local people first because prostitution takes a number of different forms in the countries that they visit, and second because they buy into highly sexualised forms of racism.[11] Similarly, in Kibicho's chapter on sex tourism in Kenya in this volume, none of the tourist respondents involved in sexual relationships with local men while on holiday in Malindi would accept being labelled as sex tourists.

There is, however, considerable debate surrounding such viewpoints, the nature of bumster-host relationships involved in 'romance tourism', and whether or how it is different from male sex tourism.[12] Sanchez-Taylor argues that, whilst social researchers have not been blind to the phenomenon of female sex tourism, there is a tendency for it to be treated as qualitatively different from male sex tourism.[13] Several authors, such as Pruitt and LaFont, use the term 'romance

11 J. O'Connell Davidson, 'British sex tourists in Thailand', in M. Maynard & J. Purvis, eds., *(Hetero) Sexual Politics,* (London: Taylor and Francis, 1995).
12 Albuquerque, 'Sex, Beach Boys, and Female Tourists', 1998; E. Herold & R. Garcia, and T. DeMoya,T. 'Female tourists and Beach Boys Romance or Sex Tourism?' *Annals of Tourism Research,* 28, 4 (2001): 978-97.
13 J. Sanchez-Taylor, in Maynard and Purvis eds., *Tourism and Sex: Culture, Commerce and Coercion*

tourism' to refer to female sex tourism and imply that it could hold possibilities for positive changes.[14] Female sex tourists are sometimes sympathetically construed as 'lonely women' whose 'economic and social ability to travel alone is being exploited by Caribbean tourism and the 'beach boys' who either offer the possibility of a 'holiday romance' or sexual harassment'.[15] However, Sanchez-Taylor argues that the tendency to de-sexualise female sex tourism by labelling it as 'romance' hides the complexities involved in the social interaction between affluent, western women and poor black men from the host destinations. She argues that the differences between male and female sex tourism may not be as great as has often been assumed.[16] Conversely, many others argue that romance tourism does in fact often lead to the development of relationships involving love, romance and companionship – something generally absent from sex tourism.

So the literature suggests that romance tourism in The Gambia, in common with other countries in Africa and the Caribbean, poses numerous questions – is it really different to sex tourism? Is romance or love involved in these relationships? Who exploits who? What do these relationships mean to those involved?

Characteristics of romance tourism encounters in The Gambia

To be better placed to answer some of these questions, I take the view that there is a need to look beyond the prostitute-client relationship that is typically assumed to exist between tourists and bumsters engaged in romance tourism. There is also a need to be more self-conscious of the traditional, ethnocentric oppositional dichotomy of 'economic interests' and 'emotional attachment' that is frequently used to assess such relationships.[17] As summarised by Helle-Valle, the common Western privileging of '...romantic love and/or personal pleasure (physical and psychological)...[as]...the "proper" motives for engaging in sex...' has led to a gaze on African intimate relationships whereby '...strategic, materially oriented uses of sexuality are strictly tabooed – being forcefully embodied in our image of "the prostitute".'[18]

Thus a closer look at some of the dynamics and characteristics of relationships which exist between tourists and bumsters reveals a range of factors which affect the nature of this interaction. This section outlines these different influencing factors and characteristics

14 D. Pruitt & S. LaFont, 'For Love and Money: Romance Tourism in Jamaica', *Annals of Tourism Research*, 22, 2, (1995): 422-40.
15 D, Momsen. 'Tourism, Gender and Development in the Caribbean', in V. Kinnaird, & D. Hall, eds., *Tourism: A Gender Analysis* (Chichester,West Sussex: Wiley, 2000).
16 Sanchez-Taylor, in *Tourism and Sex: Culture, Commerce and Coercion.*
17 Chant & Evans, 'Looking for the One(s): Young Love and Urban Poverty in The Gambia', *Environment and Urbanization* 22 (Sage Publications on behalf of IIED, 2010).
18 J. Helle-Valle. 'Understanding Sexuality in Africa: Diversity and Contextualized Dividuality' in Arnfred, S. (ed.), *Rethinking Sexualities in Africa* (Nordic Africa Institute, Uppsala, 2006) cited in Chant and Evans, 'Looking for the One(s):' 354.

of romance tourism from the perspectives of bumsters, tourists and formal tourism industry stakeholders which provides food for thought on some of the old debates surrounding romance tourism – thus, in effect, providing a 'bubble history' for the Gambian context.

Much of the findings in this chapter draw on my study which investigated the factors affecting the nature of the tourist-host encounter between package tourists and bumsters in Kololi and Kotu resorts in The Gambia. It involved an 'interrogation' of existing anthropological and sociological literature to identify a conceptual framework for analysing factors argued to affect the nature of tourist-host encounters. For this I identified five broad categories of factors, namely:

- Bumster and tourist individual characteristics
- Type of tourism characteristics
- Destination characteristics
- Characteristics/context of the encounter
- Outside influences

I also supposed that different variables/factors can have either a positive or negative impact on the nature of the encounter between tourists and bumsters. This conceptual framework and other emergent themes informed the design of the research questions of a questionnaire survey of 52 package tourists[19] (mainly British); participant observation (both covert and overt)[20] of 40 bumsters; and in-depth interviews with 36 informants[21] from the tourism industry. Thus, since the sample sizes are very small, the findings from this research can only be interpreted as indicative of trends and issues rather than being statistically accurate.

To summarise, this research considered the encounters between tourists and bumsters from the three different perspectives of tourists,

19 Of this sample of tourists, 42 per cent were male and 58 per cent female with an age profile predominantly in the range from 26 to 65 years. The majority were British (71 per cent) with the remainder being a mixture of other European nationalities plus one Australian. All those interviewed were on a package deal using a variety of hotels and tour operators, 65 per cent on a one week package and 35 per cent staying between 11 and 18 days.

20 The covert participation observation of bumsters raises ethical issues about the rights of individuals who were not aware of the specific research project nor asked to give their informed consent for participating in the research. The justification for using this method is that the researcher felt that if bumsters were informed about the specific research then this might have had a number of negative effects on its validity. For example, they might not have behaved 'naturally' and modified their behaviour, chose not to divulge any information, or said what they thought the researcher wanted to hear and thus increased the 'Hawthorne Effect' which refers to the unintentional impact of observers on a setting. However, there is nothing to suggest that any of the participants were harmed in any way by their involvement as data collected in field notes. Field notes was treated confidentially and the identity of all involved has been kept anonymous. In addition, the observation was done in an unobtrusive manner by only observing those bumsters who approached the researcher to engage in conversation.

21 All key informants were stakeholders in the tourism industry in The Gambia with extensive knowledge and experience of bumsters in the TDA. Five were resident expatriates, the rest were Gambians, and only eleven of this group were women. In terms of age profile, all key informants were estimated to be in between the age range of 30-65 years. Therefore these characteristics reflect a bias and gender imbalance of the sample.

bumsters and tourism industry stakeholders (largely Gambians). The findings showed that romance tourism or sexual relations is a 'service' that was often offered to tourists by the majority of bumsters, and the approach used by the latter to develop relations with tourists was often clearly sexual – whether tourists were interested or not. In fact, 58 per cent of the tourist sample reported that a sexual or 'lechy' approach was a factor contributing to their negative experiences with bumsters. Similarly, my own participant observation showed that an uninvited sexual and intimate approach was attempted by approximately half of the bumster sample who would indicate their 'romantic' intentions almost immediately and request a phone number – a level of attention I do not often receive in the UK!

Thus, although my research did not directly target those involved in romance tourism, sexual relations is obviously a central dynamic in many tourist-bumster relations and was frequently referred to by participants. Furthermore, many of the findings on the factors which affect the nature of the general interaction between package tourists and bumsters are also relevant here for understanding the relationships involved in Gambian romance tourism. These findings, in addition to other research in romance tourism destinations, are used to illustrate the following characteristics, dynamics and influencing factors which shape romance tourism in The Gambia.

Historical origins of the bumster phenomenon

To understand the nature of the interaction between tourists and bumsters for sex or romance tourism today it is essential to take into account the wider context, including the origins of the bumster phenomenon and mass tourism in The Gambia. This continues to shape expectations within such tourist-host relations, the nature of the tourist bubble and its intermediary organisations.

Until the advent of tourism, the main form of contact for most Gambians with white people *(toubabs)* was during the slave trade, the two World Wars (1917-18 and 1939-45), the missionaries who came to proselytise, and the colonial administrators who only mingled with the higher ranking Gambian Civil Servants. The nature of interaction changed in the 1960s with the arrival of Scandinavian tourists who were amongst the first white people who wanted to mingle with local Gambians and find out about their culture, lifestyles, and food, in informal settings. These package tourists were usually middle-aged retired people who were high spenders with specific needs and demands for goods and services, many of which the country did not have. However, as a traditionally hospitable culture, the Gambian people were well disposed to work towards meeting the needs of their 'guests.'[22]

This new kind of interaction and the inter-cultural exchanges with

22 A. Bah, A., H. Sallah, H. and S. Tijan, S. *Problems and Benefits of Tourism in The Gambia* (Action Aid, 2005).

the Scandinavians led to new relations and friendships. Some of the well-meaning tourists who made friends with Gambian families took some members back for educational and other purposes and thus a new type of migration and a dependency culture started. The Swedish and Gambian Governments developed protocols and for a period Gambians did not require visas to travel to Sweden.[23]

However, not everybody had the opportunity to make 'friends' or be a 'special guide' and form mutually beneficial relationships with tourists (referred to locally as 'chanting'). Thus, as competition for these relationships developed, the approach changed to a more aggressive form of hassle for which the term 'bumstering' was coined, and which set the scene for some of the current interactions between tourists and local people and the mindset and expectations of many locals that tourists *should* help them.

Some of these 'friendships' and expectations between tourists and local people evolved to plant the first seeds for romance tourism. As opposed to sex tourism, it is likely that this historical background of 'friendships' fitted well with the development of romance tourism in which the economic component is hidden (or at least more subtle), and where courtship is a central characteristic in meeting the demands of those Western women with ideals of sexual intimacy and romance.

Destination characteristics
Bounded on its three landward sides by Senegal, The Gambia is the smallest mainland country in Africa, covering an area of 4,361 square miles. The country occupies a thin ribbon of land bordering both banks of the River Gambia in West Africa. It has a pleasant sub-tropical climate with two distinct seasons reflected by a seasonal tourism industry.

In terms of its economy, it is ranked 168th out of 187 countries with comparable data in the 2011 UNDP Human Development Index.[24] Poverty remains high: according to the UNDP, 60.4 per cent of the population suffer multiple deprivations.[25] The country has no important mineral or other natural resources and has a limited agricultural base. Some 75-80 per cent of the population depends on crops and livestock for its livelihood, and its agricultural base is vulnerable to drought and locusts. Tourism is the second largest employer, the main foreign exchange earner, and currently accounts for a significant proportion of the nation's GDP.[26] Given the small size

23 Ministry of Tourism and Culture, (June, 1995) National Policy for Tourism Development 1995-2000.
24 UNDP, *Human Development Report 2011, Sustainability and Equity: A Better Future for All* (UNDP, 2011. http://hdr.undp.org/en/reports/global/hdr2011 (accessed 12 November 2011).
25 UNDP, *Human Development Report 2011, Sustainability and Equity: A Better Future for All, Explanatory Note for The Gambia.* http://hdrstats.undp.org/images/explanations/GMB.pdf (accessed 12 November 2011)
26 Department for International Development (DFID) (2007), Gambia Country Profile Available from: http://www.dfid.gov.uk/countries/africa/gambia.asp [accessed 12 November 2011].

of the domestic market and limited opportunities for other forms of economic activity such as manufacturing, tourism is one of the few economic sectors that offer significant growth potential.

The significance of these socio-economic characteristics on host-guest encounters was recognised by my key informants. They identified a number of issues in The Gambia which they felt caused and perpetuated the bumster phenomenon and acted as push factors for these men to engage in romance tourism, namely: poverty; lack of natural resources; decline of agriculture and the consequent rural–urban drift; lack of alternative employment opportunities; government's poor provision of education; the low wages of legitimate tourism workers; and a lack of linkages between the tourism industry and the agricultural and industrial base of the economy. Thus economic disparities, and the comparative poverty and limited opportunities for economic advancement for bumsters, are clearly key aspects in their relationships with tourists.

Cultural difference and cultural change
The Gambia is home to a wide diversity of different cultures including five main ethnic groups, the Mandinka, Fula, Wollof, Jola and Sarahule. As a former British colony until Independence in 1965, English is the official language. Islam is the main religion (about 90 per cent of the population), with the remainder being Christian or practising a traditional African religion. In spite of this ethnic diversity, there are several common strands such as communal lifestyles, family networks, and patriarchy.

This cultural context is clearly very different from the culture of European tourists who come to The Gambia, and thus cultural difference was recognised by all three of my sample groups as a key factor affecting the cross-cultural interaction between bumsters and tourists. However, the specific nature of these cultural differences was either not understood or elaborated upon in much detail by participants.

Although this research did not analyse the nature of such culture differences between tourists and bumsters in The Gambia, it is important to understand their significance and consider existing work in this area. For example, Reisinger and Turner reviewed the literature on this subject and summarised some of the key aspects of culture that are significant for the understanding of culture differences such as: communication (verbal and non-verbal), social categories (role, status, class, hierarchy, attitudes towards human nature, activity, time and relationships between individuals), social behaviour, concept of service, and social interaction.[27] Also, three studies, Czinkota & Ronkainen, Hofstede, and Trompenaars, have suggested a range of elements that generate cultural differences, such as: language, social

27 Reisinger, Y. and L.Turner, *Cross-Cultural Behaviour in Tourism: Concepts and Analysis* (Butterworth-Heinemann, 2003).

institutions, social classes, family structure, customs, economics, values, material items, religion, attitudes, aesthetics, politics, manners and education.[28]

Thus the relevant point here is that culture differences play a large role in determining the behaviour of both parties, the potential impact of social contact between them, the nature of their interaction and communication, and the potential for causing conflict and misunderstanding in the relationships involved in romance tourism. Culture difference is an important characteristic of romance tourism in The Gambia that needs to better researched and understood.

Another important aspect of the cultural context in The Gambia, identified by some informants as affecting the interaction between tourists and bumsters, is the changes in Gambian society and acculturation brought about by a wide range of influences including tourism. To summarise the views expressed, they felt that the traditional values of 'looking after each other', and a village approach to rearing children, is being replaced by a Western culture more focused on the individual and material possessions. Consequently, it was felt that there are changes in 'home training', where different social norms and values are imposed on the younger generations who are behaving differently, living alone, and aspiring to greener pastures. Such aspirations are encouraging younger generations to want relationships with tourists for opportunities to travel or find wealth. This change in society was thought to be affecting the mindset of bumsters towards tourists, as well as perpetuating the bumster phenomenon and romance tourism.

Bumster motivations
The key informants and tourists agreed that bumsters are primarily looking to gain some sort of advantage from tourists. Benefits sought were described as follows:

- Obtaining a passport and means to get to Europe
- Financial gain (i.e. tourists seen as 'cash cows' or 'money bags')
- In-kind payment or gifts (e.g. mobile phones, watches, food, cigarettes)
- Sponsorship for study or employment to 'succeed in life'
- Genuine friendship or pride in being a traditional host

In comparison, approximately one-third of the bumster sample justified their activities as a means to help their families, village and wider community by actively exposing tourists to the reality of life in The Gambia and encouraging them to sponsor individuals and community development projects. A number were also vocal about

28 A. Czinkota and I. Ronkainen, *International Marketing* (Orlando: The Dryden Press, 3rd edn 1993). G. Hofstede, *Cultures and Organizations: Software of the Mind* (New York: McGraw-Hill International, 1991/97). F. Trompenaars, *Riding the Waves of Culture: Understanding Cultural Diversity in Business* (London: Nicholas Brealey Publishing 1993/97).

the enjoyment they got out of being a bumster and experiencing the company of strangers and the romance. The latter was identified by 13 per cent of bumsters as a factor contributing to positive encounters with tourists, with one bumster adding that 'sometimes they even do it for free!'

The research did not include much discussion on the Gambian ideals of beauty or how attractive European women are to Gambian men although this would have been an interesting line of investigation: physical attraction as a motivation. However, some bumsters identified 'false love', age difference and a lack of sexual attraction in their relationships with older female tourists as examples of negative encounters, indicating an absence of mutual physical attraction in some instances.

Overall, there was a convincing amount of anecdotal and qualitative evidence that many bumsters enter into sexual relations with tourists not through personal desire but in order implicitly or explicitly to obtain money or goods of some sort and the possibility of upward social mobility. This motivation is often referred to as the 'Babylon syndrome' in which 'Babylon' is the emic name for 'the West', a dream destination flowing with wealth which forms the core of bumsters' fantasies and aspirations to travel abroad and escape their own poverty.[29]

Thus bumsters' motivations for being involved with romance tourism are inextricably linked with their reasons for becoming a bumster, and support the view that in a context of resource scarcity young men and women regard their sexuality as a livelihood asset.[30] Further insight on bumsters' motivations is provided by the study carried out by Carlisle-Gaye and Green for the Gambia Security and Sensitisation Committee on the reasons for youth involvement in bumstering and prostitution. Reasons identified were attributed to a combination of poverty, lack of education and employment opportunities, a change in cultural values, peer pressure and bad marriages.[31] In addition, Sosseh identified with bumsters the following reasons for hassling tourists: inaccessibility to the TDA; lack of coordination amongst bumsters; despair; unemployment; nature of the job; and lack of alternatives.[32] Finally, it is argued by Brown that another motivation for being a bumster is the fact that some Gambian youths identify with it as a lifestyle and sub-culture which offers an alternative to the traditional world of their elders, a world from which some feel marginalised and which they consequently reject as irrelevant to their own needs and wants, which are often focused on Europe.[33]

29 Nyanzi et al, 'Bumsters, big Black Organs and Old White Gold', 557.
30 Chant & Evans, A. 'Looking for the One(s)', 366.
31 S. Carlisle-Gaye and C. Green, *A Report on the Security and Sensitisation Committee Workshop held on Saturday 18 June 2005. Theme: the Bumster Menace And Prostitution.*
32 A. Sosseh, *Assessment of the Needs of Bumsters in The Gambia* (Responsible Tourism Partnership, 1997).
33 N. Brown, 'Beachboys as Culture Brokers in Bakau Town, The Gambia', *Community Development Journal*, 27, 4 (1992): 361-70.

Tourist motivations

Tourists' motivations for engaging in sexual and romantic relations with bumsters were not a focus of my research but they have been covered in a number of other works looking at other romance tourism destinations, particularly the Caribbean. Although there is no scope to do this topic justice here, it is still helpful to consider briefly some of the reasons tourists engage in these sexual relations as this will obviously affect the nature of their relationships with bumsters.

The most obvious motivations for romance tourists in The Gambia are the spectrum of sexual relations including sex, love and romance depending upon the type and personal characteristics of the individual tourist in question. In support of this, Albuquerque categorised female sex tourists in Barbados into four different types in which the centrality of sex as a motivator varies: the *first timers or neophytes*; the *situational* sex tourists who have sex with beach boys but do not travel specifically with that intention; the *veterans* whose objective is to engage in anonymous sex; and the *returnee* who has established an ongoing relationship.[34] In contrast, Herold (et al.) argue that female tourism is more complicated than being either a matter of sex or romance. For example it may involve a desire for 'companionship'. They suggest that there is a need to take into account other motivations and prior expectations when developing female sex tourist categories and propose five types for the Dominican Republic. First, *first time romantic tourists* who do not anticipate ahead of time that they might become involved with a local male, and who largely view their relationship as romantic rather than sexual; second, *first time sex tourists* who anticipate involvement and focus on the sexual aspects; third, *romantic returnees* who have been to the Dominican Republic before, had a romantic relationship with a local man, and who return because they wish to maintain this love relationship; fourth, *committed sex tourists* who return with the objective of maximising their sexual pleasure with one partner; and fifth, *adventurer sex tourists* who have casual sex with a number of partners. Thus, using this model, tourist-bumster relationships can be placed on a continuum with a focus on sex at one end and a focus on romance at the other.[35]

Other works highlight the desire of female tourists to experiment with new gender roles and power. Pruitt and LaFont suggest that in romance tourism in Jamaica, gender roles are reversed and that relations with beach boys are shaped and defined by the fact that it is the women who have the power, freedom and money to engage in these liaisons. Also, such female tourists are often seeking authentic, cultural and enriching holiday experiences which take them away from the package tourist resorts in favour of locally owned guest houses

34 Albuquerque, 'Sex, Beach Boys, and Female Tourists in the Caribbean'.
35 E. Herold et al., 'Female Tourists and Beach Boys: Romance or Sex Tourism?'.

and local hang-outs. [36] Such motivations would appear to fit for The Gambia where romance tourists are in a powerful economic position in their relationship with bumsters. They often want to 'experience Africa' so they spend a lot of time interacting with local people in tourism's informal sector, or outside of the tourist bubble completely, including spending time with the families of their bumster partner.

Quite how these examples of tourist motivation for romance tourism in the Caribbean compare with The Gambia has not come under much scrutiny but it would seem there are many similarities. For example, Nyanzi (et al.'s) research in The Gambia showed that some female tourists were motivated by a desire to experience different types of relationships (e.g. with different race, sex, background, or gender) and that sexual fantasies and racial myths about male black bodies were part of it . They postulate that

> the narratives about their (bumsters) sexuality reveal an enactment of myths about the male Black body and superior sexual performance on the one hand, and images of plundered wealth sitting in 'the West' – a dream destination flowing with milk and honey, and physically represented by the toubab – a local label for White foreigners – on the other. [37]

This study also noted that some of the female tourists in the sample are exposed to the poverty of The Gambia and the bumsters and wish to help them escape the hardships, adding a humanitarian dimension to the relationship. This dimension is interpreted by Sanchez-Taylor in Negril, Jamaica as meeting tourists' romantic ideas of caring for and taming a 'noble savage' which 'gigolos' or beach boys take advantage of by making spurious claims to be 'country farmers' who live simple lives, and so on. [38]

Finally, a useful theoretical concept to bear in mind when considering motivations is that tourism is a kind of ritual, one in which the special occasions of leisure and travel stand in opposition to everyday life at home and work. [39] Therefore, the nature of tourist travel and experience is understood in terms of the contrasts between the special period of life spent in tourist travel and the more ordinary aspects of the tourist's life at home. Linked to this theory is the Turnerian concept that tourists are in a 'liminal state', 'betwixt and between' ordinary life, when they travel overseas to 'exotic' locations where there feel outside the social norms and codes of behaviour that exist in their home destinations. [40] It is this state of mind that is argued accounts for the tendency for tourists to have reduced inhibitions and behave out of the norm, even naughtily, for example by having sexual relationships

36 D. Pruitt & S. LaFont, 'Romance Tourism'.
37 Nyanzi et al., 'Bumsters, Big Black Organs and Old White Gold', 557.
38 J, Sanchez-Taylor, in *Tourism and Sex: Culture, Commerce and Coercion*.
39 See Mbaiwa's discussion of 'the myth of the unrestrained', this volume, and N. Graburn, 'Tourism: The Sacred Journey', in V.Smith, *Hosts and Guests: The Anthropology of Tourism*, (University of Pennsylvania Press, 2nd edn 1989).
40 V. and E. Turner, *Image and Pilgrimage in Christian Culture*, (New York: Columbia University Press, 1978).

with bumsters which they can then either hide from people at home or alternatively boast about. As part of this, one should also consider the tourists' desire to experience something different or authentic.[41]

Individual/personal attributes
As with all relationships, the individual or personal attributes of those involved in romance tourism will affect the nature of these encounters. In common with the key informants and bumsters, 58 per cent of the tourist sample felt that a bumster's friendly/good personality was a main factor contributing to a positive encounter with tourists. Also, being well educated/having the required knowledge (26 per cent), good communication/language/conversational skills with tourists (19 per cent), and dressing 'appropriately'/smartly (19 per cent) were personal characteristics of bumsters that tourists felt contributed to positive interaction. On the other side of the coin, the tourist sample showed that the 'dodgy'/Rasta/unkempt/intimidating/'flash' appearance of bumsters (19 per cent) and selling/using drugs (14 per cent) were felt to have a negative impact on the nature of interaction with tourists, in addition to a rude/aggressive personality (10 per cent) and begging attitude (4 per cent).

In terms of tourists' personal attributes, key informants and bumsters identified modest appearance, appropriate/'open-minded' personality, philanthropic motivations, an interest in interacting with local people, accurate knowledge of local culture, experience/length of time spent in the Gambia, and (British) nationality, as variables which might help towards positive interaction with bumsters.

Rasta image
During my participant observation I found that approximately half of the bumster sample chose to adopt the Rasta image in their clothing, use the dialect and grow dreadlocks. This was not discussed in depth although a number did state that they were not practising Rastafarians but just liked the image. A more in depth explanation is provided by Pruitt and LaFont who studied the 'Rasta appeal' in Jamaica. They proposed that in Jamaica

> whether due to an agreement with the Rasta political philosophy and a desire to demonstrate lack of prejudice, or an attraction to the powerful masculinity projected by the Rastas, or both, men who assume the Rastafarian identity have proven to be particularly popular with the female European and American tourists with a lust for the exotic... Therefore, those men interested in trading with foreigners, whether selling marijuana (associated with the Rastas and an important tourism commodity), or generally acting as a companion to ease the way of foreigners through the largely informal society, have increasingly styled themselves as Rastafarian. They 'locks' their hair, speak in the Rasta dialect,

41 D, MacCannell, *The Tourist: A New Theory of the Leisure Class*, (London: Macmillan, 2nd edn 1989).

and develop a presentation that expresses the Rastafarian emphasis on simplicity and living in harmony with nature, in effect, constructing a 'staged authenticity'.

Furthermore, they argued that the Rasta identity is attractive to the Jamaican man involved in the tourist hustle because

[it] provides a model of masculinity that is not dependent upon the dominant ideology that places Eurocentric achievement of occupational success and money at the centre of the status system. Rather, it is developed around an articulation of the forces that prohibit the African-Jamaican man from achieving economic success. No one expects a Rastaman to be rich.[42]

Such reasons may well explain some bumsters' adoption of the Rasta identity in The Gambia.

Bumster tactics

Participants in my research revealed a range of tactics and approaches used by bumsters to try and initiate relationships, provide a service or seduce tourists. Based on the nature of the approach and the different tactics referred to, I identified a rudimentary kind of bumster typology as summarised below:[43]

- Mr Friendly
- Mr Businessman/Entrepreneur
- Mr Casanova
- Mr Criminal/Scammer
- Mr Disguised/Sophisticated bumster
- Mr Sympathy Seeker

These various tactics reflect the fact that bumsters are informal intermediaries who need to use their initiative to get access to tourists. The choice of approach used was seen as a reflection of a bumster's personal qualities, as well as determining the negative or positive nature of a tourist-bumster encounter.

Such tactics include a range of 'seduction' techniques such as smiling, eye contact, flattery, romance, strategies to get noticed or display skills, or encouraging tourists to drink or go dancing. Once noticed, bumsters often play on sexual and racial myths about the exotic African Other by offering tourists unlimited virility and other such sexual experiences.

Alternatively, some bumsters manipulate economic and racial differences by trying to make tourists feel guilty if they are not interested in having a relationship with them, or in helping them out financially in one way or another. Other more subtle approaches used by bumsters are to initiate conversation through the guise of a more respectable activity, such as providing a sun bed; giving a tourist a

42 D. Pruitt & S. LaFont, 'Romance Tourism', 326.
43 A bumster may fit into more than one typology.

'free gift' or a glass of African tea and then obliging them to stay and talk or return the favour.

In fact my participant observation with bumsters revealed that they are very astute in how they select someone, the techniques of their approach and in their use of certain cues or signals, such as a tourist's sun-tan, activity, dress, age and nationality, in determining their tactics. They also explained that their typical line of questioning of tourists, such as asking tourists their nationality, choice of hotel, length of stay, holiday activities, marital status, and feelings about the Gambia enables them to determine what the tourist might be interested in. To use the words of one bumster: 'We engage in friendly conversation with tourists as a way to get them to tell you the story of the day and night they want so that we can understand what the tourist likes and doesn't like.' Or, as another bumster put it: 'If you let me walk with you along the beach I guarantee to find out soon what you want and to get some money out of you!'

These findings resonate with other anthropological works such as those of Simoni who looks at strategies and tactics deployed by Cubans *jineteros* in the course of their informal encounters with tourists. He identifies the use of nationality, or 'nationality talks', as a discursive resource and framing device while interfacing with tourists, including the use of 'Cuban' stereotypes and features such as sexuality and ways of making love. He also describes a range of similar techniques used by *jineteros* for classifying tourists, of capturing their attention and creating profitable attachments.[44]

On a range of continuums: exploitative to 'voluntary', commercial to non-commercial, and enhancing to degrading self-identity
A key question in romance tourism is about power relations and who exploits who in these relations, or whether it is a mutually beneficial arrangement. There are competing theoretical conceptions of bumsters and prostitutes as either sexual victims or empowered sexual actors.[45]

In the case of The Gambia, some argue that bumsters are often exploited by female tourists (in the same way that men exploit female prostitutes). It is felt that in many of the tourist-bumster relationships, the economic power and idiosyncrasies of the tourist determine the nature of their relationship with Gambian youths:

> Their momentary economic power enabled them to draw Gambian youths into their own social and cultural milieu. Some would sit and drink alcohol with them, contrary to the quasi-Islamic and traditional cultural values of abstention from alcohol use. Some would pursue sexual passions to the point of holding hands with their host in public, contrary to the conservative quasi-Islamic and traditional norms of displaying

---

44 V. Simoni, '"Riding" Diversity: Cubans'/Jineteros' Uses of "Nationality-talks" in the Realm of their Informal Encounters with Tourists' (PhD diss. Leeds Metropolitan University Press, 2008).
45 Herold, et al., 'Female tourists'.

sexual passions only in private. Some elderly citizens from Europe have even decided to transform their position of patronage into intimate relationships by marrying Gambians young enough to be their children or grandchildren.[46]

On the other hand, some take the view that tourists 'looking for love' are exploited and manipulated by those bumsters who are only 'in it for the money'. It is argued that some bumsters enter into these relationships with tourists without sexual desire or genuine affection, but rather with the hope that sex may end up in a relationship that will earn them a visa in Europe, or get them out of the poverty trap. The *Rough Guide to The Gambia* states that: 'The Gambia has plenty of stories of European women who have fallen in love with Gambians (male and female) and arranged their passage to Europe, only for them to turn abusive or disappear without a trace.'[47] Consistent with this, many of the bumsters reported in Nyanzi argued that, whilst many bumsters were acutely aware of the negative attitudes towards such behaviour, they were willing participants who were neither abused nor used by their older, wealthier tourist partners. Instead they viewed them as 'stepping stones to the West', whilst others argued it was love.[48]

In reality, romance tourism relationships in The Gambia, as elsewhere, do not all fit neatly into one category or another, but rather bumsters provide sexual services on a range of terms depending on the individual relationship in question. Generally, however, they are voluntary and mutually beneficial, albeit in very different ways, and often asymmetrical in terms of economic and power relations. There is also substantial anecdotal evidence that they are often relatively long-term relationships which fits with the notion of romance and companionship. It could also be construed from the point of view of the bumster that the longer the relationship lasts with a tourist, the more benefits and money he will receive. Another advantage of lasting relations is a reduced need to compete for the attentions of other tourists in a competitive market, although several bumsters in the research joked about having several tourist girlfriends 'on the go' at the same time.

Thus the types of relationships that are involved in romance tourism in The Gambia can conveniently be positioned using Ryan's three sets of continua for analysing paradigms of sex tourism, namely whether it is voluntary or exploitative; commercial or non-commercial (i.e. an interaction not marked by set prices or which involves payment in kind); enhancing or degrading of self-identity. In this sense, the nature of these encounters can also be placed on a continuum with mutually beneficial and positive experiences at the one end, and

46 Bah et al., *Problems and Benefits.*
47 E. Gregg, E. & R. Trillo, *The Rough Guide to The Gambia* (Rough Guide Publications, 2006).
48 Nyanzi et al., 'Bumsters, Big Black Organs and Old White Gold', 557.

detrimental and negative experiences at the other.[49] This and other similar models are useful tools for taking into account wider variables than economic gain in reaching conclusions about the nature of relationships involved in romance tourism, but they do not, by any means, take into account all of them.

Impact of formal and informal intermediaries in the tourist 'love' bubble

The Gambia is primarily a winter-sun, package holiday destination. The country markets itself using a number of selling points, namely the semi-tropical climate and the Atlantic coast, its rich African heritage (largely based on its cultural history and the slave trade), and the relaxing, unsophisticated atmosphere of the Gambian people who, as a result of their friendly welcome, have earned their country the title 'The Smiling Coast' – a marketing strapline used by the Gambia Tourism Authority.[50] Both the formal and informal intermediaries and infrastructure surrounding this package tourism industry create the tourist bubble in which romantic host-guest encounters take place.

Figure 15.1 depicts the nature of this tourist 'love' bubble in The Gambia which is centred on the formal intermediaries associated with the package tourism industry, such as tour operators, ground handlers, airlines, local shops and restaurants, tourist taxis, official tourist guides, and other formalised tourist services. The diagram also illustrates how the informal tourism sector's intermediaries,

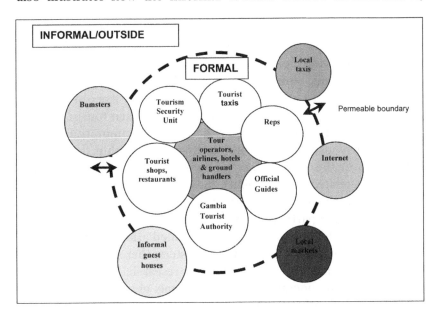

15.1 Intermediaries in The Gambian tourist bubble (© Lucy McCombes)

49 C. Ryan, 'Sex tourism: paradigms of confusion', in S. Carter and S. Clift, eds., *Tourism and Sex: Culture, Commerce and Coercion* (London: Cassell, 2000), 23-40. See also Bauer & Mc-Kercher, *Sex and Tourism*.
50 Became Gambia Tourism Board in October 2011.

including the bumsters and unlicensed local guesthouses where some romance tourists stay, operate at the margins of the tourist bubble and the formalised tourism industry. Thus it is suggested here that the Gambian tourist bubble has permeable boundaries where, depending on the individual relationship in question, romantic encounters between tourists and bumsters can flit in and out of both the intangible and physical boundaries of the formal tourism industry marked by the resorts, tourist restaurants, tour operator excursions and the tourist beaches.

As informal intermediaries, bumsters, as well as offering sexual relations, act as culture brokers and informal guides and provide opportunities for their tourist partners to meet the local community outside of the tourist bubble, for example when travelling to the bumsters village to meet his family. Therefore, operating in what Bruner describes as the 'touristic border zone' which is a zone of interaction between natives, tourists and ethnographers which is described as a creative space that allows for the invention of culture.[51]

During such interaction romance tourists often surrender control of their interaction with local people to bumsters who explain to their tourist partners about life and cultural norms in The Gambia, and assist in mediating and communicating with other local people and negotiating cultural difference between the different parties. It is in this way that bumsters help to cushion the shock for tourists venturing outside the tourist bubble, as well as influencing the understanding, behaviour and attitudes that tourists have towards local people. It is in this role, and through exposing tourists to the poverty in The Gambia, that bumsters can inform tourists in a subtle way about the needs of their family/community members and inspire them to help economically. Thus, bumsters' informal role in and outside the tourist bubble as a sexual partner, local guide and cultural broker can influence the nature of the relationship between them and their tourist partner, and for both parties' relationship with the local community. However, bumsters may also interact with tourists solely within the physical boundaries of the Tourist Development Area (i.e. land designated for tourism-related development), the heart of the Gambian tourist bubble, in which case their tourist partners experience much less of the reality of their partner's Gambian life.

In terms of the impact of formal intermediaries on the nature of relationships between tourists and bumsters, there are a number of significant impacts emerging from my research. The information which many tour operators, reps and hotels give to tourists about bumsters was shown to affect tourists' understanding and attitudes and can deter many from interacting with them. For example, 35 per cent of bumsters and 32 per cent of tourists whom I interviewed complained that tour operators were not giving balanced information

51 E.M. Bruner, 'Tourism in the Balinese borderzone', in S. Lavie, & T. Swedenburg, eds., *Displacement, Diaspora, and Geographies of Identity* (NC: Duke University Press, 1996) 157-79.

about the former, which affected tourists' behaviour by making them cautious/afraid to interact with bumsters and other local people who they meet informally.

Second, a number of formal intermediaries physically discourage encounters between bumsters and tourists. These are the Tourism Security Unit's policing in the resorts, the effect of the Tourism Offences Act (2002) which made hassling illegal, and the restriction of locals' access to hotels and restaurants and certain areas within the Tourism Development Area (TDA). This, in addition to the competitive environment between formal tourism stakeholders and bumsters, was seen by key informants as perpetuating the bumsters' aggressive approaches to tourists in order to initiate a relationship. It could also be argued that such legislation and policing, restricting access to tourists, reinforces romance tourism as there are so few alternatives for many local people to earn a good income from other forms of tourism.

Third, the package-tour industry is a facilitator of romance tourism by accommodating and transporting holiday-makers to 'honey pot' resorts, providing rich pickings for bumsters and likewise a central point for tourists interested in having a romantic or sexual relationship. Similarly, tourist infrastructure such as bars and night-clubs provide an environment conducive to bumsters' seducing and charming tourists with alcohol, marijuana, and R&B music. From a different angle, informal networks of people associated with the tourism industry act as a facilitator of romance tourism. For example, ECPAT research found that some ground staff, security men, hotel cleaners and waiters identify potential tourist partners for bumsters, or act as pimps by connecting two interested parties.[52]

Fourth, there was a general consensus amongst all three sample groups that the nature of package tourism in The Gambia does little to encourage positive interaction between local people/bumsters. It was felt that package tourism typically attracts tourists who are motivated primarily to 'just lie on the beach and get a tan' rather than to explore Africa, and who have 'very limited knowledge about the country, little time to learn, and unrealistic expectations'.

Finally, intermediaries such as the internet and certain types of tourism marketing sometimes promote The Gambia as a sex or romance destination and perpetuate racial myths and stereotypes about African men. This in turn affects the expectations and the type of tourist attracted to The Gambia which maintains the bumster phenomenon.

Thus it is evident from the range of impacts that intermediaries have on the relationship between tourists and bumsters that the nature of tourism or the 'tourist bubble' is an important variable

---

52 End Child Prostitution, Pornography and Trafficking (ECPAT), 'Sustainable tourism development and the protection of child from sexual exploitation: New research to shed light on child sex tourism in The Gambia'. *ECPAT International Newsletter,* 41, October (2002).

in understanding sex or romance tourism. A similar conclusion is drawn in Chapter 14 (this volume) on sex tourism in Malindi where uncoordinated mass tourism has created an institutional vacuum for an upsurge of sex tourism. As in The Gambia, the tourism industry in Malindi is dominated by foreigners who control much of the tourist bubble, leaving many local residents with the sole option of trading in small-scale businesses in the informal sector – in other words, on the permeable boundary of the tourist bubble.[53]

Local consequences

Lastly, we consider here the impact of romance tourism in The Gambia on the relations between bumsters and the local community, and on the local population as hosts to tourists in general.

In terms of their relations with local people, bumsters' sexual activities with tourists have been met with a mixed response. On the one hand, in support of Brown, my findings in The Gambia suggest that many elders do not look favourably on the behaviour of bumsters and disapprove when youths imitate tourists in terms of dress, drink alcohol, have relationships with older white women, and disrespect traditional authority. Such negative views of bumsters are also symptomatic of a local concern expressed by informants that the former's sexual activities, and their embrace of western culture, whether in fashions, products and values, is potentially damaging to Gambian cultural traditions such as hosting guests, extended family, and a sense of community. It is in this sense that a bumster could damage his own identity, status and self-respect in the local community. Tension with the elders is also identified by Brown who finds that the divide between the old and the young men has been exacerbated by tourism and the evolution of bumsters who some elders feel demonstrate a lack of respect, disobedience, a disregard for Islamic faith and failure in their lack of formal paid work.[54]

Similarly, in Chapter 14 (this volume), Wanjohi Kibicho quotes a veteran fisherman in Malindi, Kenya, complaining that 'Tourism has destroyed our youngsters. You can no longer teach them to fish. Today, they want easy and fast cash; they want the tourists' lifestyles...' Kibicho also points out that 'Malindi's strong socially determined link between sex trade and immorality punishes the sex worker and shows how the local people feel offended as the whole community becomes tarnished.' However, in contrast, in The Gambia, some informants argued that elders also acknowledge that change must happen and that they are happy to take advantage of the opportunities to better their lives in material terms through income earned by bumsters' contacts with tourists. Thus elders in the community appear to be

53 W. Kibicho, this volume.
54 N. Brown, 'Beachboys as Culture Brokers in Bakau Town, The Gambia'.

torn between trying to maintain a balance between their traditional authority and social structures and the lure of the material benefits brought by social change.

Interviews with bumsters conducted by myself, Sosseh and Brown also identified a more positive perspective on bumsters from others in the local community.[55] Many justified bumsters' relationships with tourists in terms of the contribution they make to the socio-economic development of their communities and indeed The Gambia, based on the donations that they encourage tourists to make. Some argued that bumsters are intelligent entrepreneurs who are meeting the tourist demand for authentic, cultural and 'real Gambian' experiences. This has resulted in many successful bumsters, and their families or communities, benefitting from money, education and travel experiences provided by their tourist partner. These men are given high status in the local community and are perceived as role models for many of the younger generation. Such a scenario is made much easier by the particular nature of romance tourism whereby it is often not viewed by participants as prostitution, but rather something involving genuine romance, or at least a mutually beneficial relationship.

On another level, my interviews with key stakeholders in The Gambia highlighted a number of tensions between bumsters and local people who work in the tourism industry. Whilst they recognised that bumsters are, to quote one informant, 'just poor Gambians who want the nice things in life just like anyone else', the way they go about their activities was heavily criticised. Primary tourism stakeholders, such as hoteliers, beach bar and restaurant owners, tourist taxi drivers, craft market vendors, official tourist guides, fruit sellers, juice pressers, tour operators and ground handlers, criticised bumsters for competing unfairly, 'stealing' tourist business, harassing and scamming tourists which negatively affects their holiday experiences and deters repeat custom. Secondary tourism stakeholders, such as the Gambia Tourism Authority, the Tourism and Travel Association of The Gambia and the Tourism Security Unit were critical that bumsters operate without licenses, taxes or insurance when they act as local guides.

Also, many from both these primary and secondary stakeholders resented the impact that bumsters have in giving The Gambia a reputation as a sex tourism destination, as well as threatening the tourist experience. A few also highlighted the social dangers commonly associated with sex tourism including the spread of sexually transmitted diseases, increases in prostitution and child sex tourism. This final point is illustrated by a study conducted by UNICEF which provides evidence of some bumsters acting as intermediaries between sex tourists and child and adult prostitutes.[56]

---

55 Ibid. See also L. McCombes, *Ingredients*; A. Sosseh, *Assessment.*
56 UNICEF, *Study on the Sexual Abuse.*

It was widely recognised therefore by key informants that bumsters and the reputation of The Gambia as a romance tourism destination is bad for business and contrary to the aspirations that many in the community have for the tourism industry in this country. The fact that bumsters' activities pose a real threat is demonstrated by the airport exit survey carried out for the 2006 Gambian Tourism Development Masterplan on a sample of 2,000 tourists which indicated that the bumster syndrome (i.e. tourist harassment) is the biggest threat to tourism. Some two-thirds (68 per cent) of respondents identified bumsters as a substantial disappointment (in particular at the airport, beach, and on the street), and 43 per cent suggested that bumsters needed to be stopped.[57]

Conclusion

It appears that people in The Gambia remain divided in their opinion as to whether it is appropriate or in the interests of local people to take action to burst the Gambian 'love' bubble for some host-guest encounters. Although, encouragingly, there is a growing number of tourism stakeholders who are starting to challenge the notion that bumsters are like leopards in that they don't 'change their spots', and are increasingly starting to believe that if interesting and worthwhile alternatives to romance tourism are provided (as part of an holistic approach to addressing the issue) then behaviour change could result.

Whatever course of action is agreed, this chapter has attempted to demonstrate that romance tourism in The Gambia needs to be understood and addressed as a socio-cultural reality rather than simply as a menace or problem that can only be contained by strengthening the police apparatus. Furthermore, that the role of tourists and other intermediaries in romance tourism should also be put more under the spotlight when considering management solutions rather than the finger of blame resting solely with the bumsters.

I have also argued here that romance tourism involves relationships that are much more complex than a simple sex for money or in-kind payment arrangement. These relationships in The Gambia are shaped by a wide range of factors and intermediaries, and exhibit a number of typical characteristics. These variables influence the supply and demand, and pull and push factors, for entry into romance tourism in the first place. They also affect the overall nature of relationships such as the degree to which these relationships are exploitative or beneficial to those involved, and the local community around them. The findings in The Gambia also show that the relationships in romance tourism do not fit neatly into one category, but rather incorporate a range of relationships which, whilst not generally being socially acceptable, are

57 DOSTC. *The Gambia Tourism Development Master Plan, Final Report (Main volume).* July, 2006.

largely entered upon on a 'voluntary' basis by those involved due to divergent motivations.

Unsurprisingly, therefore, romance tourism in The Gambia has been shown to be a double-edged sword. On the one hand it poses a threat to the long-term wellbeing of those involved, and to the reputation and economic benefits of The Gambia as a holiday destination. On the other hand it offers rapid social mobility for those bumsters who are successful in their charming of tourists, as well as benefiting their extended families and communities. It is fuelled by tourist motivations such as escaping the norm, authentic African experiences, sexual myths and fantasies about the exotic other, and by bumster motivations to experience Babylon and a rapid escape from poverty. Also, importantly, it is sometimes fuelled by a common motivation for love of one form or another and companionship ...thus forming a genuine love bubble on occasion.[58] With these powerful drivers the Gambian love bubble is very unlikely to either burst or float off to a happy ending.

58 There will never be consensus on a definition for love but it is useful here to note the three main types of love identified by sociologist Lee (1976): first, *eros*, characterised by immediate physical attraction, sensuality, self-confidence, fascination with beauty, close intimacy, and rapport with partner; second, *ludus*, characterised by love that is playful, hedonistic and free of commitment; and third, *storge*, characterised by love which is affectionate, companionate and devoid of passion.

REFERENCES

Albuquerque, K. de. 'Sex, Beach Boys, and Female Tourists in the Caribbean', *Sexuality and Culture*, 2, (1998): 87-111.

Bah, A., Carlie, H. Sallah and S. Tijan. *Problems and Benefits of Tourism in The Gambia* (Action Aid, 2005).

Bauer, T. and B. McKercher. *Sex and Tourism: Journeys of Romance, Love, and Lust* (The Haworth Hospitality Press, London, 2003).

Brown, N. 'Beachboys as Culture Brokers in Bakau Town, The Gambia', *Community Development Journal*, 27, 4, (1992): 361-70.

Bruner, E.M. 'Tourism in the Balinese borderzone', in S. Lavie and T. Swedenburg, eds., *Displacement, Diaspora, and Geographies of Identity* (Duke University Press, 1996), 157-79.

Carlisle-Gaye, S. and C. Green. *A Report on the Security and Sensitisation Committee workshop held on Saturday 18 June 2005. Theme: the Bumster Menace and Prostitution* (Security and Sensitisation Committee, 2005).

Carter, S. and S. Clift. *Tourism and Sex: Culture, Commerce and Coercion* (London and New York: Pinter, 2000).

Chant, S. and A. Evans. 'Looking for the One(S): Young Love and Urban Poverty in The Gambia', *Environment and Urbanization* 22 (Sage Publications on behalf of IIED, 2010).

Child Protection Alliance and Terres des Hommes. '*Gambia...the Smiling Coast!': A Study of Child Sex Tourism in The Gambia and the Involvement of Dutch Tourists* (Netherlands: Terres des Hommes, 2003).

Czinkota, A. and I. Ronkainen. *International Marketing* (Orlando: The

Dryden Press, 3rd edn, 1993).

Department for International Development (DFID). *Gambia Country Profile* Available from: http://www.dfid.gov.uk/countries/africa/gambia.asp (accessed 28th March, 2007).

Department of State for Tourism and Culture, Banjul, The Gambia, and African Development Bank, *The Gambia Tourism Development Master Plan, Final Report (Main volume)* (July, 2006).

ECPAT (End Child Prostitution, Pornography and Trafficking) 'Sustainable Tourism Development and the Protection of Children from Sexual Exploitation: New Research to Shed Light on Child Sex Tourism in The Gambia' (*ECPAT International Newsletter* (2002, 41, Oct).

Graburn, N. 'Tourism: The Sacred Journey', in V. Smith, ed., *Hosts and Guests: The Anthropology of Tourism* (University of Pennsylvania Press, 2nd edn 1989).

Gregg, E. and Trillo, R. *The Rough Guide to The Gambia* (Rough Guide Publications, 2006).

Gupta, T. *Sugar Mummies*, Royal Court Theatre, London, 2006.

Herold, E., Garcia, R. and T. DeMoya. 'Female Tourists and Beach Boys: Romance or Sex Tourism?' *Annals of Tourism Research*, 28, 4 (2001) 978-97.

Hofstede, G. *Cultures and Organizations: Software of the Mind* (New York: McGraw-Hill International, 1991/97).

Jaakson, R. 'Beyond the Tourist Bubble: Cruisehip Passengers in Port', *Annals of Tourism Research*, 31,1,(2004): 44-60.

Jacobsen, J.K. 'The Tourist Bubble and the Europeanisation of Holiday Travel', *Journal of Tourism and Cultural Change* (Leeds Metropolitan University, 2010).

MacCannell, D. *The Tourist: A New Theory of the Leisure Class* (London: Macmillan, 2nd edn 1989).

McCombes, L. *Ingredients for Positive Tourist-Host Encounters: A Study to Investigate the Factors that Affect the Nature of the Tourist-Host Encounter Between Tourists and 'Bumsters' in Kololi and Kotu, The Gambia*, University of Greenwich (unpublished dissertation), 2007.

Ministry of Tourism and Culture, *National Policy for Tourism Development 1995-2000* (June, 1995)

Momsen, S. 'Tourism, Gender and Development in the Caribbean', in V. Kinnaird, V. & D. Hall, eds., *Tourism: A Gender Analysis* (Chichester, West Sussex: Wiley, 1994).

Nyanzi, S., O. Rosenberg-Jallow, O. Bah. 'Bumsters, Big Black Organs and Old White Gold: Embodied Racial Myths in Sexual Relationships of Gambian Beach Boys' in *Culture, Health & Sexuality* (Health Policy Unit, London School of Hygiene and Tropical Medicine, London, 2007).

O'Connell Davidson, J. 'British Sex Tourists in Thailand', in M. Maynard and J.Purvis, eds. *(Hetero) Sexual Politics* (London: Taylor and Francis, 1995).

Pruitt, D. and LaFont. S., 'For Love and Money: Romance Tourism in Jamaica', *Annals of Tourism Research* 22, 2, (1995): 422-40.

Pruitt, D. and LaFont, S. 'Romance Tourism: Gender, Race and Power in Jamaica', in Sharon B. Gmelch, ed., *Tourists and Tourism: A Reader* (Waveland Press, Inc., 2004).

Reisinger, Y. and Turner, L. *Cross-Cultural Behaviour in Tourism: Concepts and Analysis* (Butterworth-Heinemann, 2003).

Ryan, C. 'Sex Tourism: Paradigms of Confusion', in S. Carter and S. Clift, eds., *Tourism and Sex: Culture, Commerce and Coercion* (London: Cassell, 2000), 23-40.

Simoni, V. *'Riding' Diversity: Cubans'/Jineteros' Uses of 'Nationality-talks' in the Realm of their Informal Encounters with Tourists* (Leeds Metropolitan University Press, 2008).

Sosseh, A. *Assessment of the Needs of Bumsters in The Gambia* (Responsible Tourism Partnership, 1997).

Trompenaars, F. *Riding the Waves of Culture: Understanding Cultural Diversity in Business* (London: Nicholas Brealey Publishing, 1993/97).

Turner, V. & Turner, E. *Image and Pilgrimage in Christian Culture* (New York: Columbia University Press, 1978).

UNICEF. *Study on the Sexual Abuse and Exploitation of Children in The Gambia* (Geneva: UNICEF, 2003).

Van Beek, W. E.A. 'Approaching African Tourism: Paradigms and Paradoxes', in Patrick Chabal, Ulf Engel & Leo de Haan, eds., *African Alternatives* (Leiden: Brill, 2007), 145-72.

Van Beek, W.E.A. 'African Tourist Encounters: Effects of Tourism on Two West African Societies', *Africa. Journal of the International African Institute*, 73, 2, (2003): 251-98.

Afterword
Trouble in the bubble: Comparing African tourism with the Andes Trail

Annelou Ypeij

As the chapters in this volume show, tourism in Africa is characterised by heterogeneity and complexity. Though wildlife tourism is the continent's main tourist attraction, all kinds of cultural tourism and sea, sand, sun (and sex) tourism can also be found. Small-scale tourism developments directed at niche markets, such as those of the Dogon, Touareg, volunteer, roots, chief and community-based tourism, exist shoulder to shoulder with large-scale industries with a mix of foreign and domestic investment, as the Kenyan and South African cases show. This diversity means contradictory outcomes for local populations. While some local people and communities are able to benefit from tourists, others are excluded from tourism revenues. The paradoxes and contradictions of the African case that are so eloquently described and analysed in the preceding chapters raise the question of what is specifically 'African' about African tourism. Or in other words: how can African tourism be compared to developments on other continents? In this Afterword, I want to sketch my own research in the Cusco-Machu Picchu region of Peru[1] and show some of the similarities to and differences from the cases presented in this volume. I will focus on the formation of the tourist bubble, (the leading concept for all the authors here), and its main participants, i.e. the state, mediators or middle men and women, and the local men and women who work in the lowest echelons of the tourism labour market.

As the contributions by van Kessel, van Egmond and Koot indicate here, tourism needs a bubble, a fact against which only a small minority of tourists, the so-called pioneer backpackers, react. Tourists have no business in places where there is not at least one person willing to offer food and a place to sleep, as tourism always needs some basic infrastructure. It would appear from this volume that in contrast to the Peruvian case, the tourist bubble in Africa has not yet fully developed and the actors who are creating the bubble are often limited to the local hosts and international travel agencies. In Peru, most tourists arrive at the Jorge Chavez international airport in Lima, from where Peru's tourist bubble extends in all directions.

---

1 I did this research within the framework of the WOTRO Science for Development research programme at CEDLA, Amsterdam between September 2003 and September 2007. The project was entitled 'Incatourism in the Andean Highlands; Prospects and Ambivalences of the Idea of SustainableTourism (Bolivia, Peru).'

Actors in all echelons, from the huge international companies to the very small local travel agencies and individual guides, are active in the bubble. The Peruvian bubble is probably most developed in the Cusco-Machu Picchu area and from Cusco tourists can visit Machu Picchu and the Sacred Valley and travel south to Puno and the islands in Lake Titicaca (Ypeij & Zoomers 2006). Especially in the centre of Cusco and on their way to Machu Picchu, tourists can drink red wine or Coca Cola and eat pizza or hamburgers at ever corner, with the more adventurous sampling specialities such as guinea pig or Cusqueña, the local Cusco beer. The Andean bubble is well organised and allows all tourists – from those travelling on a shoestring to the big spenders seeking luxury – to access the products they are looking for.

State involvement

The government plays an important role in the construction of the Peruvian tourist bubble. The state actively promotes Peru through its website by broadcasting promotional films internationally and other activities. The media's message is that Peru's exotic, indigenous populations and its mystical Inca history create an overwhelming experience that is worthy of a visit. The romantic images that circulate in the bubble of exotic Indians with a mystical culture and authentic unspoilt communities uncontaminated by the achievemens of modern consumerism are thus state-approved, as are the false sentiments these images appeal to (cf. van Egmond; Finlay & Barnabas; Mbaiwa; Wijngaarden, this volume).

The general policy is important here also, as the state shapes the tourist bubble with its neo-liberal economic policy by attracting foreign investment and allotting concessions to international companies. Perurail, the railway operator that connects Cusco with Machu Picchu is partly owned by Orient Express Ltd, an international travel company that is listed on the New York Stock Exchange. The presence of this international player is all the more remarkable as the only means of transport to Machu Picchu is indeed by train (for walkers there is the Inca Trail), so the state has given the monopoly on this crucial route to a partly foreign-owned company.

The Peruvian state wants to keep its most important tourist sites clear of informal workers. In Chapter 10 here, Brooks, Spierenburg and Wels, looking at a comparable situation, (the farm dwellers in future game farming projects in South Africa) mention Mary Douglas's concept of dirt as 'matter out of place'. The municipality of Cusco views itinerant vendors in the streets of the historic centre of Cusco as 'causing congestion, immobility, public disorder, noise and pollution'.[2] After Cusco's historic centre was declared a UNESCO

2 Master Plan for the Historical Centre of Cuzo (Municipalidad del Cuzco 2000) in Steel, G.

World Heritage site, the municipality, under Mayor Carlos Valencia (in office 1998-2006), introduced a policy to stop informal vendors and street children from working in the historic city centre.[3] The local vendors were harassed, intimidated and forcefully chased away. Their merchandise was confiscated as it was felt that the image of poverty that they and the street children exuded did not fit the official tourism project. Fortunately for the vendors and the children, a change of mayor has also meant a change in policy.

Park management

One other way in which the state plays an important role in the formation of the bubble is through its development and implementation of nature parks. Based on the views expressed by contributors to these pages, my impression is that African governments do not participate as strongly in their national tourism projects as the Peruvian state does. This may be an important reason why Africa offers more possibilities for local control and ownership, and thus for direct contact between local hosts and their guests, as well as between international tourist agencies and community-based developments. Having said this, and as the chapters in Section II that deal with African nature parks and conservation areas show, the state is present when its park management is concerned. Just as in the Peruvian case, the African state cannot be said to represent its entire population. On the contrary, Africa is a front-runner in the way it excludes the local population and indigenous minorities from park management, so it is not without reason that the four articles on parks project a real sense of injustice. As both Koot (Chapter 8) and Brooks et al. (10) indicate, local people can lose their land due to the creation of parks and often experience trouble over the ownership of land and relocation. Finlay & Barnabas (7) as well as Wijngaarden (9) show that local people's culture tends to become frozen in time, implying they are denied development and are excluded from serious tourism revenues. In these cases, the state inclines towards preservation instead of development.

The state in Peru is omnipresent in park management and its policies are often not beneficial for the people who live in them. The management of the Historic Sanctuary of Machu Picchu – where the ruins of Machu Picchu are located and through which the Inca Trail runs, bringing in hundreds of tourists every day – views the local inhabitants negatively. The approximately 250 peasant families who

'Dishing up the City. Tourism and Street Vendors in Cuzco', in M. Baud & A. Ypeij, eds., *Cultural Tourism in Latin America. The Politics of Space and Imagery* (Leiden: Brill, 2009), 161-176.
3 Steel, G. *Vulnerable Careers. Tourism and Livelihood Dynamics among Street Vendors in Cuzco, Peru* (Amsterdam: Rozenberg, 2008), and 'Dishing up the City. Tourism and Street Vendors in Cuzco', 161-76.

live in the park are said not to belong in the area because they are thought to be non-indigenous and do not own the land.[4] The state envisages a park without people because 'the presence of humans weakens the concept of nature as magical and renewing' (Koot, Chapter 8). Nature is perceived as something in which people have no place, as something pristine, untouched. The agricultural activities of the Machu Picchu peasants are restricted, as are the number of cattle they are allowed to keep since these practices are considered to harm the natural surroundings. This is ironic considering the number of tourists who walk through the park every day. Though the peasants are proud Quechua speakers who have lived in the area for generations, it is true that there are many problems over landownership. The main reason is that only a decade before the area was turned into the nature park as we know it today, the area consisted of *haciendas*. For centuries, the peasants living in the area were forced to work for the *hacendados*, farming the land of the landowners and herding their cattle in return for the usufruct rights to small plots of land for subsistence farming and cattle grazing. Land reforms were only half completed when the area received its protected status. Thus, power inequalities with a long history in the *hacienda* system are being revived through the park management's policies.

Resistance against the state

What sets the Peruvian case apart from the African tourism project is the fierce resistance of the local population to the state. Not only are the peasants of Machu Picchu determined to stay, and are engaged in legal procedures and other forms of resistance, other local groups too are also not shying away from violence. Small-scale business owners and other local stakeholders in the tourists villages of Machu Picchu (where the entrance to the ruins are located) and Ollantaytambo have used blockades, occupations and hunger strikes in their struggle against the Peruvian authorities. The government has even needed the army to protect tourists. At stake is the very ownership of the tourism project. Local small-scale entrepreneurs detest the presence of foreign investments and international companies that inevitably leads to the leakage of tourism profits abroad. Protesters from other areas of Peru with different agendas have entered the bubble and blocked the railway, on one occasion even derailing an engine. Although there were no casualties, this incident shows that attacks on the tourism project are perceived as a way of resisting the state.[5]

4   Maxwell, K. & A. Ypeij. 'Caught between Nature and Culture. Making a Living in the World Heritage Site of Machu Picchu (Peru)', in M. Baud & A. Ypeij, eds., *Cultural Tourism in Latin America. The Politics of Space and Imagery* (Leiden: Brill, 2009), 177-98.
5   22 June 2009, Terra Noticias 'Suspenden trenes a Machu Picchu por las protestas de campesinos en el Cuzco'; 19 February 2008, ADNMUNDO.com 'Bloqueado el paso a Machu Picchu'; 12 July 2007, Terra Noticias 'Se descarrila locomotora que llevaba turistas a Machu Picchu en Perú'.

From the tourist perspective, this struggle in the Peruvian bubble means that the bubble does not always offer tourists a safe haven or the feeling of being in paradise. Then there is the danger that their train may not run because of blockades and they might miss their flight home, which is the ultimate nightmare.

Guides and other middlemen

Subjects in this volume that are less prominent[6] are guides and other mediators in the tourist bubble. The reason for this may be to do with the business chain that organizes tourism. In Africa, this chain mainly consists of international travel agencies that have direct contact with the representatives of local people and communities, providing tickets, accommodation and transport. In the Peruvian case, the chain of businesses is more complex because between the international travel agencies and the local populations there are national and regional entrepreneurs, local operators of all sizes, and individual workers. An important reason for this is that the Peruvian tourism project has turned into a massive phenomenon since the 1990s with more than 800,000 tourists a year visiting the Cusco-Machu Picchu region.[7] People from all sectors of the local economy are seeing their chance to get a slice of the tourism pie. One of the most popular courses is to train as a tourist guide, and many parents and students are investing a fortune in these. Guides work under the authority of local travel agencies and accompany tourists on excursions, for example the three- or four-day hikes along the Inca Trail. They are usually from Cusco or other Peruvian cities and their mother tongue is Spanish, i.e. they are of *mestizo* origin. This is important because they literally stand between the tourists and the indigenous population. Though the Peruvian tourism project is built around the supposed exoticism of the indigenous population, authentic Indian communities, and the mystics of the Inca history, this does not mean that indigenous people are readily accepted as equal partners. Centuries of racism are difficult to erase and indigenous people are often only allowed to be present in the tourism bubble as passive decoration and frozen representatives of the exotic Other.[8] The similarities with the chapters by Koot (8) and Wijngaarden (9) in this respect are striking. In the Cusco-Machu Picchu case, guides determine the contact between the tourist and the indigenous population, telling tourists who is 'authentic' and who is not, and where to buy and where not to.[9] This power play is evident

6 With the exception of Warren & MacGonagle, Klute, Steegstra, Swan and van Beek.
7 MINCETUR Cusco: Llegada de visitantes al Santuario Histórico de Machu Picchu, Enero 2004-Febrero 2010 (www.mincetur.gob.pe).
8 Cf. Hill, M.D. 'Contesting Patrimony: Cusco's Mystical Tourist Industry and the Politics of Incanismo', *Ethnos* 72, 4 (2007): 433-460.
9 Bosman, K. 'Ofreciendo un mundo imaginario: los guías de turismo en el Cuzco', in A. Ypeij & A. Zoomers eds., *La Ruta Andina. Turismo y desarrollo sostenible en Perú y Bolivia* (Quito:

from experiences on the Lake Titicaca island of Taquile, where the inhabitants were in full control of the tourism project for two decades. However, since 2000, they have lost control of it due to the aggressive tactics of small-scale travel agencies and their guides. Increasingly, tourists are visiting Taquile by booking an excursion through an agency in the nearby city of Puno instead of travelling independently. The guides who accompany tourists to Taquile advise them not to buy Taquilean weavings on the island because of their poor quality and high prices, whereas in the US they are valued museum pieces.[10] Instead the guides take their clients to on-shore sellers, who probably pay the guides more commission. Whereas guides are Maasai and Bushmen in the African case, there are hardly any indigenous guides in Cusco. It is only recently that people from Huayllabamba (on the Inca Trail) and the Uros Islands and Taquile (both in Lake Titicaca) have started to send their children to train as guides. I am convinced that this development will contribute to the agency of the indigenous populations involved in the tourism project.

Local people and communities

Most of the contributors to this volume (including the Foreword) discuss the effect the bubble is having on the host populations. They assume that the bubble consists mostly of local people, in addition to the sending tourist organisations, but that the influence on the communities comes from the partial participation of community members in the bubble (as van Beek shows for the Dogon in Chapter 2). The Andean tourist bubble seems to be more complex and with more actors but one that does include local hosts and populations in a quite specific role. One could say that, in addition to the state, international businesses, local operators of all sizes and *mestizo* mediators, the people from the lowest echelons of the local economy are a minor but still obvious part of the bubble. For example, tourists visiting the historic centre of Cusco can hardly avoid seeing the street children who sell postcards and candy or offer their services as shoe-shine boys. These children, usually boys, actively connect with tourists and try to speak a few words of English with them. Many of them do not only want to earn some quick money but also to develop a deeper relationship with tourists who might take them out for dinner or arrange for a stay for them in a children's shelter. With the internet, some children maintain long-lasting relationships with tourists who, for example, pay for their education. The tourists are moved by the stories of misery and poverty that these 'cute little boys' tell them in broken English. Needless to say the children are

Abya Yala; Cuzco: CBS; Amsterdam: CEDLA; Lima: IEP, 2006), 199-218.
10 Ypeij, A. & E. Zorn. 'Taquile: A Peruvian Tourist Island Struggling for Control', *European Review of Latin American and Caribbean Studies* 82, (April 2007): 119-128.

quite capable of manipulating these sentiments. The children form part of the well-developed informal sector on the tourist route. Most informal workers – and they can be found everywhere that tourists are – sell handicrafts, jewellery, sweets, soft drinks and cigarettes. As Kibicho's chapter on Kenya (14) indicates, the domination of foreign investments pushes local people into the informal sector, and the Cusco case is a good example of this tendency. Tourists also inevitably meet women dressed in their most beautiful indigenous clothing who offer to pose for tourists' cameras in return for money. These women, who come down on their own initiative from the mountain villages of the Sacred Valley to the tourist village of Pisac and to Cusco, are called *sácamefotos* ('take-my-pictures'). They are specially dressed for the occasion, often carrying a child or have brought along a lama or a goat. They undeniably add flavour to the tourists' experience as they offer a rare chance to talk to indigenous women and to gaze at them.[11]

Although, in the Cusco-Machu Picchu region, mediators such as guides and local travel agencies may use racist notions to limit the agency of informal workers and other local people, there are other examples of tourism offering the possibility of escaping poverty. As the chapters in this volume show, local hosts and communities can only benefit from tourism if they are proactive and keep control over developments. In the Cusco-Machu Picchu region one can find cases of indigenous women who are in control of their tourism activities and have become remarkably successful. The women of the tourist village of Chinchero make good money from selling their weavings directly to tourists instead of to a wholesaler and are in full control of cloth production too. All the women are members of the market association that has decided that all vendors have to wear indigenous clothing. The colourful scene they offer tourists has turned their village's market into an important tourist attraction. Weaving art has strengthened women's feelings of cultural pride, standing, and ethnic identity in a way similar to that described by Klute (Chapter 3) for the Tuareg.

As this volume indicates, tourism studies have moved beyond the 'is-tourism-good-or-is-tourism-bad' discussion. Tourism is nowadays a given in many localities and regions. More often than not, the local communities visited have high expectations of the benefits that tourism will bring. Situations of subordination and exploitation exist alongside examples of cultural pride, profits and strengthened ethnic identities. But while the African case offers tourism on a smaller scale and has created several niche markets in which locals are able to work on their own terms, tourism in the Cusco-Machu Picchu region has

---

11 Henrici, J. '"Calling to the Money": Gender and Tourism in Peru', in M. Byrne Swain & J. Henshall Momsen, eds., *Gender/Tourism/Fun* (New York: Cognizant Communication 2002), 118-33. Simon, B. 'Sacamefotos and Tegedoras: Frontstage Performance and Backstage Meaning in a Peruvian Context', in M. Baud & A. Ypeij, eds., *Cultural Tourism in Latin America. The Politics of Space and Imagery* (Leiden: Brill, 2009), 117-40.

grown beyond recognition. Many investors are only motivated by the idea of rapid profits. In combination with racist attitudes towards the indigenous population, this has turned the Andean bubble into an arena of struggle and trouble. When protesters block the railway, the tourist bubble bursts and tourists perceive the 'real Peru' as their safety is put at risk.

REFERENCES

Bosman, K. 'Ofreciendo un mundo imaginario: los guías de turismo en el Cuzco', in Annelou Ypeij & Annelies Zoomers, eds., *La Ruta Andina. Turismo y desarrollo sostenible en Perú y Bolivia* (Quito: Abya Yala; Cuzco: CBS; Amsterdam: CEDLA; Lima: IEP, 2006, 199-218).

Hill, M.D. 'Contesting Patrimony: Cusco's Mystical Tourist Industry and the Politics of Incanismo', *Ethnos*, 72 (2007) 4: 433-60.

Henrici, J. '"Calling to the Money": Gender and Tourism in Peru', in Margeret Byrne Swain & Janet Henshall Momsen, eds., *Gender/Tourism/Fun* (New York: Cognizant Communication 2002), 118-33.

Maxwell, K. & A. Ypeij. 'Caught between Nature and Culture. Making a Living in the World Heritage Site of Machu Picchu (Peru)', in M. Baud & A. Ypeij, eds., *Cultural Tourism in Latin America. The Politics of Space and Imagery* (Leiden: Brill, 2009), 177-98.

Simon, B. 'Sacamefotos and tegedoras: Frontstage Performance and Backstage Meaning in a Peruvian Context', in M. Baud & A.Ypeij, eds., *Cultural Tourism in Latin America* (2009), 117-40.

Steel, G. *Vulnerable Careers. Tourism and Livelihood Dynamics among Street Vendors in Cuzco, Peru* (Amsterdam: Rozenberg, 2008).

—— 'Dishing up the City. Tourism and Street Vendors in Cuzco', in M. Baud & A. Ypeij, eds., *Cultural Tourism in Latin America* (2009), 161-76.

Ypeij, A. & A. Zoomers (eds) *La Ruta Andina. Turismo y desarrollo sostenible en Perú y Bolivia* (Quito: Abya Yala; Cuzco: CBS; Amsterdam: CEDLA; Lima: IEP, 2006).

—— and E. Zorn. 'Taquile: A Peruvian Tourist Island Struggling for Control', *European Review of Latin American and Caribbean Studies* 82, (April 2007): 119-28.

Notes on Contributors

Shanade
Barnabas

Shanade Barnabas is a doctoral student in the Centre for Communication, Media and Society at the University of KwaZulu-Natal. Both her
Master's degree and doctoral studies are based on the CCMS Kalahari
Research Project Rethinking Indigeneity which involves studies with
the !Xun, Khwe and ≠Khomani Bushmen of the Northern Cape and
the !Xoo in Botswana. Shanade is presently working as an editorial
assistant on Prof. Keyan Tomaselli's forthcoming book, *Cultural
Tourism, Methods and Identity: Rethinking Indigeneity*.

Walter van Beek

Walter van Beek is full Professor of Anthropology at Tilburg University,
as well as Senior Researcher at the African Studies Centre, Leiden. He
has done intensive longitudinal fieldwork in North Cameroon among
the Kapsiki/Higi, in Central Mali among the Dogon, and has published
extensively on the two cultures. The most recent one is *The Dancing
Dead. Ritual and Religion among the Kapsiki/Higi of North Cameroon
and Northeastern Nigeria*, New York, Oxford University Press,
2012. His major interest is religion, and he is currently publishing
monographs on both groups. As both areas, the Mandara Mountains
and the 'Pays Dogon' are tourist attractions and have been so for a
long time, he entered into studies of the impact of tourism on local
communities, publishing several articles comparing these two cases,
as well as general analyses of tourism in Africa. His teaching duties
have brought him to Namibia and South Africa, and he is currently
engaged in PhD training programmes in Southern Africa.

Shirley Brooks

Shirley Brooks holds a doctorate in human geography and environmental history with a particular interest in South African land and
conservation issues. She taught geography at the University of Natal
(later the University of KwaZulu-Natal) and the University of the Free
State, and is soon to take up an Associate Professorship in Geography
at the University of the Western Cape. Her work explores the historical
and contemporary geographies of wilderness tourism. In addition
to conducting collaborative research with Dutch colleagues on the
politics of game farming, Shirley Brooks is currently preparing a book
entitled *Making Colonial Wilderness*, on the history of conservation
and game reserves in Zululand.

Ton van Egmond studied social psychology at the University of Leiden and graduated in 1974. From 1974 onwards he has been working as a lecturer and consultant in tourism at NHTV Breda University of Applied Sciences, Breda, the Netherlands. Ton van Egmond has taught a number of courses in consumer behaviour and psychology of tourism. He has been involved in the development of tourism curricula and tourism staff training all over Eastern Europe and the developing world. Currently, his educational activities focus on sustainable tourism planning and development, particularly in rural areas in developing countries. His research interests chiefly lie in the area of tourism demand, i.e. tourists' motivations and market analysis. Ton van Egmond received his PhD in 2006. His thesis, *Understanding Western Tourists in Developing Countries*, was published by CABI in the UK (2007).

Ton van Egmond

Kate Finlay holds a Master of Social Science (*cum laude*) from the Culture, Communication and Media Studies (CCMS) department at the University of KwaZulu-Natal. She is presently involved in the tourism industry, having previously worked as editorial coordinator for the *Journal of African Cinemas*, as a media researcher for CCMS, and for the eThekwini Municipality.

Kate Finlay

Ineke van Kessel holds a doctorate in the history of Africa and is a journalist. She is a senior researcher at the African Studies Centre in Leiden, Netherlands, where her research focuses mainly on contemporary South Africa and on the historical relations between Ghana and the Netherlands. Her main publications include: *'Beyond Our Wildest Dreams': the United Democratic Front and the Transformation of South Africa* (2000); *Zwarte Hollanders: Afrikaanse soldaten in Nederlands Indië* (2005) and *Nelson Mandela in een notendop* (2010) . She has also edited several volumes in her field.

Ineke van Kessel

Wanjohi Kibicho teaches tourism at Moi University, Kenya, and is director of the Centre for Tourism Research and Development. His took a master's degree in tourism management, and his doctorate (Université Lyon 2, France) focused on community-based tourism in Kenya. His research interests include sustainable tourism and tourism destination management. He has published articles in a variety of journals on sex tourism, as well as the service quality of and impacts of tourism. His third book on sex tourism in Africa will be launched by Ashgate Publishing (UK) later this year.

Wanjohi Kibicho

Georg Klute has been full Professor of African Anthropology at the University of Bayreuth, Germany since 2003. His main research interests are in Economic Anthropology, the Anthropology of Work, Political Anthropology, the Anthropology of Violence, Ethnicity

Georg Klute

and Ethnic Conflicts, the State in Africa, the emergence of non-state forms of power, Nomadism/Nomads and the State, as well as African Anthropology. He is currently conducting research in the Southern Sahara (Algeria, Mali, Niger) and in West-Africa (Guinea-Bissau). His recent publications are, with Birgit Embaló, *The Problem of Violence. Local Conflict Settlement in Contemporary Africa* (Köln: Rüdiger Köppe Verlag, 2011); with Alice Bellagamba, *Beside the State. Emergent Powers in Contemporary Africa* (Köln: Rüdiger Köppe Verlag 2008).

Stasja Koot Stasja Koot (1974) holds Master's degrees in both cultural anthropology and environmental studies from Utrecht University, the Netherlands. From 2003 until 2007 he has lived and worked in Namibia, where he has assisted the community of Tsintsabis to build up a community-based tourism project: Treesleeper Camp. In 2007 he started working as a fundraiser (with major donors) for a Dutch non-profit organisation to support education in developing countries. Simultaneously, he embarked on his doctoral research in 2009 at Tilburg University, the Netherlands, in co-operation with the Africa Studies Centre Leiden. His field is the dynamics of marginalised groups in tourism, focusing on the relationships between Bushmen, wildlife parks and tourism.

Elizabeth MacGonagle Elizabeth MacGonagle is Associate Professor of African History and African and African American Studies at the University of Kansas. Her research focuses on processes of identity formation in African and Diasporan settings. Her first book, *Creating Identity in Zimbabwe and Mozambique* (Rochester, 2007), examined four centuries of history in southeastern Africa, challenging popular notions about tribalism. She is currently analysing the intersections between history and memory on the African continent at four sites of memory steeped in history that UNESCO recognises as World Heritage Sites for their outstanding cultural importance to humanity. An article on the significance of Ghana's slave forts in our collective memory, from their use during the transatlantic slave trade, appeared in the *Journal of Contemporary African Studies* in 2006.

Lucy McCombes With a background in the social anthropology of development, Lucy McCombes has worked on community development initiatives in Jamaica, Mali and the UK. In 2005 she began her studies for an MSc in Responsible Tourism Management at the International Centre for Responsible Tourism (ICRT), graduating in 2008. Her dissertation took her to The Gambia where she researched the factors that affect the nature of host-guest interaction between package tourists and 'bumsters', i.e., beach boys. During her time in The Gambia, Lucy worked as a temporary coordinator for the Association of Small-Scale Enterprises in Tourism (ASSET), supporting members with marketing, training and product development. In 2009, after a year working with a private consultancy company in Yorkshire, Lucy joined ICRT as a Research Fellow where she is involved in a range of consultancy, research and teaching work.

Joseph Mbaiwa holds a Ph.D. in Tourism Sciences from Texas A&M University (USA). He is currently working as an Associate Professor (Tourism Studies) at the University of Botswana and is based at the Okavango Research Centre in Maun. His research interests are tourism development, rural livelihoods and conservation, with particular interest in the Okavango Delta. Joseph Mbaiwa has wide experience in research and consultancy work on tourism development, rural livelihoods, community-based natural resource management, natural resource use and biodiversity conservation in Botswana and in other Southern African developing countries.

Joseph Mbaiwa

Annette Schmidt, the co-editor of this volume, is an archaeologist with a vast experience in the tourist zones of Mali, such as the Inner Niger Delta. Her PhD thesis provides a comprehensive description and analysis of the excavations in Dia, as well in the Djenné area. She is Curator of the African department at the National Museum of Ethnology in Leiden and continues her affiliation with Mali in several cultural heritage projects financed by the Dutch Ministry of Foreign Affairs. Her research focuses is on the history, archaeology and material culture of West Africa, cultural heritage management, illegal trade in cultural heritage and mud architecture.

Annette Schmidt

Valene Smith, author of this volume's Foreword, is one of the intellectual founders of the anthropology of tourism. She has published widely on local aspects of tourism, with a general and lasting fascination of the Arctic. Her book *Hosts and Guests*, in its first edition, marked the start of the sub-discipline as a serious area of research at a time when anthropologists were still wary of tourism studies. In the second version of her volume the sub-discipline was further developed, while the third and completely distinct published work opened up yet more vistas. She is Emeritus Professor of Anthropology at the University of Chico State.

Valene Smith

Marja Spierenburg is Associate Professor/Senior Lecturer at the VU University Amsterdam, the Netherlands, in the Department of Organization Sciences. She is currently involved in several research projects focusing on the role of the private (for-profit and non-profit) sector in nature conservation as well as in land reforms in Southern Africa. Her research investigates the negotiations between the various interested parties, but also within the different partner organisations, concerning the meaning of the concepts of development and

Marja Spierenburg

conservation. It also addresses the impact of the growing importance of public-private partnerships in conservation on the land rights of local communities and the latter's possibilities to participate in the management of and benefit from conservation and land reform projects. Her earlier publications include *Strangers, Spirits and Land Reforms, Conflicts about Land in Dande, northern Zimbabwe* (Brill 2004) and, together with Sandra Evers and Harry Wels, *Competing Jurisdictions. Settling Land Claims in Africa* (Brill 2005).

Marijke Steegstra Marijke Steegstra is a cultural anthropologist. She has worked as a researcher and lecturer at the Department of Anthropology and Development Studies of the Radboud University of Nijmegen, the Netherlands, where she also received her PhD in 2004. Her book, *Resilient Rituals. Krobo Initiation and the Politics of Culture in Ghana* (LIT Verlag/Transaction Publishers, 2004) analyses how the contemporary performance of Krobo girls' initiation rites relates to and is shaped by Krobo encounters with missionary Christianity, colonial intervention, and modern nationalism in Ghana. She has carried out further research with the support of the Netherlands Foundation for Scientific Research (NWO), focusing on traditional rule and the popularity of foreign 'development chiefs' in Ghana.

Eiliadh Swan Eiliadh Swan is a doctoral candidate in Social Anthropology at the University of St Andrews, under the supervision of Professor Roy Dilley. Her thesis is based on eighteen months of research in Ho, Ghana between 2007 and 2009 and focuses on the contemporary nature of Ewe chiefly authority and chiefs' changing role within modern democratic Ghana. Before these studies, Eiliadh Swan spent three months in 2005 as a volunteer in Ho where in addition to teaching English she conducted research into local international volunteering organisations. This research focused on the interactions between volunteers, the people with whom they worked and members of the community more generally. It sought to elucidate the different ideas held by volunteers and their Ghanaian hosts on the status of international volunteerism in relation to tourism and development.

Kim Warren Kim Warren is Assistant Professor of United States History at the University of Kansas. She is the author of *The Quest for Citizenship: African American and Native American Education in Kansas, 1880-1935* (Chapel Hill: University of North Carolina Press (2010), a comparative study of race in the United States, examining identity and belonging among two minority populations. Her articles on race and gender in 19th- and 20-century America have appeared in *Kansas History: A Journal of the Central Plains* and *History Compass*. She is currently working on a study of African American women's civil rights from a national and global perspective.

Harry Wels is Associate Professor at the Department Culture, Organisation and Management, VU University Amsterdam. He is author of *Private Wildlife Conservation in Zimbabwe: Joint Ventures and Reciprocity* (Brill, 2003); co-author (with Marja Spierenburg) of 'Securing space: mapping and fencing in transfrontier conservation in southern Africa' (*Space and Culture*, 2006) and co-editor (with Sierk Ybema, Dvora Yanow and Frans Kamsteeg) of *Organisational Ethnography: Studying the Complexity of Everyday Life* (Sage, 2009).

Harry Wels

Vanessa Wijngaarden is currently a Junior Fellow at the Bayreuth International Graduate School of African Studies (BIGSAS). She has graduated in Political Science (specialising in International Relations) with a research project at the International School for Humanities and Social Sciences (ISHSS) in Amsterdam. Previously she studied Cultural Anthropology at the Universities of Amsterdam and Leiden (the Netherlands) and Calgary (Canada). Combining her interests in culture and power, she focuses on the relationships between the actions and ideas of Western citizens, international institutions, the images and discourses they produce, and the daily livelihoods of people in Africa. During five months of fieldwork in Masai and Taita communities in Kenya, she observed the local people's interactions with charismatic mega-fauna, the Kenyan state and international tourists.

Vanessa Wijngaarden

Annelou Ypeij is an anthropologist and works at Cedla (the Centre for Latin American Research and Documentation). Her research on tourism focuses on the Cuzco-Machu Picchu region of Peru and deals with the role of local populations in tourism development. She co-edited, with Michiel Baud, *Cultural Tourism in Latin America. The Politics of Space and Imagery* (Leiden/Boston: Brill, 2009)

Annelou Ypeij

Index

Printed and bound by CPI Group (UK) Ltd, Croydon, CR0 4YY

23/04/2025

14661046-0001